The Marriage License

Joanna Hager-Smith

Distributed by
Logos International
Plainfield, New Jersey 07060

I dedicate this love story to my family
with thanks to God for making each of them
an instrument of His love
William, Susan, Geoffrey, Roderick, Gregory
Anthony and Moria

I wish to thank Eveline Robinson whom the Lord sent in answer to my prayer for a typist and who became both helper and friend.

Table of Contents

PART I

A Weekend in May

The Judge's Decision

Weatherbird satellite stared down at the beautiful blue orb 22,591 miles below, keeping twenty-four hour watch on planet Earth. Its video cameras relayed high resolution photos of atmospheric storms, sending down a new one every thirty minutes. Alas, no instruments of advanced design can see the storms within the human heart and hear its cry. Even as Weatherbird reported a rare day with clear skies from coast to coast, there was a storm brewing in a valley down below: a legal decision was being made that would cause a tempest in the hearts of men and women.

The eye of the coming storm was a lovely little town in the mountains somewhere north of where you live—a beautiful place called Temagami Springs, U.S.A. It is a place where people go in summer to enjoy the beauty of the cool green mountains and breathe the fresh clear air.

It was the fifteenth of May and the citizens of Temagami Springs went to their work rejoicing in the first warm day in months. Public law 04Y4 was on the shelf awaiting a decision on its legality and had long since been more or less forgotten. Like many laws passed in the name of freedom, its implications had gone unrecognized by the public at large. But that was about to change. Before the midnight hour a cry would be heard on the wind, "Why? Why me?"

What was the law that struck like lightning on a summer day? It sounded simple, even harmless, and this in ordinary English is what it said: When the younger party of any marriage reaches the age of forty-five, the couple must go to the county courthouse within four months and file for a new marriage license at a fee of ten dollars.

That sounds simple enough, doesn't it? Like getting a new hunting or fishing license. (The fee was reasonable considering that the young middle-aged were the citizens most able to pay new taxes. And the income from it would cover the appropriations for the new lulus for the state lawmakers.)

Then there was the other side of the law: Should such consensual filing (that's legalese for both partners filing together) not take place, then the couple would be divorced and the children protected by the divorce laws of the state.

"Now," they asked, "what's wrong with that?" And they were quick to add, "Half the population is being divorced anyway and this law makes it so much easier." The press dubbed it E-Z OUT.

There was no debate over this new licensing act. Public Law 04Y4 was tacked on to an appropriations bill the previous year and sped through both houses and across the governor's desk for rapid signing in the midnight hours before adjournment. When the churches woke up to the fact that it might be a threat to the American home, the evangelicals and the Catholics got together long enough to file suit in the Judges' Court for a ruling on its constitutionality. Months had gone by and everyone forgot about Public Law 04Y4.

On May 15 the weather forecast was for cloudless skies from coast to coast, a rare day in the United States of

America. But weathermen are sometimes wrong: the winds were beginning to blow. Had there been a supernatural satellite to sense a human tempest in the making, it would have turned its cameras on an old-fashioned brick building, a two-story walk-up on Main Street, and peering through damask drapes have focused on the man in whose hands, by law, the peoples' future lay: Judge John Freund II, sixteen years on the bench and a lifelong resident of Temagami Springs.

Judge Freund swivelled away from the long mahogany table covered with legal papers. He was satisfied he had made a great decision. Reaching for the telephone, he briskly dialed his stockbroker in her office down the street. Now it was time for an investment that just might be the best one he ever made. He picked up his briar pipe with shamrocks on it and, filling it with aromatic tobacco, he smoked and smiled while he waited for someone to answer.

"Anderson, Chase, Jong and McVay."

"Judge Freund here," he said in his wheezy voice. "Give me Mrs. Jong please."

In a few moments Margo picked up her phone. "Mrs. Jong speaking," she answered in crisp, businesslike tones.

"Margo? John Freund."

"Oh, Judge! It's you. How's everything?" exclaimed the lady stockbroker, hoping for some word about the ruling.

"Fine, Margo, fine; everything's fine. How's the market today?" He wondered whether he should tell her the news. It would be a little unethical, of course, but it was hard to keep a secret from Margo. She was one wonderful woman— his favorite, in fact—after his wife, Tulie. The judge smiled a foxy smile, thinking of his friends at the club who would never have a lady broker. He took a lot of good-natured kidding about Margo over his daily lunch at the Elks, but he never revealed to the boys that his luck in the market skyrocketed after he switched his account from Bill Jong to his wife, Margo.

It was Margo who got him into McDonald's before it split. The profits from that beautiful investment turned into an Italian trap gun with silver inlay and a pair of special trap and skeet shoes! Judge Freund grinned because it gave him unending satisfaction that the gun was to this day a secret from his wife.

His thoughts were interrupted by Margo. "The market is quiet. Very quiet. It usually is on Fridays, you know. What can I do for you, Judge?" asked Margo, curious to know why he called.

John Freund took the pipe from his mouth and exhaled abruptly. Something about her tone told him it would be a mistake to mention the ruling. "I just want to buy a little Mother Bell today—for my wife's account. Say, one thousand shares for Tulie," he said.

"How come, Judge?" Margo asked as she swiftly executed his rather large order. "That's been pretty stagnant lately. The antitrust action isn't helping. It seems to have plat-formed."

"No reason. Just one of my famous hunches. How can I lose the way Tulie uses the telephone? Mrs. Freund keeps the Bell system in business!"

"Whatever you say, Judge," mused Margo. "Jong's going to get a kick out of it. Mind if I tell him?"

"No, no. Goodbye," he said abruptly, still tempted to let out the news.

"Goodbye, Judge." As she hung up, Margo Jong's nerves were tingling; from her long acquaintance with Judge

Freund, she knew his purchase indicated something. He had bought no stocks since Temagami Downs Track opened for the season. This buying today could only indicate a decision on 04Y4. She was excited, because she knew from sixteen years of stock market experience that if the ruling had been made, the market would go up on Monday. Her intuitions on the market were seldom wrong.

Judge John Freund hung up the telephone after his conversation with his broker and relit his pipe. He felt satisfied that a difficult decision had been made. This new law would be a good thing. It would make people feel a little freer. That's what everyone wanted—freedom to do what they pleased. The churches had complained—said it was another abortion law—but law was law and morals, morals. Modern man had his choice and if the churches didn't like the fact, it was up to them to improve the behavior of their members. If they disapproved of divorce, let them stay married—like himself.

He would never divorce Tulie. She was a great cook. A bit old-fashioned perhaps, and not a size ten anymore, but as comfortable as his old army boots. He remembered when she was Tallulah Redford, Judge Redford's daughter. To think he had married Judge Redford's daughter! Wouldn't the old man be pleased if he could see him now?

A smile quivered on John's face as he blew out the match and leaned back in his comfortable leather chair. Surely, he was glad his marriage was one that was not in trouble. Why should it be? He was a good husband and he never doubted it. He had given his wife everything. He allowed her to do pretty much as she pleased—even encouraged her to collect all that old stuff she didn't need, and he never interfered with her having the kids around. Tulie had a comfortable home and lots of friends; what else did a woman want? Nothing he knew of. Nothing at all.

He was proud of himself as a judge—and as a husband.
Reaching in his drawer for a tranquilizer, John Freund
popped it in his mouth and swallowed hard. Yes, indeed, he
had a fine reputation as a liberal judge and he expected a
favorable reaction towards his ruling from most of the
people that mattered. He relished public approval the more
because he didn't get much from his family. No matter; he
was pleased with himself. A look of contentment spread up
and down John's usually doleful face and erased his tired
look. He leafed through his calendar. It seemed there was a
free week ahead. Judge Freund never took a long vacation;
vacations made him restless. His wife called him a workaho-
lic. But it was time to plant his garden.

He decided to spend mornings spading and planting and
afternoons at the track. With his favorite pastimes to look
forward to, life was sweet indeed, and there was his new
investment to keep an eye on. It would be fun to watch
AT&T move up the chart. He smiled, chuckling to himself:
one thousand shares of AT&T. What an idea! What an
inspiration! Ah, he hadn't dealt with widows for years
without knowing something about women, enough to
predict a further immediate rise in the profits of Mother
Bell; and no one could call his purchase unethical, not
AT&T, not the stock of widows and orphans. No one
would expect him to buy that old stalwart for himself, not
young high-flying Freund. Anyway, it was safe in Tulie's
account.

The judge, in his simple way, still thought of AT&T as a
telephone company rather than as a data communication
business. However, it was true that since Strolly Paddock
introduced 04Y4 to the legislature, phone company profits
had been edging up and there was talk of increasing the

dividends. The judge knew that, thanks to him, long-distance calling would immediately skyrocket. His wife, Tulie, would be the first to pick up the phone to talk things over with her sister in Santa Fe. Indeed the whole country was about to have something to talk about. Maybe other states would like the idea of 04Y4!

There was a certain measure of revenge in the judge's glee. He hated his wife's excessive use of the phone; but it was not until her sister moved to New Mexico and young John went to college that her monthly phone bill became intolerable. Tulie called their son on the slightest pretext and, worse still, he called her back collect. What was there for them to talk about? Nothing important. She said she liked to hear his voice. "After all, he is my only son" was her usual remark.

Now his wife could be forgiven. "I'll get back that $109. I'll get it all back and a whole lot more. And then I'll sell!" The $109 was the loathsome bill the month young John dropped out of college. Spoiled kid, thought his father, I don't know what will become of him.

Just then John Freund III, the subject of these irritating thoughts, passed through the office. John, whose friends called him Freud, carefully looked straight ahead; in his hand was a long legal document.

"What's that?" snapped his father, his eyes hard and critical. The shaggy appearance of his only son was a great affront to the proper man and elicited very short behavior on the judge's part.

"Just an agreement, that's all," replied Freud, hastily stuffing the paper into his briefcase. Freud, aged twenty-two, had quit the university at Christmastime—three semesters short of graduation—and after a few futile weeks hunting for a job with short hours and high wages and being told he was overqualified, had reluctantly accepted his father's suggestion that he come into the law office to lend a hand and help out. He did library work, docketed cases and decisions, and went to court to serve as clerk to swear in witnesses.

"You'll see what it's like to be a lawyer," his father had said, harboring a bruised hope that Freud might become a partner some day. The kid had been noncommittal all along, very closemouthed, but now he had been in the office almost four months and was doing a credible job. Perhaps he would go back to school in the fall and get on with being the lawyer his father felt he should be.

Freud, of course, had other ideas; today he was thinking about something very big and very secret. "By the way, Dad, I have the papers ready on that land Brig Bantley is buying, the new parking lot for Glory Land. Shall I take them over for his signature?"

His father answered abruptly as he left the room to go to have a smoke in the library. "No, not today. His secretary called and left word he's gone to his place at the beach. We'll get to him Monday," Judge Freund replied. The judge was glad that Freud was taking this responsibility.

And Freud too was glad—glad that his dad had surmised the papers in his hands were for Mr. Bantley. "What if he knew they were for me?" Freud asked himself. And he began to hum, excited as he was by his recent brainstorm—a really big idea—something he had come upon while searching titles at the county courthouse. If things worked out he would soon be a property owner, maybe even a notorious person in Temagami Springs.

All he needed now was to use his powers of persuasion, which were well known to himself and to his mother as well as his friends, and with a small loan from these same friends he would become a property owner and move out of the family home forever. Oh, happy day. It was an idea packed with promise.

A vague "shh, shh" from the secretary's office reminded him of where he was and he ceased humming aloud, but a smile lingered on his big bewhiskered face. Shall I quit my job today? he mused. After all, it is Friday. No, maybe I'd better wait till I have this agreement signed and the money to buy my land. Maybe Monday. I hope I can get the money tonight. Five thousand dollars should do it; maybe she'll accept one thousand down, Freud thought to himself, but he'd have to act fast or it would be futile. These were very special acres, which might be worth even more than he could pay. The very thought that someone else might have the same idea or discover his secret gave him a tight feeling in the chest.

But Freud remained confident that he knew what he was doing. He always felt that way about things. Even as a small child he had never been deterred when he had an idea, and he had developed into a young man of great enterprise and enthusiasm, with a certain charisma that elicited support from his peers. When he had an inspiration he never hesitated or procrastinated and this one was the best he ever had. His shaggy appearance—thick, wild, curly blond hair, thick lenses, mustache and brown beard—hid his capacity from some of his elders, certainly from his father. However, his mother regarded him as a prodigy. This morning Freud's thoughts about the shiny future he envisioned were interrupted by the buzzing of the telephone. Rosa DeLuca, the judge's secretary, came around the partition and picked up the receiver. She signaled the judge, who came back into his office to take the call.

As Freud was leaving the office, his father called, "John!

That was your mother. I knew she'd call," he added with a smug smile of satisfaction. "She's having a roundup tonight" (which was his satirical expression for a family party). "I think maybe it's her birthday. Better be there," he added as he walked back into the library, looking sideways at the briefcase in Freud's hand.

"How old is Mom, Dad?" asked Freud.

"I'm not sure. I'd have to think—forty-two, maybe forty-three," he replied absently, his mind elsewhere. Freud went out and the large door went shut behind him. Rosa looked up at the serious expression and flickering half smile on Judge Freund's face. Something in that fleeting look of satisfaction prompted her to ask, "The decision? Has it been made, Mr. Freund?"

"It's been made," was all he said, but he went on muttering to himself. "A simple little law," he puffed. "I don't know why no one thought of it sooner." Noting the doubt on his young secretary's face, he continued, "That law will simplify things for those who want out and the rest can just sign the forms. Yes, a harmless idea," he snorted. "Like getting a fishing license."

The judge, thought by his colleagues to be rather naïve, was given to sweeping statements and this was a classic example. His young secretary was shocked at the news. " 'Harmless'? Harmless, indeed!" Her parents were nearly fifty years old and fought lovingly every day of their lives. She couldn't contemplate the fights this would cause at home. She just shook her head, a disbelieving look on her face, and went on typing, her anguish converted into pressure on the keys. Bang–bang–bang–bang. Her fingers attacked the keyboard.

The door opened and Freud reappeared. "I think I'd better call Mom," said Freud aloud to Rosa.

"Hi, Mom. You called?"

"Yes, Freud. There will be company for dinner tonight. It's my birthday, you know, so don't disappoint me."

"Happy birthday, Mom. Why didn't you tell us? By the way, how many, Mom?"

"Ten or twelve, I guess."

"No, not people—years, Mom."

"Would you believe forty-five?" she sighed. He thought it was about that, but since his father was uncertain in the matter, Freud had asked her because he had to be sure.

"Great! That's a nice number. Four-five—like something to bet on at the races," he laughed awkwardly. "I'll give that tip to Dad. The fourth in the fifth, when he goes to Temagami Downs tomorrow!"

"Don't mention it, Freud," Tallulah said emphatically. She didn't like the judge's gambling, but there was nothing she could do about it. He was as poor at the races as he was in the stock market. Such silly systems he devised; she supposed 4-5 for her birthday was as good as any. But his losing their savings was a continuous burden. She remembered the period he bought stocks by ticker symbol SEX, EGG, PEG, NOC, anything that spelled something. His success with them had been short-lived and he switched to mutual funds just prior to their collapse in 1974. She never talked about the judge's bad investments with his children but, of course, they knew he had more prestige than money—and living with his stuffiness, his narrow-mindedness and his lack of feeling, as they did, they couldn't understand the prestige.

"Don't worry, Mother, I heard him say he's working in the garden tomorrow."

Tulie continued on. "Freud, you will come to dinner tonight, won't you?" She hesitated to push her needs upon him; she knew he was a man now and must answer to his own demands, but tonight was different. "I must know now, Freud, because I'll be at Lost Friday all afternoon. I want you to be there. You see, dear, we're getting company, special company."

"You know I wouldn't miss one of your parties, Mom. Who's the special company?"

"Phlox, Phlox Fontaine. I'm afraid she's coming to stay for the summer, at least."

"Phlox Fontaine? Where have I heard that name before?" asked Freud, making a face.

"It's Jean Fontaine's daughter. You know Jean, my college roommate. Remember? Well, Phlox has been giving her parents trouble; they just brought her back from some boarding school in California and now Jean thinks I'd be a good influence. She wants her to stay with us till their new home is built. Just like Jean," Tulie sighed heavily, "to give me a job I can't refuse. But I'll try to help—with a few pointers from you on how to handle young ladies. I'm rather behind the times since Linda married." If Tulie could have seen her son's determined expression she would have been worried.

Freud stiffened as he thought to himself, Uh-uh. No involvements for Freud. Not now. Not when I have something big coming up. Not with a girl with a name like Phlox! Aloud he said, "Phlox; no wonder she's having trouble with a name like that." He said it sarcastically for something to say. "How could your roommate inflict her on us?"

"Well, she could," answered Tulie. "She was fond of shock treatment."

"Life-long shock?"

"Yes, even that; but I do think Phlox has a pretty name.

It's so like Jean to send her daughter away and I'm not surprised that Phlox is a handful. Her mother was a problem to all who knew her. But we'll try to make up for it with Phlox."

"Oh, Mom, you're so simplistic. I doubt we'll change Phlox one iota, and she may be a big pain in the neck." Freud thought of his property and of his secret plans that were to come to fruition in the weeks ahead. *Just so this female doesn't interfere.* Aloud he continued, "Well, Mom, I have some important agreements and deeds to see to this afternoon, but I'll be there at six thirty. Bye now." And he hung up.

"Rosa, get me Crabbe Grass on the phone." Rosa smiled at Freud. She liked him. He had the zest his father lacked and just his presence in the office had turned her job of legal secretary into an adventure. She didn't know it was the effect he had on everyone.

"Crabbe Grass, what a name! Who is he?" she asked smiling.

"Oh," laughed Freud, "I thought everyone knew ol' Crabbie. He's a freak, a friend of mine. His number is 987-0666. If he's not in, try The Sesame Seed Bakery. I'll take it in my office."

He hastened into his room, which was also used as a storage cabinet. The coffee pot was kept plugged in on the table that served as Freud's desk. Brooms stood against the wall and cartons of forms and typing paper were stacked on the chair. It was a mess but he didn't care.

Rosa smiled questioningly. Fresh out of the local business school, she had never met anyone like Freud. She was not alone in this; few young girls had met anyone so exciting to be with. It was impossible to say no to him.

"Yes, Mr. Freund." She was mystified and intrigued as

she dialed the telephone number. Who could Crabbe Grass be with a name like that? It suggested something undesirable, omnipresent, difficult to eradicate, certainly something out of place. Well, Crabbe Grass was all that, and owner of the freakiest pad in town. However, he was thought of as a man with money, and a loan was what Freud had in mind.

"Hello, Crabbie; Freud speaking. Where have I been? I'm workin' for my old man," he laughed. "Just called to say I'd like to come down to your place tonight. It might be ten—eleven o'clock. I see. I'll look for you. I have business to discuss."

"What business?" Crabbe asked in a slow drawn-out voice, puffing on a cigarette.

"You'll see. High finance. Bye." With that Freud rang off.

"Thanks, Rosa," he said, and he thought for a moment of asking her to join the crowd downtown. She seemed lonely and tense and so straight. She needed some color in her life. Yes, she ought to meet Crabbie. However, what they were going to discuss was not for his old man's ears and maybe she had some sort of loyalty to him. Another time, he thought, shrugging his shoulders. Then he placed his checkbook into his briefcase, retied his open tie and put on his brown sweater.

"Where are you going?" demanded his father.

"Out on business," Freud smiled.

"Humph, why don't you go for a shave or a clip or something? If you're going to be a lawyer you ought to look like a lawyer."

Same old dad, thought Freud, but he said nothing and ran his fingers through his curly hair, which only made his big head bigger. Smoothing his tangled sideburns by way of accommodation, he was about to say, "But I may become a historian, not a lawyer," when he checked himself. He sensed his father was in a bluff mood this afternoon. Freud gave Rosa a wink and a smile and went out.

"By the way, Judge Freund, when will the decision be handed down?" asked Rosa.

"The decision was handed down today. 04Y4 is legal. I'm releasing it to the press at ten p.m." Rosa, now the only living person to know the news, looked up at her employer. He didn't meet her eye as he laid papers on her desk. "Type these," he said and walked quickly out of the room.

"Santo dio," muttered Rosa, crossing herself. She put a sheet of legal-size paper in her typewriter and this is what she typed:

(P.L. 04Y4): Whereas, recognizing the right of the individual to freedom of choice, it is hereby declared that when the younger spouse of any marriage contracted under the laws of this state shall reach the age of forty-five, said license of marriage must be renewed by the signature of both parties appearing in person four months from said date before a duly designated officer of this court.

Should said consensual filing not take place, the marriage contract will terminate on said date and be declared null and void. The rights of minor issue of such parties will be protected by the jurisdiction of the court under the divorce laws of this state.

Rosa stopped her machine and put her head in her hands. "Oh, how awful! Don't they see what will happen? It's a coiled snake! God, help us all!"

Goodbye at The Bantleys'

Two beautiful people stood in the morning room of their large and elegant home overlooking the Valley of Springs and looked at one another. They had been married for twenty-four years and they could find nothing to say. Brigham Bantley and his wife, Lucy Lorenson Bantley, stood waiting, perfectly matched, like a pair of Russian figure skaters competing in the World Championships; he—athletic, tall, rugged; she—slender and svelte and beautifully attired. And like a pair of skaters, they were stylish, poised and tense—tense over what was about to happen. The female half of this well-known pair was leaving. Oh, not forever, but at times a summer season is forever and so it seemed today.

This handsome couple and their three good-looking and well-educated children were everybody's idea of a family to be envied. As owners of the unique and beloved entertainment center known as Glory Land, they were the first family of the town of Temagami Springs. The affluence and prestige they enjoyed were the results of the vision and old-fashioned hard work of Brigham Bantley, founder of Glory Land. However, Lucy was less than pleased with the demands the business made upon her husband; and every summer, as opening day approached, she absented herself from home on a long tour to some exotic place, seeking source material, so she said, for articles on music she wrote for the local newspaper.

Today, May 15, she was ready to depart on an extended tour along the coast of Africa. She would return in September via the Orient. Dressed in a tan knit suit with a cream and azure scarf at the throat, and holding her beige makeup bag in one hand and her elegant carry-all in the other, she stood before Brig in the large front hall, known as the morning room; and neither of them could think of anything to say.

For one thing, it had all been said many times at other partings—take care of yourself, write, I'll miss you, come back soon, remember, have you forgotten anything? Yes, the usual pleasantries had all been said before; however, today these platitudes were inadequate to cover the concern they felt, and so they were silent, waiting, half hoping the other would say whatever it was they should be saying to one another. Yet neither could speak the proper words. They could no longer communicate, because there was a growing difference of direction and viewpoint between them, and so they kept silent about what they were thinking. The less often they discussed their important concerns with one another, and the more often they pursued individual paths, the less able they were to agree about anything. Their relationship one way or another had almost ceased to exist. Furthermore, after twenty-four years of matrimony, each harbored a profound feeling that the other could never change and would never understand if his partner acted out of the character long assumed, quite mistakenly, to be his. How could one explain one's self to someone with whom one has lived so long, explain one's other self, a secret self, unfulfilled and undiscovered? Only a stranger would take that self on say-so, someone without habit and preconceptions, and give it serious consideration. A partner would say, "I don't believe it," or laugh, "My wife?" And so it was that on this fragrant spring day all the old platitudes were inadequate to cover their frustration with one another. And the silence between them was deep.

At length Lucy, remembering something, set down her bag and opened her purse. "Here," she said, handing her car keys to Brig, "don't forget to run my Triumph now and then."

He nodded. "Do you have your passport?"

"Yes." She stepped up to him and kissed him on the cheek. "Goodbye, dear. See you." She looked at him for an instant. Brig wanted to grab her and hold her back, to forbid her to go. It would have been reassuring to both of them if he had done that. However, as he knew she would go anyway he refrained from it, hugging her quickly instead, and she fled out the front door into the bright sunlight. She was followed close behind by Skip, her twenty-year-old son, who put her bags under the hood of his Volkswagen and got into the driver's seat for the short ride to the airport.

Brig stood for a moment where she left him. He watched his beautiful wife leave. At forty-five she was as lovely as ever. Her auburn hair, worn in a ponytail, framed her oval face. She had a Latin beauty with dark oval eyes and fair Castillian skin. He watched the car go down the drive and disappear into the woods and there were tears in his dark violet eyes.

"Oh, well, that's that," he sighed. He too was leaving, though only for the weekend. After a moment he sprang back to life and threw a few things into a rucksack; in no time at all Brig Bantley drove noisily out of the garage in his new Mercedes 240D. He had wanted a 450SL but, due to the energy crisis, had compromised on a diesel instead. It was well with a business such as his to be mindful of the energy crisis. Without cars, no one would come to his park in the country. Now this afternoon belonged to him and he was happy to be going away—away from the scene of all his problems, running away to be alone and to have time to think great thoughts. How rare an opportunity it was. But as he drove south toward the sea he felt no happiness; he was as lonely as a man could be, already missing his wife. This would be the fifth time she had flown away for the summer. She had been to see turtles on the Galapagos, dragons in Sumatra and penguins in the Antarctic. Now she was off, so she said, to hear the beat of jungle drums in Africa. Each time she left he felt more depressed by her going and though he tried to rationalize this urge she had, he could not accept it. Rather than telling her that he needed her and asking her to stay and help him in some very special way, he blamed her that after so many years together she did not sense his inner needs.

However, his wife was not his only problem, nor even his biggest problem. That was the family business. The summer season would begin in less than two weeks and from then through September he would be completely involved with the problems of his successful enterprise.

There were many pressing decisions to be made about its future and there was the hiring of the temporary employees. If only his children would ask him how they might help. He couldn't understand them at all. They seemed to have no thought for the future, no sense of responsibility for the family business—Banter off to India looking for a peak experience, Savy absolutely noncommittal as to her future plans, and Skip's thinking he could live by writing songs!

If all his friends' kids weren't behaving in the same way he'd have blamed their poor attitude on Lucy, but that was unfair. They were all that way—living off the fruits of their parents' hard work. But he needed his kids' help and this summer he would have it—or else.

Another worry on his mind was his mother, living alone in her old home in Lake Placid, kept going by two very untrustworthy handmaidens. He'd have to slip away from Glory Land soon to get the old ladies in line.

He sighed. Somehow he would work out all these problems—after he relaxed and swam and rested by the sea. Water was as important to Brig as air and sunshine, and it was as sustaining.

He had all these worries, but what was really troubling him most of all was his growing realization that underneath the weight of his many responsibilities, he was feeling strangely restless. Things that never bothered him before were pressing in on him. He needed to figure out why he was vaguely dissatisfied with himself and everyone else. Probably all he needed was a rest.

With great expectations of the peace he would find, he traveled to his cabin in the dunes. It was an undemanding, absolutely private place and he loved it. Someday he would retreat to it for good—unless of course a hurricane took it away first. Today Brigham Bantley would find peace by the shores of the rolling Atlantic. The nearer he got to it the better he felt.

Turning off the car's air conditioner, Brig rolled down the windows and sniffed eagerly for the first smell of the sea. As soon as he inhaled that fresh odor of salt and fish and oxygen his spirits lifted; his foot pressed down on the accelerator and before long he turned into the sandy road to his little house among the dunes.

It was a simple sun-washed place, reminiscent of an Andrew Wyeth painting. The few things he kept there were simple but beautiful. Everything was as he had left it—a hand-woven throw, red, blue and grey, lay askew across the bed. His favorite pottery vase was on the sill, cattails and milkweed pods from last autumn dried and fallen. As he opened the door the cool salt air moved the soft light curtains; rays of sunshine, reflecting from the water, flickered on the ceiling.

Brig stepped inside and set down his rucksack. He threw his leather jacket across the wooden chair and stood for a moment, quietly absorbing the atmosphere of tranquility, so different from his buzzing office at Glory Land. He took a clean deep breath of sea air. Then quickly pulling off his boots and pants and pale blue sweater, he stood naked in the mellow sunshine. How comforting privacy can be; how great it is to be alone, he thought, stretching his arms toward the corners of the room, his lean body strong and taut.

As he pivoted around and bent to touch his toes, he noticed his old faded bathing trunks hanging behind the door where he had put them months ago. They were sandy and stiff in his hand as he lifted them off the hook. He opened the door and shook the sand on the deck; then, putting them on quickly, for the breeze was cool, he took a heavy white towel from his bag, along with his sunglasses and PABA lotion and a plastic bag (that was for the seashells he would gather and take home and then throw away). He jogged through the poverty grass, over the warm dunes to the water's edge. After a quick plunge in the cold surf he ran back to his big towel, rubbed himself hard and lay down upon his back, his hands under his black hair. He put his old floppy tennis hat over his face and lay there relaxing all over.

Brig Bantley lay for a long, long time, letting himself sink into the sand, letting go of his tensions until at length he was in a state of blissful suspension. This is what he had come for.

But such moments rarely last long. He began to think again about Lucy and about her leaving him. Why did it hurt? Was it because she left with a flair, a zeal almost religious? Or was it because there seemed such a finality about it? Was he afraid she'd never come back? He might have known before he married her that his wife loved travel and new places more than anything else. She was spoiled by her early experiences as a VIP. But how could he have known? His upbringing had been so different from hers: his with ordinary people in small places, Lake Placid and Bowdoin College; hers among the high society of a dozen countries.

When Brigham Bantley's interest in the Middle East and his need for a lucrative job took him to Saudi Arabia, Mr. Lorenson was serving the president as the American ambassador and his daughter Lucy was there on vacation from Vassar College. Brig was introduced to her at the Fourth of July reception at the U.S. Embassy and they had become friends immediately. It had been fun to be a member of her embassy crowd and be included in the heady life of outings and parties and protocol, a new experience for him. In that happy setting their love grew and flourished and the following summer the tall, handsome young geologist married the ambassador's daughter.

Looking back now, it gave him both pleasure and pain to remember those years—Lucy returning to the States after their marriage to finish her senior year at Vassar, while he, under contract to Sudarabian Oil, staying on overseas.

That had made no difference to Lucy. So accustomed was she to the varied and stimulating life of travel and foreign places that she commuted from Poughkeepsie to Dhahran as easily as to New York City. He remembered how thrilling it had been after long months apart to meet her planes, to see her descend in a flaring white dress, her brown ponytail flying. He could see her now, holding her broad-brimmed hat in her hand and running to throw her slender arms about him. And he remembered how proud he was when she graduated cum laude from a prestigious college.

He remembered that year in the desert without his bride, yearning for her and yearning to be in the green hills of home, to own a piece of his native land. It was his sadness each time Lucy went back to college that made him so eager to return to America, to buy a place and start a family, to have an old-fashioned farmhouse full of dogs and kids. My, how long ago that seemed. Now over twenty years later the white farmhouse had grown into an entertainment center and Lucy had gone back to the desert.

Heavy with bittersweet memories Brig turned over on his stomach and went to sleep. The herring gulls flew overhead croaking the news of his arrival to one another and talking about the coming storm.

Takeoff

Skip Bantley, dressed in patched and faded denims, stood beside his stylish mother. He jiggled the change in his pocket nervously and kept looking down the runway. The plane was late arriving, but his mother, veteran traveler that she was, was not worried a bit. She had carefully allowed plenty of time to connect with her flight at Kennedy International Airport. Skip, however, was anxious over her going. He would have preferred she stay home; his father was easier on everybody when she was around. Finally, when Skip's depression conveyed itself to his mother, she urged him to leave her there to wait alone; but he was stubborn like his father and he waited anyway.

It was Skip's opinion that since this was an important occasion for his mom, his dad should have come to the airport to see her off. What was wrong with his father? It wasn't as though he wasn't his own boss; sometimes Dad acted as though he worked for Glory Land instead of being its owner!

Surely this was not the send-off Lucy would have had in the old days when comings and goings were family occasions of special excitement. Skip, at twenty, could still remember when trains on the narrow gauge railway stopped at Temagami Springs, bringing Grandma Bantley. That was eleven years ago. She had come to town every few weeks and they and their three cousins had always gone to the station to meet her. They had taken their Grandma home to their house to a big dinner cooked by his mother, roast beef and chocolate layer cake—invariably roast beef and layer cake. Those were the days when Mom put real food on the table—not like now.

Furthermore, when Grandmother's visit was over on Sunday night, the whole family took her back to the station. At the time it seemed kind of a drag, all that fuss, but there had been something good about life in his childhood, more caring and sharing, more happiness—certainly more chocolate cake! Now what had happened to all of those years? If we could only bring back those years, he thought. What a title for a song: *Bring Back Those Years*! Yes, he could write a nostalgic song with that title. While he was searching for words for this song, the little plane landed and taxied to a stop at the terminal. Lucy gave him a quick kiss and walked away toward the gate.

Her kiss brought him out of his reverie. Skip looked up. "Mom, do you have to go?" he called in a low voice toward the back of his mother who was stepping rapidly away from him toward the open door of the little white commuter plane.

Lucy Bantley apparently didn't hear him and she never looked back. She was hurrying toward that open door, for many years so inviting, her gateway to new worlds, new ideas and new experiences. However, this time as she climbed to the top of the shaky stairs, she hesitated a moment. Coming in from the bright sunlight it was like looking into the black shaft of a mine; there was something forbidding about it.

But in a moment the handsome copilot was there smiling at her from under his orange beret. "Good morning, Mrs. Bantley, we're glad to have you fly Mountainair again." As if there were any other way to leave this small backwater, she thought; but she was pleased that he knew her name and, once aboard, she was her brave self again, caught up in the process of settling in and strapping down. This done, she waved feebly toward the fence and hoped Skip was not there waiting for takeoff. How sad she would have been if she had known he was wondering if his mother would ever come back. Certainly it would have made her even more nervous than she was. Quickly the door slammed shut and the little commuter fled over the taxiway; it turned and, hesitating an instant, raced faster and faster down the runway, skittering sideways as it built up speed and lifted off with wheels spinning.

Lucy Bantley clung to the window, looking down as she always did with special pleasure at the familiar places below. The trees were coming into full leaf, a sweet pale green. The apple trees were pink with blossoms and the orchards on Safflower Hill lay over the slopes like tufted bedspreads. She saw Little Bear Lake and the falls on Big Bear River; and then she sought and found the red-tile roof of her home, spread-eagled on the bluff. She looked in vain for Brig's Mercedes. He's left for the beach already, she thought.

And there below was Savernake Forest and their Glory Land. Lucy smiled to herself. The forest was a special place. Always as she flew over it on takeoff, it reminded her of being newly married and young and very much in love with Brigham Bantley. Leaning her head against the cabin window, Lucy closed her eyes and relived a special memory of a day long ago. She was in the forest with Brig. It was an afternoon in early October. They were lying under the pines on the thick cushion of the forest floor. The woods were radiant with color and overhead was a dazzling blue sky. Beyond, they could see the red-covered foothills and even redder high peaks. Lemon yellow birches filled the river valley and the sumac trees were apricot.

It was a perfect afternoon and it seemed as if they lay there forever, blissfully spellbound, his hand over hers. They talked for a time of their future. Brig suggested they buy the old Lansdown estate and while they thought about that, neither of them said anything. They lay there and enjoyed their first fall day. There had been nothing like it in Arabia.

At length Lucy sat up, and picking up a red maple leaf from the ground she stroked Brig's chin lightly with the tips of the leaf. He opened his eloquent eyes and smiled invitingly into hers, and then simultaneously they felt a tremendous love for one another. There was something extraordinarily beautiful about it, a kind of deep fulfillment, which made this autumn afternoon the most memorable day of their honeymoon.

Later, when she learned she was with child, she knew a child born of such love would be truly special. And so she was. A little daughter was born, her hair the color of the oak leaves that October afternoon in the forest. In their delight over the new baby they named her Savernake— Savy for short—after the forest that nurtured her conception.

Even now, twenty-three years later, Lucy Bantley could feel a small thrill somewhere inside her while reliving that day. Oh, what had happened to all of those years? And where had their intimacy gone—hers and Brig's—the union which had been so good to them in the days of their young love? She wondered if they would ever feel that kind of bond again.

Of course she was sure it was Brig's fault that things were like this. If only he would travel with her! But in winter when he was free to go, he took courses at the university. Always more courses. She understood he wanted to keep abreast in his field of geology and get advanced degrees. It would certainly help him find a job if she were ever to persuade him to give up his precious park and go back to the Middle East.

But until that day came she had her needs too. Life was so short—all those years gone, the eternity she'd been tied down by home and babies. If she didn't go now she might never go. Perhaps if she had been born in Temagami Springs like Tulie Freund and Surtsey Sanders, she would have been content with small-town charity affairs and committee work and parties at the country club—always the same faces everywhere. But she had had more than enough of that. As the wife of the town's leading citizen she was honorary chairman of everything. However, the prestige belonged to Brig. Indeed the social circle of Temagami Springs was much too static and provincial for Lucy Lorenson Bantley. What did all that amount to when the whole world was waiting and death never far away?

Lucy was afraid of death. It had overtaken all of her family. One by one the Lorensons died—mother, father, sister, brother. All she had left in this world were Brigham and the three children and Mother Bantley. Poor, dear, senile Mother Bantley didn't even recognize her own grandchildren anymore, one more proof that life was to be lived now, today. There might be no tomorrow.

Whenever Lucy dwelled upon the fact that her life was more than half over and that time was passing quickly by, she only needed a reason of some kind to start planning her next trip. Not a month before she had put together this present adventure. Skip was playing his tapedeck particularly loudly and offensively as she happened to be looking at an ad in *The Smithsonian* for a Sinbad cruise down the west coast of Africa. It was suggested that the passengers would be retracing the travels of Bartholomew Diaz. "I wonder whether they'd have a place for me," she exclaimed. "If I'm going to understand my boys and their loud music I must go to the source—Africa! I feel the call of jungle drums!" She jumped up and danced back and forth gleefully, her auburn hair flying.

If Skip could have heard her he would have put her down with "Mom, what about our call for a good meal, for a home with a mother in it?" But Skip was in his room behind a wall of sound when his mother be-bopped her way to the telephone and called the travel agency. Yes, she could pick up the tour on the *S.S. African Prince* in Dakar in mid-May.

As a result of that telephone call, she was on her way today to New York to catch a flight to Dakar. She would be back in four months' time with something to talk about besides Glory Land; and the family would survive as it always did. The middle-aged women who came to cook at Glory Land would take good care of "their Brig." It was Skip's sadness that worried her. He was her youngest and it was hard to leave him, but he had Savy—capable Savy— to look after him and see that he took his vitamins and got enough sleep. Yes, it would be good for all of them to do without her this summer. It was time to leave her family behind and look forward to the exciting adventure that lay ahead. She smiled to herself and when she did so, she caught the attention of an elderly couple across the aisle who thought she was smiling at them. They nodded and smiled back at the lovely lady in the expensive clothes, and soon the three of them were exchanging little comments about travel with one another. The flying time passed quickly, and while Lucy chatted with the man and his wife, the plane began to descend.

The great city of New York lay below, cubistic in the afternoon sun. Lucy tied her auburn hair back with a Pucci silk scarf from her carry-all and brought down her all-weather coat from the rack above and laid it beside her on the seat. She pulled her seat belt tighter and returned her seat to an upright position. She was ready to deplane. The big power plant was just ahead and they were about to land on the runway. By evening she would be aboard Pan Am flight 190 on her way to Africa. In her mind she was summoned by the beat of jungle drums towards an irresistible adventure. She took a long deep breath and felt absolutely free.

While he was standing in the airport terminal with his mother, an idea for a song had come to Skip Bantley. Words were running through his head. "And now what has happened to all of those years?" He must write that down. Was there a pencil in the car? Hurry—catch the words or lose them. He watched his mother until the door of the plane closed and taxied away. Then, giving a little wave, he walked quickly along the ramp, his hands in his jeans and a thoughtful stare in his grey-blue eyes, mumbling words over and over. He reached his Volkswagen and found a pen and notebook. With the words safely on paper at last, he needed his piano to work out the music.

Oblivious to all else and only vaguely aware that his mother's plane was airborne, he backed his car around and put the pedal to the floor, full speed ahead to his studio in the basement of Cornwall House. The engine missed a few times; it needed new spark plugs. But the car could wait. The song in his heart had priority. That afternoon he wrote and rewrote, trying the words and the beat, and at length he was satisfied the song was good enough that he could put it aside and go home for something to eat. He was starving, even after eating the pie and coffee that Anna Maria Abendtal had quietly, and without interrupting him, laid on his piano.

Anna Maria, his friend of so many years, by loaning him her piano and a private place in her cellar, had made his work possible. She also gave him a more priceless gift, the best gift of all for an artist, and that was encouragement. Skip liked the warm basement of Cornwall House, even with its noisy oil burner and ugly ducting. But best of all he liked Anna Maria herself—her tender eyes and warm, affectionate manner. He particularly liked her fussing over him in a motherly way. She was so unlike his own mother. At times he wondered how old Anna was (early forties he guessed) and he wondered if it was the fact that she had never married that made her so special. Anyway, she was a very good friend of his.

Skip Bantley left Cornwall House by the basement door, he drove his little car to the garage for a tune-up. Leaving it there, he walked home to eat supper. He was very hungry and he hoped his sister had prepared a good meal. Roast beef and homemade chocolate cake would be just right.

The Broker's Office

At forty-five, Margo Jong was as deft and trim and bright as a new clipper ship. She had sailed past the shoals on which an ambitious woman in a world of men could come to grief and had arrived at the very top of her profession, a member of the board of directors of the investment firm of Anderson, Chase, Jong and McVay. In addition, she was manager of their branch office in Temagami Springs and one of their top salespeople, serving customers in twenty counties.

Her election to the board had quite discomfited her husband, Bill, who was an account executive for Anderson, Chase, Jong and McVay. Rather than being pleased with her success, he was disappointed that he had not been chosen. It was true she had the largest clientele, including the prominent Judge Freund, and he grudgingly acknowledged that she had a certain sixth sense about the market; but nevertheless she was only a woman, and he had the biggest client of all, Brigham Bantley. Brooding over his disappointment at being outdistanced by his wife, Bill Jong had come to think the reason they had selected her was because they wanted to have a woman on the board. He comforted himself as best he could that in these times it was perhaps necessary to have a woman on the board of directors and, that being the case, Margo was as good a choice as any. He improved his toleration of the fact with dry martinis.

Following her call from Judge Freund, Margo Jong was immediately very busy. She unlocked the bottom drawer of her Monroe desk and drew out a list—her purchases and short sales and stop losses for the day—and they included no company so large and well known as AT&T. The judge could lay his bets on the blue chips, but she had small companies with thin issues in mind for her discretionary accounts, like Florida Floral and Hairdressers International— maybe even Coffins, Inc., though she was a little doubtful that enough people would die over 04Y4. Better look for a distiller instead. That thought brought to mind her husband.

If Bill knew about the ruling, what would he buy? She smiled to herself. Competing with Bill was half the fun. So she decided to tell him about the judge's call; this was an opportunity to please his most loyal customers. She crossed Coffins, Inc., off her list as too speculative. If only there were some way to invest in lawyers and plastic surgeons. She would short Levitz and Fat Boy Clothes. She added Castaway Travel to her list of buy orders. Its single weekends should at last have enough men. Thinking of men, where was Bill? He was not in the office. How like him to be gone when something was breaking!

When at length Bill returned, he was red-eyed with a vague sideways look about him, not meeting her eye, which meant he had had a three-martini lunch at the Holiday Inn.

"Bill, come over here. Guess who just called," she said to her husband.

"Who?"

"Why, our friend Judge Freund," she answered, lowering

her voice so no one would hear.

"Oh, really, what about?" he asked in a harsh, nasal voice, only mildly interested, conveying by his indifferent response his jealousy that the well-known lawyer was her customer, not his. "Was it the ruling?"

"He didn't say."

"Well, don't keep me guessing," Bill said irritably. "What's he buying?"

"You'll never guess. AT&T—a sizeable order. Could that mean anything?" Margo asked.

"I wouldn't know what," he retorted, "unless he's retiring to spend more time chasing after my wife!"

Margo bit her lip and reached in her purse for a tissue. Why did he say such terrible things? She was deeply hurt. She had devoted her life to Bill and had never been in any way unfaithful to him—certainly not unethical with her customers, which lately he was fond of implying when he was drunk. It hurt all the more today because she was trying to help him.

Bill walked off. "Well, well—AT&T. I think I'll develop some film in the darkroom while I think about that. Be a good girl and take my calls, will you?"

He knew she would and she knew that he was not going to work in his darkroom but was going into his locked office to take a nap. It wasn't the first time. He was basically lazy and he drank too much. Really, it was surprising he had any accounts at all. There weren't so many customers that one could afford sloppy service to even one of them. In Temagami Springs the least indiscretion on the part of any citizen was relayed from mouth to mouth and often magnified in the retelling; it was one of the hazards of doing busi- in a small community. She wouldn't want to live anywhere else, but if Bill kept this up his clients would learn that he drank too much. Then he'd lose his customers and maybe she'd lose hers as well. Where could they go then?

Margo Jong watched Bill walk unsteadily through the door and close it behind him. Her small-featured face lost its peppy expression. She sank back into her ivory leather swivel chair, her head back and her arms limp at her sides. What was she going to do about Bill? She knew he was an alcoholic, but she couldn't bring herself to admit it.

The personal implications of 04Y4 surfaced in her mind and washed away her earlier enthusiasm for the Monday market. To make a killing in the market was an exhilarating prospect, but it could hardly compensate for the sudden death of a marriage.

The requirements of the new law were something like an auction. Would she buy 04Y4 and sign for a new license, or would she sell and be divorced by default? There were decisions to be made that could not be put off for a better market. The date was set and the auction of her future would proceed with or without an order from her. The personal implications of the ruling became so large and heavy that Margo could not answer another phone call— not one more greedy phone call. Usually her customers, with their worries and complaints, did not seem greedy, but suddenly she was sick of them all.

Jumping up, she straightened her desk with a few deft motions and locked up her correspondence in the fireproof file. Then she referred her incoming calls to one of the junior executives and in a few minutes she hurried down the stairs, without waiting for the elevator, and emerged from the black slab office building. With quick strides she hurried to the parking lot. She was trimly dressed in a navy suit, her red purse matching her Italian leather shoes. Her short brown hair was neat and tight to her head and, as always, she looked immaculate.

"I'll drive out along the lake and think. I must think," she murmured. Margo got into her cream-colored Jaguar and drove away from Temagami Springs. She pushed the pedal to the floor.

As she passed Pat Johnson's house she noticed all the cars parked outside. Why? Had something happened to Dan? He was one of Bill's customers. Then she remembered the Lost Friday Club. Could it still be meeting after all these years? How incredible! It was years and years since she had been a member and played bridge on Fridays—back before her marriage to Bill. In those days she had interests of her own, but after she became Mrs. William Telford Jong, Bill had said *no* to everything she'd done when she was single. He said *no* to the leather-working course at night school, *no* to swimming at the Y, and *no* to the Lost Friday Club. He wanted her to do nothing except with him. And then he said *no* to the big one—to having children. He wanted to enjoy life. She had argued with him over his stand in their younger days and even threatened—in a teasing sort of way—to trick him into fatherhood; but he made it clear that if there was a child she would have to choose between them.

Much as he grieved and frustrated her, she loved him enough in those days to give in on everything and to seek her fulfillment in working together in their careers and in doing the things he liked to do. She had studied hard to become a superior broker and to help her husband, who was less gifted than she, to succeed. As the country prospered through the sixties and early seventies, the stock market was an exciting place in which to invest, and brokering was a timely vocation. It provided them every appearance of success, and yet she knew that neither she nor Bill were satisfied with their life style. They had achieved everything they ever hoped for—a beautiful home by the lake, sports cars, an air-conditioned wine cellar, a sauna bath, membership in the exclusive country club in the hills, money in the bank. And what had all that amounted to? Nothing. They were bored, like spoiled children. Bill drank and she was asking herself, "Is this all there is for me—ever?" And Margo often felt ashamed for having so much and enjoying it so little.

Worse than her shame over having a surfeit of worldly goods was the realization that had come upon her slowly over the past months that as a woman she was unfulfilled, and that at forty-five it would soon be too late to do anything about it. By denying herself motherhood she had denied her own femaleness, the very essence of her being; and she had sentenced herself to perpetual childhood and a lonely old age. Marriage was meant to be more than friendship; it was meant to be fruitful. Their marriage had been a showpiece of successful nothingness.

Having reached such a devastating conclusion, Margo Jong drew her car onto the shoulder of the road and stopped.

"I can't give up. I'm only forty-five." She sat like a stone, empty of thought, her black eyes closed. After a time the tension drained from her body and her mind became as clear as the little stream running alongside her car. From long years of practice as a stockbroker, Margo was a woman who, given an idea, knew how to jump on it. She started the automobile engine. "I'll find someone. I'll find a *child* who needs me." She roared the Jag's motor. "I'll tell Bill tonight after dinner with the Sanders. If he won't agree, I'll not sign—I'll face the future without him."

Margo felt better immediately. She decided to go for a long drive and return to Temagami Springs by the road through the mountains. She traveled east along Route 9, and along the way she passed the town's well-known eccentric pulling home her daily wagon-load of stones. "Why there's old Tatty Softshoe! How satisfied she looks." Margo Jong honked in greeting. Tatty stopped and waved. And in her rearview mirror Margo could see Tatty, a little woman in a ratty fur coat minus a sleeve, wearing a man's fedora hat. Margo could see her waving until she was no longer visible.

Tatty walked Route 9 daily. She had done so for at least ten years, in all weathers and without missing a day—a distance of five miles each way pulling a little red wagon. Her black mongrel, Shadow, invariably followed her twenty paces behind. His nose nearly touched the ground and his tail as well. At one time he had followed at ten paces, but the mutt was slowing down with age and trailing further and further behind. Occasionally someone offered Tatty Softshoe a lift, but she had never been known to accept. She lived in the swamps at the far end of Big Bear Lake, and it was said she had had a husband named Irv. Almost no one knew who Tatty really was because no one cared enough to find out. So no one understood why she walked so far for a load of stones when a stone was only a stone. They surmised she was crazy.

"I wonder if she's ever lonely like me?" asked Margo of no one. "Does anyone love her?" It made her sad to think of Tatty and her stones. Poor Tatty! Poor me. Are we all of us lonely?

Coming to a crossroad Margo suddenly wheeled her car onto the steep road up Dolman Hill, burning rubber on the turn. The narrow highway led through a forest of pine and it was cold in the deep shade. Margo closed the window and, shifting the Jaguar into second gear, she roared up the mountain.

"I'm not going to be a Tatty Softshoe," she exclaimed. "I'm not going to have a lonely old age!"

The Lost Friday Bridge Club

As Margo Jong had guessed, the cars parked at 218 Pleasant Street belonged to members of the Lost Friday Bridge Club. They were holding their three hundred and twenty-ninth card party.

The Lost Fridays (they called themselves that because they never felt like cooking dinner after club) had been meeting together every Friday for almost twenty years. The club was made up of ladies who liked the game of bridge and a few who hated it but came for the gossip. It was far better to play bridge—even losers' bridge—than to stay away and be talked about!

In the beginning, Lost Friday was an excuse to leave the house to the cleaning woman and the babies with a sitter, and spend an afternoon with one's friends. Later it became a routine happening on which to depend. More recently, quite a few members dropped out to take jobs; but for those who remained faithful, the club was a kind of nice old habit no one dared suggest be ended. They were down to three tables and these were difficult to fill. As their enthusiasm for bridge grew stale, it became their custom to break the monotony by discussing a timely topic. It was the responsibility of the hostess to pick the subject. While having dessert and coffee, the group would proceed to discuss the topic as wittily as possible. Some were better at this than others and sometimes feelings were hurt. Some chose outrageous topics. But it was invariably fun for them to let themselves go and say what they thought.

Today Pat Johnson, wife of the banker at The National, was the hostess. She had had a late baby the year before and all of the girls felt sorry for her. But it served her right—Pat was such a show-off. Today there was a large cut-crystal vase on the grand piano with twenty-two long-stemmed red roses and a conspicuous card saying, "Thanks, dearest Pat. All my love, Dan."

Pat, pressed on what had occasioned the beautiful bouquet, explained that her husband sent them to celebrate the departure of her mother-in-law. "Two roses for each day of mother's visit! No one but Dan would think of a thing like that," murmured Pat.

"No one but Pat," whispered Tulie Freund to Surtsey Sanders. There was a time when the girls had envied Pat such a thoughtful husband who sent flowers to his wife, but in recent years there were those who said she sent them to herself. Nevertheless they admired Pat's versatility, her clever choice of the events that occasioned the bouquets. However some were strangely impressed—down where it hurt—that maybe there was such a husband. And today they were especially depressed over playing the game again and being reminded that their own spouses never sent flowers.

After the scores were carefully totaled and the prize of five dollars awarded to Emily Paine, and after the booby prize of one dollar was given to Anna Maria Abendtal, the girls went to the dining room for coffee and mocha cake. When they were seated once more in the living room, Pat stood up, tapped her spoon on her cup and, looking around with a merry look, said, "The subject for today's discussion is very controversial. It is birth control. What are we intellectuals going to do about it?"

Everyone tittered. Pat, of all people, intellectual! She had been a hairdresser before she became a banker's wife. And weren't they almost past the age when birth control was any problem? While they were straightening their faces, Pat continued. "Surtsey, you have the most children. You comment first."

Surtsey Sanders, mother of six and wife of Bud Sanders, the toy manufacturer, had always been forthright and outspoken. Ordinarily she could handle any discussion, whether it was at the PTA or the League of Women Voters. There was only one subject that put her on the defensive, forcing statements she later regretted; that subject was her husband, Bud. Only afterwards, going over in her mind her stupid replies, did she think of the clever things she might have said. Her husband was a source of much embarrassment.

No one besides herself knew that behind Bud Sanders's friendly boyish face was a middle-aged child. Unfortunately for her today, Surtsey had recently read a book about sex, which explained certain things about Bud. He was, of all things, impotent. That was something no one would ever have guessed (she had never guessed!) but it accounted for his poor showing in the bedroom. It explained why certain satisfactions had been absent all along. She was comforted to learn about this. She always thought it could have been better than it was. Today she was caught off guard by Pat's question.

"Really, why ask me?" she said. "Ask Bud. He doesn't believe in birth control." The girls looked at each other and lifted their eyebrows. After all, six children, and probably a miscarriage or two—there were those times she sent a substitute to club. Yes, it was obvious he didn't believe in birth control.

Discomfited by the stir she detected, Surtsey entertained them further by adding, "He says it spoils his enjoyment."

"Is Bud a Catholic?" asked Jean Fontaine, knowing quite well he was not.

"No, he's not. That isn't it. It's just that, well he's not—I should say he never seemed—dangerous," said Surtsey. She picked up a deck of cards and shuffled them as she spoke, not daring to look up.

Again significant looks traveled around among the girls. Someone stifled a laugh. Bud was known in Temagami Springs as a swinger. Perhaps Surtsey didn't know. To break the embarrassment she felt, Tulie Freund interrupted with a question. "Did you all know that Lucy Bantley is going on a trip to Africa? She's leaving this afternoon."

"That's one form of birth control," said Jean Fontaine testily. She was irked because she was asked to drive fifty miles to substitute at the Lost Friday Club. It hurt her feelings to be asked to substitute—but she always came.

"Well, if I were she," remarked Pat, "I'd never *ever* leave Brig home by himself with all those women in Glory Land!"

"Yes," sighed Olivia Dupre. "As one of those women I often ask myself how anyone could leave Brig." Brigham Bantley, handsome and affluent and downright nice to everybody, was the idol of all the women of the town. Olivia Dupre was his art director and greatest admirer.

Anna Maria Abendtal, the unmarried curator of the local museum and an occasional substitute, spoke up. "Would you girls believe it, I've never met Brig Bantley?"

"Never met Brig!" they exclaimed in unison.

She shook her head. "I guess I've missed something. But I know his sons and if he's anything like them he must be a fine man."

"Oh, yes—fine and good-looking and kind. What sort of father he is I wouldn't know. But he's my kind of man," breathed Pat Johnson.

"And mine."

"And mine."

"And mine."

Anna Maria laughed heartily at their enthusiasm. Jean interrupted them. "I say never trust a handsome man," she said, rattling her charm bracelet for emphasis and looking very wise and experienced.

"Don't you trust Frank—I mean François?" asked someone.

"My husband? Well, I know him too well to think he's handsome," replied Jean, blowing circles of smoke in the air.

Peggy Jones, whose claim to attention lay in her fashion-model figure—she could still wear a bikini—jumped to her feet and waved her napkin for attention. "The pill. Let's talk about the pill. Do any of you think the pill is safe?" she asked. Answering her own question she said, "I went on the pill and in three weeks I put on ten pounds. Then I spent three months losing it at Weight Watchers. No man is worth that. No tiddly—" (She was about to say something but thought better of it.) "No tiddly man is worth that!" So saying she sat down.

"We should form a live-dangerously club," said one of the members.

"You can live dangerously. I read in *The Enquirer* about a woman who had twins at fifty-two. I'll bet they were a surprise!" Everyone groaned.

"You know, men get me," offered Zelda McVay. "They think because they have showy external plumbing and Y chromosomes that they are automatically great lovers. Why don't women tell them otherwise?"

"Who's going to face a man by herself and tell him he's not a lover and leave him naked and shivering? That would be too cruel," answered someone. "It would turn him off entirely."

"It's the game that makes the fun—what goes before," offered another.

"Here, here, you don't speak for me," said Pat. "Dan's all I could ever ask for." Someone groaned not meaning to be audible.

Anna Maria Abendtal shook her head. She had gotten most of her education on marriage at the Lost Friday Club. They seemed silly to be talking this way. She decided it must be the suspense over 04Y4 that made them assert themselves in this fashion. She had never been married and could add nothing to the conversation.

However, Jean Fontaine, thinking about herself as usual, picked up the conversation. "Well, who is happily married? No one I know of. That's what we're getting at, isn't it?" A silence followed and some were thinking that the strain in Jean's voice suggested she was in the menopause. Poor Frank; rather, poor François, as Jean insisted he be called.

Tulie Freund got to her feet and gathered the tallies and pencils and playing cards and said, "I'm sorry, Pat. I have to leave early. Jean and her daughter are visiting us and I'm rounding up the family for dinner. It's getting harder all the time to get everybody together."

Jean stood up and looked at her friend Tulie with an appraising eye. Tulie was wearing a new two-piece dress, and Jean, who made quarterly drops in the Goodwill box before she discovered the pleasure of selling her clothes at the Nearly New, was jealous and depressed that she herself had not come to club in a new outfit.

Surtsey Sanders joined the two of them and spoke to Tulie. "Have you ever thought of getting a job, Tulie? I think I would if I didn't have three young children. It would be an outlet for us."

"Me, a job? Why, I have a job," said Tulie. "The judge is my job—and my big house. And, as you know, Johnny's living at home now. I've quite enough work for me at my age. And I still love to entertain!" she added happily.

"But you don't entertain much," interrupted Jean, the very Jean who had just foisted her daughter on dear old Tulie for the summer.

After all these years she's still a pill, thought Tulie, and she answered, "You know the judge is a busy man. He doesn't like people. I do entertain my whole family as often as I can. Tonight, as you know, we're celebrating my birthday."

"How old are you?" asked Jean, arching her mobile brows. It was a nasty sort of question and typical of Jean, who having been Tulie's college roommate knew perfectly well how old she was.

"Here, here, an unfair question," said one of the others.

"I can't fool you girls. I'm forty-five! I just hope the judge will make it to my party tonight. He has some important case in the works today," replied Tulie.

Tulie Freund thanked her hostess and walked to the door, followed by Jean Fontaine. The others rose to leave, and as these old friends said goodbye to one another they were unaware that they had met as a club for the last time.

Club members everywhere would soon be too preoccupied with urgent matters to shuffle and deal and tally—too busy chasing their own husbands and other people's, too busy hiring detectives and visiting psychiatrists, too busy writing legislators and praying for help, too busy playing for keeps to make small bets.

Indeed, before winter came again many an American home would tremble on its foundations (a devastating 6.9 on the Richter scale); and every one of the bridge players would be clinging to her own small strengths and values as never before. Yes, it was "goodbye forever" to Lost Friday that sunny day the fifteenth of May. It had been good while it lasted. It had had a long life.

The Dune House

Brigham Bantley slept upon the sand. Not far off, the sea lay flat and the water stroked the shore with long affectionate licks. There was a deep solid quiet broken only by the strident voices of the gulls. Later that afternoon, a dark malevolent shadow passed over the sea and a sudden cool stroke of air upon his cheek woke the sleeping man. He turned over and looked up at the rolling black cumulus clouds. He watched them move rapidly to the east, and after a brief blow there was quiet again and he was at peace. He turned back onto his stomach and buried his head in his arms.

A few moments later he was startled out of his rest by someone tickling the soles of his feet.

"What's going on here?" Brig exclaimed, leaning on one elbow. "Well, what a surprise," he added as he looked up into the cool eyes of a golden imp with short-cropped yellow hair. She was all round and brown in her brief, gold metallic bikini and she had a teasing expression on her face. In her hand was a purple Frisbee.

Say, do that again, will you? thought Brig who liked to have his feet tickled.

"How about a little Frisbee?" she said. Brig Bantley had

never played Frisbee, but why not try? There was something about her—he felt he'd do anything for this imp, even play Frisbee. So he sat up and struggled to his feet while she stood with her round muscled legs planted firmly in the sand and watched him.

Brig pulled in his stomach, yanked his swim suit higher on his hips and drew himself up to his full height, six feet two—the male bird preening before the female, making, he hoped, an impression on this little five-foot imp.

"You're the only one on the beach and I'm bored. I think it's important not to have a day you don't enjoy, don't you?" she asked in a matter-of-fact way, at the same time deflating his flash of ego. "I'm a member of the Ultimate Frisbee team at Jersey High and I've got to keep in practice. Even if you've never played Frisbee before, you're better than no one."

She stretched out her golden arm and flung the purple Frisbee towards him. Brig caught it and tossed it back.

The sand runt bent to retrieve the disc, exposing the white skin of her lower back. As she lifted the Frisbee up and over her shoulder Brig was so entranced by the line and movements of her breasts and the slight pouch of her belly button that he missed catching it entirely and had an ignominious chase down the beach as it rolled away from him.

The game went on and Brig improved as he made an effort to focus on the Frisbee. He was relieved of his embarrassment over his ineptitude by the roll of distant thunder. The sky grew suddenly black and there came a great flash, followed in five seconds by a loud boom.

"Let's get to the house," called Brig. "I'll race you to the deck." He ran through the sand. She was ahead of him, but he caught up with her at the steps and his foot hit the

second step an instant before hers, sending them both
backward in a tangle of arms and legs.

She wasn't hurt. In fact, she was laughing and looking up
at him. Her face was close to his. "Oh, I forgot my beach
bag," she said just as he thought he was about to kiss her.
Brig, surprised by a certain stir within, untangled himself
and darted off to fetch her bag. When he came back she was
perched on the top step looking like some kind of friendly
satyr. The lightning flashed and big drops began to fall.

"Come in, quickly. I'll build a fire. The wind and rain will
be here in a moment," said Brig, watching the storm move
across the bay in their direction. "I'll fix us a hamburger. It's
all I've got. And a coke." In spite of the fact he was the
father of three children just about her age he hardly knew
how to treat this girl; but he was enjoying her presence and
wondering why she seemed so delightful. Was it the
unexpectedness of it? The Frisbee? No, it was her tickling
his feet.

"Tell me," he asked, "why did you tickle my feet?"

"I don't know," she replied, "just an impulse."

"Better not be too impulsive," Brig said. "You might get
in trouble sometime." The sand imp shrugged. It was of no
consequence to her, but to Brig it was something else. He
didn't know why he had such peculiarly sensitive feet;
something about having them tickled awakened the animal
in him. He had been tempted by this kid and he felt
embarrassed and disconcerted. What was this world coming
to that while lying alone on the sand he was suddenly in
this predicament? Was it the kid's fault or his? Anyway he
wished she'd go.

At that moment the sand satyr returned. "I'm hungry,"
she announced. "A burger sounds good." Brig went into
the kitchen, and when he came back with the snack she was

asleep on the daybed on the screened porch. He covered her with the handwoven throw and shut the door. Then he ate both hamburgers himself. "She's a cute kid. One of the 'sand runts' who lives on the beach, I guess."

With a fresh and stimulating sense of youth from his encounter with the golden satyr, Brigham Bantley felt ready to get down to work. The storm had ceased and the sun shone through the clouds. The towering cumulus in the western sky, lit from behind by the setting sun, indicated that another storm would pass in the night. Brig went into his bedroom and sat at the old pine table. He took from his rucksack a sheaf of papers—lists of all kinds, job applications and letters from clubs and corporations—and laid them in neat piles before him. It was time to think about Glory Land.

After a few moments he pushed his chair away from the table and looked out the window at the twilight deepening over the ocean. His mind traveled back in time to the years of his boyhood when he first discovered the glorious land that would someday become his own special place. He remembered he and his father camping in the meadow and looking for mushrooms in the early morning grass. In the long afternoons of his childhood the two of them walked the plowed fields beyond the banks of the Big Bear searching with their eyes on the ground for points and celts. There was great excitement the day the little boy found a big black stone axe. Brig supposed that his cache of relics, probably even the axe, were still in his mother's attic. Maybe he'd look around for them one day soon.

But his favorite memory of all was of finding the old Indian campsite under the overhanging rock by the river. He and his father cleared the brush and built a fire and cooked fish; and they sat by the campfire and ate their trout, and his father told him old Indian legends of that land. Even today he thought of the cave with the awe one reserves for a magic place.

As Brig sat dreaming about the past, the night darkened around his little house in the dunes and he went to the dresser and lit a kerosene lamp. Then he sank into his chair and closed his eyes, his feet resting on a barrel full of old magazines. He thought back to the years of his life in the Middle East, to the days in the hot desert when he wished he were spending the summer in the cool Indian cave. And he remembered so well the day he and Lucy, home from Dhahran and visiting his mother in Lake Placid, had gone to see all the old familiar places. It was the day he took his wife to see the town of Temagami Springs and there that day they learned by chance that Tyler Lansdown had died and his estate was for sale at a very fair price. It was the day that changed his life and he would never forget it.

It seemed like yesterday he and Lucy parked their new four-wheel drive Willys Jeep at the railroad station and took the shortcut from town across the river on the rocks and across the fields. He could still remember every detail of that day, even the Queen Anne's lace and the joe-pye weed. The air was heavy with the ripe smells of fall and he was struck by the peaceful beauty of the estate. He remembered looking down into the soft brown eyes of his bride, who, unaccustomed to walking through the fields, was clinging to his arm.

"I want a piece of this glorious land," he said to her. She smiled her assent and then he kissed her. Funny his remembering that kiss!

They walked along the river and rediscovered the Indian campsite covered with brush. Then they went for that memorable walk through Savernake Forest. Here at his desk twenty-four years later, Brigham Bantley smiled gently and with a pleasurable tingle as he remembered the experience of his daughter's conception, which took place there under the big oak tree.

It was after that day he decided to give up the job waiting for him in Colorado and buy the Lansdown estate. In one afternoon he had changed from a wandering geologist with a whole earth to explore into a businessman with a piece of that earth to cultivate and make bloom. It was a trade-off he had never regretted. They had been good years, he and Lucy building Glory Land and having their family and becoming part of their community. They had been satisfying years until lately. Something had gone wrong, nothing was the same as it used to be.

It's that cursed 04Y4 hanging over our heads. It's made me restless, he cried silently. How can I blame Lucy for running away? Sometimes I'd like to run away too. But she's left me alone. Alone. I don't want to be alone. What's it all been for—the work, the worry—if now I'm alone? he pleaded. And for the first time in his life he cried. He cried for himself, for his wife, for his children, and for a very difficult world.

Afterwards, feeling better as one often does after tears, he worked on his lists and studied the figures. And he wondered what had come over him.

Tulie's Birthday Party

Tulie Freund unlocked the front door of her beautiful white colonial home, and in a few moments had rearranged the *Better Homes and Gardens* on the coffee table, put little cakes into the microwave oven, observed that the roast was cooking in the second oven and had begun to prepare a white sauce for the beans. She noted with satisfaction, as she pushed back the white lock of hair hanging over her forehead, that the cleaning woman had shined the silver candelabra and set the table beautifully. The large linen napkins edged in lace, which had been her mother's, were beside the silver settings and the Limoge dinner plates were on the buffet alongside the Sevrin cups and saucers. The Georgian dining room—Williamsburg blue walls and gold linen drapes with its print of fruit and pheasants— was Tulie's special room, her pride and joy. After twenty-five years of practice she presented to her family on every conceivable occasion the most beautiful dinners served on an American table in the late twentieth century. Convenience foods in plastic containers were feeding most upper middle-class people on the kitchen table, but not in the home of Tulie Freund. Style was still worth the effort.

The great linen cloth on the table was one of her favorites

and could only be used with two leaves, that is when ten or more were coming to dinner. "But it would look nicer with the Meissen plates." So Tulie put back the Limoge and brought out the Meissen. "We must use the blue goblets and silver dessert plates. I hope they've been polished," she said, removing them their special shelf. "How exasperating. They're not! They're yellow with tarnish. I can't use them." She put them back with a look of disgust and got out her crystal plates.

The phone rang. It was Linda saying she and the children would be a little late. "Well, hurry; Freud says he has to leave early." Tulie was annoyed. Something told me this wasn't my day, she reflected, thinking the children didn't seem to enjoy her dinners like they used to. Linda's children were all in school, but just last week she had phoned to ask Linda to meet her for lunch in town and her daughter had said, "Mother, let me lead my own life. I have plans for today." Was she becoming a nuisance to her children? She hoped not. But wouldn't it have been nice if they had had a birthday party for me instead of my having it, she thought sadly, unaware that she had never given them a chance to go far enough away to come back as adults.

"Oh, well, Linda is married and I supposed she is busy with her friends and family. But I still have my Freud." She liked his nickname, for he was her joy and Tulie was sure—at least she hoped—her son's friends had given him the name because it meant "joy" in German not because it connoted "sex." Still, there was a question in her mind, especially since he frequently argued with her over the present habits of his peers and the so-called new morality. Freud argued with her but never hurt her feelings or accused her of being square—not like Linda.

Anyway, tonight the children were coming and there would also be the Fontaine family. Tulie had lived with Jean Fontaine for three years at college and they had many friends to talk about. She had known Frank then too; in fact, she had introduced him to Jean. In retrospect, she might have preferred him to the judge, but she had been no match for the beautiful red-headed Jean, not after Jean announced after one date, "I am going to marry that François—though he doesn't know it!" From then on, Jean introduced him to her friends as François Philippe Fontaine. "Isn't that a classy name?" she had said in the dorm. "Mrs. F.P.F.—and he has money too. Think how I can enjoy spending it! I'll have clothes and jewels—and lovers!" Tulie had been shocked and hurt when her roommate spoke so calculatingly of her friend Frank.

Tulie hadn't seen Frank for some time; she had heard his hair was white and he looked older than forty-five. It would be good to see him.

As Tulie gave the tablecloth a final adjustment, she said to herself, "I must hurry upstairs and shower before John gets here. He likes to shower first, but so do I." She smiled as she took his pajamas off the towel rack where he always hung them. Such annoying habits he had. Did her little habits annoy him as much as his did her? She supposed so, though his were worse.

Just as the judge hurried in and upstairs, Tulie Freund, in a long, flowered dress, her dark hair tied back in a chignon, came down the stairs. The congenital white lock on her forehead added to her sophisticated appearance. She was radiant, perfumed, and her antique diamond earrings glittered. I guess I can enjoy celebrating my forty-fifth birthday, said Tulie to herself.

The doorbell rang and she hurried to unlock it. It was her

daughter, Linda. "Oh, mother, you look beautiful. You have outdone yourself. Hasn't she, children? Happy birthday, and here is something you've always wanted," said Linda as she hung her raincoat in the hall closet. "Children, hang up your things on their hooks. Don't leave that box there for Grandpa to trip over."

Joshua picked up the box and handed it to his grandmother. "Open it, Grandma. Open it now. It's an antique." The two children danced around her clutching her sleeve.

"You know, dears, how I love antiques—anything antique. This is very special." Tulie was delighted by their attentions. "Don't tear my dress, dear. Why, you haven't given me a kiss." Sharon kissed her dutifully, but Joshua turned away embarrassed. Tulie smiled. "What could it be? It's heavy," she commented. She slowly unwrapped the pink paper and there was a beautiful round red rock.

"A lovely rock," she said, smiling at her grandson.

"Some antique," remarked Sharon. "That's a dumb present."

"Turn it over, Grandma. There's a mirror on the other side, a special mirror. I glued it to the rock." He grabbed the gift. "Look, I'm upside down. The whole world is upside down!"

The doorbell rang. Tulie laid her gift aside. "It's the Fontaines!"

"Mother, where is Freud?" asked Linda urgently. "I need moral support."

"He should be here any minute. I want him to meet Phlox; they're the same age by two weeks," said her mother.

"Jean and Frank, how good to see you! Come in, come in. It's been too long." How thin and tired he looks, she thought. "John will be down in a minute. Could this be

Phlox? How you have grown, dear. How lovely you are! I'm so glad you've come to visit us. You're just what we need around here now that Linda's married. Linda, take Phlox and her suitcase up to your room. Phlox, you'll really like it here, I hope."

Linda, impressed by the cute looks of her new guest, motioned the pouting Phlox to come away and they escaped from the room. They stayed upstairs until after the elders had their drinks.

When it was time to eat, Freud was sent to fetch them. "Hi, there," he said, stretching his big hairy arm out to shake hands. "Are you Phlox? Well, welcome to the zoo. We need new animals in this cage."

Phlox looked startled. So this is the guy I'm supposed to meet! She was doubtful that anyone who had hair like a tousled mop and called his home a zoo was her type. She liked svelt, sophisticated brittle men like her daddy, not young lions such as confronted her now. As they went downstairs Freud whispered to Linda, "Ask her what she's going to do this summer."

Dinner was somewhat desultory, that is until Phlox offered her opinion that people over thirty were hypocrites and not all that much use. Jean gave Frank a deadly look and said testily, "Phlo-ox," which Phlox ignored with practiced nonchalance.

"Well, my dear," spoke Jean sarcastically, "we do have some uses."

"I can't think of one," said Phlox, baiting her.

"Have you ever heard of perganil—one of the drugs your father sells? It is contributed by people over forty-five."

"Women," Frank interjected.

"Women," said Jean. "Anyway, it enables sterile women to have babies."

"Sometimes five or six babies," added Freud, never one to stay out of a conversation.

"Well, we solved that problem. Our generation isn't going to have children," stated Phlox. "We aren't going to have a bunch of little meanies eating up our money. That's instant poverty."

There was a certain silence at the table. Finally Linda broke in with, "Phlox, what are you going to be doing this summer?"

"Me? Oh, I'm looking around for a job. I hear they're hiring at Glory Land—a cast for their Fourth of July celebration. I've always wanted to be an actress. That's why I'm here," she said, knowing it wasn't the truth and looking at Freud.

"I don't think they're hiring yet for the Fourth of July," said Linda. "But it is a fun place to work."

Phlox looked dubious. "I hear the Bantley kids are in town this year. Do you know them, Freud?"

"Not really. I used to go to Sunday school with Banter, way back when. Crabbe tells me Banter has followed some guru to India." At the mention of Crabbe Grass, Tulie made a wry face. She hoped that the Fontaines had never heard of the infamous kid Freud regarded as one of his friends.

Just then John Freund looked at his watch and gave a loud "a-hem." The kids stopped talking. "Freud, fetch the portable television. We'll listen to the nine o'clock news."

"Not the boob tube!" moaned Phlox.

"You're not going to ruin dinner," stated Tulie with emphasis, looking at her husband. "Not on my birthday."

"You're right, my dear," said the judge, changing his mind. "I was waiting all day for this wonderful meal. No one, I mean no one, cooks like you, Tulie." And he smiled at her with his usual bleak smile. He did appreciate her cooking. It brought him home at the end of the day.

"Why, Judge, how nice!" exclaimed Tulie, always pleased by that old remark.

"I've got to go now," said Linda, jumping up. "We must get the children home to bed."

"But it's so early. And it isn't a school night," replied her mother.

"No, but there is Little League tomorrow. Joshua needs lots of sleep."

"All right, Linda. But you're not going, Freud," she said, giving him a stare that asked, "What about Phlox?" which he ignored.

"Yes, Mother, I told you before; I can't stay." He rose and said goodbye all around and turned to leave the room. His mother followed him to the door, "Will you pick up some muffins for breakfast?" He nodded okay. "And may I ask where you are going?" she added.

"Out to play bridge."

"You don't play bridge." The screen door slammed and she thought she heard him chuckle. Now where was he going?

When she returned to the dining room Jean and Frank had risen to leave. "We had a lovely time and wish you many happy birthdays. Take care of Phlox and we'll be in touch." Frank kissed Tulie and whispered in her ear, "You're a gem." Tulie blushed, a little flustered.

"Phlox wants to go over to her friend's house. We'll drop her off. Leave the front door open for her," said Jean.

"Yes, I'll be late," stated Phlox. She didn't say how late.

Tulie shut the door behind them. She was tired as she fell into the big green chair. She wondered if these parties were worth it. How much did anyone care for togetherness anymore? They didn't even stay after dinner for coffee and liqueurs. Suddenly the Sevrin cups and the Georgian spoons and the sight of the messy kitchen looked ugly and hateful. "It's not worth it," she murmured, taking off her shoes and throwing them out to the foot of the stairs. I'll ask John what he thinks. "John," she called. John didn't answer. Tulie got up, put on her apron and went in stocking feet to the kitchen to put the milk and butter in the refrigerator. Meanwhile her husband had gone to the library. He looked at his watch—nine forty-five—just time enough to pour himself a beer. He settled comfortably into his favorite chair before the television set, a tired expression in his baggy eyes. It had been a very long day. Now he would relax and listen to the ten o'clock news.

"Judge, where are you?" called Tulie, appearing from the kitchen. "Oh, no, not TV again! Must we tonight? I'd like to talk about the party."

"You don't want me to miss the news, do you?" He always watched Channel 6 at ten o'clock—*Dean Danforth and the News.* She knew that.

"No, I guess not," she answered with a sigh. "I'm going out to finish the dishes."

"Don't you have a dishwasher?" the judge called after her.

Men! They don't know that appliances do only part of the work, thought his wife.

She was scarcely gone when he called to her again. "Come here, dear. Come quickly. Listen to this." She unplugged the coffee she was reheating and accidentally knocked over and broke a goblet, one of the irreplaceable blue ones, and hurried back to the study in time to hear the corny voice of Dean Danforth say, "Now hear this, you middle-agers: news for you, news of that famous—or infamous as the case may be—bill. You know the one I mean. Here goes all you good forty-five year olds out there. Ready?" The judge leaned forward as Dean Danforth continued. "Judge John Freund has handed up his decision today that 04Y4 is constitutional! Mark your calendars. You have until September 15 to get your new licenses. Remember all you big hunters, new licenses by September 15." The TV audience could hear Dean Danforth chuckling.

"The fool. Makes it sound funny!" murmured the judge as he rose and flicked off the set. "I think I'll go upstairs to bed," he said, lighting his pipe.

Tulie flew out of her chair and grabbed his arm. "Why didn't you tell me?" she cried. "He's talking about *us*. And on my birthday?" Tulie sank to the floor, shattered by the enormity of it all. "Why didn't you tell me?"

"I didn't think it was that important," he answered, pulling away from her and going upstairs.

She looked after his retreating form. "I'll never give another birthday party as long as I live." Then she cried gently for a long time, until the phone rang. It rang again and again, all cranks. Overwhelmed by the enormity of their accusations, she took the telephone off the hook and placed a pillow over it. For a woman who loved her phone calls, it was a desperate action.

In a state of shock over finding out about the ruling from Dean Danforth instead of from John Freund, she turned out Tater, the cat, and put the light on for Phlox and went heavily up the stairs. "I must go up and talk to John."

He was watching the television set at the foot of their king-size bed. Dangerous irradiation or no, Tulie stood between him and the set, determined to gain his attention. "We have to talk," she said firmly.

"Talk? Talk about what?" he answered.

"You know what."

"There is nothing to talk about," he said, motioning her to move to the side. "Shush, turn up the television! Can't you see that was a home run? Reggie Jackson made a home run," cried John.

"A home run," breathed Tallulah Freund, her eyes bulging. Defeated at last by her thousand and first night of bedroom television, its glaring sound coming between them and cutting her off, outraged at his lack of concern and exhausted from a busy day, she put her last bit of energy into slamming the bedroom door behind her. She would sleep in the guest room.

Much later in the dead of night something woke Tulie from sleep. She awoke with a crushing feeling of incredible loneliness. There was no way she could go back to sleep. Her eyes closed again and the night seemed at a standstill. Now and then the clock chimed, always one chime—the half hour, so it was impossible to tell how deep the hour. How can a soul be so alone as I, she asked herself, with people all around? It was terrifying.

After what seemed like hours and hours she heard the four o'clock freight train coming on from the south, hooting a long E flat wail, louder and louder until finally it passed moaning away to the north. She wished she was on it, traveling away from this terrible loneliness to some warm and unearthly reception, away from this cold night to the arms of a passionate lover.

Her wool blanket was heavy and oppressive. She threw it off and went back to their bedroom and crawled under the sheet with John.

This man is my husband, she thought. Why can't I wake him up and say "I'm all alone; talk to me. Take me in your arms and comfort me." She sighed. What a futile gesture that would be! What if he rebuffed her?

He hadn't always been like this, had he? She remembered their younger days when they lay in bed together like two spent collies. Collies always looked spent to Tulie—but happy. Yes, they had been happy like two collies. Where in the succession of days and nights and years that followed had the two young collies gone? Minute by minute, cell by cell, disappointment by disappointment the collies had changed—one into an old goat! That's what he is, an old goat, an insensitive old goat, too naïve to know what is going on in this day and age. He thinks it's not important! Tears came into her eyes and fell onto the pillow and with them came resignation to her fate. "I guess I will just have to love an old goat," she murmured, patting the form beside her.

Soon after her acceptance of things as they were, the comfort of sleep came to Tulie Freund. She could never have guessed what lay ahead.

A Doubleheader

Margo Jong returned from her long drive in the country to find Bill eating a Big Mac on the kitchen table. "Aren't we going out to dinner with the Sanders?" she asked, as she hung her coat in the closet and took off her platform shoes. She went to the roll of paper towels hanging on the wall by the sink and tearing one off, cleaned her red shoes and put them away in the closet with shoe-trees in them. Then she put on a pair of neat velvet house slippers, combed her short brown hair and returned to the kitchen.

"Nah," her husband replied. "Bud called and cancelled it. He's probably taking out that schoolteacher chick," he added, his mouth full of bun. "I didn't want to miss the ball game tonight anyway. It's a doubleheader."

"Well, you shouldn't say that about Bud," said Margo, as she took a head of lettuce from the refrigerator. "After all, he is a married man. But I wonder if they're having more trouble over Mark." Like everyone else in town she heard that Mark told his father he was contaminating the world by manufacturing nonbiodegradable plastics.

"Maybe that's it," answered Bill. "I'll never know what motivates Bud Sanders. Can't you see his round eyes popping when Mark said that about the Poly-Toy Corporation?" Bill laughed and poured himself another beer. "I don't blame the kid for taking off. I can't stand his old man either."

"Would you want your son to go to the commune on Safflower Hill?" asked Margo, noting that Bill's once youthful face was wearing a purple, haunted look.

"Thank God that's one problem I don't have," said Bill. An expression of sorrow crossed Margo's face. She was tired of pretending even to Bill that she was glad they had no children, that she had never wanted any, and trying to convey the impression to her friends she could have children if she wanted to.

"Bill," she said softly, intimately, "I want to talk to you tonight about an idea I've had. I've thought of a way to enrich our lives."

Bill had started back the long hall to the bedroom, a six-pack in one hand and a box of popcorn in the other. He wasn't listening. "Okay. Later. Come on back here," he said, turning to look at her and motioning with his head. "Let's get in bed and watch the ball game."

She followed him. "We can't talk with the television on. Besides, it's only seven o'clock."

"Come on," he urged, "we'll pull up the covers, have a little booze, and after the game we can talk; and who knows what may happen? It might be just like old times—you and me after a football game!"

If only it could be like old times. Margo Jong was thinking that in those days Bill shaved twice a day and wore Woodhue cologne and he looked at her then with the same pride he now reserved for his Pontiac Trans Am. And, more importantly, in those days he had told her he loved her and she had believed it was true.

Now? Now he smelled like a sour fruit salad, his stubble

was grey, and he took his beer to bed. And he never looked at her and told her he loved her.

Bill interrupted her thoughts. "By the way, I saw a cute chick today who looked just like you looked twenty years ago." He meant it as a compliment.

"How old-fashioned! The poor kid," said Margo sarcastically. She was hurt and she cried inside at his treatment of her. A less determined woman than Margo would have been destroyed or given up long since; but she was a professional person who knew the value of appearances in maintaining her customers' trust and she kept trying to look happy. Bill didn't hear the derision in her voice or notice her feelings were hurt; he was busy tuning in a ball game and tuning out a wife.

Margo ran to the closet and grabbed her knit jacket. "Hey, where are you going?" he asked without even looking at her.

"I'm going to take the dog for a walk," she replied.

Bill was sitting in bed, his back upon a nest of pillows, looking like King Farouk. On the quilt beside him were his snacks and beer. He ate popcorn rapidly and his eyes never left the pictures of the Yankees. He paused only long enough to say, "Aren't you going to get in bed with me? Catfish Hunter's pitching!"

Margo Jong sighed. She could not bring back the old days by getting in bed and watching television—not knowing what she knew tonight, that those days were gone forever. She was not going to sink along with Bill; she would continue to grow and seek satisfaction in some new way. Perhaps Bill would someday see the need to do something for someone else. But no matter; she had set her course.

The heat lightning illuminated the street and a few drops of rain fell as Margo took her first steps toward a new life accompanied by her grey poodle.

Throughout the evening Bill Jong drank one six-pack and then another and the alcohol reached toxic levels in his bloodstream. He missed Reggie Jackson's home run and he also missed the announcement that interrupted the game. He had fallen asleep and he didn't know that his world had begun to tumble down around him, that from now on he would feel the consequences of a new law called 04Y4, unless, of course, he were to give up drinking.

The Sesame Seed Bakery

It was raining lightly when Freud left the dinner party but he didn't mind a little rain. Humidity made his white-blond hair curl and the girls said it looked cute. His face was relaxed and smiling as he jumped over the side of his old Buick convertible. What a car it was! A garage mechanic's nightmare. But it was his first car and he loved it. Anyway he had no money for a new one. And though he didn't say so, he enjoyed the visibility it afforded him. Impervious as both he and it were to wind and rain, he drove about the town in his topless car (it had been that way when he bought it) waving at every young and old person he saw. Their faces usually lit up and they waved back. "Oh, it's Freud!" He was well liked and gregarious.

Furthermore, he was a free man without hang-ups of any kind; that appealed to everybody who would like to be that way. It didn't bother Freud to be seen parking at Crabbe Grass's place or outside an X-rated movie; he was just as likely to put on a tie and appear in church and sit in the front pew. Freud, never wanting to miss any facet of life, tasted new experiences for the same reason cheese lovers taste cheese: to find the best there is. He did not allow his parents' plans for him to prevent his finding out

73

who he was, and he made up his own mind about human values by sampling the smorgasbord of life. Thus he acquired an assurance lacking in most twenty-three-year-olds which made him a leader among his peers and attracted the attention of his elders.

Freud picked up his purple bandana from the car seat and wiped his hot face. Getting away from the party had been easier than he figured, but his mother's request to buy muffins was typical of her. It was a scheme to delay his departure and, failing that, to get him back to the birthday party. He would get them because he liked to please his mother in small matters (it helped when he disagreed with her on large issues). Lest he forget all about the muffins in the excitement to come, he decided to stop in at The Sesame Seed on his way to Crabbe Grass's basement pad.

Arriving at the bakery in the old shoestore downtown, he followed the brass footprints imbedded in the sidewalk to The Sesame Seed. Three generations had followed those brass feet in the cement and the town was sentimental about them—had even passed an ordinance preserving them in perpetuity. Once they had led to the best fit in town, but now the brass soles took one to the finest pastries in Temagami Springs, made by a twenty-year-old girl who had gone to high school with John Freund III.

Freud pushed open the screen door. "Anybody here?" he called loudly, seeing perfectly well not ten feet away the startled face of Penny Dupre, rosy from the heat of the ovens over which she had been bending. Freud picked up a napkin from the nearby table and wiped the flour off her nose.

"Hello, John, I haven't seen you for a long time. How are you?" she asked timidly, smiling up at him. She'd forgotten he was so big. His shoulders were broader than ever and his eyes looked bigger than ever behind the thick lenses. But the smile spread across his wide face was the same smile she remembered.

"I'm great," he answered. "May I have a jelly doughnut? Thanks," he said, going around behind the counter as though he worked there. "You're a great cook, Penny ol' pal. Why don't you marry me?" he asked, his mouth full.

Penny was pleased. This brash man standing over her eating a doughnut was the same Freud, all right, the same one who sat behind her in Spanish class; if he wasn't begging her for a translation or passing her a note, he was gently poking her in the back. The teacher, Miss Holcomb, never guessed that the tremble on Penny's face was not shyness but rather her efforts to refrain from turning around and slapping Freud. For a second she was back in high school and she was wishing that just once she had had the courage to slap him.

Then John, licking his sticky fingers, spoke again. "I can't linger. I'm on my way to see Crabbie about a loan. Know him?" She nodded. "I presume he's still loaded."

"Oh, Freud." Her face was serious. "Don't get involved with him, not if you don't have to. He'll take you over."

"Me? Not likely, but what do you mean by that?"

"Well," answered Penny, "I guess it's a sin to hate anyone, but I—well, you know how he sticks around like an Egyptian fly. He acts threateningly and I just don't like him. I've thrown him out of The Sesame Seed more than once; but, being the leech he is, he's always coming by looking for somebody to latch on to. You'll be sorry if you get involved with him."

"I know what you mean. He's not your kind of guy, but I'm only after him for his money," joked Freud, pouring himself a cup of coffee. "I need a loan."

"Let's sit a minute while no one's here," she said. Freud pulled up two heavy oak kitchen chairs to a small oak table, one of an assortment of various shapes and sizes that were available for customers. He looked about at the nice, warm, attractive place and wondered how frail Penny had gotten up the energy to open her own business. She was maturing.

Then he heard her ask, "Isn't there anything I can do for you? I have a little money saved. Can you believe it, I've been here almost a year? I was going to have my teeth straightened but I could help you out instead. That is, if it's not too much. I thought from what people said that you had a good job at the law firm."

"I do. I have a job—until next Monday when I'm quitting. The reason? I have a great scheme, which, if all goes as I plan, should put a roof over my head for the rest of this summer. Do you live at home?"

She nodded sadly. "I do. It's a drag, but Dad's been so sick, I stay on till I build up a little equity in this place."

"I understand how you feel. I live at home too; but I have to break free. I don't agree with my old man about anything. That's why this new project of mine is so important. It's my ticket to a new planet—and one thing is for sure, it will break the monotony of living in a small town like Temagami Springs!" He reached into his jeans and took out some bubble gum.

"Care for a piece? I'm collecting baseball cards."

"No, thank you, but tell me about your plans." Penny was interested and she didn't want him to leave.

"I need a thousand bucks, which added to what I've got should finance a certain purchase—a business property; and if I hurry and get some help real quick, I can be ready for the tourist season—if not by Memorial Day, then a few weeks later."

He looked into her eyes. "Penny, do you want to join me—sight unseen?" he asked. While he waited for her to reply (she was nervously folding a pile of paper napkins) he looked about at the neat little shop. He could certainly use her business experience. "Trust your old classmate with a little money. There might even be a job in it for you," he urged.

"But I have The Sesame Seed. I don't know, Freud, till I hear what it is," she said doubtfully. "Can't you tell me more so I can decide?" He could see she was tempted.

"No, I can't say more yet," he replied, placing his big hand firmly upon her thin shoulder. "Not till I pay another woman a visit. It's top secret, Pen, but you can trust me," he said firmly, fixing her with his big blue eyes and gripping her shoulder harder.

She trembled a little at his touch. "Oh, gee, John, it sounds wild, whatever it is. Another one of your mysteries! Remember when you put the bear in the school tower? I still don't know how you got it up there." Freud grinned, laughter behind his lenses. A second later Penelope caved in. "Okay, I'll lend you five hundred dollars—at the prime rate." She didn't quite know what that was, but it sounded good.

Freud hugged her to him like a kid clutching a toy doll and then he backed away. "Mother, you drive a hard bargain. Let's say you can decide later whether you want my blood! We're partners!" He smiled. "But make it one thousand dollars!" She nodded *yes* and he shook her hand. "Say, I'm glad my mother sent me down for muffins. I would never have thought of you for a partner."

"Thanks, Freud." And I was taking it as a compliment, Penny observed to herself as she carried their cups to the sink and wiped the table. Penny was tall and slender. She was five-feet-ten and she thought she was too tall. Penny had lovely hazel eyes and a thin face with a long nose. She thought it was too long, but actually it was just right. Penny's brown hair was below her shoulders but usually tied back because she was a baker. When it was down, very little of her face showed; she liked it better that way. She hid from the world because she was shy. Penny was not quite sure of her place in life, but she was trying to find it. She was definitely searching for the meaning of Penelope Alantha Dupre.

It wasn't like her to do anything out of the ordinary. Penny was too timid for that. So her decision to help Freud was rather impulsive. She knew it was; but then again, it was rather exciting too. It would give her something to think about while kneading dough and working in her store.

She came back to Freud and they sat down and had a nice talk about all the people they'd known in high school and the new kids in town. "I haven't told you, we have these crummy guests, an ancient roommate of my mother's and her moth-eaten daughter," Freud was saying when an old jeep without a muffler pulled up outside. The screen door banged open and four Saffies came in bringing along the strong odor of the fields and barns of Safflower Hill.

They immediately occupied, with much noise and shuffling about, the round oak table in the front window of the store. "Coffee and doughnuts, Penny," the shaggy red-bearded one called, sitting backwards on his chair.

"The usual for me," said a thin, seedy, pale kid, his dirty hair tied in a pony tail down his back.

Penny got up and waited on them. The thin one had put his feet up on another chair. "Please," she said, shoving his feet down, "you know I can't allow bare feet in here."

"Okay, okay, but I didn't bring any shoes," he whined.

Penny looked irritated but rejoined Freud who had sat

down in the other window. She had tied her hair back in a red bandana, and Freud looked at her for the first time and realized she was a very pretty girl. When her long hair was down it accentuated the narrowness of her face and the length of her nose, but when her hair was pulled back, she had a romantic look about her, a trifle serious but very pleasing.

"They're good customers of mine, but they stay too long," commented Penny to Freud. "Mark Sanders is usually with them and I do like Mark. Let's say I put up with the others. But I don't know whether they're an attraction. Maybe they drive people away."

"A little of both, I'm sure," Freud answered. "Then you must know that Mark had a fight with his old man and went to live at the Hill."

"Not know, in this town? Is there anything that happens that the whole town doesn't know before nightfall?" laughed Penelope. "But, in fact, I was one of the first to know about Mark. He came in and asked me if I wouldn't show them how to start a bakery up there. They're hurting for money and I understand they're trying hard to fill any needs they can find in Temagami Springs. I give them credit for trying; but they do have a power struggle going on and a lot of big problems. Maybe they need a leader like you."

"Oh, no, not me! Are you thinking of going?" asked Freud.

"Oh, no, not me either," she exclaimed, surprised at his question. "I value my independence too much to live in a no-money economy and have all those personal hassles. I'm not an organization person and I just hate meetings."

"It's an attractive idea in some ways—to be part of a big family," said Freud.

"Especially when you've had no brothers and sisters," added Penny. "Like me. At any rate, that was one of Mark's contentions. No, I know I don't want to live there, but I am going up for contra dancing and co-counseling, and I'd like to start a Bible study." Freud no longer had to see Crabbe Grass. He took off his pink polyester dress shirt and stuffed it in his pocket and sat back down in his T-shirt to have a long talk with his new partner.

"What's co-counseling?"

"Oh, haven't you done it? You have a sort of partner, someone you don't know well, and you spend an hour every week listening to each other."

"A steam valve?"

"That's it. But you don't talk about just anything. The leader guides you. It sounds marvelous to have someone to listen to me. No one ever has and I'm so repressed. Mother says it's shyness. Is inhibition the same thing, Freud?"

"No, I think it's deeper—subconscious stifling of desires for forbidden fruit."

"That's it! Sometimes I think I want to do all these things everybody's doing, but when I go along with the crowd something inside me says not to; then I don't enjoy myself at all and I feel threatened and lonely. What's wrong with me? My friends say I'm missing a lot of fun. Maybe I am and yet—am I, Freud?"

"No," he said seriously, "I don't think you are. You have gifts. Build them up and use them. Insist upon it. You've got to be happy when you're using your talents. I'll help you keep up your resolutions. And now that we're partners, I can tell you this: woman, we are going to have fun—real fun."

Penny started to smile but closed her lips. She was self-conscious about her teeth being uneven. "John, I hope I can help you in some way," she said as though it was unlikely.

"See, we're on our way to happiness. We're co-counseling.

Penny, you have already helped me tonight more than you'll ever know. Let's have another cup of coffee," said Freud.

Penny disappeared into the kitchen and the red-bearded one helped himself to a plate of brownies. Then he snapped on the radio above the cash register to station WAMY and took from his pocket a well-worn deck of cards.

There was a light knock and through the door appeared the neat yellow head of ten-year-old Bucky Sanders. "Is my brother, Mark, here?" he asked, looking hopefully over at the Saffies.

"Come on in, Bucky, and have a brownie," called the pale thin one. "Penny, a glass of milk for our friend. Mark's back at the Hill, kid. He had work to do."

"Oh, is he?" asked Bucky disappointedly, coming on in for the brownie while looking back uncertainly toward the door. "I have to keep an eye on my bike while I buy some fudge for Mom."

"Henny Penny. You have a customer," coughed the skinny one, wondering why Penny was so involved with the guy with the white afro.

This time Penny heard him and came out of the kitchen. "Oh, hi, Bucky!" She knew this little boy well. He came here often lately looking for his brother, Mark. Because Mark was forbidden to go home, they visited each other at The Sesame Seed. Their mother, Surtsey Sanders, saw to that by being hungry for sweet things every evening. "I didn't see you come in," said Penny pleasantly. "Help yourself." She gestured toward the counter, not wanting to disturb her rapport with Freud.

The red-bearded one turned the music up louder and the Saffies banged on the table like it was bongo drums. Its one leg was a little short and the table bumped up and down, the coffee cups making their contribution to the din. Bucky was enchanted. Freud looked from them to Penny. She shrugged. "Don't mind them. They do this every time they come. They're part of the band up at the Hill. It's really not a bad group."

Just as she said this the voice of the radio announcer broke in. "Are there any swingin' oldsters out there? Listen to this. You'll all be deevorced by September fifteenth. Free, man, free. Yep. 04Y4 is lee-gall. How about that for news? And now we dedicate to you the Dreadful Diaboloes singing *Burp Me—Belt Me—Bag Me, Baby.*"

"04Y4 constitutional!" screamed the Saffies and broke up laughing.

Freud jumped to his feet. "My old man has done it again," he mumbled to himself. "My poor mother—I wonder how she'll take all this publicity!"

"Oh, John, did you hear that?" cried Penelope, running around the table to him and putting her hand on his arm. "How will my parents handle this? Mom's so high-strung, and Dad's so sick and so utterly dependent upon her. If she hurts him now I'll never get over it. He always says he can go to live at The Old Soldiers' Home. Isn't that awful?" She began to tremble all over.

The Saffies were still joking in the corner. "Let the whole generation split apart—blow up! Who cares?" said one of them.

"I think it's cool, man. Everybody divorced. I'm gonna send my old lady a singing telegram: 'Happy D-day to you,'" he sang.

"It's no joke," said the red-bearded one.

"Do they have to get divorced?" asked little Bucky, who'd been looking from one to the other with an expression of concern on his round little face.

"Sure, all of them have to if they're over forty-five years old. Big deal! They're over the hill anyway!" At that Bucky gave a small shiver of disbelief, and suddenly he turned and ran out the door with the plate of fudge in his hand. The one with the red beard looked after Bucky. "Poor kid. He's upset too."

Penny and Freud sat down again and with their heads close together they talked for some time. Finally Freud looked at his watch and stood up. "I gotta run. I'll see you soon, my little tooth fairy!"

In a second Penny heard the Buick roar off down Main Street. She wondered if he were going home or to that other woman he had to see. Who could she be? Penny, irritated by the thought of the other woman, swept the Saffies right out into the street. "Go. I'm closing." Who could that other woman be? She, Penelope Dupre, who hadn't seen Freud since high school, was jealous; and Penny found it was a stimulating feeling. She didn't know it was the way he affected everybody.

The Home of Surtsey Sanders

Heat lightning flickered across the sky and Bucky Sanders ran home in three minutes flat, taking shortcuts through parking lots and over flower beds, finally cutting across the neighbor's lawn and stumbling over their sandbox. The fudge flew off into the darkness except for one piece, which stuck to the plate. Bucky had forgotten his precious bike.

In desperation he ran straight through the hedge and into his house by the cellar door, up a short flight of steps and into the living room, which was empty.

"Mom, Mom, where are you?" he called urgently, his round face red and hot from the race and his heart pounding.

His mother, knowing through long experience something was wrong, cried, "Bucky? Are you hurt?" She pulled off her half-glasses and jumped up quickly. "Bucky, what's the matter?" He appeared in the doorway—two arms, two legs, no cuts or bruises. Seeing he looked okay she felt vastly relieved.

"What is it, Mom, when two people who are married get divided? You know what I mean."

"Divorced?"

"That's it. It's on the news, Mom. You and Dad are getting divorced! September 15th. It said so on the news. Why, Mom, why?"

"Oh, Bucky, I haven't heard the news. I've been working on your costume for the Fourth of July parade. You know I have five of them to make. Do you want to see it?"

"But what about the divorce? I don't quite understand it, Mom. Is it why Dad didn't come to school to hear my speech this morning?" he asked, his voice rising.

"No, that's not why. Of course it's not. He had to work today, Bucky. Men have to work, you know." (She hated that useful statement; it seemed to imply that women didn't work.)

"I know, but he plays golf every Wednesday. Couldn't he have worked on Wednesday and come to school today? I gave a good speech, don't you think, Mom?"

"Yes, it was an excellent speech. I was very pleased you understand so much about the entrophication of Big Bear Lake. I bet your father doesn't even know about that. You can tell him at dinner tomorrow."

"You think he'll be home for dinner? He usually isn't. That's why I thought you'd be getting a divorce—like the Guthridges. Tom says his father's never home."

"No, dear, we're not getting a divorce. We've been married a long time and we need each other. Do you think people with six children can get a divorce? My, no—we're tied together for life! Don't worry another minute about it, dear. Did you see Mark tonight?"

Bucky nodded his head. "Uh-uh."

"Well, maybe tomorrow night. It's time for bed and no TV."

"Okay, Mom. I'm sorry, Mom. Here's your fudge. I dropped most of it running home to tell you the news." He handed her a sticky piece. "Can you eat this?"

Surtsey nodded, touched by his thoughtfulness. "Thanks, Bucky. Goodnight."

"Goodnight, Ma."

Surtsey put the fudge in her mouth, but she couldn't swallow; so she put it in the disposal and washed her hands. Then she went into the living room to think. She sat down, physically drained, weak, helpless—and exposed. She knew she hadn't been truthful with Bucky. She didn't want a divorce, but she couldn't speak for her husband. Surtsey turned out the lights and sat alone in the dark. Over and over she asked herself what she would do, how she should approach the subject with Bud. He was so difficult to talk to about anything personal. It never had been easy to talk things over, but it was getting harder to reach him as he grew older. Her husband had never cared when at times she was worried about her health or about the well-being of one of the children. Consequently, after some years, she ceased to ask for his help and sympathy. How could she express herself now?

Would Bud sign? In her present mood it didn't seem likely. Not if he was the swinger her friends implied. She refused to listen to their gossip about Bud. She didn't want to know. It would be easy enough to find out, but how could she live with him if she knew for certain that he was unfaithful? Just thinking about it gave her heartburn.

Surtsey went to the kitchen for an anti-acid pill. Her friends could love their tranquilizers and their alcohol, but common sense told her not to take drugs, not with the problems she faced. It would be too easy to get hooked. She poured herself a glass of milk and turned on the television. A panel of psychiatrists and social workers, the experts with their big degrees and no brains, were talking about

04Y4. They had been waiting for this day. She snapped it off thinking, talk's cheap. How could they know if they're not forty-five? Many of them are marital dropouts anyway. How could they begin to know the truth about "till death us do part"? They have their nerve to be telling the rest of us what it's all about!

Anger at strangers helped Surtsey, and her anger was all the greater because underneath she was angry with herself over the fact that her little son had brought home the news. She was angry at herself for not taking Bucky to the movies tonight—she had put him off because she was tired—and angry at herself for her performance at the Lost Friday Club that afternoon. In retrospect, Pat's calling on her to comment on birth control seemed calculated to embarass her: anything she might have said on the subject of sex would have been worth a few laughs. Why had she fallen into the trap? And what had come over her to say what she did about Bud? It was her need, her subconscious need to talk with someone about her husband, that had prompted her to imply that Bud was impotent. Some of her friends probably suspected it was so. She herself hadn't known till she'd read that doctor's book. How times have changed, she thought. Are we any happier for knowing scientific facts about ourselves? The old standards gave us something to cling to; now we have nothing. We talk about everything and feel the worse for it.

And yet she desperately wished for someone to talk to about 04Y4. Mark would have been a comfort, if only Bud hadn't driven him away. She thought about her eldest son, twenty-two years old and as handsome a son as any mother ever had, with his flamboyant black hair and his deep-set black eyes hiding behind a black beard and mustache. She shook her head and smiled. What a joy Mark was, so compatible with her and such a pleasure to be with. But she was not with him often enough anymore. Bud had sent him away, forbidding him to come home, and now her son was living at Safflower Hill. She had done what she could to help him move to the commune. In spite of local gossip about the Hill, Mark's mother was glad he had stayed near home.

After Bud told Mark never to come home again, Surtsey thought of running away to get even with her husband. But how could a mother of six leave her life's work, her home and her children? She had always believed they were a special family. How could she leave them? Where could she go? What would it prove? She was like Penn Central— bankrupt yet needed. She was an institution; institutions don't get up and go away. Maybe Bud could shed his children like a tree sheds leaves but not Surtsey. She wanted to continue to have a role in her children's lives. No, she couldn't run away, not even for spite.

But she did find a way to help Mark, a secret between her and her son; and since then—until tonight—she had come to terms with her life. Mark moved his wooden toy business to Safflower Hill and visited with his little brother Bucky at The Sesame Seed; and the rest of them saw him from time to time when his father was out of town. They had all been getting along somehow. But now what?

Overwhelmed by the implications of 04Y4 and having no one to talk to, Surtsey sought comfort in sleep. She went to the big bed in the guest room and turned back the covers. She lay down, but sleep did not come. She lay there wondering where her marriage had gone wrong. She had married young, against the wishes of her parents. Their stand had made no sense to her because it was obvious Bud would be a success. Even in high school he had a good business going, selling candy to the kids. Anyway, she had married Bud because she was in love with him, because he was so personable and cute. But, of course, she was too young to know how people sometimes disappoint.

She remembered her best friend saying that she and Bud made a good-looking couple. Bud looked like a baby then and he still did. Surtsey looked more her age because of her snow-white hair. (Women greyed early in her family and Surtsey was white by the time she was forty.) But she comforted herself that it was attractive with her blue eyes and tan skin. And she was attractive—stunning in fact.

Surtsey had a pleasant outgoing personality and a good figure. She was well dressed and athletic. And perhaps her most outstanding characteristic was her sense of concern for the young and helpless. It made her a good mother and it also made her much sought after as a worker for good causes. The County Home, the Junior League, the Red Cross and every fund-raising drive in town had put her on the board of directors at one time or another.

But since the twins were born in her late thirties, Surtsey had been giving up charity work, saying no every time the phone rang with a new request. It was because she had so much to do at home. Life was getting more complicated every day; just paying taxes and bills and keeping up with record keeping—filing health insurance claims and the like—was taking more of her time. And bringing home groceries, and cooking, and chauffeuring the Little League. She never had any time left over.

Surtsey was the victim too of the prevailing myth that unless a woman worked outside her home, she didn't have enough to do. This convenient assumption brought her husband and children running to her with all their little chores and responsibilities. Yes, it was getting to be too much just to take care of the paraphernalia they all acquired. And, of course, with responsibilities, little and big, Bud was no help. He took care of his own little things at the office—rather his secretary did—and his wife could look after everything else because she had nothing to do. If she complained or asked his help, he replied airily, "Give up a few of your charities!" She had given a little here and a little there till there was not much left to give.

When she mentioned this to her daughter, Mary Lynn told her she should have counselling to see why she allowed this to happen. It was rather a laugh, that suggestion! But maybe Mary Lynn was right. Maybe there was something she could do; but what? And meanwhile her husband went his merry way. Living with him was like starving to death in a lifeboat with a man who is eating a picnic lunch. It didn't seem fair that he have all the fun and she be left to suffer. Such were the thoughts that bedeviled her in the dead of night, and tonight they were worse than ever.

Much later, when she heard Bud coming in from the garage, she got up and went back to the bed she shared with him. Tonight was not the night to play games—no new misunderstandings until she had decided what she wanted to do about the future. If only he would come to bed and put his arms around her and say, "Honey, did you hear about that stupid law? Aren't we lucky it has nothing to do with us, that we'll love one another forever? How could I ever be without my marvelous wife? I wouldn't trade her for anything. What a lucky guy I am!" Then they'd fall asleep snug and safe in each other's arms and let the world tear itself apart.

But that would never be Bud's style.

A Midnight Visit

Olivia Dupre flicked on her bedside radio and lit a cigarette. It had been a frantic evening and so miserably hot. She had come home from Glory Land where she worked as Director of Art and Advertising to find her husband, Rene, choking and coughing, which necessitated a fast trip to Savernake County Medical Center. Now they were back home. His emphysema was apparently worse. Why hadn't he done his exercises regularly? At any rate he was under sedation now and breathing easier, but Olivia was taut, keyed up as she always was by excitement of any kind. The littered ash tray by her bed was testimony to that.

Despite the fact the doctor had suggested she not smoke, Olivia could not quit. However, she had long since moved her bed into a room away from Rene. The room that was hers had been meant for her studio. With its north window it was fine for an artist but chilly to sleep in. Rene, unable to climb stairs, slept in the wooden lean-to at the back of the kitchen of their tiny old saltbox house.

Tonight Olivia couldn't sit still. She pushed out her cigarette and went into the living room. If only she could have a cheerful fire, but its smoke too was hard on Rene.

Anyway, it was too hot for a fire. She gazed absently at the small, colored tapestries of knotted string which hung along the walls beside Rene's mandolin and the photos of his plane and crew taken during the Korean War, his last adventure. Somehow she felt sorry for herself stuck in this little saltbox with a sick and prematurely aging man. If only I were married to Brig, she thought.

Just then came the announcement. "This is station WAMY. We bring you a bulletin. 04Y4 is constitutional."

"Eureka!" exclaimed Olivia, her arms flying up and an expression of amazement on her face. She hadn't wanted to hope, she hadn't dared to hope it would be. Nor, of course, had she really thought through all of its implications. Nor was she ready to do so now.

But she thought immediately of her secret dream to marry her boss, Brig Bantley. No one knew of her fantasy, certainly not Rene or Brig, but it had been part of her daily life for a long, long time. The more often Brig's wife traveled from home the happier Olivia was; this time Lucy might not return. Lucy wouldn't leave Brig this summer if she really loved him.

Olivia sometimes felt Brig returned her affection. But though she frequently looked invitingly across the desk at him, so far she had had to content herself with his encouragement of her talents and his appreciation of her as an employee.

"Glory Land couldn't do without you, Livy," he often said.

"You mean you can't do without me," she murmured to herself, preferring to interpret it personally.

Tonight Olivia was ecstatic. "I must reach Brig. He'll be so upset, what with Lucy just gone away again. And he'll not have heard the news. I can't reach him by phone and he'll need someone to talk to." She thought for a moment and then on impulse she decided to drive to Passion Point and tell him about the ruling.

Olivia went into her room and put on the Mexican wedding dress Brig always admired on her. On nights like tonight, when she wanted to feel seductive, she wore large Mexican silver earrings, their turning orbs dangling from her ears; and looking in the mirror, she noted with satisfaction that they emphasized her large brown-rimmed grey eyes and gaunt cheekbones. She put on the silver Navajo ring Brig had given her long ago. Did he remember? Last of all, she put on her belt made of wolves' teeth which brought her luck. Olivia was a very dramatic and arty looking person with a flair for fabric and jewelry and perfume. She was creative in every aspect of her home and dress. Olivia threw a shawl around herself, took a nerve pill, and wrote a short note to Penny (who would be home soon from the bakery) to listen for Rene during the night.

"P.S. I'll be quite late, honey. Don't worry."

For the second time that evening Olivia got into her old Ford station wagon. She wished she could buy a new car, a Firebird or something flashy, but with the increasing cost of everything and Rene's bills higher all the time she couldn't afford a new car. Of course their costs would be lower if they lived near the Vet's hospital, but it was unthinkable to leave her job. It was all that sustained her. Nothing else existed anywhere like it for Olivia, and she was near Brig and with him every day.

As she drove swiftly through the night she said to herself, I've been tied down all these years, all these years. She thought back to how it was in the beginning. Olivia had sent to the Korean War a young man with whom she was very much in love. Rene was exciting and talked incessantly of his dreams of adventure. He promised her that she'd set up her easel at Paestrum and Portofino and paint the Blue Mosque. They would visit the troglodytes in Libya and sail through the Isles of Greece. She'd bathe in the sea with Dali at Port Lligat and carve marble sculpture beside Henry Moore at Altissimo. Such beautiful dreams—she really could see Olivia Dupre with an easel seated beside the Black Sea.

How quickly shattered were all her plans for the future when her young husband returned from Korea a weak and wounded man who would never realize his dreams, who had given his dreams for his country. As Yevtushenko wrote, "When the war was over youth was over"; and so it was for them.

Rene told her quietly one afternoon when she went to the hospital that he would receive a veteran's pension for the shrapnel in his lungs but that he wouldn't work for a long, long time. She remembered how they had looked at each other, embraced and said nothing.

And so Olivia, aged twenty-four, had gone like so many young people to Glory Land to ask for a job of Brigham Bantley. He had looked at her portfolio with enthusiasm and talked with her a long time. He told her what Glory Land meant to him and how he hoped working there would help her through her crises, help her to keep faith and love each day of her life.

Yes, Brigham Bantley had helped her all these years, and she was driving through the night to be with him. She was not unmindful of how much Brig valued his privacy when he went to Passion Point. He often told her he found peace and renewal in being alone and it made her a little uneasy to violate his privacy now. Furthermore, over all the years she had never once been invited to Passion Point; so underneath she was a little doubtful of the reception she would receive tonight.

"I know what I'll tell him," she said aloud. "He wasn't at the office this afternoon when Mrs. Small phoned to say she can't cook for us this summer. That's bad news he should know at once; and I'm going to suggest he interview Anna Maria Abendtal. She's supposed to be a fabulous cake maker—surely we could use a good cake maker! People in distress always eat more carbohydrates. Rene's doctor told me that. So it should be a real coup if we can get Anna Maria on our staff this summer." I'll remind him that we open in less than two weeks, she thought to herself. But her mind was really on the new law. Olivia drove faster than usual, and in less than two hours she found the way to Passion Point. When the car door opened and the light went on, she looked at her feet; she was wearing a black sandal and a brown one. After a moment's hesitation Olivia took her shoes off and dropped them behind the seat. Then with the help of her flashlight, she walked barefoot through the sedge grass over the dunes and around to the front door of Brig's little house.

Tired of his endless list of problems, Brigham Bantley had stepped out on the deck to look at the stars and listen to the night. Olivia came upon him on the deck with his eyes fixed on the stars.

"Brig," she said softly, "it's me. Olivia."

"Olivia! You frightened me. I was feeling like the only soul in the universe and never heard you drive up. Why are you here?" he asked bluntly, looking at her bare feet.

Olivia shivered. "Can we go inside, Brig? I'm cold." She stepped towards him, pushing her dark hair back over her neck.

"I'll get you a cup of coffee. It isn't Rene, is it? He hasn't—"

"Died? No, no. It's not Rene. I did take him to the emergency room earlier tonight, but he's sleeping now and he'll be okay. It's not Rene; it's us, all of us. Have you heard?" Brig's empty face told her he had not. "04Y4—it's legal."

"So, that's all?" After a few moments he said, "Well now, I guess we'll have to face up to it, won't we? I don't think you and I have any problems there."

"Don't we?" asked Olivia as she seated herself and looked up from under her lashes without lifting her head, a question in her tone of voice. As she did so she observed with utter surprise a female beach bag on the chair. She gasped a little, her mouth fell open, and she looked at Brig with the expression of one who has had a staggering blow.

"No, we don't. We love our spouses and they need us. Now you get along back to Rene before he misses you. He shouldn't be alone tonight. At once I say," said Brig, an unaccustomed tone of command in his voice.

"But did I tell you that Mrs. Small has resigned and I suggest you interview Anna Maria Abendtal for her place as head cook? She has a great reputation as a cake maker."

"So Mrs. Small has resigned. And who is Anna Maria Abendtal? Is she the museum keeper?" asked Brig, sitting down reluctantly, anxious for her to leave.

"That's the one."

"Oh, yes. I've heard of her. I think Lucy knows her; they sometimes play bridge together. Let's talk a minute; then you must go be with Rene tonight. Has he heard about 04Y4?"

"Not yet—not till tomorrow," said Olivia. At that moment there was a stir in the bedroom. "Who is that?" exclaimed Olivia aloud. Her own question took her by surprise and she was suddenly embarrassed.

"Just a sand flea, a kid who followed me home from the beach." Before Olivia could recover from her surprise the girl wrapped in a towel, a wet bikini in her hand and her golden hair tousled, staggered through the room and out the front door.

You little imp! I could spank your round bottom, exclaimed Olivia to herself, following the girl with her eyes. The nerve of today's kids. My poor innocent Brig! She added aloud, "Brig, you don't know today's kids like I do. They can be ruthless. She's probably after you for your money!"

"Why, she doesn't even know my name. We're Frisbee partners, that's all," he added with a twinkle in his big purple eyes, amused that Olivia was behaving so protectively. Brig got up and walked over to the window and looked out and then turned back to his guest.

She looked up into his large rugged face. "Nevertheless, Brig, I had to say that. You're so innocent where women are concerned, and they all adore you. Have you never noticed the eyes of all the staff at Glory Land upon you?"

"The eyes of glory are upon me," he sang. Seeing she was serious, he said, "I'm glad about that because I'm their boss. I'm glad they care." He got to his feet and Olivia's eyes never left his face. Yes, she thought. We care. We all care.

Brig looked down at her. "It was just like you, Livy, to be so thoughtful as to come so far to tell me the news. Now get up, girl, and go home." He pulled her to her feet. "Go back to Rene. And be assured I'll go see Miss Abendtal on Monday. Now you must leave me alone. I know you understand I have to be alone to think about what this decision will mean for Glory Land this summer. Will it hurt business?" He was serious now. "Will our lady cooks come? Do we perhaps have their ages listed somewhere?" he asked, suddenly smiling.

"Not their real ages," laughed Olivia.

"I see. Well, we'll phone them on Monday." He put his arm around her shoulder and walked her to the door, still wondering why she wore no shoes. He followed behind her along the path through the wild plum bushes and opened her car door. "Goodnight, Olivia. Drive safely."

"Goodnight, Brig," she smiled sadly, fear in her round grey eyes. She felt drained of all emotion as she drove slowly back to Temagami Springs.

Back in her saltbox, utterly wrung out from her expenditure of physical and emotional energy, Olivia Dupre fell asleep and had a dream. All the women in Temagami Springs stood at a curbside on the Fourth of July, each one dress size 22½, with identical bulging purses over their right arms. They stood at military attention, while passing by in revue came their husbands—each with a clone of the sand-runt in a gold bikini on his arm. Olivia awoke sobbing and went to the bathroom for a sleeping pill, checking first to see whether Rene was still breathing. He was looking much better.

Bring Back Those Years

In the early evening hours of that Friday in mid-May, Skipper Bantley walked home from the garage where he left his car. He was six feet tall, slender and supple, and he moved along with swift strides, stopping now and then to look into the woods and watch the birds. Skip walked along rejoicing, thinking about himself and his need to write lyrics and hear them sung. He had felt compelled to make up poetry and play with words for as long as he could remember; and when he was nine years old he was writing down his ideas in little notebooks, which he kept hidden in his deepest drawer. He remembered the day he tried out his first song publicly while going through Cornwall House with the fourth grade. The curator, Anna Abendtal, had come running to see who climbed under the velvet ropes to play the piano, but she did not punish him. In fact, she liked the piece, and that was the day they became friends.

A few years later in high school, he was put on detention more than once for not listening to the teacher when lyrics were running through his head. In college it was easier. He sat in the back and when an inspiration came, he walked out of class to find a piano. However, he found that his dates never cared very much when he left them waiting while he captured an idea. Nowadays it was a well-kept secret from his father that he spent most of his time playing around with words. It was, of course, why he stared into space and seemed to look out the window so often; but how do you explain that to someone who calls you a "day dreamer"?

He wanted a piano of his own at college, which meant an apartment; this way he could compose without interruption. But his father objected, saying an apartment would be expensive and a piano would interfere with his engineering studies, that he could come home from State College on weekends and use the piano if he cared to. When he did experiment at home, his dad invariably called from wherever he was, "Play the classics! Play the classics"; and Skipper dutifully switched from his own melodies to a few lines of a Beethoven sonata, never saying a word to his father. But today he spoke, "I'm not a weekend composer. You just don't understand how hard it is." Skip threw a rock at a tree as he thought out loud. "I may have scored eight hundred on the math SAT and won a scholarship, but I do not want to be an engineer. Gosh, Dad, how dull!" he said to his father, who, of course, wasn't there.

Skip stopped to listen to the lichens. Everyone knows you can't do that, but he could. Sitting on a stump while he rested, he shook a stone from his faded sneakers. His shoe had a hole in the toe. He lingered awhile in the woods looking at the jack-in-the-pulpits and the ferns pointing up through the soil, and the white mayflowers and purple triliums, and he smelled the fertile aroma of the newly stirring earth. As he dwelled on these wonders he was filled with delight, and he sang their praises in song. He made up his mind; he knew then and there that he was not going to be an engineer. He was going to be a songwriter if he had to do without everything commonly regarded as important—

a college degree for one thing. Probably he wouldn't marry before he was forty.

Having made such momentous decisions he walked on home with faster steps; and soon, taking the back lane through the wooded hills, he reached the meadows and the paved drive, which, passing between rows of red maples, made a circle in front of the Bantley's low brick house.

Skipper could see from some distance off that his father's maroon Mercedes was gone from its usual place in the driveway. However, his sister's green Toyota was parked by the front door. He was glad Savy was home, because he wanted her approval of his big decision to quit college.

The hood of the car was up and she was bending over the car doing something with a wrench and she did not see him coming. In true brotherly fashion he approached slowly from behind and swatted her protruding backside with the evening paper. "Hi, Sis. What is my big sister doing?" She ignored him, so he took off his sunglasses and stepped closer to see what she was doing. He looked at the engine, which looked to him like any other. He liked motors as long as they worked, but he didn't find them all that interesting. Skipper preferred living, growing, changing things and he was indeed surprised to find his sister working on her car. Did she like doing mechanical things?

Savy kept on doing whatever it was she was doing and he swatted her again. "Remember me? Say, where's Dad?"

"Hey, cut it out," she laughed, looking around at him from beneath her shoulder-length red hair without lifting her hands from under the hood. "What do you think I'm doing? I'm changing my spark plugs and tuning the motor," she answered, wiping an oily glove across her brow. "I'm saving forty dollars, that's what I'm doing." She studied his amused expression. "Don't you know I took a course in auto repair?"

"At Vassar!" he exclaimed, his bluish eyes twinkling.

Savy made a snoot. "Our dinner's in the oven and I won't be much longer," she said. "Here, hold these," she added, handing him a pair of pliers.

"Seeing you like this, Sis, makes me think you chicks want to take over the world."

"Honestly, you guys. Come off it. It's a far cry from spark plugs—the world I mean. If you want the world you can have it. Temagami Springs is trouble enough. You asked me where Dad is. He's gone to Passion Point for the weekend—taking a break to plan his summer he said."

"That's a relief," commented Skip.

Savy answered, "It sure is; but, Skip, have you noticed," she continued in a voice full of concern, "how upset Dad is when Mother leaves? I think he feels rejected, left behind—like I used to feel when they went to New York to the opera and left us with Riddles." Who could forget the baby-sitter who came with her book of riddles? Skip smiled, remembering. Savy straightened up and handed her brother a screwdriver. How tall and good-looking her kid brother was; and he looked so young and innocent. "Skip, if Mom and Dad weren't my parents, I'd tell them that they've lost sight of what's important in life: people—not places and things—but people and, most of all, each other—making time to be with each other."

"Yes, you're right. Let's go into the house and eat," said Skip quietly. "Mom's gone and the summer will be over before she comes back. She said she'll phone us from Dakar to say she's safely there, so you can expect her call at one or two in the morning."

"Be patient a moment longer while I file my points," said Savy, bending over her Toyota again. "What worries me is that Mom might catch something like malaria or schisto-somiasis. Did you know that only a few years ago they only sold one-way tickets from London to the Ivory Coast? No one ever came back!"

"She's had every shot I can think of," comforted Skip.

"For llasa fever? There's no shot for that."

"You read too much, Sis. Mom's resilient. I guess she'll make it. Dad's another matter. Mom said at the airport our being here helps Dad. I'm sure glad you're going to be home this summer. I'll tell you one thing, I'd not be here right now if I could afford an apartment," said Skip. "I want to be able to work whenever I feel the urge."

"Yes, I know," said Savy.

"And if I ever start selling my songs—" Skip hesitated, his eyes following a pair of barn swallows flying in and out of the garage. "By the way," he began again, "I haven't told you the big news—I'm not going back to college in September! I'm dropping out." This had the hoped-for effect on his sister.

Savy put down her caliper and turned to look at him with open mouth. "You are!" she exclaimed. She knew it was a momentous decision for Skip, considering their father's strong feelings about the value of a college education. She was stunned.

Skip took his hands out of his pockets and gestured as he spoke. "I'm so happy when songs flow through me. Everyone says there's no money in music unless you sell. But how can I succeed without freedom to compose and exposure in the market place? People are so narrow-minded. No one understands me around here, except maybe you."

Just then a loud buzz from the stove inside the open kitchen window told them the dinners were hot. "Put down that wrench, woman. I'm starving. Let's go inside and taste your cooking. What are we having?" asked Skip.

"Mexican dinners," answered Savy.

Her brother made a face. "No roast beef and chocolate cake! Don't they teach cooking at Vassar? I walked three miles and I'm hungry," he said, sounding like a little child.

"You'll get enough. I put two dinners in the oven for you and we can make a salad. There's ice cream and cheesecake in the freezer and plenty of milk. Let's go."

As soon as they were in the kitchen, Skip went to the cellar and brought back a bottle of white wine. "I wish it were Schramsberg," he said, and his clean-shaven face wore a very happy look. "But this will have to serve as champagne tonight." He placed the bottle and two cut-glass wine glasses on the table.

"Are we celebrating having the house to ourselves for the whole weekend? Let's carry our supper outside and watch the sunset," said Savy. They picked up their food and went out onto the terrace overlooking the Valley of Springs and sat down at the white iron table beside the swimming pool. Savy raised her glass towards her baby brother. "To our weekend alone. Isn't it great?"

"You said it. It is great! But I want to celebrate something greater still." He lifted his glass and touched hers. "Here's to the song I wrote today. Here's to an album by fall. Can you believe it, Sis? I really wrote something good today. The idea came to me at the airport and I worked all afternoon over at Anna's and the time went by like ten minutes. Forgive me for raving on about it, but I'm all spaced out!"

His enthusiasm was infectious. Savy reached across the table and poked him. "When can I hear it? I know how secretive you are. When? When?" she cried.

"Well, slow up. You know my feelings are sensitive about anything I write. One family jest and I'll give it all up. That's just how it is. I can't take even well-meant criticism."

"Oh, Skip. You're too sensitive. Anyway, I'm a good critic. I won't laugh or anything."

"Let me tell you the rest," he added eagerly, brushing his wavy hair from his eyes. "I'm going to make a disc with the Safflowers. Jerry's going to help me."

"Them?" asked Savy skeptically.

"They're good," answered Skip, defensively, "and if you talk Dad into it—"

"Me? Into what?"

"I've noticed he listens to you. You're the family diplomat. If you talk Dad into it, he'll hire the Saffies group for August and then I can introduce my songs and maybe, with luck, unveil them to the world outside our little village. I have to make my debut some place. You will help persuade Dad, won't you?"

"Have you ever mentioned this idea about the Saffies to Dad?" asked Savy doubtfully. "He's not much impressed with what he calls their communal living."

"Nah, course not. He'll have to be convinced; but if I ask him, he'll lecture me about math or some irrelevancy and totally miss the importance of this to me," Skip answered. "Why is it that he always hurts me? But Anna Maria—she understands. She heard my song this afternoon and had tears in her eyes! 'How could one so young know that much about life?' was what she said. Isn't that great?"

"Won't you sing it for me—just once?" asked Savy, alive with curiosity.

Before he could answer, Skip looked at his watch. "Oh, oh—it's 9:55 and I don't want to miss Bev Jones singing her new hit on the *Back-to-Back Show*." He ran inside the house and snapped on the television.

"Ladies and gentlemen, we interrupt this broadcast for a

special NBC news report. Today Judge John Freund II ruled that 04Y4 is constitutional. There will be a special broadcast on the new law at 12:30 a.m. and our distinguished panel will include Dr. William Johnson, Dr. Virginia Masters, Dr. Benjamin Spock, Ms. Jessie Bernard and Ms. Dolly Batson. Be sure to stay tuned for their latest up-to-the-minute commentary."

"Oh, Lord," breathed Savy, dropping onto the sofa, "what will our parents do?" She shivered over the very thought of their being divorced.

"How should I know," said Skip, snapping off the television, forgetting to wait for Bev Jones. He was shaking his head. His usually merry face was grave and there was sadness in his compassionate eyes. "Any way it works out, someone—everyone—will be hurt. That's what I foresee," he said quietly, putting his empty wine glass on top of the television set.

"Why don't they think of these things before they act?" exclaimed his sister.

"Who?"

"Well, whoever got such an idea," said Savy angrily.

"Politicians? They don't think. No one has any foresight anymore or any wisdom."

"Well, I guess it's final; it's happened. When Mother calls shall we tell her?" asked the young girl.

"Of course. She must come home at once—on the next flight—and defend her rights. Dad's not unattractive you know. I think Olivia Dupre has had her eye on him for a long time!" said Skipper Bantley.

"Oh, shush, Skip," said Savy.

"If their generation acts like ours, women will be throwing themselves at him, offering sex for anything they can get. Women are dragons," continued Skip.

"Not all women."

"No, not all," he added begrudgingly.

"Maybe Dad won't sign—or whatever it is they have to do. But I really think he will. They wouldn't put away Meggido here, would they, Meggido?" she said, soothing the silky coat of the family Labrador dog. "Why would they put away each other?" She looked bleakly at her brother.

Skip shrugged his shoulders. "I'm still hungry." So saying he went to the kitchen and made himself two bologna sandwiches. "I'm tired," he said when he came back with a big full plate. "You take Mom's call. I'm going to bed."

"Isn't that just like you to get out of something unpleasant—like you always get out of going to family funerals. What'll I say to her?" asked Savy.

"I dunno. You figure it out. Tell her to come home."

"By the way, where's your car, Skip?"

"It's down at the garage having the spark plugs changed by a woman mechanic. Thanks to you girls we men are moving closer to utopia with each passing day. Will you run me down to pick it up in the morning?"

"Okay," she laughed. "I guess I have to type my thesis tonight anyway. It's due on Tuesday. It's called *The Historical Value of the Backgrounds in Medieval Paintings.* Sometime I'll read it to you; it's not bad. But, of course, I couldn't take the least bit of criticism," she kidded, adjusting the carbon paper in her typewriter.

Sometime later Savernake Bantley stopped typing to listen to the sound of Skip's music coming on the humid night air out his window and through the open kitchen door. She could hear him singing the lyrics in his small mellow voice. He sang the verses over and over, changing a word here and a word there, and as he sang and plucked his guitar he was accompanied by flashes of heat lightning.

"We have been with each other
Throughout all these years
There's been sunlight and shadow
And laughter and tears.

I loved you in the shadow
Through the sunlight and tears
And now what has happened
To all of those years?

The sun doesn't rise now days
And the nights are so chill
Your arms aren't around me
And gone is the thrill.

The sun doesn't shine
I live in the shade
My life is in shadow
And so I'm afraid.

I loved you in the shadow
Through the sunlight and tears
And now what has happened
To all of those years?

Oh, bring back the sunlight
I'll even take tears
But light up this darkness
And bring back those years."

It's lovely. Mom and Dad will like that, said Savy to herself. My little brother *is* going to be a songwriter. I do believe he is. As she said this there was a loud boom of thunder
followed by a sudden fall of heavy rain on the shake roof.
Savy got up from her typewriter to close the French doors
just as the telephone rang. It rang once. Then there was

silence. She picked up the receiver, but there was no one on the line. The storm continued and finally Savy gave up waiting for her mother's call and went to bed.

04Y4 was the law of the land.

PART II

Late May

"It's Awful to be Forty-Five"

The decision of the Judges' Court that 04Y4 was constitutional came like a sudden death in the family. In truth, it was a death—the death of married life as it had been. Those to whom the law applied went into shock when they discovered they were living in a different world. It was a world in which the future was uncertain, and the hour of this discovery was dark indeed.

The new law had been passed and delivered to the public as a simple little licensing procedure, like getting a new driver's license or a hunting license; but there was one big difference, and that was the aforementioned involved one person with one purpose, whereas 04Y4 was between two people, people at an age when purposes are many and often divergent. It was passed in the name of freedom by men who could not agree what that word meant And it was a very diabolical little law typical of the times.

In due course most of the survivors would adjust to the changes brought by this "harmless little law" because they had no alternative. But through the long night that followed the announcement, many of those concerned lay awake looking at the ceiling, each one contemplating his personal involvement, his eventual decision. As every single one was to discover, it was a lonely confrontation with far-reaching consequences.

Throughout those long, dark hours the mind of each concerned soul was prey to wild thoughts, sometimes tempting and unthinkable thoughts, which returned again and again like stubborn children refusing to be put to bed. Long-buried repression surfaced to destroy the equanimity of the spirit. Long-forgotten fears and jealousies seeped back to poison the defenseless heart. Insecurities crept out from under their blanket of material possessions to torment the sensitive nervous system.

Tranquility was gone and there was left only an overwhelming poverty of spirit as the personal implications of that simple little law danced through the psyches of those who lay awake in the night.

Is it any wonder that sleep was elusive, that tears fell and bodies tossed in their beds, that those concerned uttered the cry, "Will daybreak never come?"

Brigham Bantley was one for whom there was no sleep. He awoke unrested at dawn with the thought that he should do something about 04Y4. But what? If only his wife was here, they would talk it over and agree to sign. That would be that and they would put 04Y4 out of their minds. But Lucy was not here and he would worry till she returned. Would she come home when she found out? He could not be sure, and today there was no one to turn to because this was a curiously private affair between two married people.

By morning Brigham Bantley had decided that he must not think about the personal implications of the law. He must think only of what it might mean for Glory Land. Perhaps a swim in the frigid surf would help clear his troubled mind. He reached for his swim suit. It was clammy from the day before. Brig struggled into it with difficulty and put his damp terry robe around his body without pleasure. Then he stepped out into the wet, grey fog and stood on the deck with the mist all around him. It was an eerie, quiet dawn. Even the weather seemed to be waiting for something to happen. The only sound was from the gulls, calling to one another on a high pinging frequency, their loud, cracking voices like an oracle foretelling bad times to come.

Brig stood there motionless for some time until the fog lifted and the sky grew lighter. Then he walked across the wet deck. A light breeze fanned a spider web by the blue door and mosquitoes came from their hiding places. His towel from the previous day lay on the redwood chair as wet and heavy as his mood. He picked it up and wrung it out and wiped his face and neck. Then, dropping it, he vaulted the railing and jogged over the dunes to the shore. There was no surf. The sea was flat and expressionless.

Brig sat down on a grey driftwood log and drew patterns in the wet sand with a stick. Then he flung the stick away and stared bleakly at the cold grey water. If he expected to review his life and make decisions about September it was too soon. He sat for a time, dejected and alone.

The early morning sun was a pale disc in the platinum sky and the pewter water rushed quietly over the rocks to his feet, its tiny waves following fast upon one another, swoosh after swoosh, anesthetizing his thoughts as if to say, "Don't think. Stop trying. Then I'll be silent. Then you can find answers." But the little waves never stopped coming. He sat there awhile pressing his big foot in the sand, watching the water fill his prints and take them away, but it was hopeless. He was too unhappy to sit still; he needed to absorb himself in work. And so Brig stood up, a bit stiff from the damp and, turning his back to the sea, he walked across the dunes to his little cabin. The rhythmic lap of the waves followed him. "Go home, go back to the forest. Go home, your respite is over. Go home, go back to the town. Go home, go back. . . ."

Seeing nothing to do but obey the commands of the sea, Brigham Bantley packed his things quickly into his rucksack; tossing it into the rear seat of his car, he got into the driver's seat. The moment he turned the key in the ignition Brig felt better. The sun came out, the fog dissipated, and he drove rapidly down Lighthouse Road. Passing the town beach he was surprised to spot the sand imp in her gold bikini, vivid pink Frisbee in hand, getting out of a car with five young men. He remembered what she had said. "It's important not to have a day you don't enjoy." She was right. Maybe he could even enjoy today—maybe relax and play a little Frisbee with the kids before going home. He turned his car into the parking lot and pulled up near the suntanned girl.

Rolling down his window, Brig called to her gaily, "Hello there. Say, I want to thank you for the Frisbee lesson."

The imp turned towards him, her flat brown face tilted provocatively as though she was trying to remember who he was. After a telling pause, she said impishly, "Yes, it was better than playing with Woof Woof!" Woof Woof, a long-haired brown mutt, was running around the dunes in great circles. "Here, Woof Woof. Go fetch!" She tossed the pink Frisbee. Woof Woof ran off, his plumed tail flying, happy to retrieve the Frisbee.

Just like me, thought Brig, putting the car into reverse and spinning the wheels in the sand. As he drove off, embarrassed by her put-down, he heard the youngsters laugh. Are we all a bunch of Woof Woofs running after a plastic Frisbee? he asked bitterly.

Brigham Bantley felt a depression such as he had never known, and with it a sense of time passing. "Oh, God," he implored, "it's awful to be forty-five!" He drove faster and faster as if to out-distance time. He was in such a furious hurry that he didn't immediately notice the tailgater with two revolving red lights on his roof. Not till the tailgater swung around and nearly pushed him onto the shoulder of the road did he realize he had been caught by the radar of the state police.

"Where are you going in such a hurry?" asked a staunch-looking officer.

"Well, sir, have you ever felt you didn't know where you were going but you had to get there in a hurry?" asked Brig.

The officer's determined look disappeared as he thought about that. "You're an odd one; but I think I know what you mean. You're a forty-fiver, aren't you? Like me." He smiled a gleeful smile. "Well, being forty-five costs a lot of money these days. Like about fifty dollars," he added, flourishing a white pad while he watched the look of disappointment on the guilty party's face. "But on the other hand, I think that on account of last night, I'll just give you a warning," he added, putting away the pad. "Be careful, partner, or you won't live to enjoy your second chance!"

Brig nodded and moved on slowly. Second chance. What did he mean by that? Marriage? Would one ever go through marriage all over again, those long years of rearing a family, all the while looking forward to a kind of special someday that never comes? He didn't answer his own question and it seemed an interminable time until he turned off Route 9 and drove up the road to his house.

His unexpected arrival at home surprised his son, Skip, and his daughter, Savy, who were just diving into the cold swimming pool for a dip before breakfast. "Oh! Hi, Dad," called Savy, climbing up the ladder, her shapely body oily wet and her long red-blonde hair dripping water down her back. She gave him a wan smile, covering her disappointment over his change in plans. "Are you home already? We thought you were coming back tomorrow," she said as she wrapped her shivering body in a terry cloth blanket.

"No, I'm home," he answered abruptly. "I have work to do. You've probably heard about 04Y4. Well, I've thought it over and decided that rather than hurting us, it will increase our business. People need release in times of stress and I'd say good eating in park-like surroundings is as good a medicine for that as anything. Don't you agree with me, Skip?" he asked, looking down at his son who had surfaced below him.

"Huh? Agree? Sure, Dad, sure. That's true." Skip hadn't really heard what his dad said, so he swam over to the ladder and came out, rubbing himself all over with a towel before approaching his father. Brig sensed that, as usual, his son was not giving his full attention to the problems of their business. What was he thinking about all the time? Why was he so slow about everything?

Brig sat down by the table at poolside and motioned the children to do likewise. For a moment the father was preoccupied with making notes on a pad. At length, a puzzled frown on his tan face, he said, "I must phone all my cooks today and make sure their matrimonial problems aren't about to interfere just as we're ready to open. Mrs. Small can't be with us. Mrs. Danzig will need to be talked into coming, as she has to be every year; we can't be without her shrimp casseroles; and I don't know about Mrs. Coolidge. Her Christmas card indicated she and Elmer were separating. That certainly might keep her from coming." He shook his head and checked her name on the list with his pencil. "Olivia says we need a new pastry cook and several busboys and waitresses. I wish you could make these calls for me, Skip."

Fortunately, Brig didn't look up from his list of names and note the look of dismay on Skip's thin face. "No, on second thought, I'll have to make these calls myself. Can you think of anything else we should be doing?"

"No, Dad," answered Skip, who was putting sun lotion on his shoulders. "I think you've thought of everything. But there is something I want to tell you about. I've written a good song—at least I think it's timely, and Savy thinks it's—"

"Savy," interrupted Brig, looking up. "Where did Savy go? She could make some of these calls and maybe learn more from the ladies than I could. Tell her I'll be back this afternoon; she's to meet me at my office," he instructed as he stood up and gathered his notes. "After I change my clothes I'm going over to see Miss Abendtal, but I'll be back shortly. Stay around." Brig strode into the house.

Miss Abendtal, thought Skip. Anna? He doesn't know her! Skip was sure his father didn't realize that his son spent a lot of time in Miss Abendtal's cellar working at her piano. I hope she doesn't tell him, he thought. Dad's sure in a bad humor today.

Fifteen minutes later, while Skip was fixing himself a late breakfast in the kitchen, Brig came down and went to the garage. His face was tan from his afternoon in the sun and he had put on a coat and shirt and tie, and even Skip noticed how handsome his father was with his long sideburns, turning white below his black hair. He sure had a strong profile and a straight nose. Skip wished he looked like that, but it was Banter who resembled his father. Skip had his mother's small fine features.

Brig drove out of the garage. He had changed cars. As he drove away, Skip's eyes followed the silver limousine down the driveway. "It must be important, whatever it is. He's taking the Bentley!" His father had a rule; he used his precious old automobile on only three occasions each summer—to open and close Glory Land and on the Fourth of July. Skipper Bantley shrugged his shoulders. This was surely an exceptional day—Dad was driving the Bentley and breaking his own rule, which was absolutely unheard of.

Anna Maria Abendtal

On this beautiful morning in May, even as Brigham Bantley was on his way to see her, Anna Maria Abendtal was taking a stroll through the lovely grounds of Cornwall House. The garden was coming alive after a long season of sleep. It was a day of rebirth and renewal, a day for singing and rejoicing, a day for refreshing one's soul. Anna Maria Abendtal was doing all that. She walked slowly along the path, looking and listening. Now and then she stopped to warble with the birds building a nest in the maple tree. While she stood quietly searching above her for sight of the nest, a pair of goldfinches darted by, crying per-chik-o-ree as they flew to the nearby fields, and in the top of the highest elm, a Baltimore oriole sang in flute-like tones. In the bushes the robins whistled and the sparrows twittered. Tweeter and chirp and peep—there was conversation everywhere, and Anna Maria added her voice to theirs in celebration.

Happiness shone in her soft brown eyes at being part of this coming of new life. She looked from the flower beds to the swaying trees to the clouds scudding across the sky, and it came to her in a flash that it is an awesome thing, a very rare and precious thing to be born, to be living at all!

Anna Maria breathed deeply of the fresh humusy smell of spring, and as she gazed at each new leaf, each little shoot, and every fragrant growing plant blessing her garden anew, she felt a kinship with all living things and a sense of belonging to mother earth with its cycles of life and death and life again.

In many ways human beings are like plants—each one a wonder of creation, each serving his own function, each with its season. And in their uniqueness and design people are as diverse as all other living things. Some are beautiful to look upon; some stand strong and tall. Some are tiny and fragile, some wildly luxurious. And there are rare ones— often plain but sturdy ones not found in every garden, scarcely to be found at all. Such a person was Anna Maria Abendtal.

Should you happen to meet her in the supermarket or at the savings bank you would have a happier day because of it. Anna Maria, called Anna by her friends, had a rare capacity for caring about people, and she radiated such happiness and good will that meeting her was like standing beside shiny rippling waters on a warm sunny day.

If you were to describe this remarkable woman to a friend, you might say her manner was unassuming and so was her appearance. Her brown hair was short and wavy and her eyes were very dark; the pupils and iris were of the same brown-black color and gave her a deep and mellow look. Her profile was one quite often seen in Switzerland, the country where she was born; she had a prominent nose, angled parallel with her forehead and set ahead of her wide mouth and chin. Anna Maria was not very tall; her figure might be called motherly. She dressed casually, fond of hand-knit sweaters, tweed skirts and loafers—not exactly up on the new look in clothes!

But if her clothes were old-fashioned for reasons of thrift, her outlook on life was always up-to-date—so much so that people of all ages were comfortable with Anna Maria. There was just something special about her, an indefinable quality which magnified and enlivened all those who knew her.

This same indefinable something filled the gardens and permeated the rooms of the lovely eighteenth-century home where she lived and worked, the place called Cornwall House. When the Historical Society acquired it some fifteen years before, Anna Maria Abendtal was the ideal choice for the job as curator, because she was a single woman who lived by herself and because she knew all about the old house. Indeed the Savernake Historical Society couldn't have found a better person for the job.

In that house and garden so alive with her presence lived Anna Maria, ever tending, ever caring. Although her life was quiet and confining, it was a full one because she had so many friends; people of all ages came to her for helpful advice or just to be with her, for she made them feel good. She was always there when they needed her, which made her a true friend.

Through her helpfulness to young people, Anna was an influence for good in the little town of Temagami Springs. Fortunately, there were people like her in every city and village, and it was well for all that they would not trade whatever it was they had for the honors and rewards of worldly success.

But in the evenings, after her friends went home to their families, Anna Maria Abendtal felt the loneliness of her life. The large empty rooms of the old house seemed to stand around her and ask, "Why have you become like us? Isn't there something more interesting you want to do with your life? Isn't it time for a change?"

Within the limits of her modest income, Anna was doing all she could do—namely, helping in many little ways a dozen children in distant lands. It wasn't much, but it gave her great satisfaction. She filled her lonely evenings reading and writing to her godchildren, her *Enkelkindern,* as she called them. She tried in her letters to share more with them than her money could buy. In order to do this she went frequently to the library, always looking for new books about the homelands of her children. And as a result of her reading, Anna knew more about their countries than the children did themselves. When her adoptees grew old enough for her correspondence school she became their teacher, seeking like all good teachers to enlarge their horizons and increase their understanding. She loved hearing from them—oh, it was a day of joy when Anna Maria found a letter from an *Enkelkind* in her mailbox!

So, in a small sense these children were her family. But letters are not the same as having loved ones coming and going, conversing over dinner, saying goodnight at the end of the day—sharing not only the triumphs but also the little intimacies, the small daily happenings that make for the fullness of family life.

And in the deep hours of night there were moments when she longed to start over again, to be young, to marry and have a family of her own. But it was too late for that. She needed companionship; sometimes she even wished she were having an affair. But it seemed that neither love nor matrimony nor children were for her. There was no reason; it was just the way things turned out for Anna. She was what she was and that included being lonely and middle-aged.

However, Anna was not entirely without family in this world. She wrote frequent letters to her Uncle Werner in the small village of Zweisimmen in the Bernese Oberland in Switzerland. She hadn't seen him for thirty years. And although Anna shared with everyone who has ever left his land of birth for a different land the passionate desire and intention to return, she had never been back to Switzerland. There were always reasons to postpone the trip for a better time—like another child needing help. And so it happened that she had waited too long to go home; the Swiss franc was increasingly expensive and inflation was demanding a rearrangement of her priorities. Anna Maria was beginning to realize she would never go back. Perhaps it was just as well, she thought. There's always a touch of heartbreak in trying to relive the past.

To keep alive her ties, Anna corresponded faithfully year after year with Uncle Werner, and somewhere over the years they found they were very close in spirit. They were delighted to discover they enjoyed the same books. Not only did they both love the Bible, but they also read the lives of the saints and enjoyed the mystical works of Dante and Pascal and Blake. The old man and his niece discussed Dietrich Bonhoeffer and C.S. Lewis. He sent her translations of Simone Weil and she sent him Thomas Merton. They made small contributions to Mother Teresa in India and wrote of it to each other. For more than twenty years there had been a frequent exchange of long letters and books which engendered a heart-warming relationship between Anna and her uncle.

Unfortunately, within the last year, Uncle Werner showed signs of slowing down. He wrote less often and when he wrote, his letters were short and complained of his worsening sight. How sad old age is. And it's coming right along for all of us, thought Anna Maria, when she received an infrequent letter—a letter that filled her with *Heimweh* for her native land and for a sight of the old man's face. And it made her lonely to think that he would soon be gone and she would be alone in the world.

Anna Maria was in her early forties and for some time Uncle Werner was the only male in her life. There were few men her age who were not attached. Sometimes she looked back, for long ago there had been a love in her life, a man in a uniform—handsome and brave but lacking in understanding; she had said goodbye and sent him away and as the years passed by and no other appeared, there were times when Anna thought she had made a mistake; it might have been better to have risked an unhappy marriage than never to have married at all!

Nowadays Anna rarely entertained a male contemporary—unless one could call the occasional teacher and history professor who stopped to talk on his way through Cornwall House a guest. Consequently this day was to be an unusual day for Anna Maria Abendtal because Brigham Bantley, the town's leading male citizen, was on his way to call on her.

Anna Maria was not expecting a man to come calling, but she was thinking that since it was the first warm day in May, tourists would come to Cornwall House. And so she mixed up a batter and while the cakes were baking in the oven she went for a stroll in her garden. She had found that while waiting for visitors to show up, cake-making made a very pleasant little hobby. The fragrance of cakes baking was appreciated by the visitors and when they commented on the smell, she explained to them that she used old-fashioned recipes and expensive ingredients—butter and egg whites, real chocolate and natural vanilla. Anna Maria did not mention the extra ingredient which made her cakes welcomed as something special by those lucky enough to receive them as gifts—that same tender loving care she gave to house and garden and everything she did.

Today Anna had cakes in both ovens, gifts for the girls in the Lost Friday Club. One after the other had been phoning in great distress since six o'clock in the morning. How thankful Anna was that she was not experiencing the terrible trauma of 04Y4. It was a shocking thing.

The unhappiest person of all over the new law was her dearest friend, Tulie Freund. Tulie was absolutely inconsolable, which seemed natural enough, considering Judge Freund's part in the matter. With her powers of intuition and understanding, Anna Maria realized immediately from the nature of the crank calls they were receiving that the Freunds were facing serious trouble, aside from any personal matrimonial conflict of their own. There was every chance that Judge Freund would become a scapegoat for the unstable and politically motivated. As their friend of many years, Anna sorrowed over the unfortunate situation in which the Freunds found themselves.

Anna Abendtal held a sentimental place in her heart for Judge Freund because he presided as the U.S. Court Judge in the District Court that proud day in 1954 when she became an American citizen. She also met Tallulah for the first time that day at the DAR reception for new citizens. Tulie had been one of the hostesses. Anna Maria would never forget Tulie's friendliness, even remembering that she had volunteered to find out whether a naturalized adopted daughter of an old American family could join the DAR.

In the years which followed "day one" as a U.S. citizen, Anna Abendtal had come to know the Freunds well.

Certainly she was fond of both them, but she had to admit, Tallulah deserved a bigger man than John Freund. Poor Tulie—had John even thought what 04Y4 would do to his wife? Probably not; wisdom was not one of John's attributes. Anna shook her head. Marriage was such a lottery— sometimes the prize seemed hardly worth the price!

Yes, she thought, sighing to herself, there is something to be said for being an independent woman. That's what I am! A few seconds later, she chuckled. No one but a fool could think he is independent, not completely so; we all need each other and we're not free till we recognize that fact!

She thought of what Skip Bantley had said about his parents the previous day. When she asked him what gave him the idea for his new song, *Bring Back Those Years,* he replied that his mother had left for Africa and his Father needed her now more than ever before, and he wished things were as they used to be. I wonder if Lucy Bantley knows she's needed, thought Anna. I bet those men of hers never told her so. Why do people hesitate to speak of their need for one another until it's too late? Tulie Freund was one who needed someone to need her now, so Anna would show her she cared by giving her a cake, a pink cake with candy-tuft and forget-me-nots in the center.

While Anna thought about her friends, she picked the flowers from the garden. There were not many tulips and daffodils left after the recent rains, but she gathered what few there were to take indoors. Bouquets were a tradition at Cornwall House, flowers in every room all summer long. In the days of her youth, with the coming of May, Anna's stepmother, Monica, had invariably put pink tulips and golden daffodils in the sitting room. Now Anna did likewise because she too loved the way the spring flowers harmonized with the red and yellow Persian carpet and the ancient brown wallpaper. Anyway, it was fun to follow her stepmother's custom. Soon, with tulips almost gone it would be time for bouquets of snowballs and peonies and iris—red, white and blue for Memorial Day—another tradition at Cornwall House.

Mindful of the cakes baking in the oven, Anna stepped back inside the house, letting the wooden screen door bang behind her. She went into the kitchen and put the flowers in the white porcelain sink while she opened the oven and looked at her cakes. The kitchen was hidden in an old summer pantry behind the round hearth. The historical society, as a concession to her privacy, had agreed to let it be closed off from the public part of the house. But strangers, following the sweet scent of cakes, sometimes peeked in anyway and were rewarded with a sample. (They were surprised she cooked on a twentieth-century stove.)

After taking the cake pans from the oven, Anna put the flowers she had gathered into cut-glass vases and carried them to the parlor. Then she went back to the kitchen. As she placed a second round of cake pans into the ovens she heard a car drive up in front of Cornwall House. Looking out, Anna Maria saw a long silver-grey automobile backing up to park alongside the white picket fence. "Why that looks like Mr. Bantley's car!" She knew who Brig was— everybody knew who he was, and everybody in Temagami Springs recognized his famous silver car, the former Lansdown limousine, now called the Bantley Bentley or the B.B., as his sons dubbed it. She knew Skip and Banter Bantley well enough to know they were never allowed to drive the precious B.B. Apparently their father was coming to see her and she was about to meet the owner of that famous car.

In a moment the front door bell chimed, and a deep resonant voice called, "Miss Abendtal, may I see you for a minute? Is it convenient?"

"Could you come over to the kitchen door?" she called back, quickly throwing off her potholder mitt, removing her flour-dusted apron and smoothing her short brown hair. It was a little embarrassing to be caught in her work clothes by the town's leading citizen.

In a moment he came around and she looked up to see, behind the screen, as good-looking a man as she had ever seen, well over six feet tall with black hair greying at the temples and large features—what her stepmother would call a strong chin. And what eyes!

She unlocked and opened the screen door. "Hello, you're Mr. Bantley, aren't you? It's nice to have company on this beautiful day. Do come in." She smiled, noticing the same soft sympathetic look in his eye that she saw in his son's expression. "Do you mind if we sit here in the kitchen? I have cakes in the oven." She led him to a little round table and pulled up two carved Swiss chairs. "Let's have coffee and soon we'll have cake, Mr. Bantley." She looked at him curiously. Why had he come? Could it be about Skip's new song? Probably not. From what his son said it wouldn't be that. No, she couldn't begin to guess why.

So she sat down and poured him a cup of coffee. Brig, charmed by her warm friendly welcome to this attractive kitchen, took a deep breath of the aroma of cakes baking and smiled as he sat down. "It smells great in here—like my mother's kitchen long ago." He closed his eyes and journeyed back. He was a little boy again licking the spoon, waiting around, hoping for a piece of fresh cake. He inhaled a sweet mouth-watering smell and opened his eyes and looked straight into the coffee-brown eyes of Anna Maria.

He noticed in their return gaze understanding and tranquility and possibly a lurking sense of humor. "I can smell that we're going to get along famously," he said, grinning at her.

For an instant she looked startled. Then she laughed and smiled back at Brigham Bantley. No wonder all the Lost Fridays sigh over him, she thought—he is very handsome. She said aloud, "I feel I already know you through your sons. I'm very fond of them."

"My sons?" He looked at her inquiringly.

"Yes, indeed. They're friends of mine. Skip has your eyes, I think."

"It seems my sons get around more than I do!" exclaimed Brig.

"Oh, I've known Skip and Banter for years since the first time their classes toured the museum. It's a very special pleasure to meet the father of so talented a pair of young men."

"Talented?" replied Brig, plainly surprised at her giving them such an inappropriate compliment.

"Yes, talented. Why only yesterday—" Somehow by the look on his face she knew he hadn't come to talk about them. Maybe later she'd ask him how he liked *Bring Back Those Years*. If only she could tell him of his son's sympathy with his father. But she knew from the boys that Mr. Bantley was a proud man who did not communicate well with his sons. He might misunderstand her, and so she said nothing. How sad that is, she thought. Then jumping up she opened the oven door and exclaimed, "I very nearly forgot my layer cakes. Well, I see they're done. I'll just take them out and put a little sugar and cinnamon on top, since there isn't time for icing. Would you like a sandwich? There's ham in the refrigerator. Yes, let's have a real lunch." She busied herself while waiting for Brig to explain his visit.

Brig watched her. "Oh, no, the cake will be just fine. I really came over to talk to you." Anna Maria kept on making lunch." Tell me, Miss Abendtal, how did you come to occupy this charming old house?" asked Brig, looking about him.

"This old museum, you're thinking," she said, smiling and turning toward him with the carving knife in one hand and the ham in the other. "But it's not a museum to me; it's my ancestral home, in my stepmother's family to be exact," answered Anna Maria. "She bequeathed it to me along with her great love for the place. It was built in 1782 by her ancestors, refugees from Canada. It's a pleasant old home, don't you think?"

Anna cut the sandwiches in two and laid them on black plates, continuing to chat as she did so. "Nowadays I'm its employee. You see there came a time after my father died when I overextended my commitments and I couldn't afford its upkeep. The house needed a new roof and the city put in sewers and raised my taxes." She gestured skywards with the knife. "I had to sell out. I'd have lost it entirely but for a stroke of good luck," she said, putting down the knife and pouring him a fresh mug of coffee in a white mug.

"What was that?" asked Brig.

"Well," she continued, "just at that time when my world came tumbling down, in a manner of speaking, an unknown benefactor—so the paper said—gave the Savernake County Historical Society a gift of twenty-five thousand dollars. And wonder of wonders, they offered it to me for this house. My hesitation was overcome completely when they asked me to be its curator. So here I am where I've always been! And I don't have to pay any taxes."

As she told her story, Brig's mind flashed back fifteen years to the days of his first big success with Glory Land, when he had made a contribution of twenty-five thousand dollars to the society with the understanding that they would take their eyes off his Indian campsite, which rumor had it they hoped to acquire. Apparently the gift had worked, for no one came to him about the site; and his favorite spot on the distant side of the river remained to this day a part of Glory Land, undisturbed and unspoiled. Could this be the same twenty-five thousand dollars that saved this old house for its comely occupant? If so, it was another one of those amazing circles of coincidence that revolved in his life. "I hope the arrangement was a happy one for you, Miss Abendtal," he commented.

"Oh, it was—at least for a time," laughed Anna Maria, "because of Isaiah—my first *Enkelkind*. You see I had just adopted him. The Feed Africa Society was looking for sponsors to adopt starving children. There was the saddest picture of this little boy in the paper. I wish I could find it to show you. He was just skin and bones! Anyway, I had to help Isaiah. He couldn't go hungry." Her face wore a look of anguish as she remembered the little swollen belly and the stick-like limbs. "I sent him my first month's check the day I signed this house over to the Historical Society. But I have to admit, since you asked me, that my life in Cornwall House has been what I would call a mixed blessing. Can you imagine the joy and the pain of being paid to keep your own house?" she asked her guest, wiping her eyes on a tea towel as she spoke.

"What Shakespeare might have called 'a sweet sorrow.'"

"Yes, a sweet sorrow." How understanding he is, she thought.

Brig could see she was upset for some reason and while

she was recovering her equanimity, he continued to converse. "You mentioned Africa. My wife's in Africa; and I must say that although she left only yesterday, it seems like years ago. I miss her already and I worry about her safety. Today I feel especially unsettled due, quite naturally, to the new law. You know about it, I suppose?"

His hostess nodded sympathetically. Should I tell him what Skip said, thought Anna to herself. Aloud she said, "I'm sure you miss your wife. I know what living alone is like." She rose from the table as she continued to talk. "Now we'll have cake and ice cream." Brig protested, but it was no use. Anna was getting the ice cream. Having had nothing since the hamburgers at his dune house, it took no persuasion for him to enjoy a delightful lunch with Miss Abendtal. Why had he never met this charming woman before? He felt the thrill of surprise that comes with discovering unexpected treasure in a long familiar place. As he laid down his linen napkin a half hour later, Brig said, "Your cake was certainly delicious. Thank you so much for lunch. Now since you must be wondering why I came, I'll tell you. I came to see you about cakes." There was a mischievous look in his purple eyes.

"Cakes!" exclaimed Anna Maria. "Oh," she added, disappointed that such a nice man was merely interested in one of her lesser talents. "What about cakes?" she asked, somewhat let-down.

"I hate to talk business, but I guess I should explain myself further." She nodded. "As you must know, I own—rather the family owns—a special sort of park and restaurant. We struggle to operate an old-fashioned kitchen, specializing in certain dishes. Our menu is somewhat limited, but quality is the big thing; and I have to say it's hard not to take all the shortcuts. But so far, thanks to our superb cooks, we manage to retain our reputation for real old-fashioned dining. This year I'd like to add a new specialty for people to talk about. Just between us, I expect 04Y4 to give us our best summer—I may be wrong but I think it will."

"So you want me to sell you my cakes?" asked Anna, visualizing cakes jumping out of her oven and running to Glory Land like the gingerbread man.

"No, no," demurred Brig, "not exactly. There's more to it than that. You'd make the cakes—five-layer cakes, all natural and organic ingredients no additives—I'm fanatic about that. You'd make them at Glory Land behind a window so our patrons could watch and see all those good ingredients. You'd be something of a performer, a Julia Child with a live audience, and our customers would go home talking about our home-cooked, old-fashioned food!"

Anna pulled her green sweater around her shoulders, lowering her head as she did so to hide the doubtful look in her eyes. What next, she asked herself as Mr. Bantley continued. "If you could get away from here you could live at Glory Land. Each of my ladies" (Anna put her hand over her mouth to hide her smile) "lives in her own Airstream trailer in Bakersville. It's hidden in the pines beside the lake and a very pleasant place to spend the summer. Some of them call it a vacation. I don't know whether you know the story of Bakersville," he continued, unbuttoning the top button of his shirt and loosening his tie, "but I'll tell you about it because it was the best idea I ever had!" His face was animated and he had the rapt and amused attention of his hostess.

"One day when Lucy was off on one of her trips—maybe ten years ago—I ate one TV dinner too many and I said to myself, 'What I wouldn't give for a good meal!' They

were showing on the news a woman who had just won a
bake-off contest. Why don't I hire her, I thought—there
must be many cooks who make one dish well for which
they are famous in their communities. I'll hire them. I fixed
up the village by the lake by way of inducement and I set
out to find those women. My girls now come from
seventeen states and several foreign countries, and some
bring their husbands—at least I hope they are their
husbands—but we don't have even one lady from Europe,"
he added, smiling directly at Anna Maria.

She was at a loss for words. She knew all about
Bakersville and had been a customer of the Pink Pavillion
from time to time, but she never thought of herself as a
pastry cook. True, keeping Cornwall House required no
advanced degrees—although she knew as much colonial
history as any college professor—but the role of curator
did seem more special than being a cook. Nevertheless the
proposition had possibilities, and in a curious indefinable
way it was a tempting offer. To think that this man, of all
people, needed her *was* rather delightful.

"Oh, my, you've taken me by surprise. I'd like to think it
over. I do have this museum to take care of and we too are
expecting a big summer." She stopped talking in order to
think. Perhaps she could find someone to take her place at
the house. But do I really want to make all those cakes?
Me? With people watching? She looked over at Mr. Bantley
somewhat skeptically.

He sensed her need to be alone and stepped into the
hallway. "Mind if I look into the parlor?" he asked. "I love
old houses." He disappeared and she heard him exclaim,
"Look at this Rittenhouse clock!"

Her guest walked about and discovered, as his sons had
long since, that this old house was a museum with a

difference. It had, of course, many antique furnishings: an Empire style sofa, a card table with canted corners, and a handsome Chippendale highboy too tall to be useful; there were other antique pieces that were attractive but spelled a certain amount of discomfort, which was usual in a prosperous nineteeth-century home. But for all that, standing there alone in the parlor, he felt the presence of its occupant and he felt the presence of a love he had never felt in a parlor before; maybe it was the hanging plants and the flowers, the photos of young and smiling faces—he didn't know exactly what there was about it, but it felt good. He was glad when Anna Maria joined him. He was looking at a cross-stitch dated 1827 and he read aloud,

> "Bless this house
> And bless these lands
> Keep us safe
> In your loving hands. Amen.

I like that," he exclaimed.

"I do too," said Anna." Come, let's sit here and talk further." She sat down on a straight-back chair and smoothed her denim skirt, a little self-conscious about her old sweater and tennis shoes. "I don't know how to say this. It's true I have made many cakes and people seem to like them, but it has been more of a nice way to fill the odd moment than—well, than something I'd consider a fulfilling job. I'm speaking bluntly, but one does have to decide how one wishes to spend one's life. I have only half my life left to live: the question is, shall I turn it into cake! I don't know about being a performer either, I can't see myself doing that," she added, nodding dubiously.

"A summer is not a lifetime, Miss Abendtal. And you do have a reputation as a cook, you know. Please join us," said

Brigham Bantley. "I promise you we'll use all your talents."

"Thank you," she replied. He was so irresistable, so flattering, like his son Skipper. "I'll think it over," she added.

"Please do, Anna; I must go soon," said Brig, standing up. "But before I leave, let me tell you a favorite story of mine about a famous cook in my own family, my great grand-mother Green who was a Mormon. You're not a Mormon by any chance?" She shook her head. "I told this story to two fresh-faced elders who came to my house to call and they fled speechless. I really thought it gave us something in common and I'm sorry I offended them. I guess it's safe to tell you." He sat down again on the Empire sofa.

"As I said, great grandmother was a Mormon. She went west from Missouri on the second wagon train to Utah and she was expecting a child. Can you imagine—in a bumpy wagon? Sometimes I shut my eyes and see her trekking west alongside the wagon. There was no doctor saying, 'Don't travel in the ninth month'; and she surely took her chances."

"Faith in God gave her stamina," murmured Anna Maria. "Go on."

"Soon after she got to Salt Lake, she gave birth to my grandfather," said Mr. Bantley. He pushed his black, wavy hair back from his face and crossed his long legs.

"Yes, go on," said Anna.

"I gather from the tale handed down to me by my mother, that Great Grandma Green was satisfied with her hard life in Utah until one day Great Grandpa met an incoming wagon train and brought home number two wife, ten years my grandma's junior and the hungriest, most insufferable critic in the West! The new arrangements lasted only a couple of months. After extreme controversy

Great Grandma Green took my grandfather, Brigham, from his bed one dark night and joined a peddlar going east."

"Did she ever go back?"

"No, she never went back; and great talker that she was, never ceased to say to all who would listen: 'Judge not until you have trekked two thousand miles in search of God.'

"She won a second husband with her cooking—a traveling preacher—and had ten more children. In spite of her religious husbands, and because it was a family scandal, everything about her was sort of hush-hush. When I mentioned her name, I got a very short answer. Her son was my mother's beloved father and I'm named after him, so Great Grandmother Green is one of my heroines! Nowadays she'd be called a women's libber. Maybe an ecumenical too," he laughed. "We Americans are a remarkable mixture, aren't we?"

"Yes," Anna Maria answered. "We are a wonderful mixture of cultures and customs; and little by little, we do seem to be learning to tolerate one another. Sometimes I think God himself selected the people to come to this continent, bringing as they did so much energy and ambition and faith. Our ancestors crossed great depths and distances to reach these shores. They crossed a sea of deep, black water and a gulf of even deeper loneliness. How did they cope with it? Have you ever thought about that?"

Brig Bantley was enthralled by her seriousness, by her compassion. Anna continued. "They came, some by the southern route following the Church, some by the northern route to escape that same church and worship as they would. They crossed hills and valleys, deserts and wild plains, and spoke of their love of God—each sure that his group alone had the true word. They made judgments of

each other that were God's alone to make; but in four
centuries, having suffered hardship and loneliness side-by-
side, we've come so very far." She shook her head and said,
"Even so—even though we climb mountains in His name,
sometimes we can't seem to go as far as next door. It seems
so very hard to love our neighbor. If only we could, what a
world this would be!" Anna Maria was thinking, perhaps of
the children at Safflower Hill whom the people of Temagami Springs were finding difficult to love. And as she
spoke, her gaze was infinite and her face was radiant. Her
eyes glistened. Brig had heard no one speak with such
fervor since his mother sank away into senility almost ten
years ago.

When his hostess's gaze came back to his face he said,
"Tell me about your ancestors, Miss Abendtal. From where
did they come and with what beliefs? Your name is
German. It means *evening valley*, does it not?" Brig picked
up a Murano glass ash tray from the coffee table and then
he set it down again. Anna didn't notice.

She was thinking what a pleasure it was to meet
someone like him; she wanted to talk forever. "My ancestors?" she said. "I've been thinking a lot about them lately. I
suppose one does as one gets older. Mine have certainly
affected my life. Lately I've come to believe that their very
strengths have robbed me of being myself. But my ancestors were Swiss not German."

Brig was arrested by her seriousness. There was something special about this unmarried woman with her twinkling eyes and merry face that fascinated him. He didn't
want to leave. "Tell me what you mean about their
strengths, Miss Abendtal." Before she could continue, the
door bell rang, startling them both.

"Oh-oh," said Anna disappointedly, "that will be tourists.

I'm sorry, but we do have to please our tourists, don't we?" She sighed, "Please come see me again. I've so enjoyed our talk and I'll decide on your offer tomorrow. I'll send Bucky Sanders over on his bicycle with my decision. He's my errand boy." She was already planning to send along a cake.

Brig left then, and he knew he would return because for the first time in years, he felt like the same promising young man who came to Temagami Springs full of eager enthusiasm and boyish dreams.

As for Anna Maria Abendtal, she felt she had known Brigham Bantley all her life. And though she doubted she would go to Glory Land, it was stimulating to have something new to think about.

Lucy Arrives in Africa

Through the long night full of stars into the sudden dawn of low latitudes flew the old 707, journeying back to the continent that nurtured the birth of humankind. And from it into the light of her first African day stepped Mrs. Brigham Bantley. Lucy was tired beyond feeling! It was because she never slept aboard any conveyance save a ship, not since a traumatic experience years before when, during college days after doing an all-nighter (as her daughter called studying all night), she fell asleep on a train to New York and failed to get off at Harmon where her date from Yale was waiting with a yellow mum tied in a blue and white ribbon. He had outdone himself. But her late arrival spoiled their weekend plans. They missed most of the Yale-Harvard football game, which Yale, the underdog, had won. Her boyfriend never forgave her. Perhaps but for that inopportune nap, she would have married Stubie and become in time the wife of a celebrated senator.

She thought about that quirk of fate once in a while. Would she have been happier married to a senator at the pinnacle of power than to a man with a kingdom of his own in a small town? Was it better "to be first in a little Allyrian village than second in Rome?" Maybe yes—maybe no.

What about her children? Married to Stubie she would have had other children, but not the wonderful, special combination of sperm and egg, the fruits of her marriage to Brig, not Savernake and Banter and Skip. There was pain in that terrible thought. And although the memory of her early love had long since faded, the knowledge that she could have been a senator's wife played havoc in her psyche every now and then. And the emotional trauma left from that day long ago was still capable of robbing her of her rest when she traveled.

Arriving in the early morning with her body tuned to a different sunrise, Lucy Bantley wanted only a bed in an air-conditioned hotel. It would soon be hers. She passed through customs without search or delay, journeying on that special passport carried by beautiful women that turns customs officials into civilized men.

Stepping outside the terminal into a dazzling sunlight such as she had never experienced, she felt frightened. She had been set down so far from home so quickly, so anonymously. Lucy Bantley was overwhelmed, like an earthling stepping from his spaceship onto a far planet. To remind her further that she was on new terrain, hot winds blowing south from the Sahara desert swirled around her, flinging red grit into her face. She was glad wh. she was tagged by a taxi driver sent by Sinbad to take her to her hotel.

She was glad too that reservations had been made at a hostelry in the heart of Dakar, the new Hotel Teranga. From it she could walk out to explore her first African city. During the ride to town Lucy observed that there were many strange sights to see. But before exploring this new scene she must telephone home and catch up on her sleep.

Once alone in her room, waiting for the international

operator to return her call to America, Lucy Bantley stepped out onto her balcony and looked across the city. Beyond the boulevards full of traffic was the white mosque and in every direction lay the sea. It was a marvelous view, but it was the beautiful black people who fascinated her. In the courtyard just below her balcony, a woman with a baby on her back was washing clothes in a large enamel basin. What kept the baby from falling on its head? Why not let the child sit nearby? It seemed so cruel, but it was practical. Maybe the baby derived comfort and exercise from its mother's movements.

Overhead a blackbird flew back and forth from roof to tree. How comical it looked, so different from the ones at home. This bird looked like it was wearing a white tank shirt. Somewhere she must find a bird book to identify that crow. Following its flight to a big tree Lucy observed a man doing something under the tree, which was behind a high wall. As she watched him, she realized that he lived outdoors under that tree. She watched him wash and dress and prepare his breakfast. She looked away when he urinated into a pot he placed on the roof of an adjacent hut. Watching for a little while, it became apparent he sold bread from his hut to passers-by; a truck arrived and from it—hand to hand like a bucket brigade—passed dozens of unwrapped loaves of French bread! It certainly is a contrast in every way to The Sesame Seed Bakery back home, thought the spell-bound traveler.

As she looked beyond the little hut, to the gardens of the house next door, she saw a row of large, limpid, green *casa marina* trees—those wondrous trees that grow almost without water. She was elated because she had planted one on a hillside in Jerusalem. She hadn't thought about it since, but she hoped it was growing. Looking again today at that graceful dusty tree here in Dakar, Lucy Bantley felt one of those thrilling cosmic moments peculiar to travel when things one has known in far places meet together in one's heart; in that moment one encompasses the world. This was what she had left home to experience!

But why did her telephone call not go through? Lucy Bantley stepped back into her room and opened her suitcase. Usually she traveled lightly, but for this long trip down the west coast of Africa she had packed as though she were going up the Congo River with Joseph Conrad. She had everything she could think of—antibiotics, stomach sedatives, quinine and aspirin, plastic bags and kleenex and curlers, paper and pencils, pencil sharpeners, make-up of all kinds, much too much underwear and nothing at all to read, the books having been taken out of her suitcase when its weight exceeded forty-three pounds.

The telephone rang: it was the operator speaking. "We are sorry all circuits are busy now. We hope it will be convenient for you to place your call later." Circuits busy? At three a.m. back home? How could that be? Probably some local inefficiency. It never occurred to her that 04Y4 had been declared constitutional and that the phone lines in the U.S.A. were as busy as on Mother's Day. She decided to try again later after she slept.

Her nap extended into the afternoon and when she awoke she was hungry. Lucy looked at the watch on her slender wrist. In half an hour the dining room would close. She quickly put on her pink cotton polyester sleeveless dress and zipped it up the front. She brushed and combed her auburn hair, put on light peach lipstick and a little matching eye shadow, locked her suitcase with a practiced hand and in twenty minutes descended to the dining room.

Lucy was a rather formal, somewhat self-conscious

person, who was not quite at ease by herself. She would be more comfortable when she joined up with her tour companions. However, she was trying very hard to overcome her insecurities and be self-sufficient, and so when she felt a certain sinking feeling coming on as she crossed the lobby of the hotel, she lifted her pointed chin high and carried her head back and walked rapidly towards the dining room as though she had been there before.

Seeing her swift approach, the headwaiter looked at his watch to remind her that closing time was near—his French resentment of the American barely hidden. Then he confronted her with ever so slight a bow. "Madame, zeez way pleez." He gestured towards a seat by the window overlooking a broad view of the sea. Lucy looked at the magnificent view for a moment. A giant tanker was on the horizon and a ship with a Russian flag was coming into port. Small fishing and pleasure vessels passed in the bay and a ferry was making for Ile de Gore. Somewhere across that sea Brig was weekending at the dunes. Was he thinking of her? Lucy came out of her reverie aware that the waiter was standing behind her chair waiting. He stood there upright and straight like a clarinet, his smile was as warm as the early sun on a dewy morning. "What a handsome young man," she thought.

"Pleez," he said as he pushed the chair under her and presented her with a large menu. "You like Dakar?" he asked.

"Why, I don't really know; I've only come," Lucy replied. He smiled straight at her, his eyes round, expectant, and she added, "Well, I suppose I do. Yes, I do—but I'm not very hungry. I'm fatigued—*fatiguée*—you understand?" She was wondering if he understood. Few seemed to speak or understand any English. She had found that out immediately, having had some little difficulty with the taxi driver over his tip.

"You, madame, an *Américaine?*"

"Yes," she said, surprised he recognized her nationality. Why was she never taken for a European? It was always puzzling that a foreigner knew right away.

The waiter put his long thin arm to his head still smiling dazzlingly at her. "Mostly speak French here. I'm from Gambia. South. Speak English there," he added in a proud voice.

"Oh, Gambia," said Lucy nodding. "I'd forgotten they speak English there. Good. Maybe they'll have books I can read."

"You go to Gambia soon?" the young man questioned.

"Yes," she said, wishing he'd go away so she could study the menu. "I think there's a bus tour tomorrow. I'm waiting for the *African Prince.* It docks in a few days." Her waiter nodded as though he knew all about that.

Lucy relaxed into her chair. She felt more secure somehow since meeting this friendly young man who spoke English. He looked about the age of Banter. She'd like to ask him his name. So when he came back with her filet of sole *flambé* she said to her cheerful new acquaintance, "You remind me so much of my son. What is your name? I'd like to tell him about you."

"My name is Mamadoo," he replied, his eyes never leaving her face.

"Mamadoo?"

"Yes. You like?"

"Oh, yes." She smiled as she repeated the strange name silently to herself. What an agreeable Mamadoo. There was something very enlivening about him. She asked him to bring her coffee with her dessert.

After he returned and placed a *crème glacée* before her, he paused, silver coffee pot in his right hand, and lifting her cup he said quite matter-of-factly, "I go along to Gambia tomorrow?"

"You do!" she exclaimed in surprise. Then realizing that he was asking a question, she was flustered. Did he mean that he wanted to come with her? Apparently he did because he was nodding his neat round head up and down, his black eyes begging. "Pleez, I like to go. I have day off. Yes? Maybe I go to America too."

"Well, I don't know about Gambia," she replied, ignoring the preposterous go-to-America gambit. "You'll have to ask the tour guide about that." She stood up and took her cream-colored purse from the chair. "I hope I'll see you again before I sail," she said, returning his smile. What a forward young man.

She did not know that Mamadoo was no ordinary foreigner who wanted to go to America. He had a reason of his own, known only to himself; and he was so blessed with an optimistic spirit and so determined by nature that to him 'no' was an unknown word. He would go on asking every American he met and someday, somehow he would go to America. Oh, maybe he was a waiter now, but a good job like his was hard to get. It had taken special qualities like effort and willingness and diplomacy to become a waiter in the Hotel Teranga in Dakar. He was luckier than his friends. Some of them raised crops and fell victim to every drought; others had worse lives on ships at sea. As a consequence of Mamadoo's good fortune, he was a big man in his small village. Seventeen people depended on him for their bread, indeed for life itself.

There was something about Mamadoo that prompted Lucy to stop at the desk in the lobby and seek further information about him. It seems he was an entertainer as well as a waiter and she was very interested to learn that he would be opening his new act in the supper club that evening. "What fun it will be to hear him tonight," she said to herself, pleased that she had recognized that he was a very unusual waiter.

Walking out into the city in the direction of the Place d'Independence, her heart was at ease. It felt good to be in a new country with funny coins in her purse and to talk with strangers who, no matter how humble, invariably seemed more interesting and more eminent than the people back home. She looked out across the ocean and thought about Brig and felt sorry for herself that he had not come with her. But the city of Dakar, the "Paris of Africa," was too interesting a place to waste time thinking of home. Better to watch the beautiful women walking about majestically in their striking clothes. Each wore a four-piece costume of dramatic simplicity; the most beautiful, though apparently not the most treasured clothes, were made of batik, dark-dyed cotton fabric patterned with fish and fowl and geometric designs of rich colors, both color and design enhancing the black beauty of their skin. How pale and uninteresting I am; how out-of-place, she thought to herself somewhat wistfully. After a time Lucy grew tired and wanted to rest, but it was a city in which it was impossible to sit down out-of-doors. If she did so, she was surrounded by persistent vendors and the little beggars who walked beside her. Away from the main boulevard she was likely to step in a hole or on some unsavory object like a dead, bloated goat. And so she eventually returned to the Teranga. Lucy took a hot tub bath and rested on her bed until it was time to go to the supper club.

In honor of the opening appearance of her new friend she wore a long Chinese mandarin gown and lots of costume jewelry. When she entered the ballroom a French group was playing hard rock, and although the noise was enormous and punishing to tired ears, she watched with curiosity. And people watched her too. A Frenchman nearby whispered little compliments and gestured for her attention. He continued making provocative little speeches in a low tone, but Lucy concentrated on the stage, waiting for Mamadoo to appear. She was a good judge of talent in performers, had listened to many with Brig over the years, and was always looking for someone the Glory Land customer would pay to see. If only Brig were by her side to hear Mamadoo and protect her from this French pest.

It seemed that her husband was always on her mind. Why was it so? And why had Brig accused her of running away from Glory Land when she was just doing her thing? Was she running away from her marriage? Surely not. It had been a good marriage; it was only that law hanging over everybody's head that made it seem necessary to evaluate one's spouse. That frightened her. How dared one assess one's own past? Even the very idea of making such a summation was a threat to one's ego, for what if she were to conclude that the sacrifices and demands of marriage had not been worthwhile? What then? There could be no regaining those years. She shuddered at the idea of giving any heed to it at all.

Lucy Bantley was lifted from the clamor of her inner turmoil back to her surroundings by the sudden cessation of acid rock. The silence was delicious. The French entertainers from Grenoble were leaving the dance floor and an expectant hush fell over the large audience of multinationals and prosperous Dakarians.

After what seemed a long deliberate silence, there began ever so slowly off-stage the slow beat of jungle drums and the beat grew louder and louder in a steady rhythm. The pounding went on and on and on. It seemed as though it would never stop. And then the drums made an even louder cyclone of sound and the terrace doors opened and in stepped Mamadoo in a white kaftan. A single warm spotlight illuminated him from above. He lifted his quivering arms over his head and the wide sleeves fell in folds on his shoulders. He looked into the faces of his audience and smiled a blissful smile. Reaching out as though to embrace them all, he danced jubilantly around in circles apparently moving through the round huts in his village.

Then as suddenly as they had begun, the drums ceased beating. The light grew colder and Mamadoo's arms fell limply to his sides. He was another man—thinner, sadder, wiser. Was this the same person? Was it Mamadoo? His gaze grew distant and his kaftan fell open revealing a white city shirt and a thin black tie. He sang a song in French, a sad song—hauntingly beautiful. The listener followed this other man into a different world and sorrowed with him. The young black man finished his song, and after a moment the drums began to beat again their loud throbbing beat, and Mamadoo broke into shouts of joy; his face radiant as the drums built up into a throb of heavy sound. And the listener's heart accompanied the sound in a tachycardia of its own. Then abruptly there was utter silence, leaving the audience trembling and exhausted. For a moment no one moved. Then the overly familiar French-man at the nearby table leaned across to Lucy to explain the music to the beautiful dumb American. He whispered in funny English that what they had heard was the song of a man torn between two cultures—that of the city and that of the bush. The man lived in the city and went home to his tribe and the two ways clashed in his soul. Lucy nodded at the Frenchman. Her own soul had conveyed to her the same meaning and it was an experience she would certainly never forget.

A little later, when the Frenchman was looking away, Lucy Lorenson Bantley went swiftly to her room and got into bed. She took up her diary and wrote, "My Trip to Africa, Saturday May 16th, Dakar, Senegal. I met a talented boy who wants to go to America. . . ." While she was writing she fell asleep, happy with her first day in the footsteps of Bartholomew Diaz.

Freud Meets Tatty Softshoe

Freud, heavy hiking boots in hand, carefully descended the back stairs. He went slowly, one step at a time—very quietly for a big man—but he knew every creak in the old floor. This was the one day in his life when he must not awaken his parents or that terrible Phlox. She'd been at his home less than two days, but it was time enough to see she was the pushy type who would ask questions. No one must know where he was going this morning. He went slowly past the living room where his mother lay asleep.

Freud sneaked out the back door without any breakfast. It was hard to go hungry, but the sacrifice was necessary. He stepped outside and looked around. The day was going to be warm and dry and perfect for what Freud had in mind, which was to walk over the land he was about to buy. What a stroke of fortune it had been to get Penelope Dupre for his partner. Imagine, a quiet chick like her volunteering her savings—her tooth money! She had a lot to lose so she could be trusted not to give it all away too soon. But having her for a partner, a girl he wouldn't ordinarily go around with, was just one more heavy thing about the whole unbelievable adventure.

Freud gave his sagging blue convertible a little push,

jumped in and coasted down the sloping drive, well away from the house before releasing the clutch. As far as he knew, no one had seen him go. He squared his shoulders and leaned back against the seat. It was a very satisfying thing—acquiring one's first piece of one's native land—and he was going to enjoy every minute of it.

Phlox Fontaine, who had come home stoned and couldn't find the front door, spent the night in her sleeping bag under the pines beside the porch. As Freud drove away, she crawled out from under the trees, her hair disshevelled and her jeans rumpled. She stared after the disappearing Buick through grey and red-veined eyes. Phlox wondered where he was going so early on Sunday morning. "I hope not to church," she muttered. "Maybe he's a religious freak." Slowly and deliberately she rolled up her bag and dragged it into the garage. Then she helped herself to a ginger ale. My, she was thirsty! Leaving the glass on the table, she went up the back stairs to her room. She'd catch up with Freud later after she had more sleep.

Freud drove through the slumbering town of Temagami Springs. It was exhilarating to be driving through empty streets and feel a new day come to life. Early worshippers were walking to the Church of St. Anne's and a group of nurses were leaving the hospital after a long night of duty. They looked tired—no way to be on such a beautiful morning.

Freud had found out by a little checking around that Glory Land would be quiet at this time of day. He was glad it was May 17th; in another two weeks the park would be alive with early morning activity. During the summer, Sunday breakfast was the event, like the arrival of the Big Top, to which the local people came. Tourists came later in the day for dinner and supper, but Temagami Springs went for pancakes and sausage in the early hours. It was Brig Bantley's gift to the town he loved.

In ten minutes more, Freud arrived at his destination on the near side of Glory Land and parked his car close by the forest where it was not visible from the highway. A long roll of papers and measuring tape in his hand, he jumped nimbly over the rail fence and walked barefoot through the white mayflowers, across the dewy lawns. A pink fog hid the distant lake from view and curled up from the river, making it difficult to find the markings for which he was looking and lending an air of unreality to his plans.

When he got to the river bank, Freud stopped and, unrolling the paper in his hand, he read aloud slowly the description of a property as it had been recorded many years before. "Starting at a stone cistern near the easterly end of Big Bear River southwest a distance of 1000 feet to the corner of a stone wall." He looked about. Where was the stone wall? There was only one so that had to be it. "Then in a northwesterly direction a distance of 2000 feet to a depression in a muffin-shaped rock." That he knew would be the famous Muffin on which the high school picnics were held year after year. Its round top was big enough for all one hundred kids in the senior class. Yes, there was the saucer-like depression! "Then in a northeasterly direction a distance of 750 feet to a stone marker." That would have to be in the hills on the farther shore of Big Bear River. "Then southeast to the point of beginning." Such a primitive description—but quite close enough for his purposes. It was right in the heart of Glory Land Park!

He laid the papers on the Muffin and climbed to the top, his eyes twinkling and his face a picture of joy. Then in true Freudian form he raised his arms heavenward and cried aloud, "Victory! Riches! Glory! Mine, all mine!"

An echo came back from the hills beyond. "Victory! Riches! Glory! Mine, all mine!"

"No, mine," he called again.

"No, mine," came the answer.

Flushed with excitement, Freud sat upon the rock and, taking from his pocket a pad of paper, he drew a small sketch of the landmarks. There was the river, of course, then the paths that met not far from where he was sitting, coming together just beyond the big oak tree. He stopped sketching for a moment to stare admiringly at that tree. It must be eighty feet tall.

Freud loved trees—birch trees, elm trees, maple trees, spruce trees—any trees, all trees. He just had a thing about trees. To find this magnificent tall Northern red oak with its wide spreading limbs in the center of the property he was about to buy was a special thrill. While he sat on the Muffin looking at the tree and studying this piece of ground, Freud began to realize that it was in the heart of Glory Land in a very strategic location. It was a part of Savernake Forest. It was worth a ransom!

The exuberant young man got up and scrambled to the highest spot on the big rock. He took a chance that someone might see him up there, but he had to see what lay across the river. From on top he had a better view; indeed, there was a faint glimpse of an old bridge across the Big Bear. "That must be mine too!" he exclaimed. "I'll control the river!"

Freud was beginning to see that there was a lot he could do with this place. It did not escape him that he was in the heart of a famous entertainment center to which people came from everywhere. O happy day for John Freund.

"I have a gold mine here!" he exclaimed, leaping off the Muffin and doing a war dance round the big oak tree. It may not have been the first dance round this oak; local Indian legend made mention of just such a tree. Had anyone seen him there in the woods with his arms stretched heavenward, they would have thought he had gone mad— or was a hippie heathen worshipping the sun. But he was merely a young man rejoicing with boyish vigor at having outwitted his elders. John Freund III, while searching titles in the County Court House, had found, through diligence and incredible perspicacity and with some luck that deep in the heart of Glory Land lay this corner of ground not owned by its presumed owners, the Bantley family. And now, having visited the property, he was about to make use of his secret information to buy it from someone who had no possible use for it. Then he, Freud Freund, would spring up in the forest like a deadly amanita!

Suddenly he stopped dancing. "Easy now, boy, easy. It's not yours yet. In other words, Freund, get out of here quick before all is lost and what was yours be yours no more," he said to himself. If Tony DeLuca, the caretaker, happened along he might recognize the judge's son. After all, Tony's daughter, Rosa, worked in the law office.

John Freund III lost no time in running through the woods and springing into the driver's seat of his car. As soon as he was well away from the park, he pulled off the road and wiped the sweat from his face. Then he put the plat maps back in his briefcase and locked them in the trunk. It was time to visit Tatty Softshoe.

Who was she anyway? That's what everyone asked. Wasn't she that oddball who walked along Route 9 with a wagonload of stones? Was her name really Tatty Softshoe? Probably not. That was an epitaph, perhaps a play on the old muskrat coat and carpet slippers she always wore. The town records listed her as Kaleri Tuttle; it had taken Freud

awhile to figure out she was the same person Temagami
Springs people referred to as "the rock lady" or Tatty Softshoe. Her being known by several names was Freud's good
fortune. It contributed to the fact that no one knew she
owned part of Glory Land.

Thinking about what little he knew about her—peculiar,
poor, shrewd—he was less certain than before that she
would want to sell the land. It had always been Freud's
experience that no one said *no* to him for long. People sometimes held out, but they always came round when subject
to his powers of persuasion. He shook his head. This was a
new problem. He had never confronted an eccentric old lady
before, maybe too senile to understand. What if she wanted
more money than he could pay? Freud laughed to himself.
Now that he had seen that tree and that bridge he would
acquire that land if he had to marry the girl! What a wonderful sensation she would make riding like a princess in his
open Buick waving her fedora to the crowds.

Freud did not know that according to legend Tatty was a
princess, an Algonquin descended from a Mohawk chief.
Her ancestors had hunted beaver along the tributaries to
the Big Bear River, and at the turn of the twentieth century
Tatty's father owned a thousand acres in the mountains
hereabout. He had sold much of his land to Tyler Lansdown,
millionaire inventor of something to do with steam loco-
motives. And the rest, including the oak tree, which legend
had was sacred, went to Tatty on her father's death. After
her marriage to Irving Tuttle, the young couple had moved
to the old Berry farm at the east end of the lake. They
gardened and raised chickens and fished in the lake and,
aside from an occasional trip to town, they kept pretty
much to themselves.

Then one windy night, ten years before, the diners in the

Pink Pavillion saw flames at the far end of the lake. Mr. Bantley summoned the volunteer fire department, but by the time they drove over the rough road to the Tuttle place the house had burned to the ground. Irv had died looking for Tatty.

Poor Tatty! She had loved and respected Irv as few men are loved, and she grieved for him still. As if his loss was not terrible enough, the fire destroyed the barns and cattle too, and nothing was insured.

And although there were unfounded rumors of hidden treasure on the old Berry farm, it was obvious that Tatty was poor. A few people—Brig Bantley for one—kept an eye on her, but no one ever went to her house because Tatty had a gun. She lived alone in the swamps.

It seemed obvious too that she was crazy. Why would anyone who wasn't crazy walk ten miles for a few dozen stones? Maybe once—but every day? In all weathers? Yet, it was true; she did that. Everyone had seen her walking along Route 9. As invariably as the sun rises in the heavens, she walked five miles to the river bank and five miles back every day for a load of flat round red stones, and no one knew why. Crazy, crazy Tatty, always in her funny fur coat, even in summer. But Tatty had more purpose to her life than many of them. Day after day she was walking to provide for her future security. She pursued her course as diligently as a chipmunk storing seeds for the winter.

Freud parked his car carefully in a dry ditch full of new cattails. With his hands in his jeans and his head low, he walked swiftly down the trail that disappeared into the dark woods. He was anxious now to get their meeting over with. Anyway, he had to hurry, because in an hour she would leave on her daily walk. He observed that at one time the path had been wide enough for a car; but now it was overgrown with tall weeds and only a footpath and two little tracks wound through the trees and over the roots and stones.

Freud skirted a fallen tree and carefully bypassed the black marshy places, and soon he came out of the woods into a grassy clearing that had been the farm. The path divided, the left one going to the lake, so he took the trail to his right and coming around an outcrop of rock, he saw before him the strangest little house he had ever seen. It was hard to believe that Tatty lived in what had been the top of the old wooden silo, but that's what it was. The same wind that whipped the flames and destroyed her house and took her Irv had provided her with her present dwelling place.

To John Freund, student of history and anthropology, Tatty's round house reminded him of a mud hut in the kingdom of Meli and of the eighth-century huts of St. Brendan in Ireland. It also had the shape of a yurt. This primitive house, this American original, struck Freud as tremendous; in that moment he could see that black or Irish or Indian, the peoples of the world were somehow much alike.

He stood for a long moment looking at this strange, inviting place. Tatty's house sat back against an outcrop of rock and was partly surrounded by a high stone wall. There was a little door which had once been many feet above the ground, the loading door, and there was a sort of window. The round walls were faced with stones, red and smooth and perfectly matched. From the octagonal roof sprouted a crooked stovepipe with many wires holding it in place to the rocks behind. On a porch of sorts, there was her chair, what was left of a chair, much sat-in and rained upon and often repaired—one arm gone—a faded flowery cushion stuffed into the hole which had been its seat. Over to the side were piles of bottles, neatly collected. The whole place

was an incredible piece of primitive art. Everything seemed
to belong.

Yellow butterflies flitted among the wildflowers and
black and yellow bumble bees traveled about in the warm
sun. Blue jays were feeding from a rusty pan and red-
winged blackbirds flew low over the grassland. To his right
were the remains of a horse stall and in it was what looked
like an old car, carefully wrapped in plastic.

As he studied the place, he suddenly saw what Tatty did
with her stones. The high piece of wall was a wall in the
making. She was encircling her house with a wall six feet
high! Very impressive, but why did she need a wall in this
enchanted place? He took a deep breath. The air was sweet
and fragrant with the smell of lilacs.

Freud had not till then noticed the crooked sign hanging
from a cherry tree. It said, "Privat property, no huntin, no
fishin, no nuttin, U keep owt, vissus dog." Surely, thought
Freud, the "vissus dog" was not the black one that followed
Tatty on her walks with its tail between its legs. Surely the
"vissus dog" was not Shadow! Freud picked up a stick just
in case there was a German Shepherd; but thinking better
of it, he threw the stick away. He heard no barking. Perhaps it was a mystical dog! That thought completed the
other-worldly atmosphere of Tatty's place. Summoning
strength for his encounter with whomever he met, with
either a wicked witch or a good fairy, Freud straightened
his sweater and ran his fingers through his wild hair and,
opening his big mouth, crooned what he hoped was a call
an Indian would recognize as friendly. "Tat-tee Tut-tul.
Tat-tee Tut-tul!" For a time there was no answer.

Since yesterday Tatty Softshoe had had a premonition
that some change was coming in her life. She had worked a
little longer than usual on her wall, trying to finish it to be

safe. It was a strain; she was getting old and her hips and legs were full of pain. So she had a little nip of strong brew, curled up with Shadow and slept till morning. But she had awakened at dawn with a feeling that something was going to happen.

It was while she was up in the garden above the house planting petunias that she heard heavy footsteps on the gravel. She peered out over her house, shading her eyes with her hand, and she made out the silhouette of a big man, his arms hanging from his shoulders like paddles, his hair shining like the sun, and big glittering eyes. She trembled in fear.

Freud, gazing at the house and looking for some sign of its inhabitant, gradually became aware of a head in a man's fedora peering over the rocks behind the house. In a moment she emerged. It was Tatty herself, in the familiar coat and bedroom slippers. She scrambled down over the rocks and stopped by the door, motioning him to stay where he was. Then she vanished inside and in an instant reappeared with an old rifle. For one heart-quickening moment, as she pointed it right at him, his curly hair stood out all around his head. He grinned when she lowered it, and then he bravely took a few steps closer and saw that the gun was old and rusty and would never fire again.

"Mrs. Tuttle?" he asked loudly, in case she was deaf. She drew back into the doorway and squinted at him as if she were trying to find him someplace in her memory. "Uh!" she answered. Who was he? No one ever called her that. She waited for him to speak. Then she reached behind her and opened the screen. "Go get em." Blind old Shadow came out into the morning sun, sniffing and blinking; and while the dog waddled toward the unwelcome stranger, Tatty slipped inside and sought safety behind her bed.

Freud followed her up the steps to her door, Shadow licking at his heels. As he stepped into the door frame he filled the small doorway. Tatty turned towards him and blinked her eyes, unable to make out his face. He loomed so large in the tiny room that she crouched back afraid, but there was no way to escape the intruder. An ugly grey and black cat jumped to Tatty's shoulder, purring threateningly, and together they advanced toward Freud.

She came close enough to make out his face. Her lips were ashen and she grinned a tortured grimace as she croaked, "Ya come fer me? Ya come to take me away?" Tatty sometimes wondered if she was getting old. She'd been expecting someone to come for her and so she built her wall higher every day, higher before it was too late. Now he had come and she was terrified.

"Well," he answered, touched by her agitation, "I came to see you about business."

She looked at him sideways out of her one good eye. "Business? What kinder business?"

"I want to buy something."

Now this was more like it, she thought, but buy what? She'd got nothing but Whiskers, the cat, and old Shadow. She panicked; maybe it was the shotgun he was after.

"I got nothin' to sell!"

"Yes, I think you have, Mrs. Tuttle." She stiffened in alarm. No one had called Tatty Mrs. Tuttle since that lady from the church had come to take her into town to sign up for Medicaid. Mighty suspicious that lady was. After that, Tatty avoided her and never walked by that church, with the thought in her mind someone might take her to a nursing home.

"You have a husband—Irving Tuttle. You are Kaleri and Irving Tuttle?" asked John Freund III.

It sounded familiar. She nodded. It would be safer not to tell a stranger that Irv was dead. If only Irv were here now.

"Well, Mrs. Tuttle," continued Freud, smiling benignly down on her, "you have something I need. It's worth a lot of money and I'll pay you fair market value." He couldn't bring himself to say what and where it was, but she looked so hostile he hastened on—after all, she didn't know what he was talking about. "Land. You don't use it. Forty acres by the river—near the old covered bridge. I'll pay you $2,000 down and $4,000 more by the month for your land by the river."

Tatty sucked in her breath; a faraway look veiled her little black eyes and tears welled up. At length she spoke. "I'd forgotten—land by the river. It was our wedding present from Pa, but we never could use it. Too rocky to farm. No way to get to it either except through that fancy park." Then Tatty fell silent and shut her eyes. Freud thought she had fallen asleep, maybe had a stroke or something. He was beginning to wonder what to do when Tatty shook herself and sat upright. "Did you say two thousand dollars now?" she asked, examining her black nails, a look of intense interest in her beady black eyes.

Freud nodded. Tatty was thinking of something she'd been wishing for for ten years. She's seen it every day at Homer's junk yard. It was a big iron gate with spikes on top and it would be just right for her wall. She could buy it and maybe a new shotgun and shells and a padlock—no more big strangers in the doorway and no nursing home for her. A huge weight was lifted from her heart and she looked up into the confident, trustworthy face above her and grinned. "You've got yourself a deal, whoever you are." She took Freud's big, soft hands in her two little sandpaper fists and Freud knew he had made a deal.

"When do I get the money?" was Tatty's next question.

"How about the day after tomorrow?"

"How about tomorrow—early?" rebutted Tatty. There was too much at stake to trust him longer than that.

Freud looked at his watch. He could drop by the office and type up the deed, but he'd have to bring Penny along. "I'll return in the morning and bring along my partner," he said. "But please don't tell anyone. There are lots of sharks in the sea, Mrs. Tuttle."

He left hurriedly and Tatty had a little openin' up to celebrate this unusual event. But oh, how she wished Irv were here! Irv always liked the feel of greenbacks, but he never touched no two thousand dollars. She'd have to enjoy them enough for both of them. That was just what she was going to do tomorrow.

The Gambia

The day after Lucy Bantley arrived in Senegal, the international operator was still assuring her that her call to America would be put through at the earliest possible moment. Lucy was disgusted and annoyed because she had promised to telephone Skip, but she was leaving for Gambia, so she sent an aerogram instead. It was a hasty note written with one eye on a big green tour bus, which stood waiting in front of the Hotel Teranga. Her traveling companions were beginning to gather around it.

Handing her letter to the concierge, Lucy hurried outside and was the first to board the bus. She took a front row seat and, experienced traveler that she was, she carefully spread her things over most of the seat. She focused her eyes on a travel brochure as the other passengers boarded the bus. If this seemed selfish, it was not: Lucy was a veteran traveler; her actions were prudent to prevent herself from sitting all day beside the tour bore, or worse still, beside the tour wolf. She must not wait too long or she would attract the tour drunk who was always the last to board, having invariably gone off for a quick drink at the final moment.

This morning Mrs. Bantley's attention was drawn from

the papers in her hand by the sound of a familiar voice. It was her waiter of the day before and he was going, as he had said, to Gambia. Obviously he wanted to sit beside her.

The French tour director, seeing Mamadoo's intention, shouted, "No, no, not zair," gesturing frantically. "Not with madame. Zeet zair," he said, pointing toward the seat beside the driver.

"Oh, it's all right, sir," said Lucy. "I want to talk to this young man." The guide looked at the American tourist with contempt, but Lucy paid no attention to him. She moved her things and made a place for Mamadoo to sit down. She had so many questions to ask him about his country and his family. She just hoped he wouldn't bring up about America again, because she didn't know how to respond without running the risk of hurting his feelings.

It was important to tell him how much she enjoyed his performance in the supper club and she would tell him too about her son who wrote songs.

The bus was quickly out of the city and rolling through the semi-arid and monotonous desert. Occasionally the driver stopped the bus so the tourists could photograph something unusual. Once it was to see a troop of monkeys swinging in a baobub tree and then it was to watch a seven-foot monitor lizard cross the road and disappear into the desert. That was a sight as exciting as seeing its cousin in Indonesia, the Komodo dragon. Lucy had seen the Komodo and she told her interested seatmate about her trip to the Lesser Sundas. She stopped talking as they approached a village of round huts. The bus slowed down to allow the passengers to photograph an elderly woman in a topless dress. Some of the tourists thought the sight comical, but Lucy was embarrassed by their laughter. She covered her chagrin by talking once more to her friend.

Had he ever heard of the famous flyer called Charles Lindbergh, she asked. Maybe he had. She told him that Lindy was a famous American pilot and that he and his wife, Ann, had visited the Gambia and landed on the river, in fact had trouble taking off from it. Mamadoo was very interested in that story and Lucy had a pleasant sense of importance to be following such distinguished American travelers to the Gambia. Would they see the river today? Mamadoo's face lit up; most assuredly they would and very soon, just a few kilometers.

The only other single thing that Lucy knew about Gambia was that Bathhurst had a new name. It was called Banjul, a melodic name, sonorous and majestic like this young man beside her. She loved the romance of names, but how she wished she hadn't studied geography so long ago. New math was puzzle enough, but new geography was out of this world!

They passed farmers preparing their dusty fields to plant peanuts and meager gardens of lentils and okra and eggplant. Everything depended on the rains coming soon. A drought lay hot upon the land, but the bus was cool, air-conditioned. Another paradox thought Lucy.

A short time later the bus sped by a waving border guard, leaving the soldier in cloud of dust, and after a few bends in the road, it came to a stop where a small crowd was waiting for the ferry to cross the Gambia River.

The crowd swarmed around the bus—vendors and beggars and friendly children. A little girl approached Lucy. She was wearing a castoff lady's slip, nylon with lace trim, in lieu of a dress. The other children too were dashingly dressed in a mad array of American give-away clothes. Some missionary was obviously busy in this place.

Lucy had packed many relief boxes at her church and

worked for the Red Cross, but she never imagined the other end of the pipeline of good intentions would affect her like this. She was both touched and shocked. It made her wonder how she could share more with these people than old clothes. Was there any way to send them opportunities? She did not know the answer, but she would think about it. Did any of the other passengers feel this paradox? Apparently not—the Minoltas and Exzactars snapped and snapped, and the children laughed and tumbled happily in the dirt.

But what was this coming to the dock? It looked like a child's fort on a homemade raft, a most unlikely craft in which to cross the wide river, being less seaworthy looking than the Monitor raised from the deep. Was it a child's boat? "Not at all," said Mamadoo, "It is the ferry to Banjul!"

Lucy was very relieved when she reached the other side of the river. She was a little too old to play Huck Finn. As she and Mamadoo walked down the pier toward the town, he said, "You like to walk, Mrs. Bantley? Come home with me, ma'am."

"How far?" Lucy asked in a skeptical voice.

"Short walk. Five, six kilometers."

"Oh, no, I couldn't, thank you," she answered, looking at her flimsy shoes and wishing she had more courage. Anyway, it was too hot to be in the sun all day and she wanted to go for a swim in the ocean and see the sights.

"Okay, ma'am," he said, and pulling a woolen cap from his pants, he put it on his head and walked away down the dusty road home.

Lucy watched him go and then she approached the tour guide and asked him what there was to see in Banjul. His mouth turned down at the corners. "Maybe you see a Swede. They come to walk naked in zee African sun. Lunch in two hours. Zee hotel is zair, just beyond zee park," he said, pointing up a squalid street to a dusty tree-lined square.

I guess I'll look for a naked Swede, but first I'll take a walk, thought Lucy, laughing to herself. Apparently there wasn't much to see!

Lucy's assumption was right. There was nothing to see and the streets had open sewers. It would be better to walk on the beach. Following lunch at the hotel, she took off her shoes and strolled along the sand. Some distance down the beach she met an elderly American who had been riding in the back of the bus. The woman asked her what she had found to see in Gambia. Lucy replied just for the fun of it that she was looking for naked Swedes! The old lady, who it turned out was a missionary from Kenya, was horrified at the possibility of finding any, and she took Lucy by the arm and hustled her back to town to visit the mission bookstore. There Lucy supplied herself with several little books, ones which she would never have bought ordinarily. In them she was later to discover another side of Africa, that of the poor brave white missionary. All in all, it was an interesting day in spite of the heat—a Sunday school lesson come to life.

Mrs. Bantley and her missionary friend journeyed back across the Gambia River together, both of them more nervous than before over the crude and unseaworthy raft. It carried two small trucks and all the passengers who could squeeze aboard. A Moslem sat on the back of his truck saying his beads. Lucy didn't know what sort of a prayer he was saying, but it seemed like a good thing to be doing. She looked around for her native friend whose face would stand out even on this crowded ferry. Apparently he had not returned from home.

The craft was pulling away from the dock when Mamadoo came running, his striped gown flowing behind him, and jumped aboard clinging to the stern with both hands. His face looked strained and his smile was gone, but his eyes sought hers and seemed to be asking her to save him the seat beside her on the bus. This she could not do. Much as she wanted to hear how he had found things in his village, she could not sit anywhere but with her new elderly friend. If only the poor soul didn't talk so much—she was obviously hungry for American company.

Mamadoo came aboard last and took the seat in the back of the bus. It had been a very hot and tiring day and it was a long trip back to Dakar. Lucy was glad when they arrived at the Teranga. While her friend from Kenya kept repeating goodbye and asking Lucy to promise to write, Mamadoo disappeared. Finally Lucy was able to break away and retire to her room. She was exhausted and glad that tomorrow she would be at sea resting in a deck chair, but she was disappointed that she had not said goodbye to Mamadoo.

Lucy made a pretty picture as she alighted from a taxi at the pier the next afternoon with her last-minute shopping in her hand. Looking the tourist, she was wearing a new seed necklace and carrying a wooden carving set. She walked through the crowd on the wharf and much to her surprise, there was Mamadoo! He was waiting for her by the gangplank, holding a bunch of orange flowers in his black hand; taller than most of the crowd, he made a striking figure in a royal blue kaftan. When she caught his eye, he made his way through the throng and held out the flowers awkwardly. "Have good trip. Some day I go with you to America. I get rich in America." He smiled, but there was a look of sadness in his eyes.

"How is your brother?" Lucy asked with concern.

His smile vanished. "He died—five more mouths for Mamadoo to feed." The young man looked desolate.

"I'm so sorry," said Lucy, taking the flowers and lifting them to her nose. "These flowers are lovely—they smell very sweet. Thank you so much, Mr. Mamadoo." She looked up at the tall youth as a mother looks at her son. "I hope you get to America someday and if—when you do— please come to visit us in Temagami Springs." She could think of nothing more to say to this charming and impulsive young singer, so she shook his hand and turned and walked up the gangplank onto the *S.S. African Prince*. She stood for a moment by the rail to smile and wave and then she went to her stateroom.

Mamadoo disappeared in the crowd. Two hours later when the ship was under way, Lucy spotted him through her field glasses. He was standing on the ramparts of the old fort waving his white knit cap at the ship as it sailed out into the open sea. Lucy waved from the stern until she could see him no longer. Then she shook her head sadly, thinking about the nice young man and his impossible American dream.

The *S.S. African Prince* sailed down the coast carrying Lucy Bantley, carrying her back in time, back to her geography lessons about diamonds and copper and bauxite, back to her history lessons on slave trading and colonial explorations, back to her earliest Sunday school lessons. She sighed because she knew from a United Nations report that slavery was still practiced in parts of Africa.

As the ship sailed on, Lucy Bantley spent the long hours

at sea sitting in her deck chair reading her little books and thinking about brotherhood. Among the books was one about the White Fathers who were martyred in Africa. Many had gone forth from France, obeying Jesus' command to "love one another, even as I have loved you" and had found death. Such sacrifice was theirs, and yet a century later the need for love was undiminished. What could anyone do in the face of so much suffering and sorrow?

Every time Lucy Bantley paused to look away from her book, she was met by a refrain in her own heart: "Help Mamadoo, help him. He needs your help. You can do that."

As the ship sailed on through southern seas, Lucy dwelled upon the idea that perhaps she could help him; and day by day what at first seemed preposterous began to seem possible. Who could help Mamadoo better than she? She could give him a job at Glory Land. Could Mamadoo be happy? Yes; her children would help make the transition easy by taking him to their hearts. For don't young people today grow up loving everybody?

Helping the young Gambian was an idea that would not go away. It would accompany her everywhere, through villages and jungles, on mountains, at sea. She knew she would not escape from it until she went back home across the ocean, back home where everything was more difficult.

She would not forget until time and distance intervened to wipe away the memory of a young man of talent and his hungry family.

Lucy sailed through the summer and her mind was on Mamadoo. What could she do for him?

Pizza Maxima

The sun was shining in the west windows of Cornwall House and the last Sunday visitors were leaving. It was late afternoon, the time of day when the old house was most beautiful. Its creamy walls, accented by windows with black shutters and white trim, glowed pink against the blue sky. The sun shone through the fanlights over the front door and illuminated the blooming plants in the windows; the polished brass knobs on the stair railing reflected its afternoon glow.

Anna Maria Abendtal followed the tourists out into the sunshine. She was looking for her next-door neighbor, Bucky Sanders, to deliver her cakes. Walking back from the Sanders' house, it occurred to her that she had not thought much about Brig Bantley's offer of a job. What a preposterous idea, she said to herself. It's not as though I was looking for a job. No, I can't do that—and yet, it is rather a tempting idea. When will I ever again get an opportunity to do something different? He certainly has asked me at a restless moment in my life. I didn't know how much I needed a change until he offered me this one. Ordinarily I'd never be a cook. What shall I tell him? It's absurd. And yet why not try it—just for this summer? I really should ask Tulie what

she thinks. But I won't make cakes with people watching.
That I will not do.

Anna Maria stopped to peek into a robin's nest in the
cedar tree. Then she continued her walk, stooping to pull a
weed from her garden every here and there and thinking
about Mr. Bantley's offer. I wonder whom I could get to
work here, she thought. I know—I'll ask one of the Safflowers; maybe one of them will take over for me. Thinking
of this made up her mind for her. "I'll call them right away,"
she said, "before I change my mind." She hurried into the
house to the telephone. Anna knew that the Safflowers,
who tried to follow the command from God to love one another, were struggling to survive financially. The thought
that she could help them lent attractiveness to the whole
idea of her going to Glory Land. All that cake baking would
make sense if it would help the Safflowers.

Should she call Surtsey Sanders, who was on the board
of the Historical Society, or should she call Surtsey's son
who had gone to live at the Hill? While trying to make up
her mind which one to phone first, she thought about Mark
Sanders. What led him to go up there to live a life style so
much more primitive than any he had ever known? Rumor
had it his father had put him out of the house. Apparently
he and Bud had nothing in common and the manufacturer
was embarrassed to have a wood carver for a son. But how
could Bud Sanders do that to his own child, she wondered.
The very thought made Anna sad for both of them. However, it was reassuring to know from Surtsey that Mark
was getting along just fine, making and selling wooden toys
and even taking over the management of the commune. So
perhaps given a little help, things would work out for him
and all the other young people up there. Perhaps she'd be in
a position to hire a few for Glory Land if she were to accept

Brig's offer.

Anna Maria now had sufficient incentive to hasten her on her way to her new job. She decided to call Mark first. She dialed the Hill and talked to him for quite some time. Yes, he'd be delighted to find two helpers to take turns with himself in coming to help out at Cornwall House. After everything was arranged, Anna went into the parlor and turned on the television, which was hidden in the heavy old buffet. Then she went to the kitchen and washed the cake pans. Not very hungry after making such a big decision, she fried herself a leftover potato and made a tossed salad. Then she carried her plate into the living room on a tray. After supper she would send word of her decision to Brigham Bantley along with a nice chocolate cake that she had made for him.

At the same time, Brigham Bantley returned home and walked through his kitchen and out onto the terrace looking for his children. He had reached all his cooks by telephone and they were coming as planned. Thank God for that. Only one felt she might have to stay home to keep an eye on her husband. Brig countered with a job offer for the husband which solved her problem. And he was pleased that Savy had made some of the calls for him graciously and efficiently. However, that was yesterday. Today she drove away with her friends after breakfast without saying where she was going or when she would be back. Now there was no one around. There was only an empty milk carton on the kitchen table to testify to the recent presence of Skip.

Brigham Bantley looked at his watch. It was time for supper. He opened the refrigerator and the shelves were all but empty. Taking out a can of tomato juice, he sat down at the table in his large and expensively cabineted kitchen.

The appliances stood around him, new and unused. What was it for anyway? He'd built it for Lucy, a fine house for her and the kids; now they were never in it when he needed them. What was it all for, all his concern and worry? Feeling hungry, he remembered yesterday's lunch at Cornwall House and the friendly woman who served it. Would Miss Abendtal accept his offer? She had certainly been disconcertingly noncommittal.

Brig got to his feet. Why not make sure of her coming by going back to ask her again? Why not invite her out to dinner and for a drive along Big Bear Lake? He'd find out how she happened to know his sons and why she spoke as she did of Cornwall House. And he would persuade her to leave it for Glory Land. He had already decided it would be a better summer if she were to come to the park.

Brig took a quick shower and changed into slacks and a sport-shirt, and forty minutes later he rapped on the screen door of number 10 Main Street. "Anna Maria. Anna Maria. Open the door. I've come back. Anybody here?" he called.

Hearing the commotion, Anna Maria jumped up from her chair and opened the screen door as the announcer intoned, "Merrill Lynch is bullish on America."

"I'm bullish on Anna Abendtal," said Brig. "I've come back to hear about your ancestors and I propose to do it over dinner at The Casa. Do you like pizza?"

Anna began to reply that she had already eaten, but she stopped herself. It would spoil something—she didn't quite know what—to refuse his invitation. Inside somewhere she knew that with this strong fascinating man she would eat pizza anytime, anyplace, anywhere. She seldom ate pizza, but she surprised herself by saying, "I love pizza— with everything on it!"

"You'll have it—peppers, bacon, mushrooms, pepperoni—

the works. A pizza maxima. And I'll give you five minutes to get ready."

"Oh, I just remembered," said Anna, "I have an appointment tonight. A friend of mine is coming over to talk about her troubles."

"04Y4, I suppose."

She nodded. "But I'll give her a call and ask her to come a little later." In a few moments she came back and handed him a stereopticon and a stack of photos. "Here, Mr. Bantley, look at these while I get ready. You won't recognize any of these people—they are my ancestors."

While Anna went to dress, Brig looked at the device. My grandfather had one of these, he thought. How I loved it. He held it up to his eyes and looked into it. It's the Alps, the beautiful Alps. When Anna reappeared he said, "We've been to Switzerland a few times. Lucy and I took the boys to the *Jungfraujoch* several years ago. These men look like early mountain climbers," he added.

"They are," she replied. "It's my great-grandfather—and the little boy with the pick in his hand is my grandfather. They were mountain guides."

A half hour later Brig and Anna Maria were seated in a dark wooden booth in the back room of The Casa drinking ginger beer and waiting for a pizza maxima. Their being together in a cramped little eating place seemed a bit awkward at first, but Brig quickly offered the explanation of their coming here: his fondness for pizza was not shared by Lucy and so he had the habit of coming to The Casa by himself from time to time. It wasn't much of a place, but he thought that tonight the privacy of the booths would give them a chance to talk about Glory Land. And talk they did; it soon became apparent that a man whose wife is away and a woman who lives alone have a lot to say to one another!

Anna Maria opened the conversation. "As I said yesterday, I feel I know you because I see in you things that make me think of both Skip and Banter. Shall we talk about your sons? I'd like to!"

"Since you really want to; but we'll talk about them later," answered Brig. "First let's talk about you. I enjoyed those old photos of your family. Tell me how you came to emigrate from Switzerland."

"It's rather a long story," she replied, "but one I like to recall. You see my mother, Elsa, died when I was ten years old, not long after World War II ended, and we lived for a time with my uncle in the little village of Zweisimmen. My father was terribly restless after mother's death, and when he was offered a job as a ski instructor at Snow Slide—you know where it is?" Brig nodded. "He got a job there and we left our little homeland for America.

"I missed my mother terribly, and I grieved for her so much that I became a difficult child for a man to handle. I was certainly a misfit at school and my father couldn't understand why I was so miserable. I can see myself now— my hair in pigtails, hand-knitted stockings and heavy workshoes on my feet, and an apron. Can you believe it? That's how I went to an American school! Naturally the other children made fun of me, and when I complained to my father he said I was good advertising for Alpen Lodge! All this, of course, was before Dad met Monica Monet.

"Monica was the greatest thing that ever happened to me. She was quite a few years younger than my father and we were like sisters. To show you the kind of person she was, the day of their wedding she took me to the store and bought me new clothes."

"She understood," commented Brig, propping his head on his hand and looking straight into the eyes of his guest.

Brig was an expert listener, which was one of the reasons he was so appealing to women. "Go on," he said.

"Yes, she did understand. As I look back I think she was sent by God to save me from becoming a delinquent. Monica was the daughter of old Doctor Monet, who owned Cornwall House. They were very proud of their early American ancestry, which was French and English, and they loved the history of that old house.

"To make a long story short, Monica eventually adopted me; and on the day she signed the papers, she hugged and kissed me and said, 'Now you are my own dear daughter and Cornwall House will one day be yours, along with all my ancestors who fought in the American Revolution. On second thought all of them are yours now! To my new American daughter I make a gift of ancestors.' How's that for a gift?" Brig smiled at her question.

"Monica died before I was twenty and, sure enough, beautiful Cornwall House became mine when I was twenty-one, much to the disappointment of my European-style father who felt that it should have been his. I think Monica left it to me because I appreciated the ancestors, whereas my father couldn't care less. And his dismay made me even more aware of my responsibility to those ancestors. I was thrilled by my inheritance; that house became my Rock of Gibraltar in my new country because, believe me, we first-generation Americans never quite belong. We love the new but miss the old. Anyway, now here I am, middle-aged, I've sold my house and I have no one to whom to leave the ancestors! That's kind of a sad joke, don't you think?" Her voice softened. "And I lost the only man I ever had on account of Cornwall House." Obviously she had said all she cared to. Her voice brightened again. "But that's another story. Let's talk about your boys. They're favorites of mine.

Skip and Banter are rather fond of my house too. Do you know how I got to know them?"

"I can't possibly guess. Shall I order coffee?" Mr. Bantley signaled the waitress and Anna continued. "Skip must have been a fourth grader and Bant a sixth grader when they came to my house on a school tour. I had an old piano of Monica's in the living room, and after the others left I heard someone playing a pretty little tune. Naturally I went to see who was playing, and there was Skip making up a song. I could tell by his look of concentration that the inspiration came from within. He's been writing songs at my piano ever since—some very good lyrics—and I've moved the piano to the cellar so he can have privacy at all times.

"Bant had other interests in my museum, especially the war uniforms, and he came back often bringing his friends to see them. I'd get them out of the old trunk in the attic for him to show the other boys. He particularly liked the story of the Revolutionary War soldier buried in my back yard. Do you know Banter has put flowers on that soldier's grave every Memorial Day since he was a child? In fact I had a card from India last week reminding me to put flowers on the grave for him. That's the Banter I know and love!"

Brigham stared at her in disbelief. It is always a disconcerting experience to hear a stranger discuss one's children with intimacy, and Brig felt somewhat discomfitted to have been left out of what they shared with Miss Abendtal.

If she noticed the change in her host she said nothing, continuing, "I do think young people should be encouraged to use their talents, don't you?"

"Yes, certainly, if they know what their interests are. Banter can't seem to find his. He's off to India on an *ozumnai*—I guess it's what Goethe called the *Wanderjahr*. In my day we were too anxious to earn a good living to go wandering about seeking spiritual enlightenment—if that's what it is. Maybe it's just a disguise for laziness, or a sur- feited appetite from having too much."

"Wouldn't you like an *ozumnai*? I would," offered Anna.

"I guess," resumed Brig, cutting a slice of the pizza. "I guess what I want for my children is that they see how lucky they are to have Glory Land in their future. It will be theirs some day and I want them to love and care for it as much as I do."

"You sound just like Monica, my stepmother, talking about Cornwall House," observed Anna. "I know that what you say is important, and in good time they will appreciate it. But if my experience has taught me anything, it's that people are more important than possessions. In their own way the kids are trying to show us this. Your children's interests and abilities will help them to bring new life and change to Glory Land in the years ahead. By the way, have you heard Skip's wonderful new song, *Bring Back Those Years*? It seems to express our nostalgia for the past."

"I can't say that I have," answered Brig, again a little embarrassed. "If only he wouldn't waste his time."

"Oh, Mr. Bantley, he has a gift for music! He must use it somehow." Brig looked at her appreciatively. She had so much enthusiasm for life. How refreshing she was. "I sup- pose you're right and I'll try to encourage him. Speaking of gifts, have you decided to bring your gifts to Glory Land?" His eyes softened. "You must use them."

"Touché. Yes," she said, her eyes glistening, "I have it all arranged. When do you want me to appear for work?"

"Tomorrow!"

"Tomorrow it is. Now we must get back to my house. I have a friend coming to see me."

Brig walked Miss Abendtal to her front door. They both

felt renewed by their evening together. She reached out for his hand. "Mr. Bantley, you've done more for the youth of our town than any other person; if our children come home to Temagami Springs it will be because you've taught them to love this land. I thank you for all of them."

"Anna Maria, I never told anyone this, not even my wife. I've been approached just recently by a lawyer representing big-money interests in Texas. They want my park for condominiums. The way things have been going I've been wondering if this was to be our last season. Now I think that with your help I can put their offer out of my mind. We'll have a great summer; I just know we will."

"I hope so, Mr. Bantley. Now just wait a minute. I have something to give you." Anna Maria ran into her kitchen and came back carrying a big three-layer chocolate cake. "This is for you and the children. See you tomorrow, Mr. Bantley."

"How wonderful of you! Please call me Brig, Anna, and thank you for everything."

She smiled, "See you tomorrow, Brig."

That night they both slept well: Brig, because everything was in order for the summer, and Anna, because her life was heading in a new direction. At Anna's age a change was the best thing that could happen.

Freud Closes the Deal

No one ever anticipated the signing of a real estate transaction with greater pleasure than John Freund III on the morning of May 18. He was looking forward to buying forty acres of choice real estate in the very heart of an enterprise worth millions, and it was his own well-kept secret. He got up early; it was no day for savoring sweet moments of sleep. He brushed his teeth and combed his hair. He tried to keep calm, to seem normal in every way. This was the day of triumph come at last. This was the day he would sign the final papers and take possession of his piece of Glory Land. He was anxious for the deal to be closed, because secrets were not well kept in Temagami Springs. Furthermore, there was an agent on his trail— none other than the sexy little houseguest, Phlox Fontaine. She was following him about and checking on his where-abouts. Fortunately, she was not a morning person and had yet to show up for breakfast (which was very annoying to a proper hostess like Mrs. Freund). Therefore he felt safe in sitting down with his mother to eat breakfast, two soft-boiled eggs served in Royal Dalton egg cups. Excitement always gave Freud a good appetite, but this morning he ate fast. After he finished his second cup of coffee from a

Haviland cup, he went to the door and looked outside toward the cluster of pine trees. "Where is she, Mom?" he asked.

"Still in bed, I suppose," replied Tulie. "The child will have to make her own breakfast because I'm going antiquing in Duxbury with Pat Johnson and I'll be gone all day."

That's good, thought Freud. He wished she'd take Phlox with her, but he didn't dare suggest it. At any rate it was high time to sneak away fast before Phlox appeared.

In a few moments he was out of the garage, which closed automatically behind him, and on his way to pick up his partner. What a great day it was going to be! He began to whistle something he made up. However, happy thoughts are often quickly quelled by unexpected happenings. As Freud coasted in neutral down the drive and turned into the street, he saw a dreadful apparition. There at the far end of the hedge was Phlox with her thumb in the air. Her blonde hair was curly all over and her lips were pursed as though for kissing. Seductive creature—she looks like she just got out of bed. I wonder where she hid her sleeping bag, thought Freud.

It was too late to back up and go the other way, so Freud pulled up beside her and stopped. Quickly she opened the door and jumped in.

"Where are you going?" he said abruptly.

"Down to the bank," she replied in a tone one might use to say "just one more kiss."

"The bank's not open for a half an hour."

"Could you lend me fifty dollars, Freud? I have to have wheels. I need it to put down on a cycle—something cheap. Please, Freud. What's fifty dollars to you?"

Freud looked exasperated. "I don't have it, Phlox, but I tell you what," he said impulsively, "I'll lend you my very special Falcon Olympic ten-speed. I don't usually lend it to anyone, but I will to you," he said, forcing a smile. "Let's just go back and get it. Then I'll drop you at the bike shop. By the way," he went on quickly, giving her no time to comment, "I don't think my mother will like your sleeping in the front yard. It might not be safe with people out to get Dad. You are aware he's had threats, aren't you? Someone might throw a Molotov cocktail."

"Gee, I hadn't thought about that! But I like fresh air and I hate coming home late to a strange house," she said. She didn't add that she had no intentions of sleeping inside. After all, it had been her mother's idea she visit them to get to know Freud, and she had posted herself under the shrubbery to watch his comings and goings because he was very hard to get to know.

"Do you want to change your pants while I get the bicycle?" he asked. Phlox shook her head and smoothed her pant leg with her little hands. Who was he to imply she didn't look good? Anyway, given a chance, he might drive away without her. She didn't trust him at all.

Freud had only one idea—get rid of Phlox as quickly as possible. So he drove fast, parked and went with her into the shop with his bike. He asked the owner to put on a new tire. "And charge it, okay?" he said loudly for Phlox's benefit. It was the time for generosity on his part. Mr. Freeroder nodded, wondering what it was like to be the son of Judge Freund and who the cute chick was. Freud, inspired by the glint in Mr. Freeroder's eye, said, "Mr. Freeroder, meet Phlox Fontaine; she's a stranger in town. Fix up my bike for her."

"Why, certainly," he said, and he took over at once, leading Phlox into the back of the shop and, giving Freud his chance to escape.

Freud raced away to The Sesame Seed with a sense of relief at having pulled off the impossible. Fortunately, Penny was waiting for him in front of the store, a box under her arm.

"Hello, beautiful," said Freud.

"Hello, partner," smiled Penny. "I brought along some cupcakes for lunch. Do you think she'll make coffee?"

"Who knows, she may serve celandine tea," he said mischievously. Penny looked dubious for an instant, but then she smiled. Most of the time her long, thin face looked serious, but today her mouth turned up at the corners and she had a sweet expression. "Oh," she said, "I'm so happy; I haven't had such fun in ages. I do feel poor though, Freud, carrying this check for all my savings. Are you sure it's a good investment?" She was thinking of how long she'd saved to have her teeth straightened.

"You're getting more like a businessman every day, my dear," said Freud, putting his arm around her and pulling her closer to him. Penny, responding to his tenderness, put her dark head on his shoulder, her shiny sweet-smelling hair tickling his bare arm. She was so happy and so grateful that Freud, big Freud, was paying attention to someone like her that she forgot her crooked teeth for a moment and rested in his strength. Suddenly she sat upright, all business. "You know, we're almost there. Don't you think you should tell me what we're partners in? Maybe we're out to rob a bank."

"All in good time, lass. I want you to get the full flavor of what's to happen." That was Freud for you, always squeezing the maximum pleasure out of everything he did. "Let's pull into The Burger and get some sandwiches to eat with your cupcakes."

Tatty hadn't missed a day collectin' stones for years. Not since she had chilblains, the year Irv died. But something told her it would be okay today. Everything was going to be okay today, for she was gonna git that gate. Tally didn't think very long thoughts and she didn't think very hard thoughts, but this mornin' she had been thinkin' and thinkin' and she finally thought as how she'd need some help with that gate. She'd even said a little prayer in the direction of the sky above about that gate. And quick as lightnin' she thought of that big man with hair like an angel who was bringing her two thousand dollars cash. He'd know how to get that gate. Meanwhile, there was work to do on the wall.

As Freud led Penny along the path through the swamp to Tatty's house, taking time now and then to disentangle Penny's skirt from the briars, a light rain began to fall. When they came out of the woods and around the rock, there was Tatty—rain or no rain, high up on the wall, happily placing stones and humming to herself. And through the cool, wet air it sounded to them like "No nursin' home. No nursin' home fer me."

"Mrs. Tuttle," called Freud, waving his briefcase and smiling. "We're here with your money. What are you doing up there?"

"I'm gittin' ready for my gate, that's what," she commented, climbing down. "Come on inside—the ink might run out here in the rain. Hello, young lady," she added, giving Penny a quick once-over. Tatty led the way through the screen door—its purpose purely illusory—and, pushing Whiskers off the table and taking a pile of old newspapers off the only chair, she cleared a small spot for their business transaction. Penny in all her life had never been in such a place. She was appalled, repelled, yet enchanted by Tatty's nest, and a little bit scared at how her savings fit into all this. Surely Freud wasn't going to buy this strange place, this dump, with her one thousand dollars. It looked like part of an old silo—and that funny stone wall all around. What could he have in mind? Freud was enjoying the look on her face. Finally he winked at her and she felt better, though she'd never liked boys who winked.

Freud, with a certain clumsiness, brought in the old rickety chair from the porch and set it inside. No one could move. "Mrs. Tuttle, please sit down and we'll proceed." He handed her the deed. "Now read this."

Tatty didn't tell him she couldn't read; why, he might put sumpin' over on her. She ran her crafty black eyes down the page and looked up warily.

"Now sign here," continued Freud.

"Wait a minute, young fella. You got the money with you?"

"Yes, I have a check."

"A check! I got no use for a check. I want *cash*," she said emphatically.

"Cash? Are you going to spend it right away?" Freud looked distressed.

"Right away! Today! With your help. So I won't sign no papers till you promise to help me and till you pay me in cash," she said stubbornly. She liked that word "cash."

"Sure, anything you say," Freud stated, looking at Penny. "I'll take our checks to the bank in town. You stay here, Penny."

"Let's have lunch first, Freud," Penny said, turning to Tatty. "We brought some sandwiches and cake." Freud didn't want to be delayed, but he wanted to please; so he squeezed into the chair, his chin almost in his lap as he sank through the hole in the seat.

Tatty smiled bleakly. When you have lived off nuts, berries, corn and fish, this kind of fare might make you suffer, but she was too happy to care. "Okay, let's us eat," she said.

"May I call you Tatty?" asked Penny.

"Seein' as how we're lunchin' together, you can call me by my real name. It's Kaleri—after an Indian saint, Kaleri Tekuhuacha." Freud took one bite of a sandwich and, picking up a cupcake while Penny and Kaleri were talking, he struggled out of the chair and backed through the door. "I gotta rush to the bank. Be back in half an hour." He ran away quickly down the path, letting the door slap behind him.

"What are you going to do with so much money, Kaleri?" asked Penny.

"Do? Why I got a dilly of an idea. I got sumpin' I want all picked out—been lookin' at it for years. Never thought I'd be so lucky. Down at Homer's." Tatty's weather-worn face was a mask as her mind went back over long years of walking by Homer's—she didn't know how many years— bringing back stones so she'd be safe. Now safety was near at hand and all she needed was that gate from Homer's. No nursin' home for her.

"You know Homer's Steel and Scrap?"

"The junk man?"

"That's the one. He's got sumpin' I need."

"A stove?" asked Penny, looking around the tiny house and thinking Tatty could use most anything.

"No, not a stove but heavy as a stove. I'm gonna need some help to lift it." She looked at Penny's thin arms thinking she'd not be much help. "It's a gate—fer m' wall."

"Oh," smiled Penny, patting Whiskers, who had jumped into her lap. "Freud will think of something," assured

Penny. Of that she had perfect confidence, but her confidence receded as the minutes passed and her partner did not return. While they waited, Tatty, fatigued by so much excitement, fell asleep in her chair. Penny went quietly outside the stifling hut to be greeted by a black hound dog, it's tail wagging gaily. Shadow sniffed and decided Penny was okay, so he took her on a walk to the lake where they both had a cool drink. From there Penny could see Glory Land way across the lake and the red roofs of the Pink Pavillion. It was a beautiful view. She sat on the sand and was lost in dreams; it seemed like days before her partner returned.

"Where's Tatty?" Freud asked, his face red and sweaty, when he came upon Penny sitting beside the lake.

"She's napping. What took you so long?"

"I ran into Phlox again. It looked like she was panhandling in front of the bank. I hope not. That would be a bummer. She ran right up to me, so I had her watch my car while I went inside to cash our checks; then I took her to The Casa for a pizza and promised to show her Safflower Hill sometime soon. I'd have done anything to get rid of her! I think I'd have given her my ten-speed to keep if she'd asked me," he laughed. "Anyway, I'm back safe and sound. Let's wake Tatty. There will be two men from the general store coming in twenty minutes to be witnesses. I thought of that at the last minute and I stopped at the store. They know Tatty; in fact they said Tatty's got a charge account with them. After this Tatty can pay all her bills. I wouldn't want to be in hock to that pair," said Freud.

Tatty shook herself awake when they spoke her name. "Oh it's you." Freud held out a sheaf of green bills.

"Let's count it." He counted it in twenty piles of ten dollars each and Tatty's eyes bulged. "Put these away in a safe place somewhere, Mrs. Tuttle, right away. There are men coming to witness your signature." Tatty looked scared. "It's all right, Mrs. Tuttle. Just a legal formality. You know the Filch brothers—it's them." Tatty looked relieved. She bought what little she needed at Filch Brothers' General Store. Tatty put the money in a coffee can and went out back with her money, returning shortly without it.

A few minutes later the Filch brothers arrived. Tatty signed the deed with some difficulty and they hurried on back to their store. Then Tatty clutched Freud's arm, suddenly remembering the gate. "Now," she said, "you take me to Homer's?"

"Sure, what for?" asked Freud.

"A gate for my wall."

Penny interrupted, "It's an iron gate, Freud, a big heavy iron gate. It must be a beautiful thing."

"Okay, Kaleri, we'll go to Homer's, but if it's an iron gate, we'll need a truck and some helpers. I'll ask Mark for some Saffies. They have an old truck, I think. We'll go ask them right away. Where are you going to put it, Tatty?"

"Here," she said, taking him to the opening between two high walls of carefully laid stone. "I'll work on it some more, but don't be too long. You're a nice little gentleman," she added, patting his arm.

"We'll be back tomorrow. Come on, Penny." The two of them ran happily down the path and Tatty, her hand shading her eyes, stood by her ladder and stared after them long after they had disappeared into the woods. "I forgot to tell 'em about the gun," she said to her dog, "but we'll git one and we'll go huntin' in the fall." Shadow looked pleased and wagged his tail.

All day long Penny had been fascinated by the eccentric old Indian who lived by herself in the swamps and appalled by the way she lived. Tatty's life style seemed to belie the contentment she showed. It was some experience seeing her house, and Penny was tormented by the idea that she and Freud were buying Tatty's place. If so, what on earth for?

As soon as they were out of earshot, Penny, trailing behind Freud, sat down on a mossy stone. "I won't go another step, John, until you tell me what we bought from Kaleri. Answer me."

Freud was laughing. "Did we buy that?" Penny pointed back over her shoulder towards Tatty's house. Freud, realizing at last how it looked to Penny, sat down beside her and laughed so hard he fell over on the ground.

"You thought we bought Tatty's house!" he sputtered between convulsions of laughter. Penny was getting excited.

"John Freund, what did we buy?"

"Glory Land, girl, Glory Land! Would you believe it? We own Glory Land!"

"What a tease you are, Freud! Be serious for once." She began walking alone toward the highway.

"My love! My tooth fairy! Wait for me!" Freud caught up with her when she came to the log. "Penny, listen. I'm serious. You and I own a nice piece of Glory Land. It belonged to Tatty, but she didn't even know it. Let's sneak over there now and I'll show you. We have to plan what we're going to do with it. But promise you won't tell anyone anything yet. It's our secret, Penny. You understand?" He put his heavy arm around her shoulder. She nodded, but she didn't believe the Glory Land bit. It was all so fantastic she couldn't utter a word. Freud, still sensing her disbelief, put his other arm around her and sealed her lips with a kiss. He made sure it was a good one.

"What time is it, Freud?" asked Penny, her legs like jelly. "My goodness, it's three o'clock and I have to make ten dozen cookies for our church reception for the new pastor by seven o'clock. I've got to go home at once!" They hurried to the car and drove back to town.

It would have been nice to ask Freud in to help her make cookies, to keep him near her; but whatever he was up to, she realized there was more to it, so she jumped out of the car, leaning into the open window to say smilingly and a bit shakily, "You are quite a guy."

"*Adios,* pardner, see you in a couple of days." He tipped his broad-brimmed straw hat and winked at her. Then Freud drove off down Main Street leaving Penny so overcome with emotion she could hardly go up the stairs into The Sesame Seed. Am I crazy or am I in love? she asked herself. Why does a couple of days away from that nut sound like forever?

Safflower Hill

Now that the deal was closed, Freud was all business. First on his list of immediate priorities was to take care of Miss Phlox Fontaine. He must divert her at once from following his activities so closely. Why not take her to Safflower Hill as he promised, introduce her around and leave her there with some male jock to look things over, while he went for a second look at his new kingdom? He wished he could move right over to Glory Land with his tent, but he must not be seen there yet—not till he found an obvious reason for being there. A job would do quite nicely; perhaps the Saffies could tell him what was available.

He felt certain Phlox would be hanging about at the Royal Purple looking for some action. It was just around the corner from Crabbe's place—thank heaven Penny had rescued him from taking Crabbie for his partner.

Sure enough Phlox was waiting right in front of the Royal Purple, chewing gum and horsing around with one of the local freaks. No doubt about it, she was a cute chick—beautiful in fact. With a figure like hers, no wonder she wore so many skimpy knit tops and tight stretch jeans. Freud was cool and unimpressed, for with him at the moment it was "handsome is as handsome does." He wondered who said that. Maybe it was a saying of Ben Franklin, his favorite historical oldie.

He drove his Buick right up over the curb as close as he could get to Phlox to gain her attention.

"Hi."

"Oh, Freud, meet Stevie," she said, introducing him to a kid about eighteen, dirt pale with long, tangled hair and a bad complexion. "Stevie's from the Hill. He's been sticking around to get a ride. And he hasn't combed his hair for a year."

"One year, nineteen days and three hours," corrected Stevie.

Freud made no comment. "Jump in, you two. Did Phlox tell you she's been thinking of moving up there?" asked Freud adroitly.

Phlox looked surprised. Had she been thinking that? As they drove through town, Stevie talked about living at the Hill. He put his skinny arm around Phlox and said right into her ear, "Don't come up unless you've got something to give." He was eyeing her tiny diamond earrings. "When I came I had nothin', and you know what I do? I wash dishes. The right kids, the ones that give them something, get the cushy jobs—'the executives,' I call them. Me—I don't even have enough to buy pot!"

Or shampoo, Phlox said to herself, adding aloud as she took his arm from around her, "Darned if I'd ever wash dishes."

Freud suggested that Phlox might think of something she had that they could use if she looked around for a while. Actually he didn't know what it would be—she didn't own a car and she was using his bike; but she probably had a fat allowance from her old man to spend on clothes.

"When we get there I advise you to stick close by me,"

said Stevie, aware he had a prize on his hands. "I'll show you around. Do you like chickens and pigs?"

Phlox made a face. "No, I'm more interested in weaving and making clothes. I love clothes. Sometimes I design my own. I'm having several of my designs made up by a Japanese dressmaker in Temagami Springs." Freud was amazed that this kid had a talent after all!

Before he could respond, Stevie exclaimed, "Say, that's great—you can bring all your clothes for our common closet. We just pick from the pile each day. How do you like this Beethoven shirt?" He laughed. "It was the only thing that fit me today because I got up late." Hair from his chest stuck out the holes, which just happened to be Beethoven's hair. It was amazing to say the least.

"You wear other people's clothes! Yuck!" exclaimed Phlox.

"They're not other people's. They're ours. We all own everything—and nothing. You have to realign your thinking. Nothing's yours. It's all ours. Doesn't it freak you out to think of owning nothing? That's freedom, man!"

"It's all in how you look at it," said Phlox. "I like to own things that no one else has. That's why I design my own clothes." By this time they had driven up the dirt road over the newly turned earth and on to Safflower Hill. They went around the barn to the front of the dilapidated red farmhouse. There were several dirty-looking children playing there and a happy group of people sitting on the steps playing banjos and fiddles and singing lustily.

"Oh," remarked Stevie, "let's go round to the back door. Those are the Saffies having a song rehearsal."

Quick as thought, Freud said, "Show Phlox everything, Stevie—the barn, the pottery, the greenhouse, everything. I just remembered I have an errand in town for my father.

I'll come back for Phlox before dinner."

Stevie gave Freud a knowing look that said thanks, and pushed Phlox into the kitchen. "Go on in. You'll like it. Just step on in." Phlox looked around the dingy room. Was this what he was calling a kitchen? It didn't look like any kitchen she'd ever seen. "Who cleans? Who runs the sweeper?"

"Oh, we all do that."

Phlox picked her way cautiously into the living room. "You do?" She looked at the dusty stairs and the dark sticky spills on the carpet. The chairs were from the Salvation Army, an odd assortment of castoffs. "How can you stand to live like this?" she asked, turning up her nose in pity and disgust.

"You see," drawled Steve, "we're not yet very well organized and we're all so busy doing our thing, we don't have time for housework. Sometimes we get sightseers—freeloaders and the like, and we have them run the vacuum cleaner. But one of these days we'll get a system," Stevie grinned at his visitor.

"This place needs a Care package," observed Phlox.

"Oh, we are a care package; yes, we care. We care about each other—and about the world. And as you can see, you'll have plenty to do if you come up here, so there isn't time to worry about how things look," said Stevie.

Phlox had decided this was no place for peons. The Freunds' comfortable, stuffy old house was better than this (not much better; without Freud it would be terrible), but she didn't think much of this life style either. Still, it was different from anything she'd ever tried.

Stevie placed his hand on her waist and turned her around. "Come now, you're not seeing what's really here. Look up from the floor into the faces and see their happiness in belonging to one another, their joy in doing what they like to do."

"And what about what you don't like to do? Who takes care of those kids?" The idea of babysitting made her shudder.

"A little of what we don't like is good for us all and many hands make light work, you know. I wouldn't stay a day if I hadn't found something special here—a love I never had at home."

"Well, I've never had any of that," admitted Phlox. "I've had a terrible life." Suddenly she was telling all of her troubles to this pale-faced stranger, and his face shone with understanding.

"I have a nice pad in the attic. I keep it clean because I sleep on the floor. Want to see it?" Phlox nodded, feeling a little less uncomfortable. Stevie continued, "Come on up and I'll play you our latest recording. Skip Bantley's new song! He writes great stuff. Say, have you got something going with that woolly-haired guy?" asked Stevie, grinning as he ran his hands through her short blonde hair.

"Hardly," offered Phlox. "He ignores me like he's my brother," she said flatly. "But keep your hands off me!" Her voice rose. "I'm not a piece of common property."

"Okay! Okay," said Stevie, thinking maybe it was time to buy himself a comb.

Homer's Steel and Scrap

In all her life Tatty Softshoe had never had two thousand dollars to spend, but like everyone else she had her dreams of what she might do if ever she should be so lucky as to find some money or be heir to an unknown relative. Over the years, as her eyesight dimmed and her fear of the future grew, she arrested her unease with dreams of providing for her own safety by keeping a hostile world from finding the path to her sanctuary in the swamps. Her ancestors had roamed widely over the mountains, hunting the deer and the bear and the beaver but always returning to the fresh clear waters of Big Bear Lake, to Savernake Forest lands and to the warm Valley of Springs, a small piece of which was hers and hers alone. She would protect it.

Now that she had received her windfall from the big blond 'un, money for land she had forgotten was hers, she intended to use the money without delay to complete her ten years of hard labor. But Tatty was romantic as well as foresighted. She loved her dead husband, Irv, and she talked to him as she tramped on her daily hike for stones. He was buried up behind the house with only a pile of stones marking his grave, but there was something down at Homer's that would be a fitting memorial to Irv and that she meant to have, if it cost fifty dollars. Irv agreed with her that it was a mighty pretty gate, and so it came about that she left her home and went with Freud and his bearded friends from Safflower Hill to Homer's Steel and Scrap.

As the young people stood around Tatty in the junkyard, staring down at a large rusty gate lying on a pile of old pipes, Freud and Mark Sanders were relieving it of its overburden of bicycle frames and baby carriages when Mr. Harry Homer, owner of the junkyard, looked out of his office window at this strange crowd. He was alarmed. What were Judge Freund's kid and that hippy crowd doing with that seedy little woman in the long fur coat, going through his scrap pile? He scrutinized them closely. Why it looks like the rock lady, he thought in amazement. What can she want? And since when does she have friends in town? His trader's instinct told him he should go out quickly and help them with whatever it was they had come to buy or chase them away if they were just looking. Harry Homer hitched up his pants around his fifty-inch waist and waddled out into the yard in his bedroom slippers. He walked up to the elbow of the well-known Freud. Freud was discussing the initials T.L. curiously intertwined in two hearts in an elaborate design at the top of the gate. Tinges of gold on the huge letters caught an occasional ray of sunshine shining between the clouds.

"I wonder who T.L. could have been," said Mark Sanders, looking over at Harry. Harry, always eager to talk, broke in, "T.L.? T.L. was Tyler Lansdown, of course. You don't remember him—'the man with the big heart,' he called himself. His place burned down and the loss busted his great big heart. Isn't that something? See those hearts. They were his trademark. How about that for a gate? I bought it at auction from the Lansdown estate when they sold the land to Brigham Bantley way back in the fifties. It hasn't been a good investment," he said, putting his foot on it. "Who wants one of them now? I wish I'd sold it for scrap during the Vietnam War when prices were high. My father always said, 'Don't invite your heart to a business trans-action'; but somehow I couldn't scrap that gate because I loved T.L. Did you know he lent me the money to buy this place? And now I'm getting old. Wanna buy a nice gate, special price for you?"

"How much?" asked Tatty from deep under her man's fedora. Her heart was beating fast.

"Oh," he said, "money can't buy what that's worth. See those gold letters. And them hearts—expensive; but I'll give it to John Freund for two-fifty."

"Two dollars and fifty cents, a fair price," commented Tatty with a confirming nod.

Freud broke in. "Make it two hundred dollars and we'll carry it away."

"Two hundred dollars? You wanna steal my gate from me," Harry shouted in practiced outrage. Then, relenting, he lowered his voice. "Will you use it for a gate?" he asked as he palmed his bald head.

"That's just what we want it for," offered all the Saffies at once.

"But I could get more money for it as scrap," Harry ut-tered disconsolately. "However, if you're gonna use it for a gate—"

"What do you think, Mrs. Tuttle," whispered Freud to the little Indian tugging his arm. "You decide."

Tatty shook her head, still in shock over the price. Two hundred dollars! That shrewd skunk, she was thinking, trying to charge me fancy city prices. Why, that would be a gate on his grave before he could sell it for two hundred dollars. The old, worthless rusty thing! But wasn't it beautiful? It would give her place class. She wavered a moment; then she drew Freud's ear down to her mouth and whispered, "Isn't that too much?"

"Tatty, don't you see that big T?"

She squinted at the gate and smiled broadly. "Why, T for Tatty and there's an I for Irv," she observed in astonishment. "I'll take it," she whispered. No one told her that the I was an L.

The deal was made and though Tatty in her excitement got in the way, the gate was loaded on the Saffies' old truck, which sagged a little under its considerable burden. Freud was thinking he would have to get Tony DeLuca to help put that into Tatty's wall—it was no job for amateurs—when Tatty said, "Now let's go get me a gun."

"A gun? What for? Do you have a license?"

"A license?" she grimaced. "No one looks after this self but me. They can't forbid that, can they? All I need is a gun."

A few days later Tatty's place was complete, thanks to the help of Tony DeLuca and his friends, experienced stonemasons working during their morning off from Glory Land. Mr. DeLuca had been very skeptical about finishing a wall that had not been done by an Italian stonemason. Indeed Tatty's creation did lack certain special effects, but Tony admitted when he saw it that it was a fair piece of work for a woman. The job of installing the heavy iron gate was a considerable challenge, but Tony was won over to full cooperation with the kids when he saw that the gate was the very gate he had dismantled at Glory Land some twenty-three years before. Tony stood in wonder at the strange way things have of turning out. Here he was years later putting a millionaire's gate in a wall around an Indian hovel!

The men went to work and the wall, ten years in the making, was finished in three hours, with its huge iron gate firmly in place. After a last look at their strange creation, the stonemasons hurried off to their jobs at Glory Land. The hinges were oiled and tested by Tatty herself; and she locked the gates together with a big padlock and chain. Finally Tatty went inside and got her old gun and, propping it against the house, she sat down on her rocker to enjoy the results of so much effort. She hadn't known security since Irv died, but now she rocked and rested in perfect happiness. As she rocked back and forth she crooned a prayer of thanksgiving to God for giving her this peace at last. She was tired, but she felt a warm glow of happy satisfaction. "Just try and take me to the nursin' home," she muttered sleepily. She deliberated whether to go for more stones in the morning. Maybe finally she had enough; she was tired and not young any more. Maybe she'd stay home and have a little openin' up fer her new friends. There was an old jug of Irv's special elderberry wine in the root cellar, just enough fer openin' up.

"And we'll have a little tipple to T. and I., two great lovers," she tittered. And with a smile on her face, Kaleri Tuttle fell asleep in her chair, dreaming that she was lying safe in Irv's arms.

The Peak of the Morning Light

Just before daybreak on the 28th of May, Brigham Bantley got out of bed, did five minutes of aerobic exercises and dressed quickly. A man of habit, he performed the same ritual each spring on the day before the opening of Glory Land.

He was glad everything was in readiness at the park. There had been a crisis a few days before when the restaurant manager took a fatal dose of sleeping pills; however, Anna Maria Abendtal had agreed, albeit reluctantly, to take the position. Thanks to the recent rains, the lawns were in splendid condition, mowed smooth as a golf course under the direction of Tony DeLuca, the groundskeeper for twenty years. Olivia Dupre had seen to the redecoration of the theater green room and the art gallery and invited the town fathers to a reception there on the morrow. The restaurant was ready to serve its guests. Even his wife had done her part by sending him a congratulatory telegram wishing him well on the opening of Glory Land. She had included the message that she was in good health and sailing south on the *S.S. African Prince*. It was a relief to Brig to hear from her and know that all was well. But she had not mentioned the new law.

Today it was time to prepare himself physically and spiritually for the arduous days ahead. To do this he had to be by himself. So it was his custom on this day of the year to go up to the mountains to a beautiful spot—a place where he could be alone with God and pray aloud if he felt like it. He would pray for wisdom and understanding and knowledge. He would need the strength of Solomon.

It was also his custom on this happy occasion to take along a picnic lunch—several slices of Brie cheese from Quebec, a loaf of homemade French bread, a hard-boiled egg and a bottle of ginger ale. After eating lunch he would come down from the mountain and back to reality better able to greet his customers with a smile.

His lunch never varied, nor did the clothes that he wore to the mountain top. Corduroy trousers and high boots, laced to the knee, with a safari jacket of tan duck. The trousers, of course, had been replaced when he was thirty by a larger size. The green plaid shirt too had been replaced and the newer one had a fine red stripe, but it was of soft Viyella flannel ordered from Abercrombie's, like its predecessor. He laughed this morning, remembering the day he had intercepted Lucy on her way to the Good-will with these old clothes. He had been angry with her for not realizing his attachment to them.

Today he was humming to himself as he put on the green shirt and tan pants and laced his high shoes. He felt younger than he had in months and he knew why. It wasn't the hike he anticipated or the fine weather. It was his having found a new friend in Anna Maria Abendtal, a person who had not come to him for anything and whom he had discovered as his own special treasure. He needed a friend, someone with whom to share deep thoughts. Funny it should be a woman.

Brig drove to the park and stopped in front of the newly painted gate. Getting out, he strode off down the main road, called the Appian Way. Turning into the woods, he followed the trail that led past his fine two-hundred-fifty-year-old oak tree. He would never forget coming here with his bride. He stopped for a moment beneath its spreading branches and looked up. It was a wonderful tree. Maybe someday his grandchildren would love it as he did.

Brig Bantley resumed his walk, crossing Big Bear River on the old bridge. It would need new planking in the fall. He made a note in his little notebook and walked on. The path divided, to the left going east to the flat rocks by the river and the Indian cave near Little Bear Lake, and to the north to the red cliffs, which formed a backdrop to the meadows and forests of Glory Land. He took the path to the left and, cutting a small hickory tree, fashioned himself a walking cane. With its help he went up the ever steeper trail, stopping at Sweetbriar Springs for a drink of pungent water, and then continued upwards on a switchback path until he came out of the woods on an outcrop of rock a thousand feet above the river. He stopped and took off his old leather knapsack. Swinging the sack down onto a flat place, he removed his jacket and laid it in the grass.

Then, his hands on his hips, Brig Bantley lifted his head and looked straight up at the great granite slab above him, scanning it with his eyes, the geologist appraising a plutonic upthrust. He looked at it carefully, studying its structure and surface for footholds and handholds. The once molten silicates, cooled slowly, had crystallized into this strong rough-textured pile of grey granite, the smallest outthrust of which would support his one hundred ninety pounds. Grasping a familiar knob of rock with his left hand, he put his right foot on a diagonal crack and with a smooth motion born of earlier practice, he maneuvered himself upward by balance and counterforce from handhold to handhold and crack to crack. Relaxed and erect he mounted the rock, solid and strong. Using a friction hold, he struggled over a small overhang and pulled himself upright on the great grey pulpit of stone. He was physically exhilarated and mentally stimulated as he stood again on the Peak of the Morning Light.

Around him was an ocean of atmosphere from which he inhaled deep breaths of oxygen. He was standing alone, gazing down on a landscape that spread from sunrise to sunset in twenty-eight waves of mountain ridges veiled in the morning mist. He looked down on tiny roads and great forests, farmlands and streams. America, the beautiful, he thought.

Then, sinking slowly to his knees on the hard abutment, he prayed to God for courage and for insight and he praised Him and thanked Him for everything, including his new friend, Anna. After a time Brig arose and, stretching his long arms high, he rotated around on that great stage and his spirit soared. There on that pinnacle, solo with God, Brigham Bantley felt magnified, overwhelmed, uplifted by the incomprehensible power of the Lord. And in that moment there alone he sensed he was part of a landscape vast beyond his own imagining.

There alone he rededicated himself to the summer ahead. It would bring forth good fruit. In his heart he was glad he was not a geologist in the hire of some eastern potentate but a small businessman in an old-fashioned town who could serve his fellow Americans. Once again he felt confident in what he was doing.

His mission accomplished, Brigham Bantley lost no time climbing down over the rocks to the grassy place below. He was hungry; the Brie would taste good and so would the pear and the pickle and the hard-boiled egg. He opened his lunch—it was larger than usual! Mrs. O'Leary had violated tradition and put in a chocolate bar. He opened the Temagami ginger ale with his Swiss pocket knife and poured it into a glass. Then while he ate his lunch he thought about the past. It was the twenty-second year of Glory Land. It didn't begin to grow until Olivia Dupre came to work for him. She'd been the one to suggest they place emphasis on American history and she also suggested the restaurant by the lake.

Yes, he owed a lot of his success to Olivia's help. After such a long association Brig was fond of Olivia in a sisterly way, and he usually went to see her and her husband quite regularly; but this spring he hadn't given them much personal attention. Things had been too hectic with Lucy leaving, the kids home from college, 04Y4 and the usual May rush. He supposed he should be grateful to Olivia for carrying him the news of 04Y4 and telling him about Miss Abendtal. Come to think of it, it was quite an unusual thing for her to have driven all the way to Passion Point. She must have been terribly worried about Rene. She wanted to talk but he hadn't listened. He'd sent her home to her problems, wishing to be alone with his own.

It was thoughtless of me, he said to himself. Well, I'll see her a lot from now on and I'll find out about Rene and I'll think of some way to lighten her load. Several days before, Olivia had remarked that she needed more help with publicity, that she was carrying too much on her shoulders. Now it occurred to him to take Skip away from Tony (they could surely hire a Vietnamese in his place) and send him over to help Olivia with public relations. Maybe Olivia would make him shape up and take more responsibility.

"Yes, Livy," he said aloud, "we've come a long way together, a very long way!"

At first Glory Land had been a path through the woods to the old Indian campsite and picnic tables under the trees, a sandwich and ice cream stand by the road. The second year he had put in the carousel. It was a special one, a hand-carved beauty imported from the Black Forest. This grown man still had a thing about merry-go-rounds. For a time there was a ferris wheel and small gift shop; all that was gone now except for the carousel—he'd never sell that—all gone, thanks to Olivia Dupre.

He remembered hiring Olivia because of her sad story of her war-injured husband. It was his conscience as much as anything else that made him hire an inexperienced female artist as his aide in planning and design, her husband having given to his country when he had not—uneasy thought even now.

Yes, he remembered those early days well, particularly the occasion when he told Olivia he was about to buy a roller coaster. She looked at him thoughtfully for several minutes and then, biting her fingernails, said in a nervous sort of way, "Mr. Bantley, may I say something I have on my mind? I've been thinking you don't want to have an ordinary sort of amusement park just for this small town. You want something finer—a special place for people from everywhere, a park that emphasizes the unique heritage of the American people, a place we can all take pride in. We need something special around here." She had said it all in one breath and Brig was amazed. His new helper was certainly right.

"You don't mind my saying that?" she asked.

"My girl," he replied, "you're an answer to my prayer. I haven't felt right about the direction we've been going for some time. My wife was the first to hint at it and now I've noticed she's lost interest in this place as if she's ashamed of it. But it took you to point out a solution!" Though he didn't remember, he had taken Olivia's hand in his and said, "Now I know why I hired you." She had loved that. And from then on, she was his willing slave.

They'd done good things together and created one of the most beautiful places in the whole country, its streams and meadows, its forests and its very stones handled with tender loving care. And they built the theater and the art gallery, the sculpture garden, the Gothic greenhouse, the teahouse and the Pink Pavillion. There were miles of paths through the woods and along the river. This year they were putting in an exercise course and a garden for meditation. Busloads of old ladies would come to spend the day and exclaim over what was new this year. He could see them now sitting on the pads in the Garden of Contemplation and doing the exercises on the new course. It was all part of the fun to have something different every year, to give people stimulating new experiences. But the feature attraction was his famous restaurant, the Pink Pavillion. It was situated on a peninsula in the Big Bear Lake, which provided splendid views both east and west and north across the lake to the pine-covered mountains and the high peaks. The food was as splendid as the view; for it alone people traveled across the state.

His biggest problem now was the continuing success of Glory Land, and yet there was no turning back. He had to go on improving it. But was he committed to endless growth? He thought not—it was the path of the country at large and it was a roadway to ultimate disaster. From now on he would add no new dimensions by way of physical attractions to his park. He would continue to stress quality and service, but he would create no new attractions.

Having made this decision, Brigham put his hand in his pocket for his pipe. Though he had given up smoking, he retained this as part of the tradition because it reminded him of his father. Once a year he smoked his redstone Indian pipe. Reaching in his pocket now for the pipe, he found the letter from Banter that had lain on his dresser unopened for three days. "Let's see what Bant has to say. When I write Lucy tonight I'll tell her about my new job for Skip and pass along the news from Bant." It was just a note; Bant never wrote much.

Dear Folks:
    My first summer away from Glory Land! I'll miss it, of course, because it's part of all that I am. But what am I? That's why I'm here at the ashram—to find out, and until I know, I can't come home. I've lost weight, which is good, and I think I've found my personal guru. I'm learning many things, but all my questions about the meaning of life are still not answered. I could use three hundred dollars.

Love,
Your son, Banter.

Funny, thought Brig, ever since childhood Bant has signed his letters "your son," as if we didn't know! Lucy thinks it's touching. Brig nodded his head. His wife just couldn't say no to Banter; why, she'd even send him the three hundred dollars! Well, he wouldn't get it from him, thought Brig as he stuffed the letter back in his pocket. But in a moment he said slowly, "You know, maybe that child of mine has something. I know who I am: I'm a church-going man, a father and a husband; I'm an educated, tax-paying citizen—that's who I am; that's the Brigham Bantley the world sees. But, by heaven, I don't know what I am or where I want to go. So far it's been onward and upward, more and more. Upward to where? More and more of what? Men have to be something more than pleasure-seeking packrats. We're higher than the animals. We're made in the image of God! What are we really meant to be? And how do we get there? I'd like to find that out. Yes, I really would, Banter. I guess I'll have to think about it later," he observed to a downy woodpecker knocking on a nearby white birch tree. "Now I must get back. It's after one o'clock and my people will be waiting for me."

The Day Before Opening

Olivia Dupre loved the day before opening. It was the beginning each year of a close association between herself and Brigham Bantley. This summer she planned to be indispensable to him and to be everything he'd ever needed in a woman—if he would let her. It was a big "if." Brig insulated himself from his employees with an invisible wall through which one did not step. From that first interview long ago, she had never been able to break this wall of authority around her employer. She had been afraid to try, fearing she might somehow lose her precious job. Probably it was necessary for him to insulate himself from women—so many of them were silly about him—but surely he didn't have to protect himself from her! It was time to break down his resistance.

Thinking about this caused Olivia to rise from her chair, go to the cabinet and switch on the electronic air cleaner that Brig had installed in her office when he gave up smoking. He had not asked her permission—he was funny that way—but it was one of the few really exasperating things he had ever done. She got the hint, but she could not give up smoking. Olivia picked up the pack from her desk and lit a fresh cigarette. Then she emptied her already full ash tray into a plastic bag and tied it shut. Brig would be down soon from the mountain.

Olivia was one of the few people who worked the day before opening. As far as she was concerned, Brig could do as he pleased as long as he didn't expect her to follow his little "ritual of spring," as she called it. Hiking in the woods was not her idea of how to spend this important morning. Nor did she pray. Olivia relied on her own resources, hard work, and creative ideas for her strength. Her husband and daughter were the religious members of the family—for all the good it did either of them. They could have all that "hallelujah and praise the Lord" talk! (It had not occurred to her that the spiritual empathy Rene had with his daughter sustained him through his sufferings as nothing else could.) She presumed that by supporting him, she was the strength in the family.

How long would her strength hold out? With Rene's health deteriorating she would soon have to hire a helper at home and that would be expensive. If only Penny would see that Rene should go to the Veterans' Hospital where he would be taken care of, but Penny wouldn't even talk about it. It was not that Olivia planned to neglect him. She would drive over every Monday to Duxbury to see him, and maybe between visits she could have some social life again. To be entertaining such thoughts after all these years surprised Olivia, but she could not help herself. She had suppressed the feeling that her marriage was not fulfilling as long as she could. Since 04Y4 came into being she had been thinking about the harsh fact that her life was half over and the only fun she ever had was her work. Since when was work all there was in life? No, it was not enough! Even though she loved Rene, her marriage had been a deep disappointment. Olivia reminded herself again and again that his being wounded in the war was not his fault, and she told herself that she was not considering divorce. She could not hurt him now when he was so sick. But Olivia also decided that one way or another she would have Brig Bantley. She knew him better than he knew himself. She had much to give and no one would blame her—not these days, not with the new morality. That is, no one but Penny and Rene, and they'd be the last to know.

Olivia rearranged her desk and moved her new schefflera plant into the corner by the bookcase. Then she watered the pink and yellow fuchsia that hung behind her desk. She moved the orange Charles Eames visitor's chair closer to her own, readying it for the boss. The Vietnamese painters had painted the walls of her office a pale, warm yellow and there was a fresh breezy atmosphere she hoped Brig would notice and appreciate.

Tony arrived to report that the lawns were mowed and the paint was dry in the toilet rooms. He was satisfied that all the preparations for summer had been taken care of. Anna Maria Abendtal phoned to say that the Pink Pavillion was ready for ten thousand guests. What a brilliant idea it had been to hire Anna, thought Olivia. Olivia had been acquainted with Anna from Lost Friday Club, but she never felt they had much in common. She admired domestically skilled women like Anna as a horse might admire a camel, acknowledging her homely talents but proud that she herself was not only talented but sophisticated, something she never regarded a homemaker as being. However, Anna would do well in the kitchen, and it was all Olivia's idea. Brig should be grateful.

To make sure she looked attractive for the boss, Olivia went into her pink-tiled bathroom and surveyed herself in the full-length mirror. Could she pass for thirty-five? She liked what she saw and she hoped Brig might notice for once. Olivia was wearing a high-style grey pantsuit she had found at a French shop in Quebec with a red scarf at her throat and a large silver pin and earrings. Her black hair was pinned back in a becoming knot and she looked glamorous and businesslike. She added fresh lipstick and a dab of Chanel 19. Brig had once asked what perfume she was wearing; it was Chanel 19, so that became "their perfume."

While she readied herself for her patron's arrival, she remembered there was one little problem left to be solved and that was the hiring of someone to portray Ben Franklin. Her new helper, Skip Bantley, had placed an ad in *The Morning Republican* and someone would turn up. Anyway, there was a month's time to prepare for the exhibit of Art Longworth's collection of Franklin memorabilia.

If necessary, she could hire a Saffie. However, she held a blanket disapproval of people who lived in communes. Who would ever want to live that way? Surely not anyone with any direction in life. No, she was not at all sure that the hiring of so many of them as busboys and waiters and ticket sellers was a good idea; but they had been hired in spite of her by Brig himself—apparently at the suggestion of Anna Maria. Olivia shrugged. Well, Anna Maria would have to train them, so she supposed they were her worry. As she thought of the children at Safflower Hill, some of them runaways, she was thankful that her daughter, Penny, was a normal child with no such nonsensical ideas. No, she would not hire a Saffie for Ben Franklin; she wanted someone whom she could trust, preferably a town boy with good references.

Olivia could not know it, but even while she sat there, Ben Franklin was being reincarnated at 210 Pleasant Street.

Freud had seen the ads for Ben Franklin. He leaped from the table and took the stairs to his room three at a time so eager was he to hurry over to Glory Land and apply for the job. He could not have been more stimulated by a message in the paper had he been the father of a kidnap victim finding a ransom note. The message was meant for him! Who else in Temagami Springs knew as much about Ben Franklin and had a big chin, a long nose and a high forehead? Everything was falling into place—click, click, click, like a digital clock. He was on his way to glory, honor, fame, fun and $2.50 an hour.

When things are meant to be, as young Freud felt they were this summer, everything one does seems to contribute to the outcome. Long before Freud had discovered the choice piece of property which did not belong to its supposed owner, long before he had plans for acres of his own, he had consented in a psychology class at Harvard University to be hypnotically regressed to a previous life. Today he had reason to be glad about that. He remembered that it had been very entertaining to his classmates when he spoke in a strange nasal voice and said he was Ben Franklin's half-brother, James. Though it was entertaining, lacking proof, it was quite meaningless; and in psych class it had mattered to no one whether or not Freud really had been Ben Franklin's brother or Franklin himself. Freud's interest in the life and times of that early American certainly came in handy that day! Today he was amazed by his good fortune in having an advantage over other applicants and quite confident that through the power of persuasion he could convince anyone that he really was Ben Franklin and the only one for the job at Glory Land.

Ruffling through his desk drawers he turned up his great-grandfather's wire-rimmed glasses—he must have been keeping them just for this. Then he dashed to his closet and

pulled out his Turkish cotton shirt with ruffled sleeves; he
never had liked it, but it was perfect for today. There was
that worn paisley vest he'd picked up at the Salvation Army
store back in high school—goodness knows why, but it had
only cost twenty-five cents. He had never worn it because
it was too small. Now scissors took care of that—snip, snip
right down the middle of the back—plus a few safety pins.
No brocade coat; then he remembered his dad's brown
velvet smoking jacket, a little small, but it ought to do.
A quick dash into enemy territory furnished that, and up
on the shelf was his mother's mink hat. Old Ben had a fur
hat—better have that too.

Everything assembled on the bed, Freud stepped to the
mirror to do what he could with his hair. In fact his biggest
problem was to simulate the wispy quality of Ben Franklin's
head. After a time, with the help of quite a few dabs of his
father's hair cream and a package of his mother's bobby-
pins, he managed to smooth his wild curls down towards his
shoulders where they turned up nicely and looked stiff, something like a white wig. It would be okay under the mink hat.

He dressed quickly in the shirt and vest and jacket and
placed Tulie's hat on his head (he took an aspirin for the
headache it gave him). He finished the costume by pulling his socks out over his pants. Then he announced, "Ben
Franklin, you have just reappeared. You are twenty-three
years old and your twentieth-century nickname is Freud and
now you are ready to proceed from the court of Louis XVI
to the banks of the Big Bear River. O, Glory Land, prepare
yourself. Ben and I are coming!"

Olivia Dupre stood up and put her pocketbook over her
shoulder. It was time to drive home to give Rene an early

lunch. At that moment there was a commanding knock on the door. She hurried back to her desk and sat down. Picking up her pen she called, "Yes, come in."

Olivia looked up into the merry eyes of a funny old gentleman. "Why, Mr. Franklin, where did you come from?" This audacious personality standing before her looked like Ben Franklin, but he also looked like someone else, someone familiar. She didn't know whether to laugh or keep a straight face, but she decided to take him seriously. "Yes?"

Freud bowed graciously and Olivia suppressed a smile. "The President sent me a cable advising that you needed me, so I flew in from Paris immediately. The Compte de Vergennes will miss me, of course, but here I am. Those new Concordes are so fast. To think I had breakfast with Louis XVI and now I will have tea with the ravishing Madame Dupre." Coming around her desk, Freud picked up her hand and kissed it, at the same time flourishing his ruffled cuffs.

"My dear Mr. Franklin," answered Olivia in astonishment. "This is too much! Why do you call on Madame Dupre?"

"Ah, my dear lady, it grieves me to say that court life is very expensive. The miserable pittance sent me by my country is not sufficient for the parties I must give. To be perfectly frank, madame, I am looking for employment."

Olivia stared up at Freud from under her dark lashes, her eyebrows raised in a look of amusement and delight. After a long moment she laughed. "You're John Freund, aren't you? I've heard about you from my daughter, Penny. Didn't you go to high school together?"

"Indeed, I remember the wench well," he muttered— mindful of the secret fact that she was presently his business partner.

Mrs. Dupre looked thoughtfully at Judge Freund's son. Was he being impertinent in calling her daughter a wench? No, of course not. It was part of the fun. "To return to the matter at hand, sir," said the Director of Art and Advertising, "it seems unseemly to ask a notorious citizen like you for a resumé and references." In a flash Freud placed his credentials before her and added, pressing forward, "I've often been told I look just like Ben Franklin."

"Well, that's no compliment; but I know a thing or two about make-up and I do believe you could be made to look like him. I'll order a wig from New York. Yes, you'll do nicely. I see you are an authority on our man," said Mrs. Dupre as she ran a pencil down over his resumé.

"Thank you, dear Madame Dupre—with your help, I know I'll be good."

She was pleased by his enthusiasm. Resting her right elbow on the desk, she pointed her pen at him. "You're hired! Tell your father I couldn't resist you." Freud didn't reply that it was unlikely he'd do that. For one thing his dad had shut himself in his room and was speaking to no one; for another thing, his dad would just say "humpf" or maybe even "she's a damned fool." So he just said, "Thank you, Madame Dupre."

"Call me Olivia. We're informal here."

"Yes, ma'am, I mean Olivia. Now, will it be all right if I take a look around the park? I really haven't been here since our senior picnic on the Muffin."

"Of course it's okay, John. Will you come back to see me Monday after opening weekend is over? Opening weekend is such a busy time."

Freud nodded assent and dashed out, heading for the men's room to change his clothes. However, he immediately thought better of it. His present costume would disguise his real identity while he had another look at his new land holdings. This was what Ben Franklin was all about, so he better take Ben along.

As Freud strode up the Appian Way he passed a beautiful girl in cut-off jeans and a halter top; her smooth, red hair turned under on her shoulders. She was walking fast and barely looked up. When she did, he waved and mumbled a hello and went quickly on. He recognized her as Savernake Bantley and he hoped she had not recognized him, but he quickened his steps, afraid to look back. My, how she had grown up! She never seemed so good-looking back there at Temagami High.

When Freud came to the old stone wall he did a ninety-degree turn to the right along his property line, going through a thicket of raspberry brambles and tearing his father's smoking jacket. Detouring a fallen tree and climbing over a ditch, he came out again on the path leading to the old plank bridge. He was looking for a place to build himself a little home, and he saw at once that there was no flat place for it on the near side of the Big Bear River. The magnificent oak tree stood in the way. However, he could not live on the far side of the river; it was not conspicuous enough and his presence could easily be ignored. He had to take physical possession of the near side and that meant removing the tree. "I can't cut down that big tree; it's too beautiful." He admired it for the second time; it was the most magnificent tree he had ever seen, its main branches radiating out twenty-five feet and some twenty feet above his head. It was hundreds of years old, probably standing there in 1776.

Freud, his adrenalin flowing, pulled himself up by the arms to the top of the Muffin to have a better look around. There were six hard ways to get up on that rock and they required a little bit of rock-climbing skill. In the good old days at the Temagami High senior class picnic there was one climb that always impressed the screaming bunch of girls who watched the boys do it. Only the strongest could make it and Freud noted with satisfaction that five years later he could still do it.

He sat down on his favorite spot, sort of a hidden shelf of rock where he used to hide with his steady girl; this time it was, in its own way, even more exciting to sit there. Freud took a pad and pencil from his pocket to make a little drawing of his domain and, as he sat sketching, he remembered coming here with his freshman art class way back when he was fourteen years old. Funny thing, here he was again sketching this spot, only this time not as a little kid who hated art class but as the owner of the Muffin! What if he'd known about this then? Funny thought. But what was he going to do with it now that he had it? Was this a place to live and be self-supporting?

As he narrowed his eyes and gave the matter his complete concentration, his mind began to sum up the assets and itemize the problems. The old bridge, though in need of some repair, was an asset. It was no architectural gem, but it was still sturdy and seemed soundly anchored to the banks of the river.

In a few minutes his look of concentration vanished and a look of pure joy came upon his broad face. Had Sigmund Freud never been born and had his name not been given to John III by his junior high classmates, Freud would have been an apt nickname for John Freund III. There was never a face like the face of John III when the big brain behind it came up with an idea.

"We'll live in that tree. Therein shall be our new home, Mr. Franklin! Every boy wants to live in a tree. Tell me,

Mr. Darwin, why, oh why, does every boy want to live in a tree?"

That question, asked in fun, brought him down to earth. There was one reason he could think of; yes, the idea had one very big advantage: a home in the tree would be easy to fortify against the prying eyes of Phlox Fontaine. She was the one person with whom he could not cope. He just couldn't get a handle on her; and she followed him wherever he went and was on his back no matter how mean he was to her.

Freud took the notebook from his pocket and made a few more sketches. His abode would be no ordinary tree house, rather a sort of spaceship draped in the crotch of the tree. He would have a lookout to see Phlox coming, retractable ladder to keep her below, and an outdoor deck for his public appearances.

Freud was so carried away that he had a little dialogue. "Mr. Franklin," he said, "you and I will have quarters on the post, as they say at West Point, which means we can walk to work! That's what I call convenient. Don't you think so, Mr. Franklin?"

"But why do we want to live in a tree, Mr. Joy?"

"Our arboreal ancestors have advised us to try it, Mr. Franklin."

"And who is to build this house in the sky, Mr. Joy?"

"Who but my friends, Mr. Franklin. My friends who dwell on Safflower Hill. They will build our house in the sky."

"How long will it take, Mr. Joy?"

"One night, Mr. Franklin. One night."

"When will we build our house in the sky?"

"Oh, Mr. Franklin, when the moon's in the sky and the stars are on high and Brig Bantley's bye-bye!"

"Now, Mr. Benjamin Franklin, let's go over to Pleasant
Street. There's much to be done. For one thing, I have to
research the subject of bridges and I must finish drawing
up my plans in some safer place than this." So the two of
them went back to town, whistling a duet, happy and full of
plans—John Freund III and Ben Franklin.

"Is It Going to Rain Tomorrow?"

At exactly one-thirty Brigham Bantley put his head into the door of Olivia's office. He was carrying a bunch of violets behind his back. "How's everything?" he asked. "May I come in?"

"Please do, Brig. Glory Land is ready. Shall we go over our list?" Brig walked over to her desk. "These are for you," he said, handing her the tiny purple wild flowers. Olivia looked at him adoringly and took the flowers tenderly in her hands and placed them in a cup of water in front of her. Brig turned around and, picking up the Eames chair, he placed it behind her desk. "Let me wash before I sit down," he said. While he went into her bathroom, where she had placed a bowl of his favorite jonquils, Olivia quickly put on another dab of perfume and smoothed her dark hair.

Brig reappeared, drying his hands on a lavender towel. "I had a wonderful morning. Did you? You know how I love the day before opening. It sets me up for the summer."

"But you always say in September that closing day is better!" said Olivia, fingering the silver beads at her neck.

"I'm afraid it won't be—not this year," replied Brig, looking beyond her through the open door into the dark pine forest and thinking about September. "But Livy," he said, snapping back to the present and looking straight at his art director, "let's keep happy no matter what happens. You know the other day a kid said to me—the one you met at the dune house—" The smile vanished from Olivia's face. She remembered the one. Brig sat down and began unlacing his high boots. "Well, that wise little kid said that it's important never to have a day you don't enjoy. I'm trying to put that idea to work in my life—not in the hedonistic sense she may have meant it, but in the sense of enjoying whatever the day brings. Already I find it gets easier with practice. For instance, I'm beginning to like talking with my children. As for this place," he said, taking off his shoes, "I'm going to make a special effort to make this summer a good one, a special one, for our patrons and employees alike." He dropped one boot to the floor and fixing her with his eyes said, "With your help, Olivia, I know I can do it." He looked away a moment and then he turned to her again. "And let me say now, thanks for all the support you've given me for all these years. You know, when the kids weren't interested and Lucy wouldn't listen, you've been the only one I could talk to about Glory Land and I'm grateful to you for that." He looked at her to see if she understood his deep gratitude.

She loved him when he looked at her like that. It seemed to have some personal significance. "Thank you, Brig," she said, squeezing his hand.

"Now, my girl," he said, withdrawing his hand from hers, "let's go down this list." It had become a ritual between them to do it in a certain way, and Brig noted approvingly that she had hired a Ben Franklin. He was somewhat surprised that John Freund III was leaving his father's law office to take a temporary job at low pay, but he was glad to hear the boy knew all about Benjamin

Franklin. That would satisfy Mr. Art Longworth, collector of Franklin memorabilia. And it crossed Brig's mind that Mr. Longworth, who was also a collector of important connections, would enjoy meeting the son of the now notorious Judge Freund. That thought made Brig smile to himself.

Putting aside the list, Brig walked over to the window in his stocking feet and drew the yellow-flowered draperies to look at the afternoon sky. Then he turned around to Olivia and asked the usual question, "Do you think it's going to rain tomorrow, Livy?"

Fond of this little ritual, she followed him to look out at the sky: but mindful of her new policy, she was bolder this time and she put her arm around Brig's waist, saying as she did every year, towering cumulus clouds notwithstanding, "It never rains when you drive the Bentley. It always brings us good luck!" Indeed it had rained the three times the Bentley was in the garage for repairs.

Brigham Bantley smiled. "You always say that, Olivia." He did not tell her that Skipper would drive the B.B. in the parade tomorrow and that Anna had given him the idea. It was a change in custom and of that Olivia would certainly disapprove.

On Saturday, the twenty-ninth of May, Glory Land opened for its twenty-second season. It was a fine day and the crowds were larger than usual. The merry-go-round went round and round all day long and everyone had a happy time hiking the new pathways, wandering through the gardens, and dining at the Pink Pavillion.

New York (UPI)—Blue Chip AT&T racked up an impressive gain of 10 points at the Friday close. Brokers attributed its strength to short covering.

PART III

June

He Went to Church Every Sunday

Just before eleven in the morning on the first Sunday in June, Judge John Freund II arrived with his wife, Tallulah, at the big greystone church on Park Place, the most fashionable church in town. The judge walked down the aisle with Tallulah on his arm and had the unpleasant feeling that people were staring at him.

This important member of the congregation sat down in the sixth row left of center, as had been his custom for twenty years, and opened his hymnal to Hymn 52, where he fixed his gaze for some time. John Freund was preoccupied with what he was going to do after the service; he didn't want to do it, but he was going to ask for help from the minister, Rev. MacMorlan. Humiliating as it was for Judge Freund to go crawling to the man he lunched with at the Elks', he had promised his wife he would. Tulie had reminded him, quite unnecessarily he thought, of their large contributions to the church and of Rev. MacMorlan's family connections in the newspaper world. Surely, she said, his friend Z.B. would suggest something he could do about the press. Tulie felt it was high time for the judge to use influence; the reporters were ruining his vacation. He couldn't garden or go to the track without them swarming all over him with their stupid questions.

The judge had another problem too, which he hadn't told Tulie about. Lawyers, friends of his, were phoning from across the state to tell him that the legislators were conspiring to place the blame for the new law on John's head, and that he should start counting his friends. John had never asked himself who his friends were. He had many connections of course—but friends?

The usually placid and stoic judge was angry over these phone calls. Those legislators had passed 04Y4 to pay for their new lulus, those secret expense accounts of theirs! Where else could they turn for new money but to the middle-aged, men like himself who put all their faith in their government? But would they tell anybody that the income from 04Y4 was for lulus? Of course not, the so-and-so's. Easier to blame him.

Personally, he didn't know why there was such a great fuss being made. What was a ten-dollar license? Weren't the people who wouldn't sign going to get divorced anyway? The divorce lawyers were mad, but they'd get all kinds of new business as a result of 04Y4, just as they did from every law they passed.

Oh, well, he thought, turning to look at the readings in the back of his hymnal, I'm going to see Z.B. today. Suddenly the judge felt very fond of Rev. MacMorlan and quite able to suffer through one of Z.B.'s moralizing sermons. Actually, the pastor's sermons were famous and well loved. He made God seem like a friendly neighbor.

Rev. Z.B. MacMorlan, pastor of Park Place Church, had a habit of coming to his study behind the sanctuary at nine-thirty on Sunday mornings to spend fifteen minutes reviewing his sermon and one hour talking to God about his work, which he hoped was also His work. Today Z.B. needed special help—the physical stamina and courage to face the summer ahead, which had turned overnight from a time for rest and contemplation into the most hectic time he had ever experienced. Much was demanded of him now that 04Y4 had become constitutional.

Z.B., ever the father to his flock, had stood by his distinguished parishioner, the Honorable John Freund II, during the six months the law was under consideration. At Z.B.'s suggestion they dined together every Thursday at the Elks' Club, but they had never discussed 04Y4. That would have been unethical. Z.B. had, of course, hoped to say a few prayers with Judge Freund for guidance, but he never found an opening. Try as he did to learn John's philosophy of life, Rev. MacMorlan had failed. He came to realize that the judge was a completely insensitive man, insensitive to the emotional needs of others and seemingly with no emotional needs of his own. He was calm, cool and unfathomable but completely unfeeling. It saddened the man of God to see a man go through life without joy, without suffering, with no spiritual comfort at all. And it saddened him too that he never got close to praying with the judge over the decision. It might have helped.

Rev. MacMorlan was himself a victim of the new law. This Sunday morning, there alone in his study, he put his head in his hands and closed his eyes to talk to God. "Oh, heavenly Father," he prayed. "Thank you for all the blessings you have bestowed upon me. Make me worthy of your trust in me. Everywhere I turn I see miserable, broken-hearted, guilty, indecisive middle-aged faces. I had no idea, Father, that so many of them feel so unloved. I want to help them, but you'll have to give me the strength to do it.

"I've cancelled my summer trip to Montana and I'll miss those hours alone in the mountains with you. If only you will help my wife to understand why I can't go. She says I neglect her and I try not to, Lord. If only I could convince her that by humoring me she serves you too.

"Oh, Lord, I am sick at heart about that widow over in Duxbury. She's very ill—writing me all those revolting notes, demanding I not get a new license but marry her! She's threatened to expose me; I don't know what that means but, dear God, she is a dreadful burden. Don't let my wife find out.

"Almighty Father, help me to make my people see that they are holy vessels full of precious oil. But the vessels are cracked and the oil is running out; inside they're empty. They don't have any values left. Help them to wrestle for their souls and seek the help of your Spirit. Help them, O Jesus, to know what matrimony is all about. How can I show them that it means to love each other as you love us? But, dear Father, it is very hard to love someone who doesn't see it our way or to love someone who doesn't love us in return. My wife says I love you more than her, but real love can't be weighed. You've got to put the answers in my heart, Lord, so I can show them what marriage means. We'll be having sermons and seminars and I'm going to need a lot of help. Teach me, O Holy Spirit. Praise you, Father, in Jesus' name. Amen."

Pastor MacMorlan arose unburdened of many things, ready to lead his flock. He put on his black robe and combed his wavy brown hair. No matter how often he made this Sunday entrance into the church it was a thrilling moment— like going onstage. He strode out.

There in the sixth row was John Freund with a remarkably

pleasant expression on his face. The service began with "We Praise Thee, O God," followed by a short invocation and the responsive reading. Tulie observed that her companion was reading the responses in an unusually strong voice and even singing the hymns. That was remarkable. John was not given to audible participation in church. John wore a little smile; he hoped Z.B. would notice how he was helping him bring the service alive by his fervor.

Having shown all this cooperation and enthusiasm, the judge was completely taken by surprise when Z.B. opened the big book upon the pulpit and, placing one hand on either side of it, leaned far out and fixed his gaze on the sixth row center while he read the lesson for the day. It was from the 26th Psalm:

> "Judge me, O Lord; for I have walked
> in my integrity. . . .
> Examine me, O Lord and prove me. . . .
> For thy loving kindness is before mine
> eyes. . . .
> I have not sat with vain persons. . . .
> I have hated the congregation of evil
> doers; and will not sit with the wicked. . . .
> I will walk in mine integrity: redeem me, and
> be merciful unto me."

Whereupon, ignoring a strange bustle in the sixth row, the pastor said, "Let us think about that for a moment. What does it mean?"

It means if you won't sit with the wicked then there go my Thursday lunches at the Elks, thought Judge Freund sadly. First the garden, then the track, now lunches with Z.B.—gone. He sighed heavily and the bags under his eyes drooped. Z.B. was only doing his job. He could accept that.

That is, he would have accepted it had it not been for the happening that was even then taking place, drawing all eyes to the sixth row left. One of the mountain people (as the summer residents were called), in this case a prominent matron from the city, stood up. She always sat next to John Freund, seeking to identify herself with the prominent people in Temagami Springs. She rose and said to her three children, who looked like new asparagus, "Come, children," and the four tall persons left the pew and went down the aisle single file and sat in the empty front row like iron spikes in a high fence. A ripple of surprise passed through the congregation.

Tulie blushed and the judge paled. He sat stony-faced throughout the sermon. He was so chagrined and affronted that he didn't hear a word Z.B. said about the blessedness of having a life-long companion. In fact he would have crawled out of the church on his hands and knees if he could have done it; but judges don't crawl on their hands and knees, so he just sat in shock. As soon as the benediction was given, he left the church rapidly by the side door.

He was angry with his wife for suggesting he talk to Z.B. in the first place and he lost no time in telling her he would never go to *her* church again. Tulie was heartbroken; not in twenty-five years had he called it "her church"!

The following week, the nightmare attack from the press worsened and the judge refused to leave the house for anything. He would not accept the suggestion of his wife on the succeeding Sunday that they drive to a church in Brownfields. Her husband had problems, to be sure, but

Tulie Freund could not give up church-going any more than she could give up antique collecting. It was an important part of her life. However, neither could she go alone; it was unthinkable that after twenty-five years on the arm of her husband she walk down the aisle of the church alone!

In her need, Tulie Freund turned to her son. Fearless as he was, Freud readily agreed to accompany her, not to Brownfields but to Park Place, sixth row left, where he was anxious to make a show of family solidarity in the face of trouble. He had other reasons for going, namely, to ask God to restore happiness to their home and then to say a few prayers over the future of his kingdom. He had an ulterior motive as well—to break it to his mother that he was leaving home. After all she had been through, he hesitated to tell her the news.

Once he and Tallulah were in their pew, Freud went down on his knees and said his prayers. Then he sat back and listened to the sermon about the beauty and the blessings of a faithful marriage; and while he listened, he occupied himself by sketching bridges on his program. He wondered if he would ever want to get married. The service was short, and after the last amen had been sounded and while the organ played the recessional, Tulie, extremely nervous over whether to shake Z.B.'s hand, had a *sotto voce* debate with her son and lost her courage. She hurried past the parson.

Freud, however, gave Rev. MacMorlan a hearty handshake.

"How is your father?" asked Z.B.

"Not good," replied Freud.

"Does he want me to come over?"

"Not yet. Thanks," answered Freud.

He rejoined his mother and invited her to have chicken dinner at the Temagami Springs Motel. He postponed telling her that he would soon be leaving home to live somewhere else. She seemed too sad to take anything more.

When they got back home after lunch, Tulie went to the garage to examine her finds of the day before and her son went into the library to research bridges. Freud threw his brown-striped seersucker jacket on the leather sofa and dropped his tie on top. Then he pulled down volume two of the Britannica and settled into his father's comfortable wing-back chair to read about bridges. The library was Freud's favorite place now that his father had moved to the apartment in the attic. Freud felt comfortable surrounded by the warm walnut paneling and all the old books. Furthermore, he felt safe here from their houseguest, Phlox. She was afraid of the judge and Freud had never seen her with a book, so this had quickly become Freud's private little hideaway. He shut himself in with a feeling of satisfaction that Sunday afternoon.

Opening his book to the "B's," he studied with interest a photo of the Pont Valentre bridge in Cahors, France, and made a sketch of it. With a little adaption and simplification it would do very nicely for the renovated span over the Big Bear. Freud was totally absorbed, when someone tiptoed softly into the room and, coming up behind him, put two small cool hands across his face and said, "Guess who?"

Freud slammed the book shut. He knew who. "I can't guess," he said sarcastically. "Who?"

"Me-ee" she said, coming around the wing chair quickly and sitting on his lap, cuddling up to him with her lips against his forehead.

Freud jumped up, dumping her and the book on the floor.

"Phlox Fontaine, remember where you are," he said sternly, picking up the heavy, black leather volume and returning it to the bookcase with one hand, as he hastily shoved his sketch in his pocket with the other. He felt like swatting her.

Phlox struggled to her feet from the floor. She had never been so put down. Freud, hiding a smile, looked out the window while she pulled up her shirt and looked under her jeans to see if she was bruised. Then she settled herself in the flowered chair he had vacated.

"How could I forget where I am? This place is a tomb." She made a face. "Where do you go all the time? I've been looking everywhere for you. I'm hungry. And you promised to take me up to Safflower Hill to see Stevie. Maybe there's something going on up there for me to do."

"Yes!" replied Freud. "Maybe there is—if only you weren't such a snob." He wished at once he hadn't said that. Phlox gave him a black look and kicked off her earth sandals. "Stevie said the kids up there love each other, which is more than I can say for this place. I thought you'd be different. I thought you'd be more fun," she added. Needing to talk, she continued. "And did I tell you Stevie said he'd comb his hair the next time I come up? After thirteen months! Would you believe it? So you see, I do have some influence!"

"Wow," said Freud, sensing an opportunity to promote a move very beneficial to his own plans. "I guess I'll have to take you there right now. Fetch your scissors and your carbon steel comb and follow me." He beckoned to her. "That sounds like the swingingest place in town," he continued. "It would surely be more fun for you to live up there than here. Think of all the improvements you can make!"

Phlox, sensing he was too enthusiastic, retorted, "Maybe eventually I'll move up there, but I have things to do first. Will you ride me downtown? I have a date at the Royal Purple in an hour. Incidentally," she continued, "I saw your mother in the garage. She wants to talk to you about something. You're lucky you can talk to your mother. My mother is hopeless; she never wants to talk to me about anything," sighed Phlox, running her fingers over her wheat blonde hair.

Freud almost felt sorry for her. He could see what her mother was—the worst kind of mother, a demanding neurotic. In other circumstances he might have felt obliged to talk to Phlox and try to show her a few things. However, Phlox wasn't his type. It was just as well it was out of the question this summer. "Okay, I'll take you downtown. I have a date too, so after I see what Mom wants I'll drop you at the Royal Purple. It might rain. I wouldn't want my bicycle to be out in the rain." He left her there and went to look for his mother.

Phlox stood up and stared after him, rubbing her behind with her hand. "He thinks he's still got that bike! He doesn't know I traded it for a Honda. If John were more sensitive he'd have tuned to my vibes by now, so it serves him right if he doesn't know what's going on!" She looked out the library window. "One of these days there'll be a big surprise for you, John dear," she said slowly.

Freud rapped on his mother's door. "What do you want, Mom?"

"Come in, John dear," called Tulie, "and lock the door." So she had put a lock on her door too!

"Yes, Mother. What do you want?" he asked, thinking as he did so that now was the time to tell her. Aloud he said, "Before you begin, I have something to tell you—good news, as a matter of fact." Freud knew she would not think so. Tulie continued to wax her latest find, a bentwood rocker. She was refinishing the chair as a gift for her husband. Perhaps a little present would help the judge feel better.

"Mom, guess what?" he said. She waited for him to continue. "I'm moving. I have a new job."

She looked surprised. "Already? At Glory Land?"

"Yes, as Ben Franklin. Now I can afford my own place. I'm planning to move out of here in a day or so."

"Oh, John dear. Won't you reconsider?" asked Tulie, her face full of sadness. "I wish you wouldn't go." She lowered her voice. "Is it Phlox? Do you dislike her that much?"

Mom wasn't dumb. "No, Mother," answered Freud, "It's not Phlox. And I don't dislike her. Aren't we supposed to love one another?" He grinned. "I love her."

"You can't stand her," replied his mother, laying down her oily rag.

"Well, you're right. You always are. I can't stand her. She's—well, she's selfish."

"But, we're doing a favor for Jean and Frank," murmured Tulie to mollify herself because she too was having a hard time liking their house guest. She stepped towards her child and looked up at him. He seemed bigger than ever. When did her little boy get so big? She looked at Freud with love and heartache. Why did he grow up so fast? "You know I hate to see you go, son. Can't you wait until September?"

"No, Mom. I can't stay on at 210 Pleasant Street any longer and I thought you would understand." He turned away. "After all, I'm over twenty-one."

"You don't have to tell me that," flashed Tulie, rubbing the rocker again with angry stokes. "You're a man now.

You have to follow your star. I don't think I'm an overly demanding person. It's just that this summer. . . ." Her voice trailed off.

"Okay, Mom. I know. I know. Don't worry. I'll still be around town. But promise me you won't tell Phlox anything at all about my whereabouts this summer." He was emphatic.

Tulie's hazel eyes were full of woe. "I won't tell," she said slowly. Then she struggled with a terrible thought. "You're not moving up to the Hill, are you?" Her voice was desperate. Freud shook his head in the negative.

"Well, that's a relief!" said his mother, rubbing the rocker again. When she looked up from her work, Freud was gone.

She hadn't told him why it was she wanted to see him— to tell him she was getting an unlisted telephone number. She couldn't take any more anonymous calls, no more threats from strangers and mean remarks from acquaintances. Half the country seemed to be angry at Judge Freund. And she had had more than she could take.

"My poor husband, he can't cope with unpopularity and he's so naive. He should have protected us from all this terrible publicity. But it's not his fault," Tulie reflected. "I think we should be proud of him for doing his duty when no one else wanted the job." Nevertheless, it was nerve wracking to have John sitting on the third floor watching television all day. If he could only go to the races. Past summers she had regretted his passion for gambling, but now she'd give anything to have him out of the house. What was she going to do with him underfoot all summer long?

Suddenly the impact of her beloved son's leaving her alone with the judge was too much for her. She stopped rubbing, giving the rocker a shove. What she was doing didn't seem important at all; nothing about her life seemed worth anything at all. She threw down the oily rag and stared out the window for a long time, and the empty rocker rocked slowly to a stop.

Tatty Softshoe's Retirement

At the far end of Big Bear Lake everything was peaceful. Tatty Softshoe sat locked behind her wall rocking in her rocker, remembering the good old days, the exciting times of the not so long ago. Somehow everything was different now that she was retired. Now that she was secure behind high stone walls, life was not the same; it was not very exciting at all.

She loved the swamps and the birds, the sounds of crickets at night and loons on the lake. For many many years she had spent her long sweet days chopping firewood, fishing for trout and wandering in the woods in search of roots and berries. She was happy with her life. She was happy until Irv died and that woman came to take her to sign for Social Security and Medicaid. On that trip she saw things she'd never seen before and she didn't like what she saw—all those old people lined up for handouts, like they had no will of their own.

They reminded her too much of the story about the Indian princess—Irv had read her that from the newspaper, figuring it would interest her because she too was an Indian princess. The story told of an old Indian who lived in the woods all her life; she had fallen sick and the authorities

took her to town, way up near Hudson Bay it was, and put
her in a nursing home. As soon as she got there, she died.
While Tatty listened to her husband read that story
something inside her recoiled. She knew why the princess
had died. She had been homesick for the woods.

Whereupon Tatty, whose Indian name was Kaleri, re-
solved then and there that she'd fight before she'd go to a
nursin' home and she'd protect herself by building an
impenetrable wall around her house, a big high stone wall,
and she'd keep Irv's gun handy and train Shadow to attack.
That's why she walked all those miles for stones. They
were special stones, round and strong like cannon balls.
After a time, Tatty began to enjoy her daily walk for
stones. It never occurred to her that her wall might have
been finished years sooner if she'd used the rocks from her
own beach. But she saw a lot of the world on those walks
and after a while "going to town," as she called it, become as
much a purpose as the wall itself.

Nevertheless, motivated as she was by fear of the
terrible fate that could befall an Indian princess, she
worked diligently on and on and finished the wall; then
God sent her a gate with T. and I. entwined in hearts upon
it. For a few days she sat on her old broken rocker and
surveyed with satisfaction the high stone walls around her
and the view through the grillwork. But today, relieved of
her fear and missing her routine, she felt empty and sick.
With no walk to take, no wall to build, her life was
uneventful; for the first time in her life she was lonely. To
fill the endless days she pulled weeds from her garden and
carried water from the lake. She picked wild strawberries
and looked for ginseng plants on the northern slopes. But
none of these activities, which had once given her pleasure,
filled the emptiness in her life. She missed walking along

the highway and waving at all those passing cars. And now there was nowhere to go in her beautiful muskrat coat. Irv had given her that coat when he saw she was so upset about the Indian princess. He had found a real nice bargain at a place with the nice name of Good Will. She had nothing to tell Irv anymore. She was sad and lost, and as her lonesomeness grew and grew, fear crept back in.

She summoned her cat, Whiskers. Whiskers could read her mind and he came and stood on her shoulder, arching his back and spitting, then settling there as if to say, "I'll take care of you." Tatty stopped shelling peas and looked about to find some comfort. As her dark suffering eyes scanned the yard about her, they lighted upon her old car, the old Chevy station wagon under the dusty burlap bags. The rust-rimmed chrome around the headlights shone in the sun. "It's just like me sitting there—not going any-place."

Then came a thought she hadn't thought in all those years. "I'll bet there's life in the old girl yet!" she observed to Whiskers. Shoving the cat off her shoulder, she pulled herself up, slowly unbending her worn-out joints. Alas, her knees, accustomed to much walking, were stiffening up now, like rusty scissors. She brushed the pea pods off her lap, put the blue tin bowl of young peas through the hole in the screen door and hobbled quickly to the old stall, the roof of which lay over the car. The car had been a beauty in its day— deep shiny green like Big Bear Lake and brown as the fall leaves.

But the years had aged the Chevrolet. The old rubber tires were long hardened in their flattened form and what was left of the wood was a weathered grey. Only the fenders and the roof showed traces of the dark green color it had been. The seat covering was cracked and its stuffing black with mildew; but to Tatty, her car was as pretty as it had ever been. My, how Irv loved that car! she thought. Maybe she could fix it up and drive downtown in it, now that she was rich. She'd ask her big blond friend to help her. "I'll tell him I've joined the station wagon set," she chuckled, not knowing quite what that meant—but it sounded good!

Even while she was looking at her ancient automobile, help was on the way. Though she did not know it, Tatty Tuttle was part of certain well-laid plans. For as it happened, the previous night had been the occasion of the weekly meeting of the community of Safflower Hill. A motion had been made by Steve Banker and duly seconded by Cheryl Gann that the residents of Safflower Hill adopt one Kaleri Tuttle as their special friend to do what they could to make her last years happy years.

It was suggested by Mark Sanders that this might not be satisfactory to Ms. Tuttle, but after discussion on the subject of loneliness, which state had indeed brought most of them to Safflower Hill, the motion carried to give Tatty a visit and try to help her in some meaningful way.

Even as the Indian princess gazed fondly at her old car from the rocking chair to which she had retired to think (she thought hard thoughts best when she was sitting down), a group from the Hill was coming her way, coming through the woods with fruit and flowers, ambassadors of love coming to find out what they might do for their new protégé. Had they known what was even then on Tatty's mind there were those among them who would have said a higher power was moving them to the little round house at the end of Big Bear Lake.

Tatty Tuttle had extrasensory perception. She could always feel when visitors were coming through the swamps. If her instincts were asleep on this day it was because Tatty herself was driving—in her fantasy—over the mountains and far away. But suddenly she stiffened and the back of her neck prickled. She shook herself back to the now and said to her old hound, "Shadow, go git 'em." She gave the old dog an urgent push in the direction of the woods below and tottered into her house for her gun.

Once Mark Sander's view had been overridden by the majority, he took charge of the mission to the Tuttle place. He led the group single-file through the woods and up the path to Tatty's house. He saw her slip inside and suspecting why, he held up his hand and motioned the line behind to stop, while he called out in a loud voice, "Lay down your gun, Tatty. We're your friends—the ones who put up your gate. We've come to say hello and visit the gate. It's a beautiful gate. May we see it?"

Tatty stood in the doorway, a thin grimace that looked like a grin on her face, her hand over her eyes, squinting to see who it was. Satisfied that the man with the black beard and wavy black hair was familiar to her, she came down as far as the gate. The Saffies edged closer to look at her.

"Oh, it's you," said Tatty, unlocking the padlock. "I was hopin' it was the big 'un with the white hair."

"You mean Freud," said Mark, recognizing whom she meant when she circled her head with her hand. "We're his friends. Can we sit down here in your front yard and look at the gate?" He motioned to the Saffies to sit on the ground. All of them sat down like Indians forming a semicircle around Tatty. Mark pointed to the gilt letters at the top of the iron gate. "Didn't I tell you it's beautiful? And look at those entwined hearts. They mean love, don't they Tatty?" Ooohs and ahhhs rose from the circle, and Tatty's wide mouth spread in a thin smile, her eyes crinkling, because they liked her new memorial to Irv.

"Why don't we have a campfire?" said someone.

"May we, Tatty?" asked Mark, adding appropriately, he thought, "Indians always have campfires."

"They do?" replied Tatty. "Then we'll have one. I got Indian blood in me, you know." She didn't tell them she was of royal blood. Tatty put her firm lower jaw over her missing uppers and watched the Safflowers build a little fire. She was happy to be the center of so much attention.

They all sat for a time in silence looking into the flames. The young people didn't quite know how to offer themselves to their hostess. But after a bit Tatty said bluntly, "I got a project for the blond 'un."

"As if Freud needs another project," whispered Laura Fogarty to Steve Banker.

"Let's ask what it is," whispered Stevie to Laura. "What is your project, Mrs. Tuttle?"

"Don't Mrs. Tuttle me, young man. I'm Tatty and I want to fix up my car. If only Irv were here I could ask him how to do it, but I need a little advice."

"Do you have a car, Tatty?" asked Steve, who was always interested in cars.

"'Deed I do. Don't ya see it over there?" She pointed to the old stall.

"Why, so you have! A Chevy. Bet it's a '46." Steve was on his feet at once and over beside it lifting off the bags. "A real jewel in its day—an early station wagon with a wooden body. Offspring of the stagecoach, I suppose. Not many of them around." Stevie was quickly joined by the other men. They pulled some rusty window screens and a pile of assorted debris from around the car and propped up the shed roof to have a better look at it.

The old automobile really belonged in the junk yard—

way back in the junk yard. It looked hopeless, but Stevie Banker gave it a thorough check-up. Had it not been for the resolution passed the night before he'd have found no way to help Tatty. Instead he pronounced his opinion that it just might run again—with enough work. Worth a try anyway!

"I think, Tatty, I can do something with it. I haven't any money now, but maybe by fall I'll have some saved—"

"No, no, young man! I may be gone to my ancestors by then. I want to ride to town *now*. I have money. Do you think I'm poor?" she challenged.

"If anyone can fix it, Stevie can; and we can get the Carpies to fix the woodwork. I'll varnish it," offered Laura. Everybody was enthusiastic and Steve hid his misgivings. Here was one way to help Tatty. They had gained a foothold in her castle!

Thereafter the young people and the Indian princess sat by the fire until midnight, eating fruit and singing and laughing and listening to Tatty crooning a lullaby. Then the Safflowers went back to their farm very happy with their new friend. Who is a friend but one whom you can help?

After that Tatty couldn't sleep for thinkin' about all their kindness, and plannin' her trips to town. I wonder where the blond 'un was. He's my favorite, she thought as she fell asleep on her buffalo-hide blanket, which had belonged to her great grandfather. She had forgotten to tell Irv the big news that they would soon join the station wagon set.

Summer Dreams

It was Tuesday morning. Skip Bantley pulled to a fast stop at the rear entrance of the Pink Pavillion in the park panel truck and walked through the kitchen, looking among smiling cooks for Miss Abendtal. He found her at the serving table giving pointers to a new girl on how to make a beautiful salad.

Anna laid down her tongs and smiled at the young man. She was always pleased to see Skipper. "Hello, Skip. Thanks for coming over right away." She turned back to the counter and continued to fix salads while she talked. "Penny Dupre is making me ten dozen brownies. Will you fetch them from The Sesame Seed Bakery by eleven o'clock?"

"What happened to Mrs. Collins? Doesn't she do all the baking?" He was pleased with himself. His question showed anyone listening that he was learning the names of the employees.

Anna replied, "That was last week. This week Mr. Collins has gone away with a topless dancer and Bertha has gone after him. I hope she comes back to us. Olivia is looking for another pastry cook, but meanwhile this is AAUW Day, and I'm told they always order summer dreams for dessert and would be very disappointed not to have any. Aren't

habits funny things? I'm finding out that even organiza-
tions have habits. Anyway, we're short ten dozen brownies
for those dreams. In fact it was a minor crisis for a time
until I thought of The Sesame Seed."

Skip agreed to go at once to the bakery, but as he put his
hand on the swinging door, Anna Maria called him back to
ask him whether he had recorded *Bring Back Those Years* with
the Saffies. He replied that they had made a preliminary
tape and that, strangely enough, before they could make
copies of it and really get it together, someone had stolen it;
they would make another in a few days. He was also writing a new song! Anna was glad to hear that and they both
laughed at that untimely happening to the tape. Then Skip
hurried away in the panel truck to drive to town for the
brownies.

Skip parked beside the bakery, went inside and explained
his mission to the girl behind the counter. Penny, who was
dressed in a long denim apron with her brown hair neatly
tied back in a red bandana, suggested they have coffee while
he waited because the brownies were still in the oven. She
carried two cups to the round oak table by the window and
they sat down together.

Skip was rather shy with girls and Penny was shy too,
but they smiled at each other, each finding the other attractive and different. She noticed he had big ears for someone
with a narrow face, a dimple in his chin and two more when
he smiled, and a rather nice curly mouth. As she looked him
over, she heard him say, "I like your place."

"Do you?" asked Penny, pleased, pushing her hair from
her eyes. "I'm glad you like it. It isn't much," she said, looking around at her shop, "but it's all mine! It took a lot of
talking to convince Mother and Dad I'd rather have this
than go to college. Do you go to college?"

"That I do! Rather I should say I did. I've quit. But I've been studying engineering, which is anything but what I want to do. I can't convince my parents I don't need that piece of paper for what I want to do."

"What's that?" asked Penny sympathetically, thinking she knew how he felt.

Looking down into his cup, he smiled a little to himself and stirred his coffee. Then he said quietly in answer to her question, "Write lyrics—compose—about love and loneliness—and about girls who make brownies," he added, smiling from beneath his brown mustache and noticing she had amber eyes.

"Is that what you do? How wonderful!" said Penny admiringly. "I can't write or paint or do anything creative."

"Don't say that," admonished Skip. "This place is very original. It's obvious to me that you are a very artistic person," he added, looking about at the rustic wood shelves full of plants and pottery and the unusual arrangement of kettles and pans hanging over the counter.

"No, my mother is the artist in the family. She helped me design my store," said Penny, sipping coffee. "I guess you know my mom. She works for your dad—Olivia Dupre."

"Of course I know her!" Skip's smile widened and his blue-grey eyes danced. "So you're her daughter—of course. I should have guessed. Say, do you remember when we went to the same Sunday school—years ago, when we were kids?"

"Did we? Were you in Junior Choir?"

"Sure I was," he answered, pausing a moment, "I think I remember which kid you were. You sang a solo, *O Holy Night* and your wing fell off! And you picked it up and didn't know what to do with it. You handed it to the kid next to you and he tried to hold it behind you, only he held it too low down.

Are you that kid? I'll never forget it. Afterwards we fell over laughing."

"That was me all right. Falling wings Dupre—the story of my life!" She stopped and her voice fell lower. "Do you think, Skip, that God has a sense of humor?"

"I never thought about that," he answered slowly. "But I will; that's a very deep question."

"I just wondered what you think." Her tone changed, "Tell me, Skip, what kind of songs do you write?"

"According to my sister, Savy, I'm hung up on loneliness, but I'm writing from my heart. Everywhere I go everyone's running from loneliness. I'm beginning to think it's part of being a human being, so there's no use running. It helps to write and sing about it. But I'd rather write about love and girls."

"No one's ever lonely if he knows God," said Penny reverently. They both sat quietly for a moment; then a timer rang, summoning Penny to her stove. Skip followed her into the kitchen and helped package the brownies. She handed him a knife and spatula and showed him how to cut them and place them in plastic containers.

While they were working together, he said, "If you hear of anyone with a studio for rent, let me know."

"I will," she replied. "I'll keep my ears open. Maybe I'll hear of a place. Say hi to Anna Maria for me."

"Sure," Skip replied. "It's too bad you don't work with us at Glory Land. There's quite a congenial group this year. We've plans for some great parties later on!" She didn't comment that she and her partner also had a few plans for the summer and that she just might be over there at Glory Land herself. Skip added, "The Saffies have a good band going—all they need is a singer. Can you sing?"

"No. I wish I could." Man, did she wish she could!

"I've been recording with them and the results aren't bad. Maybe you'd like to sit in on a session." Penny nodded yes. "I'll call you," Skip said as he was leaving. "Thanks for helping us out, Penny, and don't forget to let me know if you hear of an apartment," he called as he stepped into the truck.

Skip Bantley no sooner drove away from the bakery than the door burst open, surprising Penny who was putting the extra brownies in the showcase. She turned about, tray in hand, and looked over the counter. "Oh, it's you, Freud. Be with you in a minute."

"Okay. Hurry it up. I just passed Skip Bantley coming from here," he said curtly. "I didn't know you knew him."

"Well, I don't, but—" Freud interrupted her. "You didn't tell him about you-know-what, did you?"

"Of course not," she replied defensively. "Do you think I'm dumb?"

"You know I don't, pardner. I was just a bit nervous, that's all—for the security of our secret. Is anyone else here?" Penny shook her dark head and then she untied her bandana with trembling fingers. He had shaken her up. "Can we go into the back room?" continued Freud. "I have something to show you."

Penny took off her large blue denim apron and folded it neatly over one of the oak chairs. "What is it? Tell me quick."

She followed him into the small pantry where she mixed the dough, closing and locking the door behind them. Freud said, "Here's our plan," whispering in her ear, "our everything!"

He untied a black shoestring, opened a large roll of paper and spread it on the kneading table. "Here we are. This is our new property," he pointed with a wooden spoon, "from this old stone wall to the Muffin."

Penny interrupted. "Not *the* Muffin?"

"Yes, *the* Muffin. Our land stretches from it across the river someplace. Just for the moment there isn't time to investigate what it's really like over there in the hills. That will offer us fresh possibilities later on because more than half our property is over there. But for this summer our best bet is this old bridge across the Big Bear. The planking is shot, but the structure's sound. It never was any landmark, so I figure to replace the planking and build two towers, one on each end, and an open place in the middle for fairs and dancing. But the very first thing we're going to do is make me a place to live—a spaceship in the old oak tree. Say," he said, putting the spoon to his head, "another idea: why don't you move this business to the bridge to provide us with cash flow?"

"I don't know," said Penny doubtfully, "this is a good location and I have a six months' lease, but maybe I could open an annex." She couldn't be left out of the excitement.

"An annex! Great!" retorted Freud. "I've always liked that word 'annex.' Yes, you must have an annex of The Sesame Seed with a tea room for hungry tourists. Can you think of any more ideas for our bridge?"

"Well," answered Penny slowly, "Skip Bantley's looking for a studio. He just asked me if I knew of a place."

"Skip Bantley!" he exclaimed. "Goodness, woman, be careful of him, he still thinks he owns our land. You are aware there is a risk to our little caper, aren't you? Remember the poem 'By The Rude Bridge That Arched The Flood The World's Embattled Farmers Stood'? When we take over the Big Bear Bridge we may become the embattled farmers—you and me on the bridge with balls of dough and the Bantleys on the shore with pitchforks. Better not plan on Skip Bantley!"

"On second thought," Freud murmured, "if we appeal to

his needs, we just might win him over to our side! But his sister, Savy, looks like a very firm character—she'll be a real Tory. Well, Penny, old pal, all in good time. I just wanted to bring you up-to-date this morning. Now I have to run along to see Mark Sanders at the Cornwall House. I think he's the one to head our building crew. He's someone to whom I can safely confide our plans. After all, he's already survived his big battle with the establishment. Penny, old pal, may I seal your lips with a kiss? I've been waiting for this all my life."

She didn't know whether he meant the kiss or the secret plan, but she looked at him adoringly, hoping he meant the former.

"Gotta go start the action," he added, unlocking the door and helping himself to a fresh donut. "As soon as we hear Brig Bantley's leaving town for a weekend at his dune place," he mumbled with his mouth full of dough, "I'll let you know. Then things will happen fast. Bye, Penny, my love." And he was gone. Penny sat down. So much was happening all of a sudden.

Lunch at the Pink Pavillion

The doorbell rang at 210 Pleasant Street and Tulie Freund in jeans and an old khaki army shirt struggled up from the floor where she was kneeling, working off her tensions by oiling the underside of a parquetry commode. She had picked it up at an auction the day before at a very reasonable price. In another hour it would be transformed and worth twice what she paid for it. When the bell rang it was hard to get up from the floor. If only Phlox would sometimes answer the doorbell; as often as not it was one of her friends. But she never answered. Just this once let it ring, thought Tulie; but she couldn't do that. Tulie was too curious, and anyway she loved to talk to people. The doorbell rang again and again.

"Coming. Coming," called Tulie, wondering who could be so impatient. She opened the door to find Jean Fontaine dressed like a cockatoo, waiting nervously on the steps. Where could she be going in all that jewelry and perfume and a hat? Jean had one little fetish—she fancied herself in a picture-hat, style or no style. Tulie smiled at so much elegance in Temagami Springs. "Hi, Jean, don't you look nice? Come on in."

"Hello, Tulie," said Jean, planting a cold kiss on Tulie's

cheek and leaving a lipstick mark. Is the judge here?" she asked, looking around warily. "You know I'll never speak to him again—not ever, ever again. Not after 04Y4." Jean had a terrible problem and it was all because of the new law. For more than six years she had been telling everyone she was thirty-nine years old. And now, thanks to none other than Tulie's "dear John," she was going to be unmasked. Even the lawmakers hadn't been foresighted enough to realize how unpopular any such law would be with the likes of Jean!

"But he was only doing his job, Jean," said Tallulah defensively. "I don't know why everybody's mad at him. They should blame the state legislature."

"I couldn't agree with you less. If I lose François it will be all John's fault."

Tulie was thinking to herself that it was well Jean didn't know John was upstairs in the attic. "Is that why you came over—to tell me that?"

"No, certainly not. I've come to take Phlox out to lunch at the Pink Pavillion. What's that awful noise?" asked Jean.

"Doesn't it make a lot of noise? That's Phlox in the driveway on her motorcycle," said Tulie. "She's only just started to keep it in the garage since Freud left. I'll tell her you're here."

Sitting down on the sofa and taking out a cigarette, Jean called after her, "They say the food at the Pink Pavillion is out of this world, and Anna is decorating with *my* flowers in August; so I thought I'd drop in and show a little interest. It's about time someone asked me to show my flowers!" she commented, as Tallulah returned and sat down beside her. "Don't you have an ash tray?" Jean asked, implying that her friend was less than a perfect hostess.

"Goodness, yes," said Tulie, jumping up again to get it.

"Just look at me. I'm not dressed at all. I'm a mess. After we talk and catch up with things, I'll have to change."

Jean lit her cigarette and then she held up her arm. "Do you like my new eighteen-karat gold bracelet? I told Frank I had to have it to go with these earrings, so I got it for my birthday, Tul. My birthday's coming in August, in case you've forgotten. You know I just have to have new things. They pacify my anxieties. Feel how heavy it is," she added, taking it off and dropping it into Tulie's hand.

"It's lovely—just right for you," said Tulie, who tried very hard to be nice to her old roommate. "How did you get here, by the way? I thought you weren't driving."

"I wasn't," said Jean emphatically, "but I was going nuts waiting for my neighbor and she went off without me, so I drove over by myself. I hate driving—and in a Ford at that. Frank took the Continental just to irritate me; he knows I can't drive a stick-shift."

Phlox came reluctantly through the back door from the garage, zipping up her jeans. "Hi, mom," she said, looking away as she submitted to her mother's kiss.

"Phlox, dear," said Jean, "fetch me a couple of aspirin and do change your blouse. That pink one is too tight and I've told you before not to wear it. Don't you have a skirt? We're going to the Pink Pavillion."

Phlox went upstairs and returned after a long wait in something only slightly less revealing of her slim, shapely body. Her mother looked her up and down. "I never did like that dress; it looks wrinkled. But I guess if it's all you have, it will do. You'll drive, won't you dear? I have a headache."

Phlox looked at her with blank contempt. "Of course I'll drive," she said snappishly.

"Have you missed me, sweetheart?" asked Jean, smiling self-consciously at her daughter. Phlox did not reply.

"Well, come dear. See you Tulie. See you after lunch."

Tulie had quite naturally expected to go along with the Fontaine girls to Glory Land. She was flustered and deeply hurt. However she recovered her composure and escorted Jean and Phlox to the front door.

I don't know where I'll be, Tallulah thought, but I won't be here when you come back. Of all the selfish people, not even asking me to go along. To think I let Frank get away from me and marry her. As they departed she saw the postman coming up the drive and waited for him. "Anything for me, Bob?"

"Yep, Mrs. Freund. There's an air mail with a funny stamp. Say, can I have that stamp? It's from Liberia, I think."

"Oh, certainly," she said, looking at the envelope. "Yes, it's from Mrs. Bantley." She gave him the stamp and went into the house, reading her letter as she walked. It was a short note saying that the flight over was uneventful and Dakar was beautiful but hot. Lucy had met a talented young man whom she would like her sons to meet. He sang and danced and spoke English and was a waiter. That amused Tulie, because it was so uncharacteristic of Lucy to befriend a waiter. And she smiled as she read that Lucy wanted her to tell Brig and the kids that all was well and she felt fine. She was taking quinine.

Tulie was glad to hear from Lucy and would share the news with Anna when she phoned her later. She wondered if Lucy knew about 04Y4. I bet she doesn't, thought Tulie, adding to herself, but maybe she should. I hate to be the one to write and tell her; I might say the wrong thing. But now I must get dressed and go somewhere so I won't be here when the Fontaine ladies come back. If I only had a man to take me to the Pink Pavillion for lunch. That would jolt the Fontaine girls! But there was no mysterious man in her life, so she opted for an afternoon antiquing in Duxbury. She couldn't possibly get back until after Jean had gone home.

Jean and Phlox had a desultory lunch at the Pink Pavillion, both being on diets. Furthermore, Jean was discomfited. She would not have come had she known it was AAUW Day. She'd never graduated from college and they made her feel uncomfortable. She and her daughter talked very little, but while eating their meager desserts Jean asked, "How are you and Freud getting along, dear?"

"Oh, him—he's never home."

"Was that his cycle you were riding, dear?"

"Yes, it was," lied Phlox. "He lent it to me because he felt so sorry for me not having a car of my own. But it's no good—not enough power. It's only a 125CC Honda."

Jean said nothing for a moment. "He must like you a lot to lend you his cycle. I'm not sure I want you riding it though."

"Let's get out of here," replied Phlox. "Freud says I should get a job in this place, but I'd feel funny taking tips. Besides, I'm supposed to be on my vacation."

"I don't know, dear, whether I want you to be a waitress. We don't do that kind of work."

On the way home Jean began to cry. "Now what's the matter?" asked Phlox.

"Boo hoo. I wasn't going to tell you. Your father's in love with his secretary!"

"Oh, Mother, there goes your imagination again."

"No," sobbed Jean, "It's not. You should have heard what he said about her, that she looked so cute in her new pantsuit."

"Well, that's nothing."

"He said it was orange and with her orange shoes and orange purse she looked like a cute piece of road machinery— a cute 'piece,' if you please. Do you know what that means? Besides, he never even notices what I wear."

"Oh, Mother, sometimes I wonder about you! I don't know how Dad suffers it."

"Suffers it? There you go siding with him when I'm the one who suffers."

Phlox turned into Tulie's driveway running the tires up over the curb. "Come to my room and lie down till you pull yourself together." In a way Phlox felt sorry for her mother. She had observed that her father's secretary *was* pretty aggressive. She adored her father and she didn't like his secretary either. Who could trust a divorced woman with two children to support? Maybe this law, this signing business, had encouraged the secretary to try harder. Such nerve. Women are all witches, thought Phlox. "Lie down, Mom, and I'll play you my tapes. I got a new one written by Skip Bantley. Can you believe it, someone I know, a songwriter? Now here's one you can go for. Listen to this." She put on the tape of *Bring Back Those Years,* which she had stolen from the dining table at Safflower Hill. She played it over twice.

"Bring back those years!" exclaimed her mother. "Turn that thing off. You play it over and over. And so loud. My nerves can't stand it. Sunlight? Who has any? Bring me a cool cloth, dear."

"But mother, Skip wrote it."

"I don't care if the pope wrote it! I hate it."

"Oh, Mother, lie back down. I'll play the other side. Maybe you'll like it better. All the kids say they love this. It's called *All Alone in a Room of My Own.*"

"All alone in a room of my own!" Jean broke into fresh tears and her sobs shook the bed. While her mother wept, Phlox took the keys and forty dollars from her mother's purse, and in a few minutes the Ford could be heard driving off down the street. Jean, deep in her suffering, never noticed that Phlox, the keys, or the dollars were gone. She reached into her bag for her bottle of Valium and took two. On top of the daiquiri she had for lunch the effect was immediate and she fell quickly asleep.

The Letter

"Did you really walk out of church in the middle of a sermon, Judge? Did you?" asked a reporter from the *Morning Republican*.

"What does your wife think? Is she going to sign? Are you getting a divorce?"

"You said, I believe, and I quote you, 'This is a harmless little law.' Do you still think so, Judge?" a lady reporter asked, pursuing John Freund as he walked from his car to the front door of his house.

"Were you ever in the care of a psychiatrist?" "Are you taking a senility drug?" "Did your father have a drinking problem?" "What would your mother say?" The questions came thick and fast, inconsequential and damaging.

John lowered his eyes and pressed through the throng with only a lift of his hand and a scratchy, "Please, please let me pass," to the crowd of reporters with mikes in their hands and cameras on their shoulders. Then a distraught woman with grey hair came pushing through and spat in the judge's face. "I hate you," she cried. Judge Freund looked at her, and in that moment somewhere deep inside him something froze. Shocked by her assault John Freund gave up defending everything he had worked for and retreated inside himself.

This made life very difficult for Tallulah. It was important for her to communicate with him about what was happening, in order to find some way to handle the cruel things being directed at them. Although she always made herself available to her husband, he turned away from her and treated her as though she did not exist. After all those years of married life, he wouldn't talk to her about the things people were accusing him of. He would neither defend himself nor protect his family, and by not rising to their defense, he had in fact deserted her. This was a devastating experience for a devoted wife, and one which she could share with no one because it was so close to her heart. The wall of cruel silence her husband erected around himself, concealed as it was by a correctness of manner, in attendance to ordinary rituals between them, was invisible to everybody else. But it was in the bedroom, when the judge focused unblinkingly on a Western, never addressing, never inviting, that the coldness made itself felt. Each gesture Tulie made towards him led to a new rejection, which sent the pain deeper into her being until she cried from within, "No more. I won't take this anymore. I must do something." Do something. But what? If it weren't for her houseguest, Phlox, she'd go to her sister's in Sante Fe. It was so bad that sometimes Tulie even thought about suicide.

Then quite suddenly there came unexpected relief for Tulie. The judge went away; he went off to the north woods to a remote lake in Canada and he went without telling her he was going. Tulie found out he had gone from his broker, Margo Jong, to whom it seems he had phoned instructions about his brokerage account. Tulie pretended to Mrs. Jong that she had known he was going, but when she put down the telephone, she collapsed on the sofa and buried her face in the soft, feathered pillow for a long time. He had gone without saying goodbye.

Then suddenly, Tallulah found she could breathe freely once more. She sat up. The wall of silence was gone from her house. She rose from the wide sofa and pushed back the lock of white hair clinging to her wet face, relieved, revived, hurt but happy. Just then she heard the postman pushing letters through the slot in the front door. Surely it can't be two o'clock already, she thought.

Tulie walked swiftly to the hall and picked up a long white envelope from the floor. Whose handwriting is this? She opened it with curiosity. She was surprised to find that under the letterhead of Molico Products, Frank Fontaine, First Vice-President, had written her a letter.

Dear Tulie,

Usually Jean writes our thank-you letters, but on the chance that she may not have thanked you enough [she hadn't thanked her at all], I am writing to tell you how much we enjoyed your birthday party. [How long ago that seems, thought Tulie]. I'm at the age in life where I am assessing what it's all added up to and I must admit that when I was in your beautiful home with your happy family, your children and grandchildren around you, I felt cheated that I haven't had all that. Well, it's a fact of life that some people have more than others.

How ironic, sniffed Tulie, my life as a picture of ultimate happiness! Has his life with Jean been that bad? At least someone was thinking of her; that was some comfort. Tulie went back to the letter.

I've always blamed myself for Jean's unhappiness. I guess that's why I'm writing you. You've known her longer than I have, so maybe you know a little what she's like. [You can say that again, said Tulie to herself.] Is it all my fault?

When Phlox got into that trouble at school [Tulie wondered what trouble] and they sent her home, [It must have been some trouble!] I tried to be a real father to her, but Jean wouldn't let me. She just didn't seem to want Phlox around. I went along with her idea of sending her to you because you've always been such a strong, dependable person and I feel better knowing she'll be under your good influence. She and your son must really be enjoying each other. [I'd like to tell him thought Tulie, that that kid of his has caused my son to leave home!]

Meanwhile, I'm doing a lot of thinking. Things have to get better for me. They can't get any worse. I've been remembering The Grease Pit—didn't we have fun there?

> Fondly,
> Your old friend,
> Frank

P.S. Thanks for everything.

Tulie sat back and remembered The Grease Pit and her boyfriend Frank. She knew his letter was written under the stress of 04Y4, but always the diplomat, he hadn't mentioned it. Frank was suffering, too. "How ironic life is. Here I am taking care of his child!" she exclaimed aloud.

A long time ago Tulie had gone out with Frank for over a year and he'd never proposed. She thought that he almost did once. But on every date he seemed to be looking over her shoulder for someone else. Then he found Jean and it was all over for Tulie—such sophomoric values he had then. You can't marry for fun and keep it forever. How ironic that he envied her now. If he only knew how it was with her, how lonely, how isolated she was from her husband, how forgotten by her children, how meaningless her life was. Maybe it was good after all that she had Phlox in her charge. But such a child! She shivered.

At the thought of having a child like Phlox, Tulie Freund felt thankful for Freud and Linda. Looking through Frank's eyes, she supposed she had had a nicer life then most of her friends. Poor Frank. He had his limitations, but she wondered if he deserved Jean. She almost called him up on the telephone to tell him about her problems with John, but she thought better of it. Somehow she couldn't reveal the real judge to anyone. He was an important man in the community and she had promised before God to honor him. Her loyalty wouldn't allow herself to give him away when the world had turned against him.

Tallulah turned back to the letter in her hand and read it over again. He thinks Freud and Phlox are having a good time! He probably sees Freud in white flannels and buck shoes driving his beautiful Phlox to the country club. If only he could see that precious little flower of his hanging around the Royal Purple, he might come and take her home! Tulie smiled. My, how kids have changed! If only I wasn't too old to change, I'd find a new life myself, that's for sure!

Then reading Frank's letter a second time, she said to herself, how little we really know of one another! Most of what people think about us is just a myth. Tulie rose. Frank's letter had been good for her. She felt better as she put the letter back in its long envelope and, placing it down on a nearby table, she looked at herself in the large gilt mirror and said to her reflection, "No, Mister François Philippe Fontaine, you don't know me or my life at all. But thank you, Frank, for thinking of me. It's made me feel better to know I'm so strong and dependable."

Then she looked at herself in the glass again. "Maybe it would be more fun to be weak and dependent—and loved!"

The Kitchens of the Pink Pavillion

The early weeks of June were very busy ones for the employees of Glory Land. As predicted by its owner, park attendance was up twenty-five percent over the year before. More and more middle-aged people were escaping the confrontation of dinners at home to eat in their favorite restaurant and see their friends and neighbors.

No matter how many problems were listed on his daily agenda by his staff of secretaries, Brigham Bantley found time to drop over to the office of Anna Maria Abendtal and have a cup of coffee. He loved to slip in unobserved and see her at work among her cooks and waitresses and watch her quietly before she caught sight of him. She was so efficient and so patient and kind to her helpers, many of them first-timers, that they responded to it as happily as people have always responded to inspired teachers, by learning rapidly. It was obvious to Brig that the waitresses and the staff were devoted to their manager, and he was surprised at how hard the young people worked to please her. This was the first year that they had shown so much *esprit de corps* and the miraculous results of their efforts were obvious to the customers, who were actually coming to Mr. Bantley to thank him for the smooth service and beautiful food at the

Pink Pavillion. He expected compliments for the food, but it was rare indeed, even in fine restaurants, to hear praise for the service!

In fact, things were going so remarkably well that Brig made plans to spend the long weekend with his mother in Lake Placid. He would ask Anna Maria to substitute for him in overseeing Glory Land.

After he made this request of her one morning, Anna thought about it for a moment, flattered by his trust in her, but then she suggested it would be wiser perhaps to ask Skip and Savy to take charge of the park. "It is not fair, Mr. Bantley, to give this responsibility to me, a newcomer to Glory Land, not when your son and daughter are owners. They need to be given lots of responsibility and a sense of participation over and above that which we all feel. You know they are no longer children; they have reached a crossroads in their lives. You can help to influence whether they find their place here near you and Mrs. Bantley, or whether they go away like Banter—maybe far away. If they were mine I'd like to have them near and see them often. Do let them take charge!"

"What you say is true," agreed Brig. "But you may not have noticed that Savy's been away; she's coming back this morning. I must say my daughter picked a fine time to visit Long Island!" he added sarcastically. "But I'll put Skip in charge. Being a man, he should be in charge." Anna raised her eyebrows but said nothing. It was not her business to argue that notion. "You speak of Bant. I told you we had a letter from him about finding himself?" She nodded. "But did I tell you he made me realize that I don't think I've ever found myself either—and I'm twice his age! I've done many things and I have a lot of this world's goods and pleasures by any measure, and yet I'm not really satisfied. And I haven't used all my abilities. Furthermore, I have this sudden sense of urgency. Time has become too precious to waste! I guess it's because there's less ahead than behind. Do you know what I mean, Anna?"

"Yes, Brig, I do. I've begun to question my whole life too. Oh, how I wish I could start over! There now, you've let your coffee get cold. I'll pour you another cup," said Anna Maria, stepping over to the serving table.

While she did so, Brig continued to talk. "Anna, do you ever feel you're part of some larger plan over which you have little control, some plan wherein you're called upon to perform because you were chosen to do certain things?"

"Yes," she answered slowly. "Sometimes I feel that way about my life." She was thinking of her godchildren and certain suggestions of hers that changed their lives. She spoke aloud, looking across the table at her boss. "As a matter of fact I feel that way about Skip's coming over to my house evenings to work on his lyrics."

Brig looked up quickly from his coffee. "You shouldn't let him impose."

"Impose? It's my privilege. These young people keep me young. I feel just like them sometimes. Listening to them, I forget my grey hairs and silently I cry and sing and clap with them. Brig, why don't you help Skip get an audition? You must have some connections—a publisher perhaps, someone from your college days or someone with whom you deal when you hire performers for Glory Land. His songs are beautiful, poignant and haunting. Or why don't you have them sung here this summer—introduce them to our own special audience? They'd love him."

"Well, maybe—I'll think about it. I just don't want him to become a Mick Jagger, that's all."

"Who?"

"Never mind. Why do we always talk about the kids? There's something else on my mind this morning that I want to talk over with you, even though I'm reluctant to mention it to anyone. It's Olivia! This summer she's getting on my nerves," said Brig. "We've worked well together for years, but this summer it's different somehow. She hovers over me and fusses about little things, waiting on me hand and foot like an invalid. I'm not used to it. Ever since she drove all the way to the dune house to tell me about you, which was very uncharacteristic of her, she's been acting strangely. Don't misunderstand me, dear Anna, I'm not complaining about her suggestion. You were the best idea Olivia ever had and I should show my appreciation by telling her so," said Brig, frowning a little.

"Don't," said Anna.

"Don't? Why not?"

"Because you don't really know us women. We don't like to hear other women complimented by a man we like. It's just one of those things!"

Brigham Bantley shook his head. "I thought she'd be pleased."

"Well, I'm pleased," said Anna. "And I'm sorry Olivia is upset."

"Maybe it's not me; maybe it's Rene. Or 04Y4," said Brig. "What do you think?"

"Probably all those things," answered Anna. "Life with a sick husband must be very lonely. I think she's been going on her reserves for a long time. She needs to draw on someone else's strength, as we all do from time to time. Perhaps Rene can't give her what she needs and she's trying to get it from you. You are such a strong man." If she only knew, thought Brig, as Anna continued. "You've certainly lifted my life from the doldrums of habit; I just love being here in the middle of all this action. So," she said, embarrassed by this personal talk, "I'll try to help Olivia while you're away and maybe she'll tell me what's bothering her."

Brig stood up and smiled at her affectionately. "Tell the kids they're in charge and I'll be back Tuesday morning."

She wanted to say, "Tell them yourself," but instead she murmured, "I'll tell them."

"One more thing I've just thought of," said Brig. "I have a letter from England that a sculpture I bought at auction at Sotheby's is on its way to Montreal on a freighter. It should be here in two weeks. It's a Family Group—a Henry Moore—like the one in the Tate, only larger of course. I hope you'll approve. Come to think of it, the Henry Moore could just be why Olivia's upset with me. She said we agreed on a Giacometti for the Garden of Meditation. There never was any such plan. She suggested a Giacometti and I told her I was buying a Henry Moore. Now it seems I've let her down! Women do confound me sometimes. There's no understanding why they do and say the things they do."

"Has it occurred to you that my coming here might also be part of Olivia's trouble?" asked Anna Maria in a low voice.

Brig looked startled. "You? How could that be?"

"Well, you have given me a lot of responsibility, which she might regard as hers—like costuming the waitresses, for instance. From what I hear she didn't like my changing the color of their aprons! When I learned that, I could see her point; I'd feel the same way if someone rearranged the furniture in Cornwall House! From now on, I'll try to be more circumspect. Meantime, forgive me, I really am just learning how to handle the job," said Anna, shaking her head. "One more thing, Brig. Olivia says she's never been for a ride in the B.B. Maybe it would be nice to ask her to ride with you in the Fourth of July parade instead of me."

"If you don't mind," he said. "It was thoughtless of me never to have asked her. Thanks, Anna." He started for the door, head down, wondering if he had thought of everything he had to do before leaving for a long weekend.

Anna followed him and added softly, tongue-in-cheek, "Skip would like to take the B.B. on a date."

"That will be the day," shouted Brig, lifting his head. "Never!" Then he laughed at himself and looked at his watch. "Goodness, it's ten forty-five. I want to make Lake Placid in time for lunch with Mother. She's getting old— eighty-five this year—and I don't get over to see her as often as I'd like. Have a good weekend here and I'll be back soon. Please notify my kids." Anna Maria watched Mr. Bantley depart and in her brown eyes there was a look of admiration. She was glad he was so fond of his old mother.

As soon as Brig swung away from the Pavillion in his maroon Mercedes, Anna Maria Abendtal telephoned Savy Bantley the news that she and her brother were now in charge of Glory Land. Savy told the news to Skip, who mentioned it to Penny, who informed Freud, who called Mark, who arranged a meeting with the Safflowers for that night. Once again the grapevine in the small town was on top of the news, and big things were about to happen because Brig Bantley had gone "bye-bye."

New York (UPI)—Mother Bell led the market to new highs for the sixth straight day in a session marked by heavy trading.

The Pecan Pie

As soon as word was conveyed by the grapevine to Safflower Hill that Brigham Bantley had left town for a few days, Mark Sanders called a meeting of all the members who had pooled their lives and belongings into a group called the Safflowers. Carpenters, painters, and plumbers were urgently needed and everybody else was to come along too.

Mark Sanders was the newest member of the commune and also the most handsome. His black hair was thick and wavy, and his luxurious silky beard and mustache left little showing but suntanned cheeks and deep-set eyes. His chin was set forward giving him a romantic flamboyance. He was truly wonderful to look upon. That fact, along with a happy and positive nature and an innate managerial talent, made him a natural to move quickly into command of his well-meaning but disorganized group of peers.

Mark had moved his wooden toy-making hobby to Safflower Hill from the family home because he had been put out by his father, Bud Sanders, founder and president of Poly-Toy Industries, who saw no potential in either his son or his talent for inventing wooden toys. There was no money in the boy's handwork; it was a waste of time. Perhaps the father might have come to terms with his maverick son had not Mark, one April day, been provoked into telling his dad what he thought about plastics, plastic toys in particular. It had been a heated argument and when Mark flung, "Furthermore, your plastic toys stink" at his father, he was invited to leave the family home forever. He left at once and purposely infuriated his father by going to live at the commune on Safflower Hill. The town teletype had been exchanging opinions and taking sides ever since. Those who sided with Bud Sanders admired him for his "hail-fellow-well-met" manner and his big bank account; but his detractors said that he kept women in various places and they sided with Mark.

However, no one mentioned Mark Sanders to the one person who needed to talk about the episode; that was Surtsey, his mother. When she walked into a room people stopped talking and she knew that they had been discussing the so-called "scandal." And lately she met with an embarrassing silence from her friends when she even mentioned Mark's name. It was as though he was a social outcast or a biblical leper. They were silent, as though he had died, leaving her no opportunity to tell them about Mark's creative needs, of his plans to design quality wooden toys, or that under the circumstances, she was glad he had gone to the Hill rather than leaving town. Through her volunteer work with the young, Surtsey got to know the kids at the commune better than the skeptics. Most of the kids who lived on the Hill were decent, loving, idealistic young people trying to live up to their ideals and find out who they were. Some of their notions were impractical, of course, but all in all, group living of one sort or another had been part of the American experiment since Pilgrim times. Some sociologist had said that with the middle-class children dropping out of the establishment the next generation would be run by the poor sandal-maker's child. Why not, thought Surtsey, it wasn't much of a world at present anyway; their fresh ideas might improve things.

The commune had come to town two years before and the only person with whom Surtsey could talk about it was her friend and neighbor, Anna Maria Abendtal, who shared her confidence that the new generation of dropouts had something unique to contribute and were quite interesting people. Everybody else was disgusted with them. In fact Surtsey was surprised Brigham Bantley had hired so many of them this summer. That must have been Anna's influence.

Surtsey was thinking about this as she prepared dinner, a special dinner of Bud's favorite foods, which she always prepared for him on his birthday. She made him a pecan pie from Bud's mother's recipe and, putting it on the silver salver that had been a wedding gift from Bud's Aunt Lettie, she stood the pie in front of his place. The children would put candles on the pie and sing happy birthday and give him some gifts. How many birthdays we have celebrated and how much I wish the big children could be with us tonight, she thought. Then Surtsey opened the cupboard and, taking out the grater, she ground horseradish for the sauce for Bud's favorite shrimp cocktail.

The telephone rang. Who could that be, she asked herself as she put down the grater and picked up the phone. "Hello; Mrs. Sanders speaking. Oh, Bud—you're not coming! On your birthday!" cried Surtsey, her voice rising, then falling in disappointment. "I see. No, of course not."

Bud's voice could be heard in the next room as he

answered her. "Oh, hell, Surtsey, I can celebrate being forty-six any time, but I can't sell one hundred thousand plastic pistols every day of the year!" Had Surtsey not been such a lady she would have told him what to do with his plastic pistols, but she held her tongue. Bud continued, "If I get the order we'll celebrate tomorrow night at the Pink Pavillion."

"All right, Bud," she said flatly, "but I made you a pecan pie."

"Put it in the freezer," she heard him say as he hung up.

"That's what you think! Twenty years ago, ten years ago, even two years ago, I'd have saved it for you, but tonight this pie goes to Mark. Because of you I didn't dare invite him to the party tonight. Now here I am all alone, no one to talk to but youngsters, and all my efforts to make you a special dinner wasted. Come, children, let's eat. Daddy won't be home."

"Again," said Bucky, "not even for his birthday?" Bucky was obviously disappointed.

"Maybe he's like the old man in our storybook who hates birthdays," offered one of the twins.

"I love birthdays, don't you, Mom?" asked the other twin.

"That depends," said Surtsey thinking, *some* birthdays perhaps, but not forty-sixth birthdays—not this year. She turned to her ten-year-old son. "Bucky, after the twins go to bed I want you to take this pecan pie up to Mark. You children can have ice cream instead."

"Goody," the twins replied. "We don't like pie."

"Okay, I'll go," said Bucky, "but I wish Mark didn't live on a hill. My legs get tired, Mom. I need a ten-speed." A smile passed over Surtsey's face. How many times had Bucky said that, but Bud was adamant, "No ten-speed till he learns to take care of his bike himself. I'm not a mechanic."

Sometime later after the twins were in bed and Bucky had left to deliver the pie, Surtsey sat down with an old *Reader's Digest*. But she couldn't read; she wanted to talk to someone about herself, about Bud, about 04Y4. But she was all alone. Anyone as lonesome as I am doesn't have much of a marriage, she observed to herself. What had happened between her and Bud, to whatever they once had together? Or were all those years a mirage, a myth all her own?

Bud so seldom took any role in their lives that he sometimes seemed like a phantom; but the reputation he enjoyed as a ladies' man was hardly realistic. She knew all of her friends thought he played around; and Jean Fontaine once came out and referred to him as a great lover, but how could so many be so sure? Of course he was friendly to everybody, egocentric and cute in a baby-faced way with his round eyes and red chubby cheeks, but as a lover he was sort of an infant too. His love making had been a disappointment from the beginning. So much of the pleasure was in the drama, the buildup, the game—but with Bud it was as routine as his daily workout at the Y.

There was one evening in particular some years ago that Surtsey hated to think about even now. It would have been long buried in her subconscious except for one thing. She got her nickname that night. She remembered it well. It had been a terrible day, a day in which the demands upon her as a wife, mother, nurse and community citizen had pushed her to the end of her capabilities as a person, when she felt that her own mental survival was in question. Bud announced he was in the mood for her attentions too. "Oh, no, Bud, not tonight—I just can't. I'm too tired," she said as she flopped into bed, exhausted beyond bearing. Then her husband had said something like, "It's pretty awful to have a frigid wife." That did it—that ugly word "frigid"; she sat up, shaking with anger, and said, "Give me a compassionate man and I'll come alive like Surtsey herself!" After that, Bud taunted her by calling her Surtsey in front of her friends. How cute, they said, and Surtsey she became. Few of them knew it was a volcano that had erupted off the coast of Iceland!

It fit her more now than it ever did, fit her state of mind: seething, rebellious, frustrated, burning—in fact due to erupt. Then where will I be, she asked herself. A heap of ashes in a sea of ruin. That thought calmed her and damped the flames.

As for Bud's having affairs, the word was "perhaps." Perhaps tonight there were no one hundred thousand plastic pistols, but it was better for her not to play the game of Perhaps. It was better to think he was selling toy pistols. Bud's very lack of attachment for their children—oh, how fond he was of looking at her and hurting her by saying, "You have too many children," as though they weren't his too—this lack of fondness for them made her worry less that he would form any strong attachment for another woman. As her psychologist once said, trying to be helpful, "Bud is a simple schizoid personality incapable of forming deep relationships." And yet she felt that this lack in him was her failure too. At least she used to think so, but now she was finally questioning that feeling of guilt.

This summer her life was at an impasse. In twenty years she had become a capable, well-trained and perfect servant in a large and loving family. For them she kept a standard of living and a level of being that money couldn't buy nor help provide. They, of course, didn't realize this; for them the good life was something they were born to—a comfortable home, delicious meals, clean clothes, vacations, toys and spending money, music lessons, everything—all theirs because their father was a successful manufacturer. No, there was not a lot of reward for being the family slave. But sometimes, just sometimes, a little hint, a little word, a sentence or two giving her a little praise or credit for something they had achieved was her recompense. And to see them clean and healthy and well-dressed and to hear some adult praise them every now and then was the satisfaction she got. Surtsey had never asked for any rewards other than these small satisfactions.

But lately, quite suddenly in fact, the years of life ahead of her were shorter than those behind and more precious than before, and she questioned whether she had done enough with her life and talents. She gave her time to her family and her community, of which she was a prominent and well-liked citizen, but did Surtsey do enough for herself?

It was not a pleasant feeling to ask herself this question, to add up her life; and on certain days she was very depressed, despairing of finding the answers. But there was one thing she knew. It was too late for a career, too late to go back to school. And then there was 04Y4. The simple truth was that if she divorced Bud she'd have to support herself. How could she do that and take good care of young children at her age? Could she be a cook or a waitress or a check-out girl? Or sell real estate? It was all so unthinkable that she knew deep down she'd have to keep Bud Sanders along with all the embarrassment and pain he caused her. He was her meat and potatoes and that's all he'd ever been. Marriage is a life sentence, she thought, but why did I deserve such a sentence? Why me?

Surtsey tried to read "I am Joe's Intestines," but it just

wouldn't amuse her tonight. Maybe Bud won't sign. Then what? She turned on the television loud and waited for Bucky to return. The little boy was not long in coming with his new puppy at his heels.

"Mom," he called from the hall, "I took the pie to Safflower Hill and left it on their kitchen table. What a kitchen! It looks like Grandma's used to when I was a little kid—before you made her get it fixed up. I tried to give the pie to Mark so somebody else wouldn't eat it; but he was talking to Freud and he pushed me away and told me to buzz off fast! Why did he do that? I think they're having a secret meeting, because all the kids were coming in and sitting on the floor. That Stevie who's never combed his hair told me, 'Scram, kid.' What do you think's going on, Mom? I ought to get out my detective kit and take fingerprints."

"Well, I don't know," said Surtsey. I hope, she thought to herself, they won't make any trouble after I recommended them for Cornwall House. Surely Mark wouldn't break my trust and get me in wrong with the Historical Society. On impulse she said, "Why didn't you stay there, Bucky? Ride back over and see if you can tell me who's there."

After he left she worried. Supposing they were having a pot party or some sort of love-in—such were the rumors. Mark had assured her otherwise, but just suppose Bucky walked in on something. What got into me to send him back there? I'm no spy. Am I losing my perspective? The Saffies wouldn't risk their jobs at Glory Land, I know they wouldn't—not with jobs so scarce. Or would they? Kids can be so independent and unappreciative at times.

In her overwrought state, Surtsey Sanders paced back and forth until Bucky returned again. "Guess what," he called, "I tried the front door and it was locked, so I took a few fingerprints. Then I went to the porch window and someone pulled the curtains shut before I could see a thing. No one answered when I knocked. There's something important going on that they don't want anyone to see. Oh, and another thing, Mom, as I was riding away, a girl came up the hill on a motorcycle. I think it was that girl who's visiting the Freunds. She knocked and they wouldn't let her in either, but when I left she was crawling through the cellar window. She had on white pants too!"

"Thank you, Bucky. You're a good detective," said Surtsey Sanders, looking at her watch. "Oh, my, it's after ten—way past your bedtime."

"I'm going because my legs are tired. Two times up that hill! Now if I only had—"

"I know," laughed his mother, "a ten-speed. Well, Christmas is coming." Bucky groaned. She always said that even when Christmas was going.

A Business Meeting

Bucky was right. Something was happening at Safflower Hill. It was a business meeting. Freud in brown cowhide vest and brown jeans and high-heeled boots stood before the crowd. By the air of reverence and expectation with which they awaited his words he might have been the President of the United States. He began abruptly, looking them in the eye one by one. "I've come up here to talk to you about a business deal. It's top secret. Have you locked the door, Mark? Secured the windows? All right then, we can proceed. Recently I bought a property. Everyone should own a property, right?

"You see, I bought this business property, but I'm low on cash. I need your help to construct something on my property, a top secret something. I can use carpenters and plumbers, electricians, painters and laborers. It's a rush job at night, worker's hours. So for such a job the pay should be top pay. Right? Right. Well the pay is exactly nothing, absolutely zero, zero dollars."

A groan went up from the audience. "What? No dollars?"

"Nope, no dollars."

"Then what is the pay?"

"The pay is the special satisfaction that comes with

pulling one off or putting one over. This will make waves in Temagami Springs for years to come, go down in history, in fact. The dollar dividends will come later. You'll get your share. No, no, it's not what you might think, nothing illegal; any trouble that ensues will be in someone else's head. Are you with me?"

"No, Freud, this time you've lost us. What in the name of creation are you talking about?"

"Let me explain it another way. You've heard of the Glomar Explorer, that secret ship? Well this is like that—a secret thing till it's all in place, mission accomplished; then let the flack fly! I promise to everyone who helps me a very rewarding summer and a whale of a lot of fun.

"Cost to you? A few hours of your time this weekend and maybe two all-nighters, plus any dollars you care to contribute. Come over here and sign up if you're hiring on."

"You think we have money? We're deeply in debt," remarked a girl who resembled a mouse. "We've got a big mortgage." The Saffies looked at her and at one another, afraid to get involved financially, mystified but eager for any adventure. Mark Sanders took some folding green from his pocket. "Put me down," he said. Someone else had a buck or two, and one by one they came till everyone had signed. And the collection plate was full. "Now what, Freud?" they asked expectantly.

"All of you, please listen. I'm handing out top secret papers. I want each team to assemble the suggested things exactly as described. At least one on each team can read a drawing, I presume. Hide what you assemble until you hear from me. You have two days at most to do it so you will have to work all night tonight. If one team fails, we all fail, so let's pledge to do it—and pledge not to talk." They duly swore and he passed them sealed manila envelopes.

"And one more thing. Don't talk to the other teams about this or compare notes. Mark Sanders is coordinator. You can all talk to him if you have any questions. We should complete our caper by Monday night, but our adventure will have only begun."

No one knew what Freud was really planning, but they were willing to go along for the fun that he promised. Good old Freud, idea man of the high school senior class. College hadn't changed him at all. Their guesses were fantastic and the plans didn't show much—boards, bolts, ropes, fabric—simple carpentry for the most part. They were to build something. But what was it?

Skip and Savy Reign

A few nights later on Sunday Evening, Skip and Savy Bantley were alone together in their big empty house. Monday was a day off and their father was not due home until noon, so they were enjoying a feeling of freedom. "Let's go for a swim before we eat," said Savy.

"Good idea," replied Skip. "Am I glad you're back from Long Island; handling everything by myself has been a bit much! Say, I never did hear how your thesis came out. Did you get a four?" he asked, climbing on the board to dive into the swimming pool.

"I only got a ninety-one—a big robbery. I don't want to talk about it," replied Savy. "What about *Bring Back Those Years*? Have you found anyone to record it?"

Skip dived in and, swimming over to his sister, he climbed out beside her.

"You won't believe this, but someone stole the first tape we made. It was lying around at the Hill. But everybody likes it and I'm working on more new songs. The kids up there really dig the one I call *Seeking Love In Lonely Places*." Skip picked up his old Batman towel. It had been around for years and he liked to use it.

"Little brother, you sure do dwell on loneliness," said

Savy, kicking off her clogs and sitting down at the table.

"I know I do. It's because every one of us is lonely. Take Anna Maria—she's never had a man. And Dad without Mom. And me—even sitting in a room full of people I sometimes feel lonely. Isn't that strange?" asked Skip.

Savy interrupted him, "You know what? I'm lonely too. I'm so lonely I could cry." She put her head down on the table and really was about to do just that when he comforted her. "You need a man—even a brother can see that," said Skip, patting his sister's heaving shoulders.

"How could you tell?" she sobbed. "I haven't heard from Jack since he left for Colorado. I've written every week like he told me to—General Delivery, Boulder—but I haven't heard one word from him."

"Better get yourself a new man. Jack's not worth your tears," said Skip, which made his sister angry and stopped her from crying—which was why he said it. She gave him a poisonous look and he quickly changed the subject. "Were you over at Glory Land today? Did you talk to DeLuca? Or Olivia? Dad says we're in charge, but the way Olivia talks it's her baby."

"She would," replied Savy, recovering herself enough to move to the pool and put her bare legs in the water. "She's worked there for years. Poor woman. I can't see spending my whole life at one job, can you? I wonder why she stayed so long."

"I dunno," said Skip. "It sure would be a drag to be grounded like that. I'm glad I have a portable profession! I can get an inspiration any time, any place." Skip threw aside his Batman towel and dived into the pool, surfacing at Savy's feet.

She looked down at her brother and said, "You asked me whether I went to the park today? The answer is yes, of course I went to Glory Land today and everything is going well. Tony's team clipped the shrubbery and trimmed the borders. Olivia says we're expecting the Rock Hound Association Tuesday and the Ecological Society Seminars next weekend."

Skip interrupted. "We're almost booked full for the whole summer."

"Yes, I know, and Anna Maria phoned this afternoon and said to tell you that they set a new record for dinners served last night and that she has hired all on her own initiative a local string quartet to play in the dining room on Wednesday because she couldn't reach us in time. I told her that was okay. So it sounds as though we're doing just fine in all departments."

"Since everything's all right," said Skip, "I think I'll do thirty laps. Then let's eat. By the way, I forgot to tell you that I met John Freund III at the office while you were gone. He's the funniest guy ever in that Ben Franklin costume with his colorless beard and his wild blond hair. It seems he's a history buff. I was so curious about him that after he left I looked up his résumé. He majored in history, was president of his class at Harvard, and on every committee. A real doer, I gather. And he said to say *hello* to you; he acted like he knew you very well in high school. Did you ever go out with that guy?"

"Heavens, no!" exclaimed Savy. "He was one of the older crowd. All I remember was that he was a big show-off—not my type at all; but it would be like him to act like he knew me when he didn't. The summer's just beginning, so I suppose I am destined to make his acquaintance. But I can wait, that's for sure." Her mind was traveling far away, bound for Colorado. Why hadn't she heard from Jack? What could she do? Sometimes men could be so cruel. Savy climbed on the board and did a swan dive into the pool, and then she swam ten laps and felt a lot better.

The Two-Hundred-Year-Old Oak

Even as Skip and Savy Bantley were chatting by their poolside, the night fell over the Valley of Springs and things were happening not far away. Down Route 9 with their lights off traveled a convertible Buick, circa 1958, its contents covered like the missles on a Russian ship bound for Cuba; and behind the Buick came an old worn-out truck loaded with strangely shaped flats and pieces of lumber. The convoy came to a halt at the entrance to Glory Land just as Tony DeLuca turned out the lights in the gatehouse and was stepping outside to go home. He was confronted by this strange caravan and by a big dark hulk of a man who jumped out of the car. Was it to be 1968 all over again? Tony was apprehensive, but when he saw it was Freud he was relieved. He knew, through his daughter, Rosa, that Freud was a young man to be trusted.

"May I see you alone, Tony?" asked John. "Don't turn on any lights out here." Tony nodded. They went inside the gatehouse and DeLuca switched on a flashlight. Freud drew from his buttoned-down pocket a document. He showed it to Tony. In pencil at the bottom was written in Rosa DeLuca's hand a message. "Dad, this is a true document. I typed it myself. It won't hurt to help Freud."

When Tony looked up at him, Freud asked for help in his most persuasive way and the old Italian stonemason, his weatherworn face creased in a hundred directions, shook his head back and forth in disbelief. Tony liked young John Freund. He liked the way Freud treated the rock lady with respect and the way he'd helped her with the iron gate. It was a funny thing to do, putting a fancy gate from a fancy estate on a wall around an old silo, but it had given Tony a kick to help with that caper. He supposed this action now was another one of Freud's big ideas and he hoped it was as harmless. If Rosa, his daughter, attested to it, it must be okay. After a long pause Tony said yes.

And so it happened that a silent figure with a flashlight ran out from behind the lilac bushes and opened the gate and the strange parade resumed its motion down the Appian Way, through the pine woods and across the green swards into the forest and came to a halt below the big oak tree. The moon, just past full, hung low in the sky, giving light to their undertaking.

Swiftly as a bat swoops from tree to tree, the workmen began their well-rehearsed activity. Propane lamps were lit and hung upon the branches and the tools were laid out for the night's work on the needles under a nearby white pine.

"Did you bring the plans?" asked a wild-headed worker of the man with a black beard.

"Here they are," replied the dark one in a low voice. "We're going to put the larger platform for the sitting room just above us. We'll winch it into place between the two lowest branches and fasten it with bolt clamps. The small platform should fit on the two branches higher up. That's for your bedroom. We have two by fours drilled and ready to be bolted in place for the walls. They're made of plywood with fiberglass insulation. Then we'll cover that with slabbing. It will hardly be visible way up there. Over on that limb," he pointed, "will rest a little porch fastened in place with rope lashings. It will catch the afternoon sun. Say, Jake," he called in a loud whisper, "did you bring the rope ladder? The ladder will drop down from one end of the porch, which will be about there." The dark-haired man gestured into the dark above his head.

"Just don't damage the tree," interjected Freud. "Isn't this oak enormous? It must be two or three hundred years old; it's surely the biggest one I ever saw. Wait till the squirrels meet me, their new neighbor—and the insects, birds, larvae, bugs, caterpillars, spiders, wasps, mice, and hawks that live in oak trees. Here, let me pull on the ropes too."

"What's Brig Bantley going to say?" whispered one of the boys in Freud's ear. "We may all lose our jobs when he gets a load of this in his tree."

"Say?" repeated the fair-haired one. "He won't say anything, not when he learns that I own this tree."

"You do?"

"Darn right I do! Isn't that something?"

"Wow! Cool, man, cool." They passed the news from ear to ear and murmured their admiration in a low hum.

Quickly the climbers in the crowd went up the tree and fastened ropes and pulleys onto the big wide-reaching arms and hoisted up the prefabricated parts of what was to become a handsome cocoon. Like so many caterpillars, they wove a wonder among the leaves of the tree, and at length it was pronounced good enough for the time being. They would stabilize it better on another night. Morning would soon be here.

After the boys had finished the construction, the girls took turns going up and down the rope ladder while Freud grew impatient and began to worry that in the ever-growing sport someone might fall from the tree and be hurt, perhaps ruin everything. Tony meanwhile was watching from a distance, biting his nails to the quick. He had never heard of anything like this, but it had all happened so unexpectedly. How did Freud get a piece of Glory Land anyway?

At length Freud spoke in Mark's ear and Mark gave an agreed-upon whistle. The last girls came down from above; the Safflowers, reminded to be absolutely quiet and that the fun had only begun, drove home to their farm. Mark drove Freud's car to the Hill where he hid it in the barn until the time Freud could take it to his new place.

After the Safflowers had gone away, Penny and Freud stood alone at the foot of the tree. They were very tired and it would soon be dawn.

Freud turned to Penny and took her hand in his. "It's ours, pardner, I hope my tooth fairy likes our fairy land."

"It doesn't look big enough for both of us," she replied, seeing as she often did the negative side. "Freud, I had to tell Dad why I'd be out all night so he could make excuses to Mother, but he won't tell anyone."

"And I confided in Tony. I couldn't tie him to a chair like we'd planned—not after the help he gave Tatty—so I trusted him. That's a better way. He won't notify the Bantleys till daylight."

Penny was trembling from fatigue and nerves. "Now what?" she asked.

"Steady, lass, steady," said Freud drawing her close. "Hold on a little longer until we can build a place for you to have your tea room. Then we'll find a way to make money and pay off our debts and live happily ever after. Believe me, woman, we are going to make waves! Now we must get some sleep. I wish I could drive you home, Penny, but you understand that I have to stay here. There may well be an attack of some kind when the sun comes up, so I've got to get a little rest. Take my flashlight with you."

His tooth fairy walked away slowly, reluctant to leave but too tired to protest. He watched her go; and with some satisfaction he climbed the ladder and pulled it up behind him. It was awkward, but he would learn. Then he lay down and went to sleep in the tree. His chrysalis wobbled rather like a water bed, but he had a wonderful sleep that first night in his new home.

A Red Alert

The sun rose over the Valley at 5:10 EDT. At six o'clock the telephone rang in the Bantley home. A very sleepy young man groped his way down the hall to answer. The voice on the other end jabbered in a mixed lingo of English and Italian. Skip barely understood the message except to recognize that it was Tony and there was something wrong at Glory Land.

He trotted down the hall to Savy's room calling, "Red alert. Red alert." It took a lot of poking and tickling to get his sister to come out from under the covers.

"Go away," she shrieked, covering her face with her red hair to keep out the light. Finally, when he persisted, she sat up, clutching the covers about her. "Stop it. What's the big idea waking me up like this in the middle of the night?" she cried indignantly.

"Come on. Get up. We have to go to Glory Land. Something happened."

"Did it burn down?" she asked in a frightened voice.

"No, not that, thank God! I don't know what. But Tony's jabbering in Italian. He only does that when he's nervous. Something happened in the night."

"All right, but I'm coming in my housecoat. Warm up

your Volkswagen. I'm coming," she mumbled, slipping into her mules and following him downstairs. They rode silently along Route 9 passing only the milkman. It was already daylight and they were shortly admitted to Glory Land by a frantic but speechless Tony, who led them right along Appian Way over the fields and through the woods to the foot of the oak tree. He pointed upwards, and while they were staring up into the branches he beat a fast retreat without a word.

"What is it?" whispered Savy.

"I think it's beautiful, whatever it is."

"Will it harm the tree?" she asked.

"No, it's hanging by ropes."

"Who do you suppose is up there? 'Rapunzel, Rapunzel,'" called Savy.

"Shhhh. Don't waken anybody. I think we better leave town before Dad comes back. It's his favorite tree."

"Mine too. But it's not our fault. Are we supposed to be here all the time? No, it's not our fault, Skip. Shall we call Olivia?"

"No, no. Dad reminded me once to respect her day off. But we could notify Anna Maria. She'll tell us what to do," whispered Skip reassuringly.

"I'm glad there's someone."

"Let's go right over to her house for breakfast," said Skip.

"She won't mind?"

"Of course she won't mind. She gets up early and I'll bet she'll thank us for coming."

"In my housecoat?" asked Savy.

Skip looked at her up and down. "Why not? People wear anything these days." Skip hurried ahead and Savy flip-flapped behind him, her red hair flying in all directions. They fled from the woods like Hansel and Gretel fleeing from the witch's house.

PART IV

Early July

Brigham Bantley's Dilemma

During the night a front moved through the mountains bringing rain. By morning a heavy cloud filled the valley and covered Glory Land, hiding the peaks in grey mist. The trees in the forest were a vivid green and the grass in the fields was wet.

Tony DeLuca stood by the Appian Way and hoped the weather would improve and the ground dry so the lawns could be mowed in time for the annual meeting of the Rock Hound Society. But long before the collectors were to arrive, Brigham Bantley would return from his mother's house to be told by someone of the happenings of the night before.

This was a dreary Monday especially for old Tony. It was usually his day off. Ordinarily he enjoyed Monday. He liked to lie in bed with his wife and have a late breakfast and read the morning paper. However, since 04Y4 had become a fact in their lives, Mama spent their hours together wailing and moaning that he was going to leave her for a young *signorina*. There was no peace at home. To escape from Mama he came to the park on his days off and stayed in his tiny office in the little old farmhouse where he turned on the radio and listened to Monday afternoon baseball. Today he was too nervous to listen to the radio, so he comforted himself with his pipe while he sat by the woodstove and waited for his boss to return. He had had a reluctant hand in the whole matter of the night before; but he *had* let them do it. In retrospect he could not believe what had happened, that he, Tony DeLuca, had actually helped those kids to get into the park and hang a pod in Mr. Bantley's favorite tree. But what was done was done. If he lost his job now he'd find another—or would he at sixty-five? Why had he done such a thing? Why had he risked his job so late in life? Was it some sort of protest against things as they were? Or anger over the fact that his life seemed to be out of his control? Was it anger with Mama for her accusations, she who knew him better than to say the things she did? Why would he want to enrage Mr. Bantley who had been so good to him? He couldn't believe he was capable of such a thing, and yet he *had* done it!

Tony couldn't answer his own questions, but somewhere deep inside there was a little imp who was pleased and even curious as to how it would all come out. Tony puffed and puffed on his pipe and tried hard not to think about it at all. He had done his duty when the sun came up by summoning the Bantley kids. They'd be back with their dad after a while. Meantime, the grass was too wet for mowing. The tiny room grew hot and Tony took a nap. Sometime later he was awakened by the noise of the Bantley diesel. He could hear it coming a long way off, especially on wet days like today. Tony put on his U.S. Navy cap—he had been a sailor during World War II—and went to open the post gate for the Bantleys. They drove right on by without stopping to say hello and went to the low brown headquarters building set back in the woods behind the gardens.

Tony closed the gate and sat down again inside, but he

couldn't sit still for worrying and decided to go home to Mama after all. Miss Olivia could let herself in.

Meanwhile the Bantley children had told their father very little, only that something had happened at Glory Land that demanded his immediate attention. He felt they were being mysterious; doubtless it was some little thing Anna or Olivia or even Tony could have handled. He was glad they were finally showing some concern over their duties to their patrimony so he did not press them. He merely said calmly, "We'll go out there and you can show me what it is." On the ride he was silent, still thinking of his mother. Would he ever see her alive again?

When they arrived at Glory Land the children followed their father inside the office. He closed the door behind him. Then with his hands on his hips, Brig looked from Savy's serious face to Skip's sober one. "Okay, kids, tell me what's happened around here." They hesitated to tell him. "Hurry, tell me. I have a big day planned, a thousand urgent matters to attend to. Let's solve whatever it is that's troubling you and get on to other things."

"Oh, Dad," stalled Savy, taking the initiative as she usually did with her younger brother, "it's not that simple. How can we tell you? It's just that Tony says someone's bought part of Glory Land." She spoke in an inaudible voice, her face pale. She looked at her fingernails, awaiting his reaction and afraid to see the look on his face.

"Did I hear you say *'bought* part of Glory Land'?" exclaimed Brig. He repeated the question in louder tones.

"That's right, Dad," interrupted Skip, taking over from his sister, who looked like she might faint at her father's brusk tone. "It includes the big oak near the river. We don't know what else. Someone's built a capsule high up in that beautiful oak tree."

"My old oak tree? What stunt is this?" shouted Brig. "Who? How?"

"Well, Freud Freund, that's who," offered Savy, recovering her nerve.

"We don't know how," mumbled Skip, his blue eyes traveling from his father to his sister, who was gesturing him to say something further.

"Well, where is he?" asked Brig, his black brows tied together in a frown. Brig sat down at his desk and leaned back in a swivel chair, his hands behind his head.

"We think he's in the tree."

"All right then. Go get him at once. Bring him to me," Mr. Bantley said abruptly, reaching for the phone book. "No, on second thought, don't bring him here. Go talk to him and come back and tell me what this is all about. He can't have bought any part of this place. If he doesn't leave at once, I'll call my lawyer and have him evicted. Tell him that!" He opened the phone book to the Yellow Pages.

"Isn't Freud's father your lawyer?"

Brig looked vexed. "He was," he commented grimly. "But I'll call that young lawyer Margo Jong likes so much—what's his name—George Wescott at Wescott and Morrow. He'll straighten this out in no time." Brig stood up and pointed at one of his children and then the other, his finger moving as he lectured them. "I go away to see my old mother and leave my grown son and daughter in charge of your heritage and what happens? You sell the place!" he exploded. He brought his fist down upon the desk in anger.

"Come now, Dad, it wasn't that way at all," said Savy. "Sit down," she commanded in a tone that surprised her. Brig sat down. While she related the events of the night before, Skip slipped out the back exit. He hated unpleasantness of any kind. "Now," Savernake said, "I will go see John

Freund, Dad, but I'll say this: I don't want to go. But maybe, in a way, we kids are responsible," she said in a low voice, turning on her heels to leave the office.

As she opened the door her father called her back. "Savy, tell me," his voice softened to the tone his daughter responded to. "Have you ever played Ultimate Frisbee?"

"Ultimate Frisbee? No. Why?" she asked.

"Nothing. I hear it's a good game. Maybe we . . . ," his voice trailed off and he gazed out the window.

Dad's out of his tree, Savy thought, shaking her head. Him playing Ultimate Frisbee! What next?

Brig Bantley thought about this new dilemma. His role of creator, provider and father of Glory Land was something like that of a parent. Each day some of his employees or some of his projects or some of his customers became sick or troubled and came to him for the answers. He learned out of necessity to remain calm and externalize the stress, but lately it was getting him down.

Was it worth it to give his life and energies to so difficult a business? It was a mere three weeks into the season and already the ordinary problems were not enough. If it were true that John Freund III and a bunch of kids had taken over his favorite tree, with all the problems of liability and diplomacy their being there might entail, it was a very delicate matter indeed. He would have to find a way of outmaneuvering them, removing them from his place without offending their parents or their friends. And God forbid, if the press got the story, people would be made to think the kids had some right to be there. It did not occur to him for a moment that the property was not his.

"Rapunzel, Rapunzel"

Savy walked slowly to the foot of the huge tree. She looked up. The pod was still there, snug in the crotch of the oak as though it were built by a tent caterpillar. "Rapunzel, Rapunzel, let down your long hair," sang Savy under the red oak tree. Her sense of fun served her best when she was a little uptight.

Freud had just awakened after a hard sleep and was sitting in his sleeping bag wondering where he was; to wake as he did, in totally unfamiliar surroundings that had been built in the dark of the previous night, was a disturbing experience and so unique that he would always remember it as one of his peak experiences. He woke to see a sparrow silhouetted against the oak leaves. It was sitting on the windowsill looking in as though it was inspecting his house with nest-building in mind. Freud's place wasn't much bigger than a birdbox—just enough space for two or three to sit and talk, and two to sleep in the upper tier.

He had no idea it was nearly noon. As he sat there wishing Penny would show with breakfast, he heard a voice singing, "Rapunzel Rapunzel, let down your long hair!" That's odd, he thought, it sounds a little like Penny, but it's not her style. He decided it was one of the Saffies, so he was not prepared to see the head of copper-colored hair down below. "Hey there," he called, not recognizing her.

She looked up, and he saw it was Savy Bantley, the boss's daughter! Oh, oh, here it comes, he thought, rather pleased it was she—women were easy to get around. If he could succeed with her he'd have it made. "Come right up. I'll lower the ladder. Pardon my inexperience, but I've never tried this before." He lowered the ladder down beside her. "You see, a stork left me in this tree last night."

Savy kept a solemn expression. She grabbed the rope in both hands and expected to mount quickly to the top, but her feet kept going forward and out from under her. However, she was athletic enough and determined enough to climb the swinging ladder, although its motions made her dizzy. Why didn't I order him to come down? I'm already losing face by coming up this dumb thing, but I must keep my composure, she thought. Once on the top rung she accepted his hand and Freud helped her onto the deck. Savy stopped and looked around. It was a new experience to be high up among the oak leaves. It was fragrant and cool, the sun making lovely speckled patterns against the sweet-smelling pine boards. She would have liked to say this unusual eyrie was delightful, because it was; but Savy retained her distant tone. "This is a business matter. My father sent me," she said, looking John straight in the eye while pushing her red hair from her face. She knew the effectiveness of eye contact.

"Yes, Miss Bantley," he said soberly, his eyes never leaving hers but twinkling as they were wont to do when he was having fun.

"Well," she said.

"Well what?" he asked pleasantly.

"I want to tell you to leave Glory Land and to take this

whatever-you-call-it with you," she replied.

"Miss Bantley," he answered, drawing himself up to all of his six-feet-one-inch height so that in the confines of the deck he looked like a giant, "is that a nice thing to say on the occasion of your first visit to my new home?"

"Your new home? This pod! What do you mean putting it here without our permission? It's preposterous; it's ridiculous. We won't have it." She was what her dad called a foot-stamping redhead; however, keeping in mind that she might lose her balance and tumble overboard, Savy controlled her feet.

"Come inside and see it," replied Freud, bending down and pushing open a flap. "Of course, it isn't finished yet, but with the help of my friends I hope it will be soon. Let's sit down while we talk. We can peek through the knotholes at the ground. Look at that grey squirrel down there. He's glad he has a nice new neighbor like me!"

Savy stood there, uncertain whether to charge or retreat. There wasn't room enough for either so she sat down and stared at Freud. This big man certainly was sure of himself. He wasn't exactly handsome but there was magnetism about him. She could feel it; usually a headstrong person, in his presence she felt strangely compliant. She wanted to escape and yet she wanted to stay.

"I don't know what to say. Why are you here? Is this some stunt?" she asked.

"My child, let me show you why I'm here; let me show you this paper I have under my sleeping bag." He felt under the blue Sierra bag and brought out a stuffbag from which he took a document, attractively bound. "You see, my partner and I have purchased this property from Ms. Kaleri Tuttle and we have decided to live on our property. That it happens to be adjacent to your Glory Land should prove felicitous to all of us in the future. Here is our valid deed, duly registered at the County Court House. I have always loved my neighbor as myself and I am prepared to love you in spite of this unkind reception to the new neighborhood. Please convey my best wishes to your family and ask them to drop up and see me anytime." He held up the document for her to see. There was absolute quiet; the only noise was the chirp of sparrows in the oak tree.

Savernake Bantley listened and her hands began to tremble. "May I take that to show my father?" She looked pale; indeed, she felt sick.

"I am sorry," said Freud. "It's my only registered copy, but I will Xerox it for your scrapbook if you'll come back for it later on. This is a day we'll all want to remember! Of course if your father prefers to make trouble, we are prepared to fight fire with fire," he added as an afterthought. The pink light of the morning sun coming down through a hole in the walls shone through his wild curly hair, emphasizing his animal strength.

Savy just wanted to run. But how do you run from a capsule twenty feet up in a tree? She couldn't remember later how she got down; but somehow she made the descent in a dignified manner and walked purposefully back the way she had come. She had gotten exactly nowhere, in fact had been outmaneuvered. If the paper was valid (it certainly looked valid) then Glory Land would never be the same again. What would her father do now? No matter what her father did, she would pick up Freud's challenge. She would not let him forget that she was his neighbor.

When Savy departed from the tree, Freud looked down admiringly. Rapunzel, Rapunzel, we'll let down your hair, or my name's not John Freund, he said to himself, watching her leave.

Savy walked away with her hands in her pockets and eyes on her sandals. She went slowly back along the sandy lane towards the administration building. She was thinking about Freud. He had made quite an impression on her, but it wasn't a good one. He's a freak and so intelligent he's not for real, she thought. And his hair wouldn't look good on a Barbie doll! In fact, Savy was thinking she didn't like him at all. He talked down to her—that was it—as though she were his dog! And his story—how could he have bought those acres from Tatty Softshoe when they belonged to her dad all these years? It seemed very strange to her that anything like that could have happened. And who helped him do it?

When she told her father Freud's story and the fact that there was mention of only one partner all he could say was "well, well" and shake his head in disbelief. Then he instructed his daughter to phone Olivia Dupre to come over at three o'clock and to have Skip join them too. The lawyer would arrive as soon as he could and they would decide what course of action to take. "Meanwhile, be gone" was in his tone and so Savy went away to look for Skip.

It was very hot in the late afternoon when Savy and Skip, wet from a dip in the lake, went dutifully to headquarters. Mr. Bantley was sitting at the big table with Attorney Wescott, deeds and plat maps spread before them. Brig looked up and motioned them to sit down. His face was strained. "Savy, this is Mr. Wescott. Mr. Wescott, my son and daughter. Now I want to tell you children, you owners of Glory Land, what my thinking is on this situation with the tree. From these papers it appears that it is just possible Mr. Freund has legal title to that property. Some years ago all the land around the lake including Glory Land belonged to Tatty's parents and subsequently they sold it off piece by piece. I picked up a few pieces from the Softshoes at the time I bought the land we're sitting on here from the Tyler Lansdown Estate. Of course I thought I owned it all. It was my understanding the pieces included both sides of the river from the Little Bear to the Big Bear Lake, but deeds to the property back in 1911 when Tyler acquired his place from Tatty's father were often loosely written."

Savy spoke up. "If that's the case, I hope Freud didn't get the land from her too cheap."

"Being the son of Judge Freund, he probably did," commented Skip. No one liked Judge Freund anymore, not even Skip. "He probably put him up to it."

"Oh, no," laughed Mr. Bantley. "Judge Freund's too unimaginative for that. But I wonder how his son ever got the idea in the first place? A smart young man, I gather. However, it does make big trouble for us, which I could do without just now." At that moment Olivia rushed into the office in a highly nervous state. Her bracelets jangled on her arms and her face was streaked with tears. Brig rose and Olivia went right to him and put her arms around him and wept on his shoulder. "I've just heard about Freud," she sobbed. "I'll resign from your staff."

"Now, now," he comforted her and his face reddened. He was embarrassed by her show of emotion in front of the kids. "What would we do without you?"

"To think," she said, stepping back, "I liked John Freund and I hired him. I brought him here to be Ben Franklin and he took advantage of me!"

"Olivia, it's not your fault. I'm sure he never thought of it that way. He's young. We'll work it out together; we always have."

She interrupted. "No, I'm resigning as of tomorrow. Rene needs me now. He's worse." Before they could stop her she left the office and drove away.

Brig said sadly, thinking of Rene, "She's always upset when Rene is having an emphysema attack: by tomorrow she'll change her mind." For a moment he returned to his notes on the yellow pad in front of him. "With Mr. Wescott's help, we will try to keep this new attraction strictly off-limits as long as possible. I will instruct Tony to build a locked gate across the Appian Way at the old stone wall. Skip, do what you can to keep this from the press. Give Mr. Johnson, the editor, a call; I suppose we can trust him to put a lid on a hot story until we are absolutely sure who owns the oak tree and what our recourse is to be. Even a few days' delay will help." Mr. Wescott looked skeptical. "Savy, you go back to Freud tomorrow morning. Tell him we are getting the advice of our attorneys. Tell him what we're doing and report to me what he is doing. That's all. It's time to prepare for the Bibliopolists' exhibit, which is the day after tomorrow. Meeting dismissed." Mr. Wescott gathered up his papers and he and the kids left quickly.

Brig leaned on the desk, his face on his two hands. He smiled a wan smile. He had to admire young Freud for being so audacious. There was a time in his life when he'd have taken part in a similar caper but never as the ring leader—no, never as the leader. He had been brought up to respect other people's property. Then he remembered that, unbelievable as it seemed, the property—including his favorite tree—probably belonged to Freud. It was incredible, but so was everything these days. Everything. One no longer knew what to expect of anyone.

How right he was! Several hours later, well after dark, sounds of hammering again echoed across the Valley of

Springs. By the light of a mercury lamp, Tony DeLuca was building a gate across the road to the river. But that was not all.

Every now and then Tony stopped and stood aside to allow an old Buick, a dilapidated truck, and a tractor pulling a wobbly hayrack to pass in the direction of the oak tree. Throughout the night the activity increased, but by sunrise a heavy white paddock gate with a large lock barred the way to the river. Old Tony was home in bed and all was quiet in Glory Land.

Tony had allowed Freud a last chance to lay in his supplies before securing the fence; that the supplies were unusually large and cumbersome and took most of the night to unload did not escape his notice; but a prudent man, acting imprudently, is not likely to ask questions.

The Gynecologist

Margo Jong hurried into the kitchen on the morning of the seventeenth of June and poured Bill a glass of tomato juice. He was hung over as usual and looked awful. He sat at the table and waited for her to make his breakfast. "There will be coffee in a moment," Margo said. "Then I'll have to rush. I have an appointment with the gynecologist this morning at nine. Cover for me at the office if I'm late for the market opening, will you?"

"Uh-huh," he said sourly. "What do you have to see Mort about at his office or haven't you noticed he lives next door? Could it be, my little love, that you are a wee bit pregnant? I need a knife," he said hoarsely, expecting her to jump up and get it. "Where's the morning paper? You know I like it with my coffee."

She got up from her chair and went to the back door, picked up the paper and handed it to him. His hands trembled as he opened the paper and read the headline aloud. "Noted Doctor Attends Prominent Broker Having First Baby at Forty-Five!"

She tore the paper from his hands and hurled it toward the trash can. "Bill, you're awful!" And then she turned away and ran out of the kitchen into her bedroom and slammed the door.

Bill called after her, "We could put all our customers in Midnight Enterprises, Inc., and sell our story to a scandal sheet. Maybe you'll have triplets," he laughed.

There alone in her room she broke down and cried. She could hear him opening the cupboard where his bottles were kept, and she wept. "Bill, don't—don't hurt me like this. We'll lose everything if we go on like this," she sobbed. After she had cried hard, she felt better and firmly assured herself that it would do her good to talk to Doctor Levy.

"Be on time at the office, Bill," she said as she went through the kitchen. "We're in a bull market." She looked back, wondering whether he'd make it to the office at all. "And don't forget to shave!"

Bill looked at her with blank contempt and put his hand to his jaw. "Yeh, guess I'd better," he muttered.

Arriving five minutes early Margo Jong sat down in Doctor Levy's reception room. Minutes seemed like hours as she sat in the waiting room. Actually, it was a three-cigarette wait. She crossed and uncrossed her legs, picked up crumpled magazines and threw them down again, cast her eye on a La Leche League pamphlet entitled *How To Nurse Your Baby* (she thought that knowing how came along with the baby). Margo grew increasingly restless. It's awful sitting here among all these preggies, she thought. She looked about at two or three bedraggled females focusing on their magazines. What preggies? She looked again and couldn't distinguish any. Where have all the preggies gone? Ho hum. Here she was almost forty-five, needing a child, and no one else did. No one wanted babies. I guess I'm just behind the times. How can one get so out-of-tune with the times? She answered herself with a question. Or how did the times get out of tune with me? What has happened to our world?

"Mrs. William Jong," said the receptionist coldly. "Please come this way. I want to weigh you and take your blood pressure, Margo."

"Never mind that," said Margo, shoving her away. Why did this child call her Margo?

"Yes, ma'am; it's our procedure."

Margo allowed herself to be weighed and noted with satisfaction that she had lost three pounds. Her blood pressure was a little high but nothing to be concerned about, so the nurse said. She put up with all this impatiently, but when the nurse motioned her into a cubicle, handed her a white paper gown, and said, "Take off all your clothes and put this on, please; then lie up there," Mrs. William Telford Jong rebelled.

She dropped the gown to the tile floor and kicked it away. "That I will not do. I came here to speak to Doctor Levy as a professional person and I wish to be seated in his office beside his desk as I would seat him in my office." She was prepared to wait if need be until Mort went from cubicle to cubicle visiting other patients, but she would not stretch out half-naked with her legs in the stirrups to talk about her future—procedure be damned, she would not! She glared at the young nurse.

The young woman glared back, shocked by this outburst from so trim and sophisticated a person as Mrs. Jong. The young girl turned aside and whispered with the receptionist, then turned for a second attempt to discipline this unruly patient. Margo's Irish was up now and she was baited to teach these young ladies that middle-aged women are not to be pushed around. "Have I arrived by mistake at the Gulag Archipelago?" she asked, putting her half glasses on her nose and looking down at the youngster.

"The what?" asked the young nurse. Margo continued disdainfully, "On the other hand, perhaps to you I am just one more cow being led to an insecticide bath!"

"I don't get you, ma'am. But just come and sit in the doctor's office. It's okay, ma'am. It's okay."

"I'm okay—you're not okay," flung Margo as the door closed.

"Pfew," commented the nurse as she shut the door. Margo sat a little while strumming her fingertips on the doctor's desk. All the frustration of her many futile trips to the GYN floated to the surface of her mind. It was all useless, of course. A doctor in Atlanta had told her that Bill was sterile, but she didn't believe him. He liked sex too well to be sterile! She knew now it was true, but it was easier to keep hoping. She looked at her watch. It was nearly ten o'clock. The exchange would be opening and she didn't really trust Bill with her orders. 04Y4 had been bullish for the market as she predicted. Floral International hadn't moved yet, but Hairdressers International was up a point. Mother Bell had moved ten points, of all things. "I must go. I'll have to call Mort to come to my office."

At that moment the door opened and the doctor himself came through the door. "Why, Margo," his eyebrows lifted, "so it's you who is making this rumpus!" She rose to her feet, suppressing a smile, her fury spent, and she said very formally, as though addressing a meeting of stockholders, "In the name of women's lib, doctor, I demand to talk to you downside down, not downside up! Haven't I told you that before?"

Doctor Levy looked astonished. He interrupted her to ask, "Whatever is bothering you, Margo?"

"That's what I hoped you'd ask. You can guess, Mort, what's brought me here."

"Is it 04Y4?"

"Yes, I suppose it is. I don't know what to do about Bill. I need someone to keep me from contemplating divorce or perhaps to suggest that I should contemplate it. Though it doesn't say so in my medical records—women do lie about their ages—you know that I am forty-four years old, doctor, and I'll be forty-five in August. I don't mind that, but I do mind that after twenty years of marriage I'm not fulfilled. And yet," she continued, "I almost hate to give up Bill. He's all I have, all I may ever have." She looked at Doctor Levy. "Do you know what I mean?" He nodded. "You alone know my real problem. I've always wanted children," she blurted. "And now I know I'll never have one."

He thought she was about to cry. "In all these years," she continued, "I've never given up hope that something, some vitamins, some vacation, some accident even would happen that I'd get pregnant and have a child of my own. Oh, I suppose it was my fault. No, it wasn't my fault. No, I can't blame myself. Bill didn't want any. He was very emphatic— but you know that," she added sarcastically. "You probably have that written on that card somewhere," she said, pointing at the folder before him, her gold bracelets rattling on his desk. "But I keep telling myself," she continued, "that if there had been one anyway he might not have become a drunk—oh, I didn't mean to say that; that's privileged information." What had gotten into her to reveal Bill's weakness to Doctor Levy? Mort was one of Bill's discretionary accounts. She covered up. "Bill isn't really a drunk. He likes his whiskey now and then. I just said that because I am so very mad at him. Tell me, doctor, what am I going to do?"

Doctor Levy, already somewhat concerned about the safety of his investments, raised his eyebrows. He was impressed by Margo Jong. Why hadn't he chosen her for his broker? She's very intelligent for a woman, he thought, and I must ask her to review my investments. He was thinking to himself that she had a great need for a child and maybe he could help her. "Let us sit quietly here a moment and think," he replied. "Have you read Viktor Frankl?" She shook her head no.

"Well, as Doctor Frankl wisely observed in the prison camps in Germany, we all have to have something to give meaning to our lives, something for which to live, if we are to survive the hard things that happen to all of us from time to time. Since my divorce, I have found my work gives purpose to my life; but apparently you have special needs, which your work does not fulfill—feminine needs that work cannot satisfy. The question you pose is how to fulfill those very natural needs." Margo moved her head in agreement and folded her hands in her lap to listen, biting her lower lip.

"At your age the most feasible suggestion I can think of is adoption. You know the agencies and laws of this state now look more leniently upon the elderly and single-parent adoption."

"I'm not elderly and I'm not single either," replied Margo, affronted.

Doctor Levy was strictly professional now. "I should have said that mothers in their forties are known in my trade as elderly mothers. And should you not sign 04Y4 you would become a single parent. It is now easier for someone such as you to adopt, provided you will take a hard-to-place child."

"Well, I'm not exactly a blue-eyed blonde myself, if that's what you mean," murmured Margo, dominated now by his professional commentary.

"No, you are a talented and charming brunette," he said,

smiling at her, his eyes twinkling. Did she denote a look of invitation?

"I'm not paying you for flattery," she interrupted.

"I think an old neighbor can say free-of-charge, you're a very attractive woman. I mean it, Margo; you'd make a wonderful mother for some lucky kid. If you agree with me about that, I'll take you one step further." He was a very kind person, a perfect doctor.

She nodded. "Okay, okay," she said, embarrassed by his smile. "Well, I guess I'm ready; take me one step further."

"It just so happens I know of a baby looking for a mother." He swiveled around to look into his files. "He'll be born in two months or so and he'll be hard to place. I've been wishing I could help the parents in this tragic case; the mother is just fourteen and her only parent is dying of cancer. The father of the unborn child is an eighteen-year-old alcoholic. There's no chance they'll change their minds and keep the baby. To complicate the adoption further, it's a mixed marriage. Unfortunately, in our society this baby will face special handicaps; you see, Margo, it's not necessarily the baby for you in your business. Don't agree too readily. There will be others."

"Oh, doctor," she interrupted, jumping to her feet, "how could that make any difference to a mother?" Already thinking like a mother—a child yet to be born who needed her—a victim like herself of an alcoholic. Fate was sending her a baby now when she needed it most. "Oh, doctor," she cried, crossing her hands over her heaving chest, "you've made me very happy!" It was well the nurses weren't watching, for Margo ran around the desk and grabbed the doctor, kissing him on the top of his bald head.

"When, Mort, when?"

"Mid-August, I think—unless it's a premie," he said,

looking again at his files.

"Oh, I want that baby. Help me. Help me." Her mind raced ahead: the nursery, birth announcements, a beautiful name, private schools, college—Radcliffe, of course. Mortimer Levy smiled. Mothers-to-be made him very happy and this was a very promising mother-to-be. He escorted her to the door.

Returning speedily to her work, Margo Jong shut herself in her private office and pushed the button on the telephone to talk to her husband, Bill.

"Bill Jong speaking," said a scratchy voice.

"Bill, the doctor said I'm very healthy."

"Oh."

"He has something for us, Bill."

"A salmon from his fishing trip to Labrador?"

"No, Bill."

"Well, what is it?" His voice was irritable.

"A baby, Bill—a baby who needs us."

There was a long silence. "A *what* did you say?"

"I said he has a baby for us to adopt. Listen, Bill, we have everything we need. Let's share it with somebody. Bill, this baby's father is an alcoholic. Oh, Bill, I'm so happy. Now we'll have someone to spend our money on."

"We'll buy land."

"Oh, Bill. We can't buy what we need. We need someone to love! Please be as happy about this as I am."

"You're crazy!" He hung up. She could not see him, but she knew he was opening his desk drawer for a swig of coping juice. For the first time ever she didn't really care. She was too happy and excited about becoming a mother.

For Want of Amenities

Savy Bantley opened one eye. The rising sun caught the corner of her mirror in a way that said 6:30 a.m. Time to get up in order to catch Freud before he left for his work, indeed if he were still employed. After seeing Olivia's temper the day before, it would be surprising if Glory Land did not look for a new Ben Franklin.

"Now what shall I wear today?" Savy asked herself. "Something he'll notice, something a guy would go for." She decided on her green stretch shorts and her favorite new knit shirt. It was the color she looked best in—peach—giving her skin a warm glow, and she loved the pink and green pattern of roses over the chest. It was so yummy and good looking. She wanted to make an impression on Freud, using every feminine advantage; women's lib notwithstanding, it might be necessary with a man who seemed to get whatever he wanted—even other people's property.

Savernake Bantley was a fortunate girl, five-feet-seven inches tall, slender and supple, with smiling eyes enhanced by long dark lashes. Her soft hair was the color of copper and her skin was tawny and tight over her straight strong features: her father's features and her mother's smooth skin combined in one person in a way that could only be described as lovely.

This morning she looked delightful as she hurried out to her little car. In one hand she carried a basket, breakfast for Freud. And it was not without forethought that she left early and took along a thermos of hot coffee, a jar of honey, and a loaf of sweet-smelling homemade bread, all covered with a cloth she had embroidered herself. She knew exactly what she was doing!

Arriving at Glory Land, Savy went to the tree by way of her favorite walk, the path by the lake. The dark water of Big Bear Lake sparkled in the early morning sunshine and there were white herons standing watch in the marsh. At all hours of the day this park was a delight; there were so many varieties of beauty—some unspoiled, forever wild, others nature-trained and groomed, little waterfalls and lily ponds, wild grapes forming an arch to walk under, steps to tempt the oldest child, a cut in a big boulder leading to a bench with its own lovely view, a glimpse of water through the trees. Beyond the woodland lay a wide greensward reminiscent of the lawns at Windsor Castle, and the trees clustered at the edge of the meadow were as big as the ones on Savy's Vassar College campus. In Glory Land Park, pasture and woodland were turned into poetry, which delighted and gratified the sensitive visitor and made him feel like praising God.

Savernake was no longer a child: she was fully aware that this place was her heritage. As she walked beside the soft rippling water she wondered what John Freund was planning to do with his piece of Glory Land. What if he had some ugly noisy purpose in mind, like a drag strip or a race track? Would he ruin everything?

Turning from the lake Savy took a seldom used trail through the balsams and spruce forest. She loved the piney smell and soft needles underfoot. Would John Freund do something that would spoil this beautiful place? There was only one way to find out and that was to get to know him better.

Emerging from the woods, Savy Bantley came to a new gate in the stone wall and noted approvingly that Tony had built a strong barrier. No one could open it easily. Climbing over the wall at a low spot further along, she was soon at the foot of the oak tree and looking up at the pod hidden in the branches above her head. Hesitating only a moment to watch a chipmunk disappear into his hole, she called more bravely than the day before, "Rapunzel, Rapunzel, let down your long hair." In a moment a big blond head appeared in a hole high up among the leaves.

"Ah, my neighbor whom I have sworn to love! Come up the ladder, I pray thee; my hair is in curlers this morning so I can't come down."

Aren't you funny, Savy said to herself. "I can't come up. My hands are full. Come down at once and no more kidding around. I have further business to discuss with you, John Freund the Third. Besides, I have hot coffee!"

"Did I hear you say hot coffee? I'll be down in a second." Freud lowered the ladder and descended. "Isn't this the most beautiful day of your life? The sun is shining and the orioles are singing and the world is mine. Did you really say hot coffee?" He laid his big hand on her shoulder.

This guy is tearing me up with his beautiful world! What an egotist, thought Savy as she drew away. Should I give him the message from Dad now, or wait till after breakfast, after I've had time to figure out his intentions? She decided to wait.

"Yes, I've brought you a little snack," she replied. "We can eat while we negotiate, Mr. Freund."

"My name is John," he answered.

"King John would be more like it," Savy replied.

"King John was not a good man; he had his little ways and sometimes no one spoke to him for days and days and days," Freud recited in a sing-song voice.

"Do you like A.A. Milne?" asked Savy smiling, although she had planned not to smile at anything he said. But she did it when she remembered how her mother used to read her *Winnie-The-Pooh* and she knew the funny poem about the king whom no one loved.

"Yes, my mother read him to me when I was a kid. Maybe you are Christopher Robin and I am Winnie the Pooh," said Freud. They laughed together almost like old friends. "Just a minute," he added, "you haven't told me why you've come to see me. It doesn't seem possible it was just to be neighborly."

"Oh, yes it was. I brought you breakfast, didn't I? Can we sit down and eat?" asked Savy.

Freud motioned her to follow him to a special rock, an outcrop of the famous Muffin; he sat down, motioning her to sit on the ledge beside him. "A book of verse, a jug of wine and thou—no book of verse, green eyes? Your eyes are green, aren't they?" Before she could resist, he grabbed her arm and pulled her down close beside him and examined her eyes in detail—dark lashes, green iris, a touch of blue eyeshadow. "Ve-ry pret-ty."

"You big tease. Wait till I tell Skip about all this. He'll handle the likes of you." Savy jerked her arm from his. "He'll write a song about a bear in a tree. You did say you were Pooh Bear, didn't you? Did you know my brother writes songs? They're good songs, but he does seem to dwell a little too much on loneliness. I guess it's an emotion we all feel now and then," said Savy, picking up red and green stones and arranging them in a little design.

"Yes, I know. Miss Fontaine was playing her cassette of the one about seeking love in lonely places!" Savy looked puzzled; how did Phlox get Skip's tape? Freud interrupted her thoughts. "Now what do you have in that basket for a poor starving bear who lives all alone in a tree? I guess I'm a black bear."

You couldn't help but be entertained by this man, and Savy relaxed her guard. "I have bread and honey and a few other goodies," she said, uncovering her basket and showing him what was inside.

"Honey!" exclaimed Freud. "A peace offering! Pooh Bear loves honey. And I smell fresh bread! Ummm," he said, putting his nose down to the basket and sniffing loudly. He sniffed first the basket and then up Savy's arm, sniff-sniff-sniff. Then he saw the roses and, being Freud, he decided to sniff them too! The roses were right across Savy's shapely bosom, and when he began sniffing there, his familiarity was a little too much for Savy. She moved backwards abruptly and fell head over heels back over a rock, landing in a bed of ferns. The bread, wrapped in foil, flew over Savy's head and the honey jar rolled over the rock. Freud reached to grab the honey and somehow his teeth grazed Savy's arm, cutting through her skin. Otherwise, Savy was unhurt. But she was chagrined.

She picked herself up before Freud could reach her. Quickly he scrambled down to her side. "That's too bad," he said. "I wonder how it could have happened. Let me kiss it," he added, examining the wound. If he had seen her angry face he would have sensed what was coming. Savy wasn't worried by a little cut on her arm. It was his familiar behavior that did it. She struck him on the face. "You know exactly how that happened, you fresh—you contemptible—

you—you, you—oh, I don't know what you are!"

"Now, now. Let me wrap this bandana around Christopher Robin's arm. I'm usually not considered dangerous. I very seldom bite," he said, tearing his purple bandana into strips and bandaging her arm, unmindful of the stinging face, in fact appreciating her fiery spirit.

"Don't you ever say you're sorry?" she cried, her green eyes flashing.

"Ah, sure I do. Pooh Bear's sorry. Maybe we'd feel better if we had that cup of coffee." He retrieved the thermos and dusted the pine needles off the bread with his shirt. "Come on. Let's be friends. You're the greatest neighbor a guy ever had. And you look so beautiful that I just got carried away. Maybe I was a bit clumsy!" He looked so much like a big woolly teddy bear with his brown button eyes that Savy had an impulse to do what people do with teddy bears. Around this guy it took strength just to behave one's self.

"Well, I guess we were both a little uptight," she replied. "Perhaps now we can behave like two adults."

They began their breakfast all over again and this time it was a success, except that Freud fielded all Savy's questions about his future plans. No sooner had they finished their picnic than Freud jumped up. "I have to do something. Well, you know how it is; here in the woods we don't have certain amenities. So if you'll just excuse me and go on down by the river, you'll find my partner who's working there, and I'll be with you in a jiffy."

Savy collected the thermos and the cups, and putting them in her basket she got to her feet. "Yes, I want to talk to him too." In fact she was very eager to find out for her father who he was.

"It's not a him. It's a her!"

A her? A who? A girl! Did he live with a girl in that tree?

That would be a little too much. Savy hadn't expected his partner to be a girl; that thought aroused her personal feelings of disapproval. It seems this character never did the expected thing. Savy walked slowly and hesitatingly in the direction of the river, comforting herself that Freud seemed to be planning no further stunts to worry the Bantleys.

She followed the trail that wound around several big boulders and finally led up over the hummock of rock, from where one could see the old plank bridge below. When she came to the top and lifted her eyes from her shoes she knew in an instant that she had badly under-estimated John Freund III.

There before her was not what she expected at all. She was looking at something she had never seen in her twenty-two years in Glory Land, because it had never been there be-fore! But there it stood. It was a bridge across the waters— but not the same bridge, not an ordinary bridge. It was unique, otherworldly. Seeing it for the first time was like coming upon a foreign kingdom. She felt like a knight ar-riving in a strange land. As she gazed she became vaguely aware of a girl washing clothes in the river. It seemed an appropriate part of the scene.

What a surprise it was to discover that the old plank bridge had been transformed into a medieval bridge, a span with twin towers, one to the north, one to the south, an open stretch between. How was it built? By whom? When? It looked rather familiar, something from the background of a medieval painting. She was recognizing the bridge in Cahors, France, and at the same time watching the girl at the river turn and carry a basket of laundry up onto the bridge and hang things in the sun. Savy came quickly back across four hundred years when she realized who it was.

Penny Dupre!

Savy was shocked. Was Penny Freud's partner? Her, of all people? What a funny pair they make, thought Savy. She's so straight and he's so wild. I can't believe what I see, and I'm not going to wait to ask questions. I'm going to run right back and tell Dad. This is no little thing. This is for real. These really are towers before my eyes. What might happen here next?

With her astute mind at work, Savy began to see what had already happened. Somehow Freud must have found out that her father's heart was in the part of Glory Land across the river. So he fixed up the bridge to prevent them access to their land over there. He planned to trade for his access rights through Glory Land. He wasn't so dumb—well, she never thought he was dumb. But she was reassured about one thing: the bridge was well designed and its lines were good. Maybe he loved beauty after all. She hated to admit it, but this new idea of Freud's was exciting, even delightful.

A few minutes later Savy stood in the doorway of her father's office. Brig and Olivia were deep in conversation with Attorney Wescott. Olivia's face was lined with strain and she had black circles under her eyes. Savy waited impatiently for them to look up from their papers. At length her father raised his head and saw her there. "Savy," he said, in a serious voice, "our attorney says that a preliminary title search confirms what we thought yesterday: these young people do indeed own part—what we thought was part—of Glory Land. There is not much we can do about that! However, their rights to entrance and egress are quite unclear, and we can probably keep them from passing through Glory Land for the time being, by getting a court order to forbid it. Mr. Wescott is looking into the idea of taking them to court. All we need is some excuse."

"There's something else you should all know," interrupted Savy, speaking slowly. "They've done more: they've built towers on either end of the bridge. I guess they're going to live there!"

The three people at the table jumped up. "Built towers, you say? Going to live there?" Mr. Wescott rushed over to Mr. Bantley. "There's our charge. There it is. We'll take them to court for occupying a property too close to a public waterway without a sanitary sewer system!"

"And I can always build a footbridge or cross that river on the rocks if I have to. I don't need their bridge! They thought they could stop me," raged Brig. "We're going to sue!"

"Dad, please, Dad," Savy tugged at his elbow. "Come outside a minute. It's about something private." Her father followed her through the door.

"Dad, do you know who John Freund's partner is in all this?"

"The Saffies—that's for sure. I knew it! I told Anna. Those kids are all mixed up. They don't know right from wrong!"

"Dad, it's not the Saffies. His partner is Penny. You know, the baker." She hated to say it, but he didn't seem to understand. "Penelope Dupre. Olivia's daughter!"

"Oliv— Pen—?"

"Yes, that's why I wanted you to come out here to talk. Don't tell Olivia I said so."

"I can't believe it. Are you sure?" Savy nodded her head up and down. "I'll have to think—but even so—lack of a sewer—I'll have to think. This is madness. It's got to end. Isn't that so?"

"Yes, Dad. I'm going to look for Skip to tell him about the

towers." She walked away quickly toward the Pavillion and her father, visibly perturbed, went back inside, saying under his breath, "So that was the hammering I heard when I drove past the park last night. I thought it was Tony building the gate."

Savy hurried along the path; it was almost lunchtime and she could have cook's lunch at eleven. She would take her time about returning to the office. She entered through the heavy swinging doors and saw Skip and Anna just sitting down at Anna's private table in the far corner of the helps' dining room and she motioned them to save a place for her.

As Savy set down her tray, she watched for a reaction as she told them, "Hear this: there's more big news this morning. Freud has done it again, this time to the bridge of all places; overnight it has grown towers—twin towers!"

"You don't mean to tell me," exclaimed Anna Maria Abendtal, "that while we slept exhausted from worry over the surprise they gave us yesterday that they did even more to the park!" She set down her fork.

"Yes, they did. Father plans to get a court order putting them out—something about sewers."

"Your father shouldn't do that! It would only antagonize everybody. Let's have no more trauma," said Anna. "Tell him the Saffies are the best help we ever had. We mustn't antagonize them. We need them." Savy could see she was right. "That reminds me," added Anna Maria, "your father requested that his lunch be sent over on a tray at eleven-thirty—he's busy at some meeting. Will you take it over, Skip? I'll go get it."

As soon as she left the table, Savy whispered to her brother, "Guess who Freud's partner is? It's Penelope!"

"Not Penelope Dupre from The Sesame Seed!"

"Yep, little brother. That's the one. She's Freud's partner, believe it or not."

Skip could scarcely believe it, but he was thinking that his sister had mentioned towers. Maybe they had built him a studio, the very thing he was looking for. "There's a girl in a tower, on her I will shower my love," he sang aloud. Maybe it would be fun to live near the girl who made brownies.

Savy looked at him peculiarly. What was he thinking to make up a song like that?

"As soon as I take Dad's tray to headquarters I'm going to the river and have a look. This might be my big chance to leave home," commented Skip.

"Are you planning to be our Trojan horse?"

"I might," answered her brother. "Then again, I just might be a turncoat!"

"Skipworth Bantley! You're not going to abandon me to play good-kid and go have all the fun. Where does that leave me?"

Skip replied, "Do whatever you want to."

"Then I'm going right to Freud and warn him to get himself a lawyer. Dad's getting a court order!"

"He's not."

"Yes, he is! 'Throw the rascals out' he said."

"If you get there first, tell them I'll be over, but don't mention the idea of my renting an apartment. Freud might say no before I can talk to Penny and make special arrangements—like breakfast in bed and tea at four," he laughed. "There's more than one way to break up a power structure!" Skip smiled his cute little smile at his sister. She didn't know that he and Penny had hit it off really well that day in the bakery. "Say, what happened to your arm? Those look like teeth marks."

"You'll never guess. I was bitten by a mad bear and I think I'll get a lawyer and sue!" Savy was grinning; she didn't mean that, of course. Freud was going to have trouble enough. She knew her father well and she knew he meant business; he wasn't going to let anyone jeopardize his pride, his Glory Land. In fact she was so concerned as to the lengths her father would go that she wished she could think of some way to help John. It would serve him right to get into trouble, of course, but on the other hand, he was kind of attractive and she was beginning to hope her new neighbor would stay for the summer. She'd run right over now and warn him. It might help.

Savy hurried through the woods, now and then stopping to ask herself, "How come I'm helping John Freud all of a sudden?" Looking thoughtfully at the purple dressing on her arm she decided that those little teeth marks were a kind of blood-tie between her and her fresh-as-paint neighbor. That must be why she felt like helping him! Or was it because with him around, the old home town was beginning to come alive?

While Savy was having lunch, Penny Dupre was suffering and sobbing down on the bridge. She was full of misgivings about what they had done. When she had seen Savernake Bantley on the rocks above her, looking right at her, in that fleeting moment Penny woke up to the fact that she had compromised her mother with the Bantleys. In her excitement over being Freud's partner she had been a thoughtless daughter. Of course when she agreed to buy the property with John she didn't know what he had in mind. But how could she explain that? Only a fool would do that with her savings!

Freud, hearing sobs from the window of the tower, the window having as yet no glass pane, went down and looked inside at Penny, whose face was covered with tears. He was talking through the window, trying to reassure her that everything was working out just great, when he saw Savy coming down the hill. "Penny," he said in a loud whisper, "come on out. Here comes Savy. Don't let her find you crying or they'll think they have us just where they want us."

Penny was reluctant. She had known Savy for years; they had taken ballet lessons together. She liked her; she looked up to her, in fact. But Savy was always so sure of herself and she had everything Penny didn't have—looks, money, clothes, college. Around Savy, Penny felt insecure. She dried her eyes and went out to greet Savernake Bantley because there seemed to be no choice.

"Hello, Savy. Do you like our towers?" Before Savy could answer, Penny rushed on, a habit of hers when she was under strain. "We have such great plans for them. I'm sorry you're upset. It must be a terrible surprise [the understatement of the year, thought Savy]. You know Glory Land is all right for older people, but we need a place of our own. Can you see the potential of this? I'm putting in a bakery and there's room for a small stage on the bridge and a couple of studios there," she pointed upstairs. "Listen to the sound of rushing water and the wind in the trees. I feel close to God down here, don't you?"

Yes, thought Savy, I've been listening to the wind all my life, but before Savy could say a word, Freud asked their visitor to tell them what had been her first impression of the towers. Savy thought carefully with her pencil to her chin and then she said, "My first impression was unreal. I said to myself, this is a scene from a storybook. I was back for a moment on my grandmother's lap looking at a picture in a book of fairy tales and saying, 'Grammy, who lives in there?' Then I thought of my thesis—this is right out of the Middle Ages, you know. Of course you could use red-shingle roofing to simulate tile and harmonize with our buildings," Savy added, getting back to reality.

"If it looks like that, I'm satisfied," answered Freud. "In fact, I had great fun designing it. I'm going to become a historian, you know. I love history and I had the Middle Ages in mind. But I'm afraid we can't afford the roofing." He handed her a card on which he had printed, *Freud and Dupre Building Co.—Prefabricated Medieval Bridges.* "Want to buy a bridge?"

Savy was amused by the card and by the thought of one little thing he had forgotten! It would be a good joke on a big builder like Freud to be ousted from his dream for want of a little amenity like a bathroom with a proper sewer system. Obviously he hadn't thought that far ahead. Who ever worried in the woods? No doubt he intended to have what her mother used to call a Chic Sale on the other side of the river somewhere. It was going to be fun, she thought, to watch his face when she told him about the forthcoming legal action. So tell him she did. He was facing a restraining order and a lawsuit unless he vacated voluntarily.

"Oh, my. Who would have thought of that?" exclaimed Freud, on hearing about the proposed action. Then he turned to his partner and said, "Penny, are we going to be defeated by—a pile of dung?"

"Freud! Watch what you say!" Penny was appalled. Savy could hardly keep a straight face at this preposterous pair. Surely they weren't lovers. It was really a funny situation. "I just thought I'd warn you two so you can think what to do. Don't say I'm not your friend. Just be careful—watch where you go!" she laughed.

Sometimes Freud's sense of humor was a bit too much for Penny and he embarrassed her in front of people. She was not accustomed to anyone being so bold, and worrying about what he might say next made her nervous. To think of his saying what he did in front of Savy Bantley of all people. Penny was completely discomfited and while Savy and Freud continued to talk over the situation, she drew away from them into the woods to be by herself and think over what Savy had just said about a lawsuit.

Penny was frightened. Savy had mentioned eviction—a court order. Penny knew nothing of such things, only that her savings were tied up in this place. She had no money for lawyers. Maybe Freud had connections, but she didn't. She had no way to defend herself. As she worried about all that was happening, Penny's tongue ran over her uneven front teeth; the orthodontist had promised to make her beautiful. Now she'd never be beautiful. Why did she ever get herself involved with John in the first place? She really cared about Freud; maybe she was even in love with him. But did he return her affection? She thought he did in the beginning, but now she wasn't sure. How come Savy was wearing his bandana on her arm? For the first time since she opened The Sesame Seed, Penny was in deep despair over her future. She sat a long while on a grassy knoll hidden from sight among the pines. Finally she decided that there wasn't much left to do but trust Freud to think of a way out of their trouble. She took a long way round through the ferns and bushes to avoid Savy and John and came back to the path some distance away from the bridge.

As she was emerging from her hiding place she stopped to listen. Someone was coming through the woods from the direction of Glory Land. In a moment a young man appeared on the path ahead. He was carrying a guitar and singing as he walked, like a strolling troubadour. On his head, behind a fringe of hair, was a blue fisherman's cap and he had a yellow daisy over his ear. Suddenly she realized it was Skipper Bantley! The sweet-faced guy kept on coming right up to where she stood. He stopped and put his long leg up on a stump to bar her way. Then he gave her his little half-smile and asked pleasantly, "May I sing you a song, miss?" His blue-grey eyes were dancing like the river bubbling over the rocks, and his straight dark eyebrows were quivering. She looked up at him in surprise and was spellbound with delight as he serenaded her in song.

"I was just a little homeless waif
Afloating in the stream
When I washed up to your towered gate
And found the answer to my dream.
You invited me to come along
And stay where it was dry
So I'm heading to that wondrous place
To give your life a try."

While he sang, Penny leaned against a birch tree and her long face, so solemn in repose, came alive with pleasure and she smiled shyly at the handsome singer.

When he stopped strumming, he said, "Remember me? I'm the fellow who asked you to find him an apartment. Now I hear you've got studios of your own to rent and I want to be first in line. How about it, Penny? May I rent a room in one of your towers? I'll be ready to move in in the middle of July. Just think, after that I can stop over to your tower every morning for blueberry muffins."

"I don't know," she said, unsure whether to bring up the legal action. She didn't think Skip had any funny business in mind. "Maybe you could. I'll ask my partner what he thinks." She had already decided the answer was yes and was wondering how much the rent should be. Freud would want a lot, but she'd settle for less to have Skip there. They walked along together a little way and Penny said, "You'd like it here. I love to sit on the bridge and watch the water flow by, . . . to flow along with it into the lake and on into the sea. Maybe being here would help you write songs. I hope you can come, Skip. I'll let you know what we decide. Maybe you can have the north tower!"

Skip loved the river and he understood what she meant about the flowing water. Apparently she too had a sensitive soul. He looked at her happily, and after saying goodbye he went whistling down the path in his toeless tennis shoes, singing that funny song about the waif and strumming his guitar.

Penny watched him go and then she turned and went in the other direction to find Freud. He had gone back up into his leafy perch, but he came down when she called. "Let's rent the studio to Skip," she exclaimed. "He makes up the best songs. Are they ever good!"

"How good?" asked her partner, suddenly very interested. "Do they make you scream?"

"Not exactly, but they melt my heart," said Penny, who was no screamer. She smiled, remembering Skip's singing just for her and as she smiled she showed her not-so-even teeth. Looking at her, Freud was reminded again of his debt to her; it was happening every time his partner smiled. In fact he wished she hadn't ever told him about the tooth money. He probably should have borrowed from her instead of making her his partner. Freud was in an irritable mood after talking to Savernake. Maybe the Bantleys would somehow succeed in evicting them. The older generation had money and they had power. All he had was kid power and his own head. It would help to involve the younger Bantleys in his plans. But how? He waited for a brainstorm and it began to come.

"You say his songs melt your heart. I take it women like to have their hearts melted?" Penny nodded her head to say yes to that. "So, if we bring enough women here to the bridge and we bring *him* here, what have we got? A pile of melted hearts. Yes, and we can have another pile too." His brain was cooking up a way to make bread. "Each woman with one dollar and we have a pile of dollars too." He was thinking of some kind of entertainment for their peers— lots of them and lots of bread, and not Penny's kind of bread either. It would be a great thing to have a concert built around local talent right on the bridge! Kids would come from as far away as Duxbury to a festival and how could anyone in Glory Land not go along with that if the talent was the big man's son, Skipper Bantley?

"Settled," said Freud to Penny. "We'll invite him to come to live on the bridge and we'll make him some brownies. That's a great idea, my little tooth fairy, and I'm very glad I thought of it!" Penny walked away. She was offended that Freud had stolen her idea but glad that Skipper could come to live in the north tower.

Sweetbriar Springs

Several days later, up high in the tree on the deck of his little house, Freud was preparing himself a breakfast. Coffee was perking in a big old pot and bacon was frying in a heavy black skillet on a hibachi. Freud was euphoric over the satisfaction of having his own place—a little cozy and tight but his very own. Freud had lived well in the ample and comfortable house on Pleasant Street and it would always be his home in a certain sense, but the comfort that he felt in it never matched the pleasure he was having in this first home of his own. If he could only chase away everybody who was dropping over—everybody, that is, except his new neighbor, Savy. However, he realized that for now he would have to share the tree with all comers, friend and foe alike. He was less disturbed by Savy's news of a possible lawsuit than he had been at first, because he thought of a great idea: he would become a promoter, a producer of shows, and involve his neighborly enemies in the future plans for his bridge.

But before getting down to all that, he must face Mrs. Dupre, because he really needed that job as Ben Franklin. Freud ate his bacon and fed a curious grey squirrel crumbs of toast and thought about his boss. From all reports Olivia

Dupre was a very angry woman. Funny, Penny having a temperamental mother. His quiet little tooth fairy must take after her old man!

He looked at his watch—8:30, time to get ready to go to his job, indeed if he still had a job. He was almost afraid to find out. Anyway, it was hard to care, because his mind was on something else, someone with a hearty voice, wide-set eyes and tawny skin. Oh, that burnt-sienna hair and that "Rapunzel, Rapunzel" stuff. His friendly enemy. It was good she was a self-actualizer like himself, and he liked the fact that she was strong looking, not soft and small like Phlox nor pale and tense like Penny. Savernake Bantley was in all ways his kind of woman. It would be nice to try to please her. Freud breathed the air and it never smelled so good. Too bad he had to come down from this happy high and go to work. He'd rather dream dreams, but it was time to be practical.

Now what will I say to Olivia, he thought? He decided to be humble, maybe even apologetic, but his good intentions fled when he got to her office. His sense of fun got the better of him and he found himself soberly quoting Benjamin Franklin. "Mrs. Dupre?" She looked up coldly. "Mrs. Dupre. I have made up a saying: 'Little strokes fell great oaks.' " He was putting her on.

Olivia's eyes flashed. "I'm glad you already know that." She repressed an urge to laugh at the grotesque clown standing before her. He wore two haircurlers over each ear and his wild hair was held in place by a dozen bobby pins and a generous lacquer of hairspray. He had sewn wobbly gold buttons down the front of his corduroy jacket and he wore a red, white, and blue striped foulard around his neck. He probably had stars on his underwear! In fact he was the funniest, most maddening thing she had ever seen. She would not tell him that his real costume had arrived from New York. She hoped it would fit his successor because a successor he would have.

"I see through your disguise now, Freud Freund. You are a master mesmerizer! You conned me and you hypnotized my daughter; you brought disgrace on the Dupre family!" Lighting a cigarette with trembling hands and puffing out a long blast of smoke in his direction, Olivia added between clenched teeth, "Mr. Bantley says I'm not to fire you. But that was yesterday. I hope by today he has changed his mind and I intend to find out. I must have *some* influence around here." She glared at him. "You go about your work. You'll hear from me. Good day, Mr. Franklin."

But the Art and Advertising Director actually had a very big stroke in mind and it was not an easy one to make. She had been up half the night debating with herself whether there was anything to do but resign; and in her despair over the idea of giving up her job, she thought of another way out, which, as much as she begrudged doing it, would probably make these kids give up their devastating activities.

Olivia tried to calm down as she hurried to Brig's office. It was Freud using Penny that infuriated her. She had never believed that could happen! But she was also concerned for her standing with Brig. She had hired Freud and reluctantly agreed to the Saffies. The trouble was all due to her poor judgment and she was desperate for Brig to know how sorry she was. Olivia pushed open his door with a bang and swept into his office where he was working at his desk. She slammed the door behind her and put her back against it. Her long brown batik skirt swirled as she turned and there was gypsy passion in her eyes. Brig looked up from his desk and smiled that smile she couldn't live without. "My dear Livy, you're looking better today.

What energy you have! You must have gotten over the shock of these past few days. How is Rene?" Brig noticed the sparks in her eyes and he wondered what was coming.

"No, Brig, I have not gotten over the shock. I stayed awake all night long worrying and I have come up with a plan for counter-action. Money is the only thing that talks these days. I want you to buy out Freud. I have almost twenty thousand dollars in my savings account—that ought to do it!" she said, throwing her passbook on the desk in front of him. "Take it. It's yours. It should be enough!"

Brig looked at the little green book and stood up while Olivia went on talking and pacing back and forth. "You know how I love this place. It's my life. I don't want to leave it. I want to save it." Her deep, dark eyes looked at him, searching for some sign that he returned her feeling. She added softly, "I'd give my life for Glory Land."

"Olivia, how like you," said Brig. "You have touched me deeply. But I can't take your money." He picked up the bank book from his desk and handed it back to her. She took it reluctantly and turned away from him; what more could she do? She had nothing else to offer. She began to cry. Brig walked over to the sofa, "Come, let's sit and talk." She looked at him and her expression changed.

"No, I have a better idea," he said, springing back to his feet before she could sit beside him. There was a look in her eye that disturbed him. "I've been planning for two weeks to hike to Sweetbriar Springs and see if it's flowing. Come with me. The walk will do us good." Seeing her hesitate, he coaxed, "It is less than a mile. You can make it. Let's go. It's a lovely day and the wild roses are in bloom."

"I'll ruin my pantyhose," whimpered Olivia, turning to leave. "I think I'd rather not." He looked at her legs.

"The exercise will be good for you. Take off your

pantyhose and put on your sneakers while I get my walking boots. We can talk better alone, away from here." The boss didn't usually say personal things. Olivia decided, on second thought, to go. To be in the woods with Brig—it was a lovely idea after all.

A little later as they strolled alone side by side, Olivia felt happy and cheerful again as she usually did when she was with Brig. Perhaps all was not lost if she was regaining her standing with him. She scuffled her feet on the sandy path as she walked and stopped frequently to pick daisies. Brig looked at his watch. If they walked this slowly it would take all day. He had a lot of work to do. Looking down at his companion he said, "Have you ever tasted the water from Sweetbriar Springs, Livy?"

"No, I don't think I ever have." She smiled at him tenderly.

"I must warn you that it has a pungent taste." They approached the springs and Brig took from his pocket a collapsible tin cup. "Here," he said, handing it to her. "You drink first. On second thought, before we taste this nasty stuff, let's sit down over here while I bring you up-to-date on what has happened. First of all, we must be patient. We must lean on the advice of counsel. Attorney Wescott says it may take a couple of weeks to get matters moving. We'll let the lawyers handle everything. Meanwhile, it will be business as usual at Glory Land. We must try very hard to act as though they are not there and that we could care less. Okay? We'll act as though it never happened!"

Olivia exclaimed, "I don't agree. I think we should buy them out with a sum they can't refuse. A good offer would stop this nonsense right away."

"I'll think it over, Olivia. I really will. After all it was your suggestion that set this place on its feet twenty years ago. I haven't forgotten that, Olivia," said Brig. "Now let's drink to our future happiness."

"I'll drink to that!" exclaimed Olivia, her wrath subsiding instantly. She held her nose as she took a sip and looked up at him from under her lovely black brows. She was thinking that she was always happy in Brig's company. Maybe, he felt the same way. Maybe that's why he brought her here—just to be alone with her.

Love Finds a Way

The following day Anna Maria, unable to sleep, walked through the fields at dawn, picking meadow sage and wildflowers as she went. She was worried about the activities of the young people and she sought comfort from nature on this rare June day. Her way led to Glory Land by overgrown trails and came to the river's edge. There the Big Bear ran over great wide beds of smooth rock, swiftly falling through numerous channels, bubbling and fresh, in rivulets over the rock, and streaming with frolic and zest through the slits and furrows. Below the rocks, the shallow pools were sandy and pale, the deep ones green and shadowy, and little trout darted about in quiet places.

Anna Maria, unaccustomed to walking to work, was feeling tired when she came upon this beautiful place to rest. She looked at her watch. It was still early, barely half past seven, and there was time left to linger awhile and read a few Psalms. Choosing her way carefully around the poison ivy on the river bank, she made her way across streams of water and climbed over broken surfaces of rock to a smooth white slab glistening in the morning sun. She sat down there and enjoyed being alone with the beat of her heart and the wind in the trees and the laughter of falling water. Further downstream the river roared through a narrow crevice and fell away into a big whirlpool. Anna Maria watched it for a time and in so doing, an old memory of a terrifying encounter with rushing water came back to her. She was a little girl on holiday with her grandparents, walking down a rock-hewn path through the *Rosenlaui Chute* in Switzerland. The waters from the melting glaciers above were bombing alongside her through the declivity with such power and noise that she fled from what seemed like the most awful place in the world.

But now, grown up, she knew there was a more terrible power worse than any natural power, and that was the power of people when they lose their individual common sense, and for some emotional reason, destroy one another and all that they have achieved. When problems made by man become larger than his ability to handle them, inflamed by evil forces, he takes revenge against his fellow man. She opened her Bible, but one thought led to another.

This new law was a sleeper. It too had a destructive power latent in its hidden consequences. This business of Freud's here at the park might be a reaction of some sort to public law 04Y4. It would bear careful handling; she hoped her boss would understand that.

Anna Maria leaned back on her arms and looked up at the sky. Wasn't it a beautiful day here on the warm rocks? She put away hard thoughts and listened to the wind in the trees and the relentless noise of water. A soft breeze caressed her face. Time passed. She was drawn from her pleasant state of suspension by a familiar voice. "I didn't know you came here."

She opened her eyes and there stood Brigham Bantley. Her heart did a cartwheel. Anna was pleased to see him— too pleased for her own comfort. She smiled at him and said, "This is the first time I've been here. I was taking an early morning walk and I came upon this place. I love water and big flat rocks. When I find a perfect place, I make it my own and it stays with me forever. Somehow I feel as though I've been here before."

"That's strange," he answered. "I love this place too. There is something special about it." For a long time he stood above her watching the river and saying nothing; then he said, "I couldn't sleep last night."

"I couldn't sleep either, Brig. I feel responsible for what has happened because I asked you to hire the young people." She didn't say more, waiting for him to speak. It would do him good to express his feelings to someone. She hoped—what did she hope? She didn't know; she only knew that she cared what he was thinking and wanted everything to come out right for him.

After a time he sat down on the rock beside her, his long lean legs bent at the knee, his knees apart, two tan hairy calves showing above his white socks. Brig looked down at his sneakers rather than at her and his eyes were strained and bleak. Finally he turned and looked at her sadly. "You've asked me to to trust the kids, Anna, and I do. That is, I want to. Do you remember 1968?" She nodded. "Perhaps you've heard what the young people did to Glory Land. They marched here from town and tore down the flags, wrecked the animal exhibit, trampled the flowers and were heading for the Pavillion with bags of excrement to throw on my cooks. If Tony DeLuca hadn't kept his head and intervened, they would have destroyed my life's work. Tony delivered a speech on the privilege of being an American that moved me to tears.

"The demonstrators listened to Tony because he was a workman and not what they considered establishment.

But then their leaders, sensing sympathy towards Tony's dreams for this country, threw eggs and tomatoes at him. I was so ashamed! Before the police came, the local kids began leaving and the others followed. I'll never forget that day! How could the kids destroy what their little town has to offer when there isn't much else? Now their little brothers and sisters are giving me trouble. I can't get over it!"

"I don't wonder," she said. "It is very upsetting."

"Tell me, Anna, you understand children—what do they want? Do they plan to destroy Glory Land?" He stood up and paced back and forth across the rock. Finally he sat down beside her and put his hand on her arm. "Anna Maria, how shall I handle them?"

Anna Maria smiled at her boss. "Handle them with love no matter how hard it seems. They need love. Their world is a pretty shaky place. You'll see—love finds a way."

"I really don't see what love has to do with practical matters like managing a park and kicking out trespassers."

She hesitated. Perhaps this was her opportunity to say what she had on her mind. Anna took off her tennis shoes and put her feet in the river. It was cold. "For some reason I'm thinking of Johnny Appleseed. Remember him? He was the wanderer who walked the country roads of America in the 1830s planting apple cores. Remember the paintings of him with his flowing hair, the mush pan for a hat and the coffee sack for his shirt? He loved animals and knew about herbal medicines and was devoted to his Bible. All his possessions were wrapped in a bandana tied to a stick.

"Today he carries a backpack and a thousand dollars worth of gear and he is seeking what Johnny found. He could be any one of these young people or you or me for that matter. We are all seekers.

"We want to know why we are here and where we are going. We want to enjoy life. But how can we do that with death hanging over us? In these perilous times, no material possessions or personal success can buy us inner peace or send us happily down the road with a full pack.

"What is the answer?" Anna said nothing for a moment. The wind rustled the leaves in the forest. "It's love," she said. "But it's hard to love, isn't it?" She smiled at him. "We can't do it by ourselves. We need God, who *is* love.

"Remember when the Pharisee asked Jesus a question? 'Master, which is the great commandment in the law?' Jesus replied, 'Thou shalt love the Lord thy God with all thy heart, and with all thy soul, and with all thy mind. This is the first and great commandment. And the second is like unto it, Thou shalt love thy neighbour as thyself.'*"

"But how *do* we love?" Brig exclaimed. "What really *is* love?"

"I can't begin to tell you how often I've asked myself that question. The only definition that seems adequate is to say that 'God is love,' shown to us through Jesus Christ. What He reveals to us is love."

When Anna Maria paused a moment, Brig said, "Tell me how I can love my neighbor. I must have an answer for my problem in the oak tree."

"Remember the Golden Rule? Do unto others as you would have them do unto you. It's found in Matthew and Luke. In other words love is responding to the needs of others, as seen through their eyes. But it isn't easy. We don't usually consider the beautiful diversity of human beings, and the variety of needs they have." Anna laughed. "We should become accustomed to seeing something

---

*Matt. 22:37-39

special in everyone and be sensitive to their individuality. I look at you and say, 'God, this is one of the strongest men you've ever created!' "

Brig smiled, a little surprised. "Sometimes I don't feel strong. Not this summer. Not with Lucy gone."

"I know how much you miss her. I miss not having a family. But loneliness reaches out to God and He's there. You know, Brig, we are born alone and we die alone, and we stand before Him alone too, unless we have Jesus for our Intercessor. He meets our needs; He alone hears our prayers. Under His wings He shelters us all in a great big cloud of love!"

"You're such a comfort to me," he said. "We could talk forever, but it's time to get busy." Brig jumped to his feet and helped her up. "You still haven't told me what to do about that overgrown kid in my oak tree. Do you know the French and Indians made a treaty under that tree? We've been ignoring John and playing for time, but obviously we can't go on doing that."

Anna Maria smiled to herself. She had known young John since he was a baby. His enthusiasm, spirit and brain power might well add to Glory Land rather than posing a threat. At least she hoped so. But if all the Safflowers owned that land, there might be some cause for concern. Collectively they were beautiful children, but there were one or two who were capable of making trouble, big trouble.

"Well, does everybody own it?" she asked Brig. Anna was glad to hear they did not. It was Penelope who was Freud's sole partner.

Penelope Dupre! Then the rumors were true. What a surprise. Penny, so quiet and devout, shaking up the establishment! It was hard to believe. "I guess opposites do attract," commented Anna. "How is her mother taking it?"

"Olivia? Olivia's acting more peculiarly than ever," exclaimed Brig. "After all, she must know I don't blame her; but she weeps, she begs, she pleads with me to forgive her. She does everything but offer me herself. Isn't that something? Penny seems like such a timid kid—you wouldn't think she'd cause her mother any trouble." Brig shook his head.

"Brig," said Anna Maria, her hand on his suntanned arm, "let's handle this directly before we panic. Let us bravely walk over there and see for ourselves what they've done. I'm curious, aren't you? Maybe after we look around we can guess what they have in mind. Will they make of it something suitable to these beautiful surroundings?"

"I don't know. I've refused to look. I haven't had the courage. But when I found you here I was hoping you'd suggest it," said Brig.

"And please," commented Anna, "don't threaten them. With Rene so sick, Olivia has no one to turn to but Penelope; she needs to keep her friendship. And why make talk in the village?"

"You're a bundle of common sense, dear friend." Impulsively he gave her a little hug. "Yes, you are my dearest friend," he said looking at her with those purple eyes.

Brig helped Anna Maria over the running water onto the riverbank and held on to her hand as they walked together across the fields to the woods beyond. It felt funny to be holding a man's hand and the fact that he was a married man made it seem not quite right. Anna let go at the earliest opportunity. It was a perfect morning. Butterflies danced, bumblebees visited the flowers and brown thrushes were flying about in the grass, teaching their young ones to fly.

A short walk through the woods brought Anna and Brig to the foot of the magnificent tree where Brig stopped. Brig couldn't help but think that at the foot of this tree Glory Land was born, and he remembered that day long ago here with Lucy.

His thoughts were interrupted by his companion. "I don't see anything," said Anna.

"Wait a minute," said Brig, placing his hands on top of her head. "Now let's both look up when I count three. One. Two. Three." They raised their chins and there high above them was a little tent, a sort of chrysalis on the crotch of the tree. It was hanging by ropes from the higher branches and the limbs of the tree went through its center. From its little deck hung a three-story ladder.

They smiled at each other. "If I were only twenty years younger I'd climb up there!" exclaimed Anna.

"I had a tree fort once in our back yard at Lake Placid!" exclaimed Brig. "We must have a look. I'll have Tony bring the cherry-picker down."

"Wait a minute, Brig. From what you said, this is private property. It might be better to get an invitation first."

"I forgot about that," he said sourly, making a face.

"Wouldn't it be a delightful place to sneak off to with a book when your mother is looking for you to do the dishes?" asked Anna Maria, remembering how it was when she was young.

Brig nodded. "There seems to be no one about. Shall we be courageous and continue on to the Big Bear River to see what has happened to my bridge?"

The middle-aged couple walked along together slowly, expectantly, half afraid to go around the next bend. It was a beautiful morning in the forest. The trail, rocky and rough, was dry and the sun came through the trees giving a soft yellow-green light to the undergrowth. Passing single file up and over the ridge of rock between the tree and the river, they came immediately in sight of the bridge. They stopped in their tracks. There before their eyes was an incredible sight. The once ordinary plank bridge on stone piers was no longer visible. Instead there was a creation which, situated as it was, could only be called magical. There was something mysterious, a little frightening, and very inviting about it. One wanted to cross that bridge and peep into those towers. And the land beyond seemed like an unknown land, the river enticing one to cross over. But should one really cross to the other side?

"How enchanting!" exclaimed Anna.

"It's original, I'll have to say that," murmured Brig, trying to remember how it had looked before.

"Only the children of Tolkien would think of building towers on a humble bridge. I wonder what they plan to do with it. The further tower looks inhabited; see the clothesline strung over the river," said Anna Maria, pointing to their right as they approached a little closer.

"No, no. We'll not allow that. My lawyer is busy getting a court order to prevent its use as a habitation. The new statutes are quite explicit about sewerage facilities. And, another thing, I can deny them access through Glory Land. There's an old road to the north, but it would cost a fortune to bring it to the river. So they can't do a whole lot with this property, except camp on it, which is bad enough!"

"I have an idea," said Anna Maria. "May we sit down?" She paused to gather courage. "Brig Bantley," she began, her brown eyes focusing on him, "I think I know a better way to keep everybody happy." She looked at him, hesitating whether to say it or not, but finally she began. "Before I make my suggestion there's one thing I'd like to say first and that is that I do believe these children have the power to ruin Glory Land. It wouldn't be hard!"

"That's what Olivia says," interrupted Brig. "But first they may find out that I have the power to ruin them! With Judge Freund's present bad reputation it wouldn't be too difficult. That makes one heck of a good club with which to manipulate the press when it comes to his son!"

Anna jumped to her feet and walked back and forth. "Whatever would be gained by that?" she cried. "Let me finish what I was going to say." She fingered the belt on her hop-sacking skirt and there were tears in her eyes. Brig had never seen her upset like this before, and he stood with his hands on his hips and stared at her like a bystander. He could get angry sometimes; apparently she could get angry too. He rather enjoyed seeing her like this and he said nothing.

Finally her agitation subsided. She leaned against a tree and looked at him. "I'm sorry, Mr. Bantley. But can't you see, these children are artists! They have it in them to make something beautiful of this; but to do it they will need help from all of us. Why don't you help them out? I mean really help them. Withdraw your suit, connect them to your sewer system and allow them access through Glory Land!" Her employer looked more than a little disturbed by her suggestion. Seeing the look on his face, Anna Maria hastened to add, "It would be a great tribute to Olivia!"

"You're always thinking of others, aren't you?" said Brig. Anna shrugged. Her employer looked beyond her at the distant peaks, thinking what her suggestion would mean. He had been giving Olivia's idea of buying the property back very serious consideration. After a few minutes he replied, "I hadn't thought of it that way, but it would be something I could do for the Dupres. Maybe Rene would like it too. There's so little I can do for Rene and he did a lot for me. He fought my wars for me." Brig's voice trailed off and his purple eyes were dark.

Anna waited for his answer. He turned and stepped towards her. "I'm not going to be hasty. I'm going to give them time to change their minds. Maybe they'll sell it back to me." Again he was silent. Then he said, "I'm waiting to see what Savy can do. She's my diplomat. In that way she takes after her mother. If anyone can get Freud out of that tree, she can."

"That's good, but don't worry about John. He won't stay long in a tree," said Anna Maria. "His talents demand a wider stage. He'll come down rather soon I predict. I'm sure Tulie must hope so. I don't know how she keeps going."

"You can tell her we're trying to keep it out of the press, if that's any comfort," said Brig.

"Well, I hope so. Would you believe it's 9:30? I'm late for work." She started off the way they had come.

"Don't go that way. Take the old path along the river," instructed Brig. "It's a shortcut to the Pink Pavillion. Come, I'll go along and lead the way." He started off into the woods on a barely discernible trail through the ferns. "I'll have to have these wild berries cut and this path improved, because I'm going to name this Love's Way, short for 'Love Finds a Way'—after you, Anna Maria." She didn't mention that the path was not his to name. Most of it was on Freud and Penny's land. "Tell me one thing more, dear friend; how did you come by your special love for children?" he asked over his shoulder.

Anna Maria, who was stepping carefully along following her boss, was pleased by his question. "I've always loved children. I'm comfortable with them. They're so trusting and have so much individuality and potential. They respond so eagerly to kindness." She laughed, "Would you think me simple if I say I think they're more fun than adults? Remind me sometime to tell you about my own children."

Brig stopped and turned around. "Your children!" he exclaimed. "I didn't know you had any!" He sat down on a fallen log beside the trail and gestured her to sit beside him. She walked past him, saying over her shoulder, "Some other time, sir. I'm late for work."

"Forget it. I'm your boss. I order you to sit down beside me and explain what you said. I want to know all about you and I'm going to sit here till you tell me about your children."

Anna was gratified that this gracious and good man cared that much about her. It was a new experience for her and she turned back and sat nearby. "Let me ask you something first. Have you heard from Lucy?"

"Yes, just a note. She's been to the Gambia. Apparently it wasn't much of a place, but she made a friend there and she has an idea for Glory Land. That's a hopeful sign coming from Lucy! She also said she was sailing south on the *African Prince* for Liberia."

Anna interrupted him. "Lucy went to the Gambia! What a small world this is. I haven't heard of the Gambia for years. Remember my telling you about Isaiah, the starving child, that day we met?" Brig nodded his head. "He was a Gambian." Her voice fell and her thoughts were far away. "But he died. If I'd only had that letter in time," she murmured. "You see, I got this illegible letter from a missionary saying Isaiah had a serious infection. I sent penicillin, but I heard later that it didn't get there in time.

"As for my other orphans, what shall I say? Soon after I lost Isaiah I lost my fiancé, Neil White. Oh, he didn't die, we broke up." She laughed. "I was heartbroken and I had to have someone to care about, so I adopted other orphans. Of course I didn't really adopt them. I have helped them a little, that's all. Isaiah was the first of more than a dozen—Diago and Mikado and Erika and Haim, to mention a few. I get a new one as often as I can afford it. I'll show you their pictures when I have time. Now I must go—the antique collectors are coming." She jumped to her feet and strode off along the stream. "I can find the way—Love's Way," she called in a firm voice. "Goodbye, Mr. Bantley."

Brig stood and watched her go.

Tatty Joins the Station Wagon Set

Stevie and his friends from the Hill spent their spare time at Tatty's place working on the Chevy, and now it stood restored to its former beauty and ready to go. It had a trim shiny green cab with a smooth, wooden body, looking something like a jade and gold beetle. Even the shed in which it stood was refurbished as a garage, and a license plate had been secured. Stevie had had trouble convincing Tatty about the necessity for insurance because she knew she wasn't going to run over a single human soul—not her—and Freud had been summoned to explain to her that it was compulsory.

Tomorrow Mark was coming to take her for her driver's test. (He had carefully hidden the fact that he was doubtful of the outcome.) Tatty assured the Saffies that she had been practicing her driving—small matter that the practicing had taken place forty years ago and she was "psyched up" to drive Route 9 along which she had walked so many miles. Like Mark Twain knew the Mississippi, she knew Route 9. She knew every hill, every bend, every pothole. She was eagerly planning the whole trip. When she passed Filch Brothers' Store she intended to honk loudly and turn up her nose; she just didn't like those Filch Brothers. No one ever likes his creditor.

While she waited expectantly for the morrow to arrive, Tatty sat on her rocker and spoke to the cat in her lap. She was worried about the test. "I didn't used to have no driver's license," she said. "I guess I don't have no need now." Then she had one of her flashes of inspiration. "I'll drive right up to Safflower Hill and I'll show 'em I don't need no license. Just give 'em a little surprise."

So Tatty went inside and, despite the fact it was eighty degrees in the sun, she dressed up in her muskrat coat with the pink patch under the arm. She'd look pretty; Irv would want her to. She put on a dark red lipstick somewhat southeast of her mouth and grinned at herself in the broken glass over the sink. Then she tied a purple ribbon around her grey-black curls. She looked at herself again and was satisfied that she could pass for a member of the station wagon set. She was ready to drive.

Her new Chevy '46 wagon was also ready for its maiden voyage and stood outside the iron gate pointing down the road, which had been widened by her young friends. Tatty got inside, Whiskers on the seat beside her and Shadow in the back on her buffalo rug. Tatty's sight wasn't good anymore, so for some time she pulled and turned knobs on the dashboard. Finally, as her eyes grew accustomed to the light, she started the motor and the car took a giant leap forward. Then, after a short stall, she was off—jerking down the drive and into the woods. Somehow, by the grace of God, she managed to avoid every tree and fly out onto the highway without mishap.

Tatty didn't drive very fast, no more than 15 m.p.h., and though she smelled sumpin' bad for a time, she paid no heed. The feel was comin' back. Sniffin' again, she said it must be the brakes and she took them off; then did she go:

25—30—35! Then, remembering how she used to love to coast down hills, she turned off the key, put her slippered feet on the dash and had a nice coast down one hill and up the next, finally coming to a slow halt on the road beside Harry Homer's Steel and Scrap Yard.

"How did you like that?" she asked her silent companions. "Let's do that some more." But try as she could, she couldn't get the motor to start again. So Tatty just sat there in the middle of the road, waitin' for sumpin' to happen.

Sure enough, pretty soon out waddled Harry, pulling up his pants; he came to see what that antique Chevy was doing outside his place. If he could pick it up for two hundred dollars it would be a good buy. Not many like that left—in good condition too.

"Oh," he said, doffing his hat from his bald head, "it's you. Got a new car, eh?"

"Yep, it's the best ever made, but tonight it's like me—it doesn't go very far and it doesn't go very fast. It has to get used to going again."

"Maybe it needs gas."

"Gas? You mean benzine? Why, I do remember it uses that. You got any?"

"No, but I can get you some." Harry was very chivalrous to women. "Let's push your car inside my lot for safekeeping while we go get the gas." Tatty dismounted and it was no trouble to push the little Chevy. Then the fat man in the red suspenders held open the door of his 1975 Cadillac coupe for Ms. Kaleri Tuttle and they drove off to get some of that thrifty gas on the far side of Temagami Springs. Harry was enjoying himself as much as Tatty. He hadn't been out with a woman since Ruth died.

"My, this is comfort," sighed Tatty. "What are all 'em buttons? Don't think I could drive one of these. You know," she added, looking at him mischievously, "I got no license!"

"No license, woman. Then you can't drive. I bet you have no insurance either!"

"Maybe yes, maybe no."

"Never mind, I'm going to drive you home," said Harry helpfully. "I'd like to see ol' Tyler Lansdown's gate again. I hear it looks real swell. I sort of miss it at the junk yard." Tatty grinned. A friend of her gate was a friend of hers. A short while later they stood side by side in the cool of the evening before the big gate in mutual admiration of the intertwining leaves and the two big hearts.

Tatty asked, "Do you like fishin'?"

No one could describe the smile on her new friend's face. "Do I like fishing!" Harry exclaimed. "There's nothing I like better, except maybe sellin' junk."

Showdown at the Fontaines'

The following week, Jean Fontaine, in a black metallic swim suit, and Frank in blue tennis shorts lay on lounge chairs beside their pool. It had been a hot, dry day and Frank looked drawn and pale. His bare chest was thin and his grey eyes sunken beneath his brows. He looked older than forty-five.

It had become their evening ritual to have a scotch and soda beside the swimming pool, but there was little conversation between them. At length Jean sat up and smashed her cigarette into the ash tray. Then resetting her chair to a more upright position, she remarked, "The pool needs cleaning." When that statement fell on deaf ears she tried again. "Ye gods, isn't life drab? Here we sit doing the same old thing day after day. And I'm just a slave to bank statements, dentist appointments and supermarkets. I telephoned my psychiatrist—wouldn't you know he's going on vacation and can't see me for two weeks? How does he think I'm going to get along until then? Doctors are just rip-offs. He could care less about my recovery."

Her mentioning doctors made Frank wonder if he should tell her about the pains in his chest.

"Aren't you going to say something?" snapped Jean, a

look of disgust on her dissipated but still beautiful face.

"When you mentioned doctors I was just wishing you'd drive me to the doctor tomorrow."

"Me, drive you!" she exclaimed. "That would be a switch."

"I just wanted you to try my new Cougar, that's all," he replied, deciding not to tell her about the pains.

"Well, it's not a Lincoln; it's not even an automatic. You know I can't drive a stick shift." She intentionally didn't drive much to keep François from becoming too independent of her. She put a cigarette between her teeth and went on. "I don't drive your car unless it's an emergency—you're having a heart attack or something."

Frank took a deep breath and it hurt. Didn't this woman think she might, someday, have to get along without him? He'd already outlived his father by two years. Maybe his turn was coming. Perhaps she should be thrown on her own resources soon—before he died. Perhaps if he were not to sign 04Y4 it would be better for her.

She interrupted his thoughts. "Drive you to the doctor's, did you say? Why, you've never been sick a day in your life except for that cold the day Phlox was born." He winced. She never failed to remind him of that cold as though he'd flunked his first day of fatherhood because he couldn't hold the baby.

"No, I'm not sick. I'm just having a check-up," he said with a sigh. He fell silent, but he was thinking: after my appointment I'll go out to the new house and take a long swim and if the news is bad, who knows, we may not even have to worry about 04Y4. Only his brother knew that his home life was hell, that when it came to wives, the advertising of Mrs. François Philippe Fontaine was better than the product. She filled him with disgust because she was so completely absorbed in herself. She seemed to be getting worse. Or maybe it was him.

Unaware of his thoughts, Jean ranted on. "It's too bad you sent Phlox to Tulie's this summer. She could drive both of us around. There must be some benefits to having a child, although I haven't found any." It was Jean who had sent Phlox away, imposing her on her old roommate.

Frank looked woebegone and, putting his hand on his throbbing head, he replied, "I'm glad she's at Tulie's. It will be good for her to be around a wholesome family."

"You always did like Tulie, didn't you? After all these years you're still fond of her, and you expect me—" She got up abruptly and went into the house. "I need another drink."

Maybe he was still fond of Tulie. He began to hope that the doctor would find he was okay after all. Frank closed his eyes. Jean returned and stood over him, a highball in her hand. She looked down and said, "Well, if you can't think of anything to say I'm going out to the lake and see if the plumbers have moved my sunken tub to where it should have been in the first place. Why don't you keep an eye on things instead of leaving everything to me?" He didn't open his eyes and she went back inside.

Phlox Fontaine was also on her way to the house under construction. She had news for her mother. Ordinarily Phlox didn't tell her mother her plans. However, now that Freud was gone she had decided to move out of the Freund's home. If she didn't tell her mother, Mrs. Freund would certainly do so.

Arriving ten minutes after her mother, Phlox parked the Honda behind the workmen's shack. She wondered if Freud had got the bill for it yet; it didn't matter. Soon she wouldn't need it anyway.

Phlox found her mother stretched out on the half-built deck, a copy of *Cosmopolitan* over her eyes. "Mother, Mother, wake up." Phlox lifted the magazine and Jean opened one eye.

"Mother, Freud has invited me up the ladder. I'm going to him tonight. Here's some stuff I won't be needing." She dropped a bundle of clothes on the deck beside her mother.

"What did you say?" replied Jean, sitting up. "Make sense. You're going where?"

"Up the ladder."

"Up what ladder?"

"To live with Freud in the tree in Glory Land!" exclaimed Phlox.

"You-are-go-ing-to-live-with-Freud in a tree!" Jean shrieked, her eyes flashing and her voice rising.

"That's right. He lives in a tree in Glory Land. And I'm going to him tonight!"

"And you're not married," shrieked Jean. "You're going to disgrace me in front of all of Temagami Springs? You'll be the talk of the town. You can't do this to me!" Her face was as red as her hair.

"I'm not doing anything to you, Mother. I'm doing my own thing. Any girl in town would go to Freud if he snapped his fingers."

"With a father like his, I'm not surprised; that family will do anything! Think what people will say! My beautiful daughter who can have any man she wants, living with a fool in a tree!" Jean was almost hysterical.

"I'm going now, Mother," said Phlox, walking to the steps. "If you don't say anything—not even to Dad—no one will hear about it." She shrugged her shoulders. "Who knows? I may marry him real soon. After all, I do have certain charms and I know how to use them."

Jean knew it was hopeless to argue with Phlox. "Go then, but don't come back home without Freud. You'll see. Men aren't worth all the trouble. You don't know anything about men. Go live in a tree for all I care. You're no good anyway. You're nothing but a tramp!"

Phlox didn't hear her mother. She hopped on the cycle and roared off. It was high adventure to be going to live with a man in a tree. She'd pull the ladder up behind her and look down into the sad and wistful faces of Penelope Dupre and Savy Bantley. She drove fast because it looked like it might rain.

Bantley Bitter Water

That same afternoon, Savernake Bantley, dutifully following her father's instructions, headed for the hills beyond the river. She carried along an empty Coke bottle. Pausing a moment beneath the oak tree, Savy obeyed her impulse and called in low tones, "Rapunzel, Rapunzel."

Immediately Freud looked out between the big green leaves and answered, "Hey down there, wait for me. I'm coming right away." He swung down a big rope and landed beside his startled neighbor. "Hi!"

"Now you're playing Tarzan," said Savy. He's just a big kid, she was thinking.

Freud was so happy to see her. He grinned at her while he straightened his twisted pants. Then, gesturing toward a fallen log, he said, "Have a seat." Savy brushed away a red ant and straddled the log facing him. The two people appraised each other up and down, and both began to talk at once. There was so much to discuss. They deliberately avoided any mention of recent events but talked about everything else from old high-school friends to architecture and politics.

Savy was thinking he had more to him than she thought. "What do you really want out of life, Kingjohn?"

After a long moment he answered, "I'm not sure. I have so many interests, maybe too many interests. My first idea is to develop my kingdom, as you call it, so that it will support me. I've never seen a place with so much potential! After that I'll just let life take me by the hand. I've never been bored so far. What do you want?"

"Well," she said thoughtfully, putting the coke bottle in her pocket, "right now, I'm standing still. Obviously I can't be my father's errand girl forever. One thing I know, I expect a great deal from life. I thought for a while that I just wanted to get married." She was thinking of Jack. "But now I want a career and friends and eventually my 2.1 children— and a husband, of course, a man who will love me and share his ideas with me and listen to mine, a man who will rush to my side to sustain me in time of need, who will help me to be all that I am capable of being, who will love our children as much as I shall and enjoy them for themselves, and who will comfort and care for me all of my life. Is that too much to ask?"

"No, indeed it's not," answered John. "I hope you find all that and more, because you're no ordinary girl. You should look for someone just like yourself!" He was thinking he might know someone who would like to try to measure up. He climbed up on a fallen tree and walked along it like a balance beam, balancing himself precariously. "Say, where are you going with that bottle? Don't tell me that this is Green-up Day in my kingdom?" he said, jumping off to keep from falling.

"I'm on an errand for Dad, what else?" she replied, happy over Freud's compliment. "He's sending me to Sweetbriar Springs for a test sample of water."

"May I go with you to the springs? Maybe they're on my property and I can bottle water. I'll advertise: 'Live a long life, drink Freud's Super Special Mineral Tonic,' " he said eagerly, projecting his voice like a patent medicine man.

"They are *not* on your property," said Savy firmly. "Our attorney made sure of *that*. Furthermore, the water doesn't taste good; but for your information, legend says that it has certain special properties."

"What kind of properties?"

She hesitated, looking at him askance, "To be exact, aphrodisiac properties. Especially for men," she added to make it sound more interesting.

Freud uttered a "wow-ooey" and chinned himself on a nearby maple tree. "To think it's been there all this time and I haven't drunk any! Let's go try it at once."

Savy made a face at him, then smiled her wide smile showing her perfect teeth. One couldn't help but laugh with this guy. Somehow he made ordinary things seem special— like an errand for six ounces of bitter water.

She was still chuckling as they crossed the bridge and stopped in to say hello to Penny who was working industriously fixing up a tea room. Penny followed them to the door and watched as they vanished into the woods. Where were they going in such a chummy fashion and laughing all the way?

In fifteen minutes Freud and Savy came to a wet place in the path. An old pipe stuck out of the weedy bank and a rusty chain hung down from it, its tin cup long since gone. Water was falling from the pipe into a catch basin.

"Ladies first," said Freud, taking the coke bottle from her hand and filling it with cold clear water. Savy sniffed; there was a vague sulfuric smell about it and she wrinkled her nose. "I dunno whether I care for any," she replied, hesitating to take it.

"Are you superstitious or just too straight to try Bantley

Bitter Water?"

Savy hated that word "straight." With fire in her eyes she gulped down the entire bottle and filled herself another. "How does that grab you?" she asked, tossing back her long red hair with a quick motion of her head.

"Well, it depends," said Freud, smiling down at her eagerly. "How do you feel? We must be scientific about this."

"I feel warm," Savy answered, taking off her over-blouse.

"Well, do I look any different to you?" he asked, putting his face right next to hers.

"Maybe," she replied very tentatively.

"Am I the one guy in the world you yearn for?"

"Well, you're the only one around," she answered in jest.

"Ah-ha. So you do feel something!" He backed away. "Now, I'll drink." He drank the pungent water in one draft and quick as light he gathered her around the waist and kissed her.

She pummeled him feebly and then for a long moment she gave in. It was good to feel a man's strong arms about her again. But her heart was wary. Watch out, it said. Remember Jack and the promises he made. Be careful. You know this guy's an operator. He's got his chunk of Glory Land and now he wants you. Well, you aren't that easy. Anyway he's supposed to be Penny's man—at least Penny thinks so. He probably kisses every girl he meets.

She jumped back. "Don't trespass again, Kingjohn— kissing me just because you drank this water. You're putting me on. I don't feel a thing. Not even after two glasses. So keep away from me!"

"Maybe you'll have a delayed reaction," observed Freud with a smile on his face. "Let's go. It's going to rain." Big dark cumulous clouds were gathering overhead and it looked as though it might rain any moment. They hurried down the hill to the river and Savy left Freud at the tree. Her dad would be expecting her back with the sample. As she crossed behind the theater toward the offices she heard the putt-putt of a motor, and looking to her left, she caught a glimpse of a vivid green helmet moving through the trees. Motorcycles were forbidden in the park; who could be brassy enough to be riding through Glory Land on a motorcycle? She hoped it wasn't some girl on her way to visit Kingjohn. Savy was worried at the thought, because Freud had drunk an awful lot of that bitter water. Maybe *he* would have a delayed reaction!

Up a Tree

The person in a green helmet was not the only one on the way to the tree. That same hot evening in July there came another visitor. It was little Bucky Sanders. The very day Bucky first heard about the pod in the tree (he called it a fort) and every day thereafter, after supper, he pedaled out to stare at it. He bumped along over rocks and stones on his hand-me-down bicycle, bounced over back paths to get there unobserved, and now he stood again tonight at the foot of the tree.

When he looked around for a good spot to park his bike he noticed a blue Honda under the red oak. It looked familiar. The ten-year-old adventurer leaned his bike against a pine tree and locked it to an old chain, a cow tether which he found there.

There were sounds of voices high above and one was a girl's voice; probably it belonged to his friend, Penny Dupre. Bucky Sanders cleared away some sticks and stones and sat down to wait for Penny to come down. Maybe she'd ask Freud to let him go up into the fort. It was hot even in the forest, but it looked cool up there in the leaves. Bucky prepared for a long wait. Sitting under the tree, he looked around and wondered why that blue Honda looked familiar.

He had seen it before! Taking his notebook and pad from his pocket (he loved to make notes and his pockets were full of pencil stubs and animal erasers from his dentist) he wrote, "Blue Honda. License number 1687." A little while later someone over on the bridge turned on a stereo and the sounds of country music came through the forest. Bucky laid down his notebook, picked up a stick and sat tapping the roots of the tree in time to the music. He'd like to be a drummer some day—that is, unless he became a detective.

Now and then the sounds of music were drowned out by the low rumble of distant thunder and a rush of fine rain. The canopy of leaves above him was thick and it was dry around the trunk, but once in a while, a few drops of rain touched Bucky's face. Just in case it rained harder, Bucky (who was a scout and always prepared) put down his stick and went to his bicycle basket and brought back a yellow poncho. Putting it around him, he resumed his vigil. The voices above were low and indistinguishable.

The female voice he heard above him was not Penny's of course. Penny was indoors in her new home on the bridge praying. Under the strain of adapting to her exciting new life and worrying about her mother's fury and her dad's health, Penny began to spend a lot of time on her knees seeking God. Absorbed as she was, she did not see Bucky under the tree. Nor had she seen Phlox coming. If she had seen Phlox coming, headache or no headache, she would have rushed over to the tree immediately. Penny was not an aggressive person, but she was so utterly devoted to Freud that if she had known that Phlox had arrived with her belongings, prepared to move into the tree, she would certainly have done anything she could to protect him. But as it happened she was otherwise engaged and Phlox arrived at the foot of the tree at an opportune moment.

Freud had already grown careless and left the ladder hanging down. No one saw her mount the rungs; on the way up, her backpack wobbled so much it threatened to throw her off the ladder. However, Phlox was slight of build and agile and, after a small scare, she made it safely to the top. Before she announced herself, she wiped her rosy cheeks with a Kleenex, ran a comb through her hair, squirted herself with fragrant musk oil and only then did she tap softly on the door. In a moment the flap was pushed aside and Freud looked out.

"Oh, it's you. How did you get here? Go on home, I'm taking a nap."

"No, Freud, let me come in. I'm lonely," said Phlox. "I need someone to talk to. I don't have any friends since you left. I'm not accepted around here and I'm so lonely." Freud hesitated. He rarely felt lonely to the point of despair because of the enormous spirit inside him but, nevertheless, sometimes there were little failures and little pangs that reminded him of his human frailty. He could empathize with Phlox. The poor chick didn't have a friend in all the world—even her mother didn't love her. He hesitated just long enough to be caught off guard and Phlox slipped past him into the pod. Freud was wearing only his undershorts. While her back was turned, he reached quickly behind him for a towel and snatched it to him, wrapping it around his hips. He didn't want her saying she'd seen him in his underwear. Then he turned from the door. "Sit down, kid," he said, shoving her into the corner, "while I dress for company." He stepped backwards up onto the higher level and put on his jeans. Then he sat and looked down at her; he had noticed that to sit above and look down on someone sometimes has an intimidating effect. However, it was a useless idea.

Phlox was curled in the corner with her chin on her knees, staring up at him from beneath her painted eyelids with a look both wounded and inviting. Her soft blonde hair curled up from her damp neck and her skin was flushed. She smelled like a flower in an English garden. "Have you missed me as much as I missed you?" she asked, leaning her back against the wall and lifting her arms behind her head— a provocative pose considering her skimpy yellow bodysuit.

Freud said nothing. She rolled her blue eyes upwards. "It is so beautiful way up here. It's pure poetry. I could stay here the rest of my life." She shut her eyes. "I could design clothes here," she murmured. "It's all I've ever wanted to do."

Oh, no, you can't stay here, thought Freud to himself as he said aloud, "Maybe you think it's delightful up here, but I've been in this tree for thirty days and I have cabin fever." He had forgotten that she designed clothes and he decided not to ask her about that; the less conversation the better when you meet a dangerous person. Nevertheless, in spite of his decision, he heard himself saying, "So you are lonely. Well, aren't we all? You have to fight it by doing something you like to do. Take me—I've never had so much fun in all my life as I'm having now. I haven't time to think about myself. There's joy in creating something, in solving the problems you've laid out for yourself." (He smiled a private smile. And in taking on a big man like Brig Bantley, he thought.) "Furthermore, life is ticking by, minute by minute. We can't waste any of it. Have you ever noticed what happens when people get to be forty?" Phlox's expression showed that he had asked a question unworthy of an answer, so he continued his speech. "To put it bluntly, you can't go on forever being a scenery cat!"

"A what?" she asked.

"A scenery cat. That's a lion that just decorates the ring but doesn't perform." He paused a second and Phlox fiddled with her shoestring. "What I'm saying is that you have to do something with your life. You can't trade on your looks forever!"

Her mouth drooped like a sad fish and she bit her lower lip. She looked hurt. Seeing her distress, Freud quickly changed his tone. "I bet you design beautiful clothes. Why don't you make sketches for all the kids around this place? Some idea of yours might catch on here in Glory Land and sweep right across the country. You have to think big, dream big!" He gestured with his arms and hit the wall with his hand. "Ouch." It hurt, which consoled his visitor.

"But I haven't any place to work," she said sadly. "I can't get an inspiration in your mother's place—all that musty, old-fashioned stuff. It's suffocating!" She brightened as she said, "I could work here—or on the bridge!" The bridge would be a better place, but Penny was the troll down there.

Oh, no, you won't, thought Freud, you'll not spoil a good thing. Aloud he observed, "You were considering the Hill, weren't you? There's already one artist up there—Mark Sanders. In fact we'll soon be selling his toys in our gift shop on the bridge. You could design and make something to sell. Go on home and get started." Freud stepped down from his perch on the upper level and pulled her by the arm. He spoke roughly. "Come on. I can't have company tonight. Some of us work for a living. I have to do research for the exhibit coming up."

Just as he said that, there was a clap of thunder and a sudden rush of wind and rain on the roof. The sky blackened and the treehouse swayed on its nylon lashings.

"There's a storm coming," cried Phlox. "I can't go home when there's lightning. It isn't safe."

"I guess not," said Freud reluctantly. "Well, sit down then. Here's Kurt Vonnegut's latest book. Read it while I study, and when it stops raining I'll drive you home. You didn't bring my ten-speed, did you?" She shook her head from side to side and he failed to notice a certain look of satisfaction in her eyes.

Twenty feet below, Bucky Sanders was huddling under his yellow poncho. He had just recognized the blue Honda as belonging to that girl he met, the one who climbed through the cellar window. And when the lightning flashed, he called out to ask them if he could come up, but they didn't hear him.

Freud sat on the floor, his head in a book—*A Life Of Ben Franklin*. The thunder rumbled far off. He looked over at his guest. "Did you know," he asked Phlox, "that Ben Franklin actually electrocuted a chicken and gave it mouth to mouth resuscitation? He was a lightning freak like me. I just love storms, don't you? In fact I'm going to sit out in my lookout and watch the storm break. Want to join me?"

"Oh, no!" Phlox exclaimed, horrified. "I'll do no such thing. I'm terrified of lightning! Why did you have to tell me about that chicken?" she moaned.

Freud opened a flap in the side wall and climbed out onto the deck. The forest was unusually silent and still and bright green. The thunder rumbled. "What's this doing here?" he asked, finding Phlox's backpack and setting it inside the pod.

Phlox, with him gone, had time to plan her next move. Of one thing she was certain, she would not go back to Tulie's house. She might someday go to Safflower Hill, but not until she had something substantial to take with her to buy herself an executive position. After all, her daddy was just as rich and important as Mark's. If Mark Sanders didn't wash dishes or run the vacuum then neither would she.

Phlox had noticed that with men, if you give a little you could sometimes get a lot, that is if you pick a man with a lot to give. Freud wasn't worth all that much to her and he wasn't particularly her type. Furthermore, he seemed impossible to seduce. But, at the moment, he was her only friend, except for Stevie. Dumb Stevie, he couldn't even afford a comb or shampoo. She knew all about Mark Sanders; she could fall for him with his shiny black hair and his gorgeous beard and soulful eyes. Yes, he was the big attraction at the Hill. But there was no way she was going to leave this tree tonight.

So Phlox prepared to stay just where she was. She unrolled her sleeping bag and took off her knit shirt and jeans and sat there in her tiny bikini underwear. Phlox smiled as she thought how surprised Freud was going to be; if he didn't want her, he'd have to get her out of the tree and first he'd have to dress her—that just might not be too easy. She lay down upon the bag. At that moment the lightning flashed, lighting up the pod with an intense green flare. The thunder crashed almost simultaneously. Phlox buried her head in her sleeping bag and screamed and screamed.

Outside, water came down in great torrents. Driven by turbulent winds the rain bounced in a fine spray from the limbs and ran over the leaves. The trees stirred in all their cells, swaying and shivering with joy. The rain fell in great bursts and ran over the earth on its way to the river.

Freud sat through the downpour. His face shone at the magnificence of the storm, and he stared in awe as the whole forest was lit by a supernatural light. Water, funneled by the leaves above, poured over his head and onto his chest. He was carried away by the sensual pleasure of the cold rain on his upturned face. The thunder claps grew louder, closer, more startling, and the smell of ozone permeated the forest.

Suddenly the air was rent by an unearthly illumination, a helix of ions descended from the sky and Freud's hair stood on end. Neither he nor his guest heard the ungodly crash that followed as the lightning hit the neighboring pine and went to ground through a chain, an old bicycle and a blue Honda. The treehouse dangled at a precarious angle. Everything was still. As suddenly as it had begun, the rain stopped and the evening sun streamed forth and penetrated the wet forest with shafts of pale yellow light. The woods lay quiet—thankful—refreshed. And after a time a siren sounded, coming closer and closer.

"Anna Maria," said Tulie into the telephone. "How glad I am to reach you. Yes, I know, I don't like to telephone in a lightning storm either, but Phlox is missing—gone—clothes, Honda, everything. No, I can't believe she's gone home. I tried the Royal Purple. She's not there. She's been bird-dogging Freud. You don't suppose she's gone to that tree? Oh, Anna Maria, that would be awful!"

At that moment Tulie's house was lit by a flash of lightning and a frightening crash followed almost at once. "You say oak trees attract lightning. Oh, Anna! Yes, I heard that awful crash. Five seconds you say? Something tells me we should go see if they are all right. I'll be over to pick you up as soon as I find my raincoat. Oh, Anna, Jean will be furious with me. I should never have undertaken such responsibility." Tulie searched for her car keys; finding them, she bolted through the kitchen door towards her car.

In a few minutes they were on their way, speeding over black, wet roads to Glory Land. As they pulled up at the gatehouse an ambulance shot out over the lawns, bypassing the gate, and headed into town. Tulie Freund and Anna Abendtal circled the fountain and chased after the ambulance. "My God, it must be my son!" exclaimed Tulie.

New York (UPI)—The stock market slumped yesterday in heavy profit taking but American Telephone, the Big Board's volume leader, rose 5 points to continue its summer's climb. The rise is attributed to a recent forecast by a leading brokerage house that earnings for the quarter will be up almost fifty percent over the preceding quarter.

Savernake County Medical Center

At midnight Anna Maria telephoned Brig from the hospital to tell him of the accident. The children were in shock, but they would recover; their parents had been notified. Brig was appalled and he knew that people would ask him for an explanation. He tried to tell himself it was not his fault in any way; but the tormenting thought that he should have interrupted the whole caper was enough to send him to Glory Land in the middle of the night.

He went at once to the tree in his jeep. Branches were down and it took some time to reach the scene. Apparently lightning struck the pine and ran across to the cycle under the oak with such force as to loosen the moorings and toss the kids about. He would call the tree surgeon to come out and Bill Jong to take photos for the insurance company first thing in the morning. Now he must find out what happened. There was a faint glow of an oil lamp in one of the tower windows.

Mr. Bantley knocked on the door and Penny answered. "Penny, did you see the lightning strike the tree?" he asked. Penny had been crying, but she motioned him to come inside the gloomy room and she poured him a cup of tea. Had he come to tell her that Freud was dead?

Seeing the frightened expression on her tear-stained face, Brig said, "They're going to be all right. Now tell me what happened, Penny." He placed his tape recorder on the table between them, the question of liability on his mind.

Penny responded with a burst of speech. "Mr. Bantley, the storm came up very quickly. I wanted to go into town for cupcakes, but I didn't dare leave. I'm afraid of lightning. I stayed back from the windows and then I thought of Freud in the tree and I wondered too if Bucky Sanders might have been caught out in the rain. We're good friends, Bucky and I. He's ten years old." She babbled on. "You know how fascinated kids are by tree forts. So Bucky's been over here every evening. Anyway, there was this terrific fall of rain about nine o'clock and I looked out—nervous, you know—maybe the river was rising. I was worried about Bucky, so I went to get my raincoat to run up to the top of the rock and see if I could see him. Just then there was this terrible crash; the lightning struck close by.

"I got to the tree right afterwards. His bike lay on the ground but Bucky wasn't there. The ladder was dangling by one rope and I rushed back to phone for an ambulance.

"I was trying to figure out how to get up into the tree when the rescue squad came. After they'd gone, I came back here and collapsed. It's all so dreadful. We had such beautiful plans, Freud and I. Did you know, Mr. Bantley, that I have invested all my savings in this project?" She saw the look of incredulity on his face. "I know what you're thinking about me. But that's not the real me. That's just what people see. Only God knows what I'm really like. Do you think He was trying to destroy me for doing this to you and Mom?" She laid her head on her arms and began to cry.

Brig swallowed hard and patted her on the back, seeking to comfort her. He was strangely impressed by Penny's investing her savings in this incredible stunt. "Do you know, Penny, my customers are excited over what you have done? 'Have you seen the quaint bridge?' 'I wonder what it's going to be.' 'Why I don't remember this from last year!' I even heard one say, 'I didn't know Mr. Bantley had so much imagination!' For that compliment alone I owe you kids something in return."

"Tell me how I can help you." Penny lifted her eyes with a look of innocent hope and at that moment, Brigham Bantley made his decision, the one which had been troubling him so much: he would help the kids as Anna Maria had suggested. Somehow that would be better than Olivia's plan to buy them off. And Anna was right about something else too. Freud had come down from the tree; maybe not the way Anna anticipated, but he had come down! Brig Bantley smiled.

"Now you get some sleep, Penny, and I'll come back tomorrow and drive you to the hospital. And don't worry about anything. We'll work things out together," he said, reassuringly.

The residents of Temagami Springs who did not hear about the accident on the 1 A.M. radio broadcast heard it in the morning on the television news: "In a brief storm last night three young people, children of well-known citizens, were struck by lightning, which hit the famous three-hundred-year-old oak tree in Glory Land. Buckminster Sanders, Phlox Fontaine and John Freund III were taken to the Savernake County Medical Center where they are expected to recover. Mr. Freund had recently taken up residence in the oak. The extent of damage to the fine old tree is unknown as the owner could not be reached for comment."

The question on everybody's mind, that is everybody

who had not already heard of the goings-on at the park, was "What were they doing in that tree?"

By morning phones were ringing all over town. What had those kids been doing? Why were they allowed there? Was John Freund's son running around with that girl? Who was she anyway? What about the tree? Was it destroyed?

Word spread and everyone wanted to see the now famous tree. The whole town apparently loved that tree more than any other. Tony DeLuca spent his Monday off keeping people from trampling on the wet lawns and gardens on their way to the scene.

It was the most exciting local event since 04Y4 and almost as disturbing to those who were involved.

Tallulah Freund and Anna Abendtal sat in the hospital coffee shop, too tired from their all-night ordeal to go home to bed. But they were relieved now that the children were recovering and out of danger. Freud had been transferred from intensive care and, unless his mother could prevent it, he would probably return to his tree in three or four days.

On the other hand Phlox Fontaine and Bucky Sanders had suffered more extensive injuries and would remain in the hospital for at least five days. Phlox had been hit by a branch that fell into the pod, and she had sustained a long gash on her leg that required thirty stitches to close. Bucky was suffering from shock and torn ligaments in his shoulder. It seems he had climbed up the ladder and lifted the limb from Phlox's leg.

Tulie and Anna talked about all these things as they sat alone in the coffee shop after the staff left for their morning duties. "I wonder when Jean will come," said

Tulie. "I don't really want to run into her. She'll never forgive me."

"Not forgive you. What do you mean?"

"She'll blame me. She always blames someone when things go wrong. I could not have prevented Freud's buying that property. Just between us I think he was escaping from Phlox. I know he didn't invite her there. But Jean will never speak to me again. She's already blaming John for destroying her marriage."

"John," said Anna Maria. "Have you notified him?"

"No. No, he can't be reached. I think he had a seaplane fly him to some remote lake in Quebec. Freud will be better before John could hear of it. Anyway, John is angry at our boy for costing him his best client—Glory Land, of course. And I have to say Freud did do that to his father," said Tulie. Her face showed the strain she was under.

She lit a rare cigarette and continued. "I can understand my son. He's looking for his own life." Her voice trailed away and she stared out the window. "You are my dearest friend, Anna, and I have to talk to someone. I am so low I can't go on, unless I can find some new purpose to my life." She looked at Anna's face, which was full of concern. "I can't live a second-hand existence as Mrs. John Freund any longer. In just being his wife I'm nothing. The children don't need me. I feel like I don't even exist. I'm the loneliest person in the world."

"Maybe I could use you at Glory Land. I'll find you a job, because I know exactly how you feel. That's how it was with me before Brig came along."

"Really? You like it at Glory Land, don't you?" asked Tulie, looking at her good friend with a certain question in her eye.

Anna Maria blushed and said, "Oh, look, here comes

Surtsey."

"I know. I know. I've noticed the new color in your cheeks," said Tulie, refusing to be put off. "That's how every woman reacts to Brigham Bantley. He thinks a lot of you too." She turned around and beckoned to Surtsey. "Thanks for the job offer, but I need more than a summer's employment—I need a new life!"

They were joined shortly by Surtsey Sanders who heaved a big sigh as she set down her breakfast tray. "What a long night, but Bucky's going to be all right!" She didn't tell them her real heartache. Bud and Mark had met at the hospital and hadn't spoken to one another. If crises didn't bring families together, what could? "You know, girls, I hope Bucky soon remembers what he was doing under that tree. But it's good he was there to help Phlox, I suppose." She had been trying to tell him not to play detective and follow that girl around, but he was fascinated by her. "Did you see the headlines?" Bucky would like the publicity; children don't know the harm it can do, thought Surtsey. "Isn't that cute—my Bucky a hero?" Tulie and Anna smiled sleepily at their friend. "The paper wants his photo."

Meanwhile, upstairs the three young patients were waking up with very little recollection of the night before and sadly bemoaning the change in their lives. Freud opened his eyes to find his left arm tied in a splint; into his veins was dripping a solution of dextrose. His feet were wrapped in bandages and anchored to weights and pullies, which hung from the foot of the bed. And worst of all he had a painful headache. At the same time, his head felt different somehow. He touched it with his free hand and was shocked to feel that it was absolutely bare of any hair and covered with a greasy paste. Having cultivated a hornet's nest of curly hair for many months, he was accustomed to being beneath it, so Freud experienced a shock over the loss of his hair second only to the jolt of waking to find himself strapped to the Savernake County Medical Center. He rang for the nurse and got an unidentified buxom helper who explained, in a crude way, that the smell of singed hair was not exactly popular with the nurses who had therefore decided to remove the offensive substance. "You don't look half bad," she added by way of consolation.

Down in the lobby, Penny, who had come to the hospital to see Freud, said that she was his sister, thinking, well, I am his sister in Christ, and as a member of the family, she received a pass for a fifteen minute visit at any time.

She found Freud in Room 302 sitting up in bed, the pungent smell of ointment about him and looking as if he was bady sunburned. She took a second look and realized he was completely bald. The shock of the change in her dear friend reduced her to tears. But Freud's face lit up when he saw her. "Penny," he cried, "am I glad to see my little tooth fairy!"

"Oh, Freud, I saw it all; I saw the lightning and I couldn't do a thing to stop it," she replied, her hand stroking his free arm and tears running down her cheeks.

"Penny, ol' girl, stop the hand of God, who was sending me a message?" he asked, trying to be lighthearted about their disaster.

"Do you think He was, Freud?" she asked soberly, her tears gone. She was afraid it was true.

"Oh, I don't know Pen; but at least He didn't let me die. How are the others? Penny, run and ask one of the nurses—no one has told me anything except that Bucky Sanders and Phlox were hit too." Penny did as he asked and relayed the news that Bucky and Phlox were still in intensive care but in satisfactory condition. However, she was more interested in what Freud said about God.

"Don't you think He wants us in Glory Land?"

"Well, obviously He claims the tree as His right of way, but no, I don't think it was a message, no more than a car driving down the road is a message; but if you're hit by the car, you better get out of the road. So I must move; that's obvious."

"You can move in with me, Freud."

"Penny, m'love, the realities of our situation need now be faced. We do not live in a lonely woods; we live on a public highway. We are, in effect, a public house. We must forget our private preferences and live like our forefathers—in propriety—so I'm afraid I'll have to have my own house. Perhaps for now we could tell Skip to find some other place."

Penny's face fell. A little white lie to get in to see Freud was one thing, but to break her promise to Skip was another. "Oh, no, we can't do that. We promised. He's moving in today. He's already rented a piano. No, no. I'll never do that. I'd rather move back to town. You can have my tower."

"Miss Penny, I can't tell you how much my head aches. Forget I ever said it. Go along and tell Skip to take good care of my girl. I'll live under his eaves until I think of my next move."

"Freud, there's one more thing we should talk about and maybe you remember what that is."

Sensing by her tone some question about Phlox, Freud defended himself. "Oh, no, no, my poor head. Penny, will you love me without my hair? Get me a cold cloth for my head, please, pardner," he begged.

Penny looked at his head and smiled wanly. "I'm sure

your head hurts, but don't change the subject, Freud. Phlox was found in her underwear!" When he said nothing she grew angry. "How could you be so two-faced, telling me you couldn't stand her? And do you know who found her that way? Little Bucky Sanders, that's who! He's only ten years old. What do you suppose he thought?"

"Lightning has done stranger things! I know nothing about it. I was out on the deck studying the sky and she was inside. I told her to leave, but she was afraid of the storm. She's also afraid of dogs. So I promise you this, Pen, when I leave here I'll get me a big mean dog. It will never leave my side. And I'll be home in a couple of days and we'll have a long talk. But not now! Oh, my head," he moaned, his eyes closed.

"God help you." she murmured. "I'm glad you're all right."

Freud put his big hand over hers and opened one eye. "Tell me, Penny, m'love, how is the tree? Is my house destroyed?"

"Don't be anxious. The deck is damaged and the lashings are loose, that's all. The tree seems to have survived. Mr. Bantley's going to get a tree surgeon to check it."

"Tell him not to bother," Freud said testily.

"He wants to. He's very concerned. He feels responsible that he didn't think about lightning."

"I didn't think of it either."

"Maybe it was an act of God to save you from Phlox," Penny said and she wasn't smiling.

"Come off it, Penny. No woman but you will love old baldy now. But I do have one consolation: Ben Franklin's wig will fit a lot better. So you see, some good comes of everything!"

"I have to go back to my work, John; I promised to help Skip move his stereo and all his recording gear to the studio. Yesterday I collected two months' rent in advance from Skip. Is that what you wanted me to do?"

"That's right, pardner, keep our project moving ahead. Next time you come I'll have a list of things for you to see to."

"I'll do my best. Take care, Freud!" Penny leaned over the high bed and kissed him on the cheek.

"And keep people out of my tree!"

Penny nodded. She went away depressed. Somehow things would never be the same again. Freud made so light of everything. Was that why he was so popular and she so friendless? He didn't love her; she had come along when he needed her. And what had she done to deserve him anyway? She'd never gone to college or even lived with a man; now when he was homeless and she asked him to live with her, he refused. Her whole life had been nothing but hard work and what did she have to show—a bakery and half of a crazy bridge.

She had lost the good will of her mother and made her angrier than Penny had ever seen her. Only her father had a good word for Penny; he said she could be proud of herself, that she owned more at twenty-two than he did at forty-six. What comfort was that when she wasn't having any fun in life? Dad hadn't had much fun either, never going anywhere, tied down like herself. It occurred to her then that she could bring him to the bridge to watch the tourists and fish for salmon. He'd like that. Maybe, this afternoon, after she helped Skip move in to his studio, he'd return the favor and fetch her dad and his wheelchair in the panel truck. It would be nice for her father to go fishing.

That afternoon Phlox Fontaine and Bucky Sanders were wheeled from intensive care into a semi-private room where a special nurse was detailed to observe them for a time because of the shock they had suffered the night before. "Now," said the nurse, attaching a bottle of glucose to Bucky's arm, "now you can have visitors. But don't let them tire you. Here, Phlox, you'll want to see the headlines in the morning paper. I'll be back in a few moments to take your blood pressure." She left the cuff attached to Phlox's arm and went out.

Phlox took the paper lethargically but brightened when she saw the headlines. "Hey, kid, listen to this: 'Local boy a hero. Buckminster Sanders, known to his friends as Bucky, was the hero of the lightning bolt that struck the three-centuries-old oak in Savernake Forest last night. It was learned from reliable sources that ninety-pound Bucky, injured and in shock, climbed a broken twenty-foot ladder and lifted a limb weighing over two hundred pounds from the leg of a badly injured occupant of the tree. Doctors say Bucky may have saved the leg.' "

"Did I do that?" the young boy asked in awe. "I don't remember." But he thought to himself, Shucks, why did they have to put it in the paper? We detectives don't like publicity. What if someone asks me what I was doing there? That reminds me—I must ask Mom to bring me my supplies.

His thoughts were interrupted by Phlox. "Isn't this an awful place? I've been pushing this button for a glass of ice water for hours and no one comes. And why didn't they put me in a private room?"

"I dunno," said Bucky, thinking that it was great for a detective to share a room with his quarry. He'd need a notebook and pencil and maybe his dusting kit.

Bucky didn't have long to wait until his mother arrived. Surtsey came into the room full of a cheer, which she did not truly feel, carrying several books and a little radio for Bucky. "Hello, children, I'm glad you're all right. What a fright we had, but that's all over. Just hurry and get well. Bucky, Dad will be along later and I'm sure, Phlox, your mother will come soon." Seeing a look of doubt cross Phlox's face, Surtsey said, "She was here before you woke up and has probably gone home to change and have breakfast." Surtsey went to the bed and kissed her little son, whispering, "I love you, honey." Bucky writhed in embarrassment. Turning from him to Phlox she asked, "Can I do anything for you, dear? How is your leg? Bucky, did you really lift that big limb off her leg?"

"I dunno, Mom. I can't remember anything."

"Mrs. Sanders, would you fix my sheets? And go get me a glass of ice water. And maybe wind up the bed." Surtsey did everything. "Now hand me that old magazine. This place is just awful—people everywhere, and nobody helps the patient."

While Surtsey was making the young people comfortable, a candy-striper came along pushing a large wagon of entertainment supplies and snacks. Phlox asked for a Coke and potato chips, which Mrs. Sanders paid for, and Bucky wanted a notebook and pencil and a candy bar. "I'll get you the paper, Bucky, but not the candy bar—you know you're allergic to food additives. I'll have Daddy bring you some quality candy later on. But I doubt either of you are supposed to have anything yet."

"Okay, Mom," said Bucky, taking his first notes. "Subject likes Coke and chips, hates fat nurses and crowds of people."

Surtsey kissed Bucky again. "I'll come as often as I can, dear." Then she hurried home to make supper for the twins.

Towards suppertime a sweet-faced, elderly volunteer in a green smock handed Freud his mail. "My, you already have a lot of letters!" There were ten get-well cards and a long envelope. Freud put the cards on his night table and opened the long envelope. It was a bill from the Freeroder's Bike and Cycle Shop addressed to John Freund III. My goodness, thought Freud, I don't believe I ever paid him for that new bike tire I got for Phlox back in May. I forgot all about it. He opened the envelope and would have toppled over had he not been lying down. It read:

Blue Honda 125, Serial No. 360491	$650.00
Credit on trade-in, Falcon Olympic	75.00
Due	$575.00

Down below it was stamped, "Second Notice. Please remit within fifteen days."

Freud read and reread the bill and he just couldn't believe it. His ten-speed traded for a cycle—given away for seventy-five dollars! He paled alarmingly as he realized what had happened: his precious ten-speed had been traded for a Honda, the same Honda Phlox had said was hers. And she had sent the bill to him! His ten-speed worth almost three hundred dollars was gone.

The color mounted to the top of his head, and had his legs not been in traction (a precaution against possible damage from the fall on his back), he would have gone straightway to her room and given Phlox what she deserved—a good sound spanking. He'd felt like it ever since he met her. He probably could make good use of the Honda, but where was the money to come from? Anyway he'd have to telephone Penny to put the cycle under lock and key before Phlox could get her hands on it again. That low-down unprintable Phlox Fontaine, selling his Falcon for seventy-five dollars!

What Freud didn't know was that the blue Honda had

been parked beside the tree the night before and was even now on its way, bent and twisted, to Harry Homer's Steel and Scrap Yard. Harry had already mailed Phlox a check for fifty dollars and hauled it away, pleased that some of it was salvageable. It would bring seventy-five, maybe with luck, even a hundred dollars.

Freud lowered the head of his bed to rest from this awful surprise. A bolt of lightning was too good for Phlox; but he was angry that he, who had been flying so high, was sidelined just when things were going well. He opened his cards—nine get-wells from friends of his mother and one from Crabbe Grass. On the front of Crabbe's card was an empty coffin. The message read, "Be of good cheer, the end is near." Inside it said, "Of your stay in the hospital."

Freud managed to laugh a little. As the glucose flowed through his veins, his usual optimism was returning and his headache was going. "The end of a lot of things, Crabbie, and the beginning of other things—bigger and better things," he said aloud, winking at the cute student nurse who was taking his pulse.

Downstairs in Room 216, Bucky Sanders was talking to his teacher who had come to congratulate him for his heroism. While he was telling her all about the storm, his dad, Bud Sanders, on his way home from Poly-Toy Corporation, slipped into the room to visit his son. Seeing Bucky occupied, he glanced over at the frail pink and blonde girl in the other bed. "Well, hell-o," he said, going over beside her. "Why, you're the young lady who made the headlines this morning!" Phlox, her face full of self-pity, looked up at the nice looking middle-aged man, and nodded. "Bucky, is this the girl you saved?" Bud scanned

Phlox from her head down along the sheets to her feet. "Why, Bucky, she sure was worth saving!"

Phlox was looking vaguely interested now. "Tell me, my dear, what happened?" asked Bud.

"I was struck by lightning," said Phlox, matter-of-factly.

"No kidding!" exclaimed Bud. "Well, I'm not surprised. You are attractive. Ho-ho. Get it? 'Attract lightning'—attractive!"

"Hey, Dad," said Bucky when his teacher left, "it's me, Bucky."

"Hello, Bucky. I see you. How are you? I can't stay— gotta earn enough to pay the big hospital bill, you know. See you both later."

"Is that your old man?" asked Phlox.

"Sure," said Bucky. "But he's not so old. My grandpa's older."

"Well, he left this box of candy on my bed. I think I heard him say it's for me. I'll give you a piece after supper."

"Oh," said Bucky looking doubtful. Then he wrote in his notebook, "Likes other people's candy." He hid the notes under his pillow.

After eating a soft dinner, Freud lay on his bed trying to think. There was something he wanted to tell Savy Bantley. If only he could remember what it was, something he'd forgotten to tell her the day before. Penny had mentioned Skip. It was something about Skip. Slowly his mind began to remember. It was about planning their concert on the bridge featuring Skip and the Saffies. If all went well, the concert would bring in enough money to pay their bills and launch Skip on a career as a songwriter at the same time. It occurred to him also that any publicity about the lightning strike would help assure their success. He smiled over that. But the best part of all was he had an idea that this plan would please Savy, and for some inexplicable reason he wanted to please her.

As Freud was wondering how to get someone to bring him a telephone so he could call Penny about the Honda, the young lady he wanted to please swept into his hospital room and with a slight curtsey, handed him a large bouquet of zinnias. Then, arching one brow as Savernake was wont to do when she was play-acting, she recited a limerick.

"There once was a fool in an oak
So sure of himself when he spoke
That he challenged the sky to
    debate from on high
And he was put down with one stroke."

Freud smiled up at her appreciatively. This was the first time he had seen Savy in a dress, a soft clinging pastel nylon. Her golden red hair fell around her shoulders and her green eyes sparkled with fun. He noticed her soft skin, her smooth and glowing look, and her big smile; she was beautiful. At the sight of this lovely girl, Freud's spirits soared; and he tried to get out of bed, exclaiming, "My neighbor, whom I love. Give me a kiss!" Then he realized his predicament and fell back on his bed, his eyes inviting pity.

Savy ignored the invitation but smiled broadly. "I wouldn't take advantage of a man when he's down," she said. Freud lost no time sitting up and telling her about his ideas for featuring Skip and his songs in a concert on the bridge. Savy was so elated and thought it was such a great idea that she said, "I've changed my mind; for that you shall have a kiss and I'll forgive you everything; and tomorrow I'll bring you a box of candy!"

"A two-pound Sampler?" he asked, dreaming big.

"A five-pound Sampler!" she answered, outdoing him.

"I'll die happy." He collapsed back against the pillow.

She looked at him and began to see him for the first time as a man, a possibility. It had been a long while since Savy had met someone with mental agility to match her own and she would be glad if their relationship became more than a battle of wits. She had a feeling that they both had more, much more, deep down where it counts, to offer one another. If only he would realize that and quit kidding around. She wondered as she looked at him if this could ever be.

Freud was wondering too; in fact in his fancy he had gone well beyond her own thinking to the idea that he could go to bed with this woman. But first he wanted to share her ideas and her thoughts, to mine her emotions and search for her dreams, to know her whole person. Then if he had all that, what would follow would be paradise. That's what he was thinking as he looked at her.

"I have to run now, Kingjohn. Dad's very upset about all this." Savy took his hand. "Come home soon, neighbor. We need you." Then she gave him a happy little kiss on the cheek and went away, and Freud fell asleep with a smile on his face.

To the Rescue

It was one o'clock the next morning. In Savernake County Medical Center the long corridors were silent except for the wheezing of a respirator in the men's ward. The night was still. Nurses, putting in their long night, were having coffee and cigarettes at the other end of the hall; an aide, left in charge at the desk, was reading an article about Jackie Kennedy in an old movie magazine.

No one saw the small person come on quiet feet up the fire stairs and silently move down the hall into Room 302 where John Freund III lay dreaming that a giant bat with a face like a young girl was sitting on his shoulder.

"Ssst. Ssst," spat the figure. John came alive and sat up, his round eyes searching the dark for the bat. Then he realized he was in the hospital and there was a dark thick figure wavering at the foot of the bed. It looked more like a bear than a bat. Freud shivered a little. The monster hissed, "Young 'un, help me! Help me!" Freud held his breath and pulled the light switch. Who stood there quivering but Tatty Softshoe. Her long muskrat coat enveloped her and only her dark, dank head and penetrating black eyes were visible above the scruffy fox collar.

"Why, Tatty," exclaimed Freud in a loud whisper, "what

is it? What time is it? You frightened me. I thought I was dreaming."

"It's past midnight, young 'un, but you gotta help me." She reached in her big sleeve and brought out an official document covered in blue. "They're gonna send me to the nursin' home. Those Filch brothers down at the store. They're after my money. I never shoulda trusted no men with three wives. They're gonna take me away and come after my money and my station wagon and take everything I have. They knew they'd never get past my wall, so they're sending me to the nursin' home—probably today," she ranted, big tears in her eyes.

"Oh, no, they're not doing anything of the kind. It's good Mom brought me my glasses. Hand them here, please, Tatty, and for goodness' sake, be quiet. Now, shut the door tight and sit over there in that dark corner in case someone comes in. This place isn't private even at night. Now, let me read this paper. I'll find a way to help you, Tatty. Trust me."

She nodded her head up and down. This golden boy was like an angel and she trusted him.

By the light of the lamp hanging over his bed, Freud turned back the blue cover of the legal document in his hand and read:

A Citation

to

Tatty Softshoe Tuttle, an

alleged incompetent,

To show cause why you should not be committed to the Savernake County Nursing Home for your own safety and protection. You are hereby notified to appear in person for a hearing on this matter on the 28th day of July.

Wilbur T. Smith

Honorable Sheriff

Savernake County

Freud lay back on his pillow, pursing his lips to suppress his anger and sorrow. In his twenty-three years he had never experienced anything so tragic. For a free and stalwart soul like Tatty, who led her own life, harming no one, to have her home and her way of life taken away from her because she was different from other people and because they wanted the little bit she had, was a stunning experience for Freud. He had to do something to help her. What could he do from his hospital bed? He would have to find someone of influence who would sympathize with Tatty. Not his own dad—he was gone. Brig Bantley might help, but he wasn't about to go to him. Who then? After entertaining a number of ideas, Freud thought of Harry Homer.

Harry was a man of standing in the town and a big contributor to local charities. He had been very kind and helpful about the Tyler Lansdown gate. Besides, he was a little like Tatty in some ways; everybody in town knew from his cleaning woman that he kept fresh fruit in his drawer because he liked the smell it gave his underwear. That was kind of peculiar. And then there was his little habit of getting out of his Cadillac Eldorado and picking up aluminum cans along the highway to sell for scrap. People thought that was funny for a millionaire. Yes, he just might help Tatty if he were approached in secret. But how to do it from a hospital bed was the question in Freud's mind.

Just then Tatty, her eyes growing accustomed to the dark, came from her corner and peered down at Freud. Her eyes had begun to see that the young 'un looked different, that he was missing all his hair. "Oooh," she crooned. "Oooh, you poor, poor boy. Come away with me and I'll treat you with burdock ointment and nettle tea. Come on, I'll fix you up." She tugged at him, disregarding the tubes and pulleys tying him to the bed.

"Okay, Tatty. Okay. But listen to me first. I've thought of someone to help you—the man with the big heart."

"Harry?"

"Yes, Harry. Let's go ask him." Tatty looked a little dubious. "Well, he does like my Chevy a lot. In fact it's parked at his place right now. He's orderin' a part—fer nothing, he says."

"Good! If he's willing to fix your car for nothing he'll be willing to help you. I know he will. Now just come here and pull this needle out. That's it—ouch. Now disconnect that pulley. Easy does it. Okay. Now, while I unwrap these bandages you hand me my pants."

"If you'll excuse me," he said, turning away and pulling up his jeans, but Tatty had her eyes closed and was thankin' God for the young 'un.

"Here's to nettle tea," said Freud, tossing his throw-away pajamas into the wastebasket. Free at last! Glory Land, I will return, he said to himself. But first he would have to conquer the King of Scrap.

Harry's imposing house was designed to look like a castle. Spotlights in the grass lit up the turret roof. Freud crossed the imitation drawbridge and knocked. After a time, Harry himself opened the heavy door. He was wearing striped pajamas and slippers. While Tatty sat waiting in a taxi, Freud stepped into the antichamber and showed Harry the blue document, which Harry, putting on his trifocals, read very carefully. "Send her to the county home!" he exclaimed. "That's outrageous. I won't have it. It would kill that flinty soul. No, sir, I won't have it. Incompetent? Why, she's one smart woman, she is. She knows things about nature you and me don't know. See these red scars?" he lowered his pajama pants and displayed his fifty-inch waist. "Shingles, right there, all around. Had 'em since Ruth died. Kaleri herself healed 'em with footbaths and chest packs of crushed buttercups and linden blossoms. Send her to the home!" Harry exclaimed, pacing back and forth. "Who do you suppose is behind this desecration?" His eyes bulged as he looked at Freud.

"From what she says," explained Freud, "the Filch brothers know she's got her money hidden someplace; and after they get her in the home, they're going to go to her place and dig it up. I told her it wasn't safe to hide it in a tin can at home. Maybe she'd listen to you."

"She's got it in a tin can, has she? That's dangerous. You came to the right man. That woman needs me. I haven't had a female needing me since Ruth died!" he added, looking pleased. "You know, young man, my father taught me to be kind to women and it's paid off. You take that advice. Be kind to the weaker sex. Now Tatty isn't beautiful like Ruth was, but she's smart. However, she don't know much about money." He scratched his ear. "Why I'd 'ave let her have Tyler Lansdown's gate for one hundred dollars if she'd handled me right!" chuckled Harry.

He seemed to want to talk. "I say that woman's no incompetent. She's a live wire." Harry didn't tell Freud that Tatty had made him feel better about losing Ruth, a loss he had never gotten over. Tatty comforted him by speaking so kindly and respectfully of Irv. People did have meaning after they were gone—meaning to those with sensitivity; and Tatty had that fine tuning, that deep-felt knowledge that life is caring about living things. She also had a keen fear of not caring.

"Take Tatty home now, my son," said Harry, "and tell her I'll be there later today—as soon as I can get there—to go fishing with her; and while we're frying the fish we'll decide what to do. I'm not called King of Scrap for nothing!"

"It sure is a relief to have you helping Tatty. She thinks you're a great man," said Freud, by way of thanks.

"Does she now? Well, boy, that makes me feel good!" Harry's head nodded up and down as he undid three iron locks and let Freud out onto the drawbridge.

Tatty's Medicine

After his conversation with Harry Homer, Freud went
home to the swamps with Tatty. She ordered him to sit in
the dilapidated rocker, while she went into the fields to find
herbs for a poultice. When Kaleri came back she made a
pack of mallow roots, dandelions and burdock and placed it
on his head. Then she brewed him a cup of nettle tea. The
sun came up warm and shone through the lattice of Tatty's
gate, reflecting L (or was it I?) and T on the wall of her hut;
and Tatty forgot her troubles. She enjoyed nursin' the
young'un.

As for Freud, with the help of her tender care he
recovered quickly from his sore head and weak knees and
by noon, when Harry arrived dressed for the day in his
khaki fishing suit from L.L. Bean's, Freud left for his tree at
once. He was anxious to get back to the Big Bear and begin
to make arrangements for Skip's concert on the bridge,
which was going to solve all his problems and which he had
promised Savy. It had become very important to him to
please the beautiful redhead who he had just decided, for
the third time, was to be the new woman in his life. And he
was excited by the idea that she just might be getting
interested in him. She had been very kind and friendly in

the hospital, and with her help he felt as though he could do anything. So Freud hurried home to tell Penny all about his new ideas for the bridge. He hitchhiked down Route 9 wearing a poultice of grape leaves tied over his bald head to protect it from the sun and with it on his head he felt just fine.

When he reached his kingdom, John found Penny wading in the river. She was overjoyed to see him. "Why, Freud, you're back already. Wherever did you get that hat?" she laughed. "Skip, come and see Freud."

A few moments later Skip came out of the north tower. Freud doffed his cap. "Gosh, man, what happened to you?" asked Skip, suppressing a laugh. "Good to see you, John. I hope you don't mind that I've moved my stuff inside the far tower. Penny says you want the loft; that's okay with me."

"Good. But we have more urgent matters to discuss— your future. We gotta get you introduced, man, real quick—say next week. We can follow that up with something bigger in another month. How's that sound?"

For the next half hour the three young people laid out plans to hold an event to introduce Skip to a live audience. They would call a meeting and ask the Safflowers for their help with the details. When it was settled to his satisfaction, Freud said, "I have to check in at my tree and catch up on some sleep. But believe me, my friends, we have just begun to live!"

When he was gone, Penny said to Skip, "Doesn't he look awful with no hair at all?"

Skip tickled her in the ribs. "You asked me once if God has a sense of humor! Now I know the answer. Yes, Penny, God has a great sense of humor to make John Freund look like that!"

Penny smiled at him appreciatively. She thought to

herself that she used to think Freud was the coolest guy in town, but now that she was experiencing more of the world, her tastes were changing. She preferred more quiet and serious company, especially someone with sandy hair and twinkling blue eyes who wasn't afraid to talk about God.

Bucky the Detective

Over at the hospital, Phlox, very depressed, lay on her bed. Did this place exist for her comfort and care? No, it did not. No one paid any attention to her. It was obvious this place was to provide salaries and pensions and other benefits for its swollen staff and she was just a thing in a bed. She was sick of the place. And why did they put a kid in her room? It was crowded; oh, yes, crowded with overfed nurses and hippies pulling carts and nurses chasing married doctors around elderly volunteers. She lay there and watched it all and she was unimpressed. Besides, her leg ached and no one came to comfort her.

As her thoughts filled the room with dark vibrations, Bud Sanders came down the hall, fresh and smiling from a shower after his golf game. In his hand he carried an English bouquet of pink phlox and larkspur from his wife's garden. He winked at a nurse he knew rather well and she provided him with a vase.

Peeking into Room 216 and seeing Bucky asleep, Bud tiptoed over and stood beside Phlox. "Here I am with flowers and sympathy!"

Phlox had seen phlox in her grandmother's flower bed and she thought they were a lovely flower, the flower for which she was named. She pushed herself up on one elbow and looked at them. Her blue eyes were full of tears, which Bud was quick to notice.

"Oh, dear, don't cry. What's the matter?" He seldom affected women in this way and it was a very moving experience for him—no doubt it was the flowers!

"Now, precious baby, don't cry. What is it? Tell Buddy your troubles." And so she did tell him in a low voice that having left Tulie's house she couldn't go back there, that Freud had asked her to live with him in the tree and now he had rejected her. Her mother hated her and she had no place to go. "There, there, you poor child. Buddy will find you a place. Don't you worry another minute. I'll find you something and I'll come to see you often." Then he bent down and whispered something in her ear.

Phlox looked blandly grateful. "Do you think you could bring me some jeans, size 8, and a size 7 tank top?" Bud assured her he could and smiled at the idea. He was thinking she'd look cute in a yellow nightie.

Bucky was awake now and looking over at them. "Hi, Dad! Say, whatever happened to my bike?"

"Gee, kid, I'll have to ask your mother. I'll tell you when I come in tomorrow. Son, I'm glad you're a hero."

"Thanks, Dad."

Phlox was impressed that the president of Poly-Toy had offered to help her. Deserted by her parents, she had nowhere to turn but to Mr. Sanders. And she was no dumbbell. She knew he was not being altruistic but was expecting to be paid. Indeed the game for her was to give as little as possible while getting what she wanted most.

The more she turned that idea over in her mind the more she determined that Bud Sanders would be the key to her successful arrival at Safflower Hill. She would tap him for something big and before he had a chance to ask her to reward him, she'd dash away and take refuge among the Saffies. Phlox was already laughing at the look she projected on Bud's round face. In fact, what she decided to get from him was a big, showy, yellow pick-up truck—automatic—with a four-speaker stereo and a CB radio.

She lay back upon her pillows, her arms behind her head, and smiled over at Bucky.

"Penny for your thoughts, Phlox," said Bucky.

Phlox, flustered, said, "Oh, I was thinking of something yellow."

"Funny," said Bucky, "so was I—a nice yellow ten-speed. Say, what happened to your blue Honda?"

"Who knows," said Phlox. "Blue never was my favorite color. I prefer yellow." Bucky reached under his pillow for his notebook. "Hates blue, likes yellow. Whereabouts of Honda unknown."

An efficient nurse appeared carrying a tray with little paper cups on it. She handed one to Bucky and another one to Phlox. "Take these." She watched them do it and left as Bucky said, "Yuck. That pill left a trail like a skunk walking down my throat! Did she give you one of those tiny white ones?"

"No. She gave me one that looked like a downer; what I need are some uppers."

"You got false teeth?"

"No, kid, never mind." Bucky wrote in his notebook: "Probably has false teeth."

At 10:30 on the fifth hospital day Surtsey bustled into Bucky's room, pulled the curtains around him and told him to dress, that he was going home to a big surprise.

"Where's Phlox?" his mother asked.

"Oh, she went earlier."

"Well, I hope she's not going back to that tree."

"Oh, no, never," said Bucky, putting his head out from behind the curtain. "She hates Freud because he didn't save her. I'm her hero now."

"I see," said Surtsey, smiling at Bucky's obvious infatuation.

"What's my surprise?" quizzed her young son, no longer the subdued little patient who had lain in the bed.

"Can you guess?"

"A ten-speed!"

"How'd you guess?"

"What color?" asked Bucky.

"Yellow."

"Yellow! I can't wait to ride it!"

"Let's have lemonade on the front porch first. I still haven't heard all the story of how you came to be a hero."

Bucky agreed to the lemonade. Mom had been real nice to get him a ten-speed, and she seemed to like to drink lemonade, so he'd have some too, to please her. "Where's Dad?" asked Bucky.

"Why, I don't know. Wasn't it thoughtful of your father to bring you flowers every day and boxes of caramels?" asked Surtsey, who felt she must reassure her son that his dad really cared about him.

"He didn't bring me anything. He gave it all to Phlox. She offered me some caramels once but not enough, especially since she always had six pieces every night after the visitors left. Why didn't Dad bring me some candy?"

"Oh! I think he meant them for both of you," his mother replied, thinking, And I thought he was taking them to

Bucky! He's mean, that husband of mine, and so thoughtless to hurt a sensitive little boy. I guess he took her all the flowers in my garden too!

Bucky was pursuing his own thoughts. It made him mad when his father brought candy to Phlox because he'd planned to buy her some Tootsie Rolls when the Gray Lady came with the wagon. Now he was thinking he'd like to show Phlox his new bike, since yellow was her favorite color.

He wondered where she lived. Bucky took out his notebook when he got home and found the word "motel"— that was it, she'd said to a nurse that she lived in a motel. He'd go look for her on his new bike. Bucky wanted to take her something, maybe some Bubble Bubble. She was usually chewing gum and Bubble Bubble lasted a long time.

After having some fresh, cold lemonade, Bucky set out on his ten-speed to look for his friend. "Goodbye, Mom, I'm taking off for the planet Neptune. See ya!" He coasted away down Main Street and turned left on Thorn. There were only a few motels in town: the two big ones on Route 9, and several small ones; the Thorn was closest, so he'd try it first.

Bucky peddled around the main lodge to the path, which went behind the cabins. Stopping to get out the Bubble Bubble, he heard voices coming from an open window. He recognized Phlox's voice right away and cycled up beside the cabin. As he was putting down his kickstand, he heard his father's loud laughter. He made some notes in his little book and put the gum back in his pocket. After a time he pedaled slowly home.

It didn't seem quite right somehow, but Bucky wasn't sure why. He only knew it made him mad; he'd have to ask his mother for an explanation.

Life Is a Frisbee Game

On the day that the Society of Primitive Artists was preparing its annual juried show, Olivia walked over to the gallery to see if they were satisfied with the arrangements.

Wearing a navy tie-dyed skirt and shirt with a plunge neckline and with a red flower pinned over one ear (and a pencil inadvertently placed over the other), Mrs. Dupre stepped inside the receiving room. Because she had come in from the bright outdoors, she did not at once recognize the two men who were working there unpacking paintings. So when her eyes adjusted to the light, she was startled to see that the man in jeans and a white T-shirt was none other than her boss, and the other was Tony DeLuca. Brig rarely dressed in work clothes. Informally yes, but sloppily never. As his helper of many years who thought she knew all about him, she was discomfitted to find that she did not. His shirt was too small and he looked like a laborer. She reacted by laughing nervously. "Why, Mr. Bantley, whatever does it say on your shirt?"

Brig was pleased she had asked and he smiled at Olivia. "Come outside where the light is better and I'll show you." Brig steered her by the elbow back the way she had come and across the lawns to a bench at the back of the theater;

it was where the actors came in the afternoons to rehearse
their lines. After she sat down, he stood squarely in front
of her and said, "Take a look at me; a friend of mine left this
at the dune house." At the mention of the dune house,
Olivia remembered the sand runt in the gold bikini and her
face registered pain and disapproval; but Brig, unmindful
of her thoughts, stretched his arms wide and the white
athletic shirt he wore, a bit small, slid up his chest baring
his brown midriff. On the shirt was painted a large Frisbee
and the words, *World Frisbee Rose Bowl Championships.* "Isn't
this something?" he asked as she stared up at him.

"You're just a big kid, Brig Bantley, like everybody else
around here!" Olivia exclaimed almost angrily.

"Come on, Livy, let your hair down. Life is a kind of
game, a big Frisbee game if you like, and you and I are on
the same team. The idea is not to drop the Frisbee. We've
got to throw it back and keep the game going. Just now
we're playing against Freud and Penny. We'll win, I promise
that, but after they've had a little practice and experience,
we'll get them on our team. Meanwhile, I'm beginning to
think their challenge is keeping our minds off—well, off
worse things. That's something to be glad about, isn't it?
So here's to Ultimate Frisbee. We're never too old to learn!"

Olivia stood up and fidgeted with her pencil which, much
to her chagrin, she found behind her ear. It seemed she no
longer knew what to expect of anyone—first her daughter,
then Ben Franklin, and now her employer.

"Watch this," said Brig, picking up the Frisbee he had left
on the bench that morning. Stretching his arm back, he
said, "And now for my super throw-off. Watch this." Seeing
she was about to walk away, he lowered his arm and said,
"Wait a second." He threw down the Frisbee. It spun around
on the ground. "I have to tell Tony something. I'll be right

back. Wait here, Olivia."

In a few minutes he came hurrying back, his purple eyes crinkling with delight. "Before I demonstrate my Frisbee throw-off there is some business we have to discuss concerning the problems we have. So sit down while I tell you some very good decisions that I've made. I think they will satisfy you," he added, knowing that in Olivia Dupre's state of mind they probably would not; but this was one time when he was the boss and she the employee. "This is what I want to tell you. We will play ball—Frisbee—with Penny and Freud; by that I mean we will cooperate! I am putting in a sewer line to the bridge and am granting the kids a limited right of way, for deliveries only, through the park. Savy has suggested I give them some red roofing for the towers and I just may do that too. Maybe you can suggest additional things."

Although Olivia was still angry at Penny and Freud it was a relief that Brig was not. She looked up at him and her face showed love and gratitude. She sighed in relief and was about to reply when he held up his hand. "There's something else I've done and I hope it will please you, Livy."

When he called her Livy, she knew he was about to talk to her as a person and not an employee. What was he going to say here in the theater garden? She pushed her hair back and tilted her head and looked at him with eager eyes. "Yes, Brig," she said. "What is it?"

Brig kicked a stone into the bushes. "It's just a small thing really. I want to tell you that I—I should say Tony, because he is doing it this very moment—Tony is taking down the signs that say Appian Way and putting up new ones which read Way Dupre. I'm naming our main thoroughfare after you, dear Livy, for all you've done for Glory Land! We have walked that path so often together. And another thing,"

he motioned her to listen, "I want you and you alone to pick
the next sculpture for the Garden of Contemplation. But
please don't choose one that's underfed!" (He was referring
to a Giacometti.) Brig's face was all smiles and Olivia lowered her head so he would not see the tears in her eyes.

He put his big hand on her head. That did it. She was so
overwhelmed by his kindness after all Penny had done to
him that she dropped to her knees and kissed his sandaled
feet. Not my toes! I don't want her to kiss my toes, he
thought, controlling the sleeping animal within. "Come
now, Olivia. I want you to be happy," he said, lifting her to
her feet. To insulate himself still further from her ardent
response he used the old male gambit of mentioning his
wife. "I must run home and see if I have a letter from Lucy. I
wish she were here to see what's happening. She always
sides with the kids no matter what they do; wouldn't she
enjoy this summer's happenings? And I know she'll like
Way Dupre!"

Olivia collected herself, hoping her face was not red or
her green eyeshadow running. She was speechless, filled
with mixed emotions. With a little wave, she retreated
across the grass towards her office.

"Livy!" he called. She looked back. "Don't forget to practice your back hand and your throw-off. Here, take this
with you." He threw her the bright purple Frisbee; she
didn't even try to catch it. In fact she had to go into the
bushes to get it. The bushes caught in her hair, which had
been neatly rolled all around, and after disentangling herself, she emerged dishevelled, having completely lost her
cool. Brig had vanished and Olivia didn't know what to
make of it all.

"He's flipped his Frisbee," she moaned, shaking her head
sadly. On the way to her office she went past the new street

sign and stood there a moment turning the Frisbee over in her hand. "I used to be a good tennis player; maybe I could learn to play Frisbee and make it to the Rose Bowl!" She would do anything for Brig Bantley—anything, because he meant everything to her.

Genuine Concern

The days passed swiftly that summer in Glory Land, but all was not well with the middle-aged as they awaited September. Their need for personal decision resulted in so much inconsistent behavior that, amazingly enough, their children, who were not old enough to appreciate their parents, felt their tension and were full of concern.

Savy Bantley was one. Savy was troubled because her father, after demanding that she take an interest in her heritage, was now so preoccupied he didn't even hear her suggestions for Glory Land. What was even more uncharacteristic of him, he had stopped hounding Skip. She wondered whether her father knew Skip had dropped out of the university. If so, was that what was troubling him; or was it 04Y4?

Today, with her father on her mind, she went to the river in search of Kingjohn. More and more often she found herself following the sandy path to find her neighbor and ask his advice. She wanted to talk to him anyway about Skip's show. When she found Freud, he agreed to go with her to the beach so they could talk privately. "Wait, I'll bring along something so we can have a picnic." Freud loved picnics and Savy did too—picnics with him, that is.

447

They walked down the path through the deep shadows in the piney woods and out onto the sand spit where the Big Bear River emptied into Big Bear Lake. Freud spread out an old army blanket and they seated themselves upon it.

"Now, tell me, Savy, why you look so pensive. I hope you brought my candy."

She gave him a quick smile and then her face was sober again. "Freud, it's Dad. I think he's worried sick about Grandma. The doctors say she may have had a small stroke. And I suppose he's wondering whether Mother will give up her tour and come back for the signing. Today we had another very enthusiastic letter from her about that dancer she met. It isn't like mother to take up with anyone—well, you know what I mean—I think it's a man. Women don't get that enthusiastic about other women!" They sat thinking.

"If it's any comfort," replied John, "there's trouble at our house too. My poor mother is in hell. Dad ran off and left her to take the flak. You have no idea how cruel people can be when they're desperate. They accuse my father unjustly for 04Y4. I don't blame him for going, but he should have taken Mother along. Anyway, it's her fault too; she never would go up there to Canada with him and rough it with the moose and the mosquitoes. But it seems like this is one time they could compromise." Molding a large sand castle with his big hands, he continued to talk. "I can understand divorce. People do make mistakes. But somehow this new law is—well, it's a bureaucratic intrusion on a sacred, private matter. It has amazing ramifications. I could say something worse!" Savy was making a moat around his castle. Freud went on talking. "It's lucky Mom is so interested in antique collecting. It keeps her busy hunting and fills her days. But there is one bright thing in her life:

she no longer has Phlox to worry about. You know, Savy, that storm did us Freunds a favor—it got rid of Phlox!"

Savy patted the sand. "But now she's making big trouble over at the Sanders house."

"I regret that, I surely do." replied Freud. "*C'est la vie.* Bud and Phlox are two of a kind—exploiters. They deserve each other. I guess every generation has them."

"But Surtsey doesn't deserve to be hurt." Savy lifted her head. "Here comes Mark Sanders now. He looks the way we feel, doesn't he? Let's ask him if he has any ideas for making our parents at least think about coming back together."

They told Mark of their dilemma and he said it was the same at his house, that his dad was going to the Plastic Toy Makers' Convention in Myrtle Beach and not taking his mother along. They were silent for a time and then Mark spoke. "I know the talk—what you're probably thinking—and I happen to know it isn't true; he isn't taking *her.* In fact I really believe Dad was merely helping a kid in distress. Dad is awfully naive about the way things look; if he weren't, I think he'd cover up his tracks better." Mark bit his lower lip.

"Nevertheless," said Freud emphatically, "I know that poisonous flower better than anyone else and I say make your mother go along to the convention."

Mark shrugged. "I think she wants to go, but she says she hasn't any money for new golf clothes. Can you believe that? Anyway, it's been six years since she played."

"Can't she go without new clothes?"

"No, not my mother. Dad has a new golf wardrobe and new clubs."

"Well, I repeat. Get her to go and stay an extra week. Pack their suitcases with Bantley Bitter Water and rare perfumes—whatever it takes!"

"Kingjohn," chided Savy, "watch what you say." Freud brushed her aside and continued. "Yes, Savy, now I'll hold my tongue. But you don't attack a pillbox with a BB gun!"

Mark managed to smile. "You've given me something to think about," he said. "I'll run along. Get to bed early, you two, so you don't forget our 6:00 a.m. meeting. Everything we're working for is riding on the outcome of Skip's concert. Right?"

"Right," they said and Savy kicked over the castle. "Now for our candy," said John, taking her in his arms. This time she didn't resist.

The Cookout

Mark left the park and drove over to the family home. He was glad to see that his father's white Corvette was not in the driveway. The memory of his encounter with Bud at the hospital was too painful to his sensitive spirit to risk a second hurt; but he did want to take Freud's advice and persuade his mother to go to the plastics convention.

He found her in the back garden toasting marshmallows with Bucky. His little blond brother and two dark-headed friends were standing over the outdoor fire with dangling sticks. Mark motioned his mother to join him on the picnic chairs under the maple tree. As soon as she sat down he got right to the point.

"Mom, I've decided to take Bucky up to Safflower Hill for two weeks so you can go along with Dad to the convention. Mary Lynn will take the twins to Brownfields. A vacation together will do you both good," Mark said enthusiastically.

"Oh, I don't know, Mark. I think the Hill is not quite the place for Bucky at his age."

"Then I'll ask Carol to invite him to her house. In fact I think I'll call her to come over now so we can make our plans." Mark shouted, "Carol," loudly three or four times. At that moment Bucky interrupted, "Mom, where are the

hot dogs?" Surtsey got up and went into the kitchen to get
them. Meanwhile, Carol, who had an apartment over the
neighbor's garage, showed up in the garden and said to
Mark in a low voice, "Let me talk to Mom alone. She might
open up with me. If she's going to stay married to Dad she's
got to redevelop some kind of relationship with him. She
must not give him so much freedom—like this trip. Why
should he go alone?"

Surtsey came out of the house and the screen door
slammed behind her. "Hello, Carol. You've come just in
time for a hot dog."

"Hi, Mom. Now tell me why you won't go to South
Carolina with Dad."

Surtsey looked uncomfortable, realizing that her two
children had been talking about her. "Carol, how can I say
it? I just don't have any golf clothes and I've been trying to
cut down on our budget as much as I can, what with fuel oil
and food bills so high. I just can't afford a fancy trip and a
new wardrobe this summer. Believe it or not! And I will not
ask your father for more money."

"But Mom, what happened to the money your father left
you? You could use some of that. It's silly to put it away for
us—the government will take it in the end anyway. Use it,
have a little fun in your life."

Surtsey looked upset. Finally she said, looking over at
Mark who had turned his back, "How can I explain that I
have already used it, Carol, to fulfill a dream? Please don't
press me; I have all any woman could want and I don't need
to go away," she emphasized.

Mark came back, biting his nails. "Is she still giving lame
excuses?"

Surtsey motioned him to sit down and then she began
to talk in a very deliberate tone. "Children, you can't be

oblivious to the way your father has been acting. To tell you the truth I'm not going because he doesn't want me to go."

"Doesn't want you to go, Mom? Nonsense. Aren't wives invited? You love to play golf!" exclaimed Carol.

"Some of the girls are going—Pat Johnson for one. But no, I can't go unless he says something to me about it. Remember I'm not tax deductible, whereas a secretary is."

"Mom," shouted Carol, "that does it; we are chipping in to buy you a plane ticket!"

"Oh, children, don't do that. How will I tell Bud?" She shook her head.

"You parents are the darnedest people—married more than twenty years and you can't tell him that you're going with him to a convention! That's the living end!"

Surtsey sighed and sat in silence, thinking it over. Mark got up and went to the picnic table to light the propane lantern. "Say, you guys, you better put your tent up before it gets dark."

Carol, seeing the pain in her mother's face, went to her and put her arms around her mother's neck, "Mom," she said softly, "we kids will understand if you decide not to sign. You deserve to be free."

"Thank you, Carol," she said. "But we can't be as free as we'd like to think we could be—not if we're mature and assume our responsibilities towards others." Surtsey sighed and spoke haltingly. "We can ask someone else to carry our burdens as you are offering to do now, from time to time, but in the end we must pick up our suitcases of responsibilities or shrivel in our own esteem. The choice, I suppose, is ours, but it is not what you'd call a free choice." They were silent and the lantern flickered under the maple tree. Then she continued, thinking aloud now, letting it all hang out.

"It's not as easy as it looks to decide what to do. Don't get the idea I'm not tempted to cop out!

"I really would like to be me, the real me for a time; but perhaps this housewife is the real me, and the one still clamoring inside is only a measure of myself I made a long time ago and dressed over the years in this and that dream to make me feel greater to myself than I seem to be to others. Yes, who knows, perhaps the housewife, nurse, mother, slave, jester is the real me after all!" Speaking again to her children, who were listening with pained expressions on their faces, she went on. "Motherhood is both more difficult and wider, fuller, deeper, and more meaningful than you at your age could possibly imagine. It is a blessed tie and I couldn't have had it without your father and his support. So you see I've already had it all and should laugh and sing and rejoice!" She smiled, trying hard.

"And talk it all over with Dad," said Mark. "Start by going away with him."

"You're right. I'll go." She stood up. "Bless you both for pushing me. I do have to bring up the matter of 04Y4 with your father."

"Before it's too late!" exclaimed Carol. Mark gave her a dark look.

"Now I think I'll go in and look in my closet. There must be something I can wear. I'll leave you kids to handle the boys."

"Mom, dear," called Carol after her mother, "bring me one of those famous hand-knit sweaters from South Carolina— a yellow one, please."

"I will," called back Surtsey as she walked along the hedge to the front door. The strains of *Some Enchanted Evening* were coming from the neighbor's car radio on the other side of the hedge. "Some enchanted evening when you meet your true love," hummed Surtsey. How we used to love that song;

but now it makes me feel very sad, as though it's all over for me.

What is an enchanted evening anyway? she mused. Sexual promise is the main thing, I suppose, in the beginning. During twenty-five years that promise had been fulfilled, but something more should linger; what more was there? What was an enchanted evening? Looking into each other's eyes and feeling magnified and strengthened, feeling beautiful as never before. That was an enchanted evening, she thought. But there are no enchanted evenings for me now; there never will be again, and it makes me very sad. "But I do have wonderful children," she said aloud, consoling herself.

Penny's Plan

A few days after Freud's return from the hospital the residents of Safflower Hill gathered at the bridge to hear what he had to say about their upcoming concert. He explained that Skip would sing and they would provide the sound, sell the tickets and oversee the crowd he fully expected to come. The important thing was to get the word out to all their friends. Everyone readily agreed to make the preparations.

"Now, before I dismiss you," said Freud, "my partner has asked to say a few words." Even he didn't know what Penny would say because she was not given to speaking in front of crowds.

She flung off her apron, which made everyone laugh, and came running up front. She pushed her long brown hair out of her face with trembling hands and took a deep breath. "In a moment we'll have coffee and donuts," she stammered. A clatter of applause resounded from the hillside. The noise gave her courage and she raised her voice. "But first I have something awfully important to say and I want you to listen to me." Everyone was quiet as they listened with curiosity to what she had to say.

"Something else has been on my mind. I have been working on a plan to help our parents. But I can't do it without you. September will be a very sad month for many of us. You know what I mean. So I've been thinking that since this concert we're planning is mostly for young people, why don't we also have something for the 04Y4 generation?" She paused. "I mean a special something in a special place."

"Like what?" asked a voice.

"Where?" asked another.

"I'm thinking," continued Penny, "of something helpful, something spiritually renewing."

Savy jumped to her feet and grabbed the mike from Penny's hand. "Why not plan a ceremony, a rededication ceremony for the day of the signing on September 15?"

"Something like a Russian marriage ceremony in the Hall of Mirrors?" cried out Stevie.

"No, no," broke in Penny, taking back the mike. "It must be a holy occasion—with God invited—in a chapel of some sort."

Savy spoke again. "We can use the old barn where Tony parks his tractors. He's such a loveable guy; he won't mind."

Penny turned to Savernake. "You don't know it, but when we erected the towers, Tony said, 'Back in Italy when we wanted to build something, we built a church.' I bet he'll help us make a church out of the tool shed!"

"We'll get the ministers, the rabbis and the priests to come," offered Skip.

"Freud could conduct a remarriage ceremony," wheezed Crabbe Grass. "He has a California license." Said remark brought a quick "Shut-up, Crabbe" from Freud.

"Let's have the signing there too."

"We'll advertise for all to come—put the 04Y4s in the barn and let the onlookers sit on the hill."

"The Saffies can sing."

"And I'll compose a tune," said Skip.

"And let's have a party to remember afterwards. Oh, what a day it will be!"

"Do you suppose they'll come?"

A sudden hush fell over the crowd.

"Well, I don't know about mine."

"Maybe mine will come," murmured another.

"Mine aren't speaking to one another."

"No chance, man."

"I hope mine will!"

Everybody looked around at everybody else. Then Penny took the mike again, possessed of new strength and a sense of purpose. "The news of this ceremony will give us a way of bringing up the subject with our parents so we can get them to talk about it."

"Shall we hand-deliver the invitations each to his own parents?"

"No way—my dad would toss it in my face."

"Sending them out seems too impersonal. They might throw them in the wastebasket along with the ads."

"We could draw lots, each for someone else's parents."

"Maybe. Let's think about it."

"I know someone who can advise us. She's not an 04Y4 because she's never been married, but she knows how they think. You all know who I mean. Anna Maria Abendtal— she'll find a way to get them there!" Everyone murmured approval and Skip volunteered to ask her.

Penny said, holding up her hand, "Okay, everybody. Then it's agreed that in the little valley at the base of the high hill we'll build a chapel!"

There was no time left for coffee, but no one noticed, not even Penny who had made the coffee. It was such a relief to be doing something at last about 04Y4, and everybody was very excited.

PART VI

August

The Plastic Toy Makers' Convention

The morning of his golfing trip to Myrtle Beach Bud Sanders was hung over. "Do you really have to have a beer for breakfast?" asked his daughter Carol, who was serving her father and the children while Surtsey was upstairs putting last-minute things in her suitcase.

"No," he answered, "I'd just as soon have cognac, if you prefer." Since when did daughters police their fathers, he wondered. "Has anyone brought down the suitcases?"

"I've asked Bucky to," said Mary Lynn.

"Dad," called Bucky from upstairs, "I've got something for you. It's a going-away present."

"Bring it to the kitchen, Bucky-boy," answered Bud.

Bucky came downstairs with a suitcase in one hand and a strangely wrapped package in the other, his face shining with the thrill of giving his father a gift he had made all by himself. "I made it in the hospital," Buckminster Sanders said proudly. "I was saving it for your birthday, but I want to give it to you now!"

Bud lifted the heavy package. "Okay," he said, his cigar between his teeth. "Let's see what it is. Well, if it isn't an ash tray, a green ash tray," Bud commented, unwrapping a chunk of unfired clay painted with watercolor. "I do believe it's an ash tray."

"Yes, you'll need it in the hotel—for your cigars. Hotels don't have big ash trays like that, do they?" Bucky added, looking around at the smiling faces of his sisters.

"You're right, son. They don't. It's a great ash tray," Bud said, turning the lumpy object over in his hand.

The bustle of breakfast resumed and Bud went upstairs to get his bathing trunks. Surtsey was fetching her toothbrush. "Let me see your present from Bucky," she said, observing a strange look on his face.

"Here," he groaned, handing it to her, "what am I going to do with that thing? It's too heavy to take in the suitcase. The hotel will have plenty of ash trays. I can't take that thing to Myrtle Beach." He laid it down on the chest of drawers and left the room. Surtsey picked it up with tears in her eyes, hurt at his insensitivity. She didn't know how to answer without starting a fight.

What should she do? She considered taking it herself, but Bud had put two dozen golf balls in her suitcase and he'd be angry if she brought the ash tray because she had said there was no more space for his golf balls! However, it was clear Bud wasn't taking it, and she wouldn't want Bucky to find out. After a little thought she made a decision; had anyone been looking, they would have seen Surtsey Sanders digging a hole under the bushes back behind the maple tree and burying a very ugly, very beautiful ash tray and shedding tears the way one does at a burial. It wasn't the first such hurt Surtsey had felt over her children's efforts to please Bud—and the pain never quite went away.

"Happiness is a polyester nightgown," said Surtsey, letting her nightie slip to the floor and standing beside the bed. Happiness is taking off a polyester nightgown! Maybe she could live up to her nickname—Surtsey, the volcano! She was afraid to look at her husband to see if he still enjoyed her like this, and in fact Bud never looked up at her lovely figure but kept on reading the morning paper. Surtsey walked to the window and looked out over the sea; she felt happy and relaxed. In these unfamiliar surroundings life was different from at home; they were free from all their usual inhibitions and daily habits. She was glad the children had talked her into coming. What they both needed were more vacations like this, more togetherness.

Surtsey picked up her robe and went into the shower, gaily singing, "Oh, what a beautiful morning." She turned on the faucet and stepped into the tub. The steamy water was relaxing. How great to feel like a person instead of a mother, she thought, if only for a few days! She was vaguely aware that the telephone was ringing in their room at the Surfsider's Hotel in Myrtle Beach.

Bud was asleep again when Surtsey called from the shower, "Answer it, Bud. I can't make it!"

"Let it ring," Bud mumbled. "Probably a wrong number— some drunk dialing the wrong room." Bud made it a policy of never answering the phone. It was one of the things he had children for. Besides, he gave his friends his phone number at the office. So why should he answer it now?

On the tenth ring Surtsey dashed from the shower, wiping suds from her ears, her body dripping on the rug. "Hello. Hello. Who is this? Oh, it's you, Mark!" she said in a shaky voice. "What is it? Bucky! Oh, no. I see." She turned to Bud who had one eye open, "Bucky's in the hospital again." Turning back to the phone she said, "Why? I see—a fever and pains in his legs. Yes, yes, I know you're doing everything, but we'll take the next plane home. I'll call from New York this afternoon—maybe we can get the evening commuter."

"Bud, do you think we'll get a seat on the late commuter?"

"Huh? No, I doubt it."

"All right, Mark. Take care of Bucky. Yes, I know you're doing all you can. I'll pray. Thanks, dear. Bye."

"Oh, Bud. It's Bucky! The doctors don't know what is wrong, but it might be something awful from that bruise—osteomyelitis. What shall we do?"

"Do? Nothing we can do. Mark will handle it. I have a golf game this afternoon. We're having a rematch. That damned alligator on the sixteenth hole ruined my putt."

"A golf game! But we've got to go home!"

"I don't know about you, but I'm playing golf. These men I've met from Syracuse might mean some business to me. Prince Charles will be okay." He always called Bucky Prince Charles when he was irritated, meaning of course that she spoiled him.

Surtsey's impulse was to fly home at once, but her husband didn't share her reaction at all. Was there something wrong with her? Or was it with him? She wanted to stay here to please Bud, but on the other hand, her husband should do some of the sacrificing, take some of the load. What should she do now? She was angry, but she sat down on the bed, deflated, spent. The end of a countdown and she was a dud! She couldn't even manage a feeble explosion even though she felt she should. What if Bucky were to die? She went back to the bathroom sobbing softly and turned on the shower and cried as hard as she could. It gave her relief and the strength to do what she felt she must do. Bucky had a mother and her place was with him. She put on her clothes and went back to the bedroom. The sun poured in the window and shimmered on the surf below, which pounded like her heart.

There was a knock on the door and a bellboy came in pushing a cart with their breakfast on trays. The children had thought of everything.

Bud sat up in bed, his hairy chest naked above the covers, and motioned the bellboy to bring the tray to him.

"This is my idea of luxury," he said, lifting the silver cover. "But I need ketchup on my eggs. Boy, will you fetch me some ketchup?"

"Oh, Bud," exclaimed Surtsey, dressing quickly, watching him eat, "aren't you worried about Bucky?"

"Hell, no. You're just a worry-wart. The kid has to learn to be tough. We don't want him turning out like Mark."

"Well," answered Surtsey, her face drawn, "I'm going home. Will you come back tomorrow as planned?"

"I think so," said Bud, munching toast. "Unless the fellows want another game. You can call me tonight." The woman in his wife would have been pleased if he had tried to stop her from leaving, but he did not, figuring she wouldn't stay anyway. They'd been married a long time and he knew her well.

"Bring along my big suitcase, please," Surtsey said, kissing him on top of his round, bald head. She left quickly, shutting the door behind her, and went at once to the airlines desk. There was only one clerk for a long line of plastics manufacturers, so she sat down nervously to await her turn.

Upstairs Bud picked up the phone and made a call to Temagami Springs. "Hello, honey doll! Miss me? Just getting up, you say. I wish I were there. When am I coming home? Well, ya see, I have a golf game with the fellows this afternoon, baby doll, but maybe tomorrow. Sure, sure I

love you. You're my little chickadee. Don't be worried—
we'll pick up the truck like I said over in Duxbury. It's our
secret, right, baby doll?

"Who, Bucky—sick! At his age it's just growing pains.
Don't you worry your curly head about Bucky. Boys have
to learn to be men; they don't need so much sympathy.

"You wanna know what color? What color would it be
for my little chickie? Well, I was going to surprise you—it's
yellow like your nightie. And I've bought myself a yellow
golf shirt. I think you'll like it 'cause I look real handsome
in it."

The door opened and Bud hung up the phone quickly.
"Just calling room service for more coffee, dear. Won't you
stay and have some?"

Surtsey, her mind on other things, looked about. "I forgot
my presents for the children. Oh, my, I didn't get anything
for Carol and I promised her a yellow sweater. You'll have
time, Bud—she wears size thirty-six, but be sure it's a cable
knit. I'll tell her you're bringing it."

"Okay, okay. Sure I'll bring it," he said.

On the plane back Surtsey was in a trance, deeply troubled
by conflicting emotions, worried about Bucky and worried
about their future as a family. Bud was becoming unbearable.

She had tried her best on this trip to please him and
she was not bitter toward her husband. Or was she bitter?
Maybe a little, but she was trying hard not to be. Nevertheless every now and then, like today, she was bedeviled by
her own lack of success. She knew her husband well enough
to know he couldn't help being the way he was—he wasn't
even aware of it. He liked himself. He thought she was
the crazy one. If only she could become immunized so she

would not have this recurrent pain from his indifference to his family. Why was she wounded afresh each time he acted so unfeelingly?

Surtsey suffered all the way home, angry at Bud, worried about Bucky; it took her most of the flight to recover her equanimity. By the time she reached Temagami Springs she made up her mind that it was in the interest of everyone for her to keep trying with Bud.

When her plane landed and she saw Mary Lynn, the twins and Mark waiting for her, her heart expanded with love. "They are such a comfort," she said to herself, "and so kind-hearted to give me this trip. I'll have to say something to help them over the defeat they will feel over my coming home without their father. What will I tell them?"

A New Partnership

The partnership of Jong and Jong was disintegrating. Bill was slowly, steadily, losing his more sophisticated customers as news of his problem with alcohol spread. Now it seemed to his wife that he was about to lose his best client, Brigham Bantley; and increasingly more often, it was Margo who had to face the shame and embarrassment and censor of the firm, as well as the gossip in the community, because Bill seemed unaware of his own behavior.

It was ironic that if Bill lost the Bantley account it would come about as a consequence of Bill's hobby of photography; but it could happen. For some years past Bill Jong had been doing photo work for his clients in appreciation for the investments they made through him. They were pleased by his personal attention and for him it was a nice little business deduction at tax time. When lightning struck the tree at Glory Land and the kids took over the bridge, it occurred to Bill—with nudging from Margo—that pictures might come in handy for Brig if a court suit came about, which seemed likely. Brig was appreciative; Bill had gotten good pictures of the split pine and the tree house hanging limply from the tree. He also took a good one of two twisted cycles, a blue Honda and an old red bike. The negatives were very clear and detailed, especially considering the poor lighting in the forest. But then Bill had the finest camera and the best lenses that money could buy and he could take pictures in any light.

Today Brigham Bantley had called to ask for the photographs and Margo Jong could not find them anywhere. Bill was in no shape to be helpful; in fact he was so sick he had not been to the office for over a week. In answer to her plea for help in finding the photos, he replied in a hoarse voice, "I told him I'd do him a favor and make his prints. They didn't come out so good. They're blurry." His hands were so shaky she wasn't really surprised about that.

"Let me see the negatives," said Margo. She would take them to an all-night shop and have them finished overnight.

"What negatives?"

"Bill Jong. You're drunk. Drunk! And you're losing weight. I hadn't noticed," she added, "that you're that thin. What are we going to do?"

"Well," he drawled, "if you'd do your duty and stay home and make me some good meals—but you're a lousy cook, just like your mother. A very lousy cook."

Another time she'd have risen to that. She was a good cook just like her mother, but she controlled herself. "Now what does that have to do with Brig's film? It's important. Now where is it?"

"I don't remember."

"You don't remember! You just had it yesterday."

"I'm a good photographer, the very best," Bill drawled, his head shaking and a leer on his face. "You have to expect a few mistakes. Can't win 'em all."

"Well, who's going to tell Brig you've spoiled his film?"

"I'm not gonna tell him. He shoulda had a professional do 'em. Can't trust this cheap help," he said. "Now quit botherin' me. I'm gonna watch Milwaukee play the Red Sox."

Margo stared at him. He had no sense of responsibility for his own mistakes; he was a very sick man. "And I thought we were out of liquor." She went into the darkroom to look for the negatives. Searching everywhere, she found the film cut in little pieces in the wastebasket; and there on the counter was a large brown bottle. She took the cap off and sniffed; she tasted it on her finger. It was vodka, in a bottle marked "developer"—of all places!

"Now what am I going to do? I'll have to go to Brig myself and try to explain what happened and I suppose," she sighed, "I'll have to tell him he better take his investment business elsewhere." What a hard thing to do and all so unnecessary if only Bill would give up drinking. If Margo could blow up or cry maybe she would feel better, but she had used up her emotions over Bill long since.

And so she went reluctantly to Glory Land; someone had to tell Brig. She explained to Mr. Bantley as best she could and he made it easy for her. He didn't seem to need the pictures after all. That was a relief. It was even more fortunate that he did not bring up his account, so there was no need for her to mention it either.

Margo's mind was full of other things, of plans for her new life as a mother. Dr. Levy said the baby was due any day now and that was all that mattered. How could she have endured this long summer without a new life to look forward to? Everything the baby would need was ready: receiving blankets, little shirts, diapers, all locked in her closet at the office. There was even a sterling silver rattle and a baby cup with M.T. on it, which had been hers as a baby. To think that her cup would soon pass to the next generation! The idea that she, Margo Telford Jong, was to become by adoption a link in the great chain of life was a thought that filled her with awe.

Tonight, after suffering the burden of her husband's latest embarrassing behavior, it was a relief to be driving through the dusk with pleasant thoughts in her head. Margo was so glad that Brig didn't care about the photos and that he had treated her with his customary enthusiasm and good manners, that she decided not to rush back to her irritable husband but to drive home by the long way round over Dolman Hill. And it was just when she roared up the hill in her Jaguar and out of the dark woods that suddenly, from one second to the next, what had seemed like such a large and heavy decision became absolutely easy. In that split second she knew she would not renew her marriage license in September. What a relief it was to have come to a decision at last!

Four o'clock the next morning the telephone rang in Margo Jong's bedroom. It was Dr. Levy saying her little daughter had just arrived—four pounds fifteen ounces; and though the adoption wasn't final and couldn't be until her own affairs were straightened out, if she came right over he'd give her a peek.

Now there was no turning back! For obvious reasons she had never said anything to Bill after he said she was crazy even to think of adopting. When she told her friends of her hopes for a child they invariably exclaimed, "Not at your age!" And so this baby was her own well-kept secret. Margo was a mother and no one knew or cared. But she cared.

She jumped into her freshly pressed white linen dress with blue sailboats on it and into her white clogs. She tied back her brown hair with a red ribbon and she looked like a twenty-five-year-old girl ready for a date. Then Margo went into the adjacent bedroom and, looking down at Bill who slept sonorously, she whispered, "Goodbye, Bill. It was good at times. Now I'm going away on an adventure you too could share, if only you would. I'm going to welcome a new soul to this world because you see, dear, I've just had a baby."

Having spoken those beautiful words, Margo Jong felt like a different woman—elevated, inspired, more important. On light feet she ran to her sports car; she felt as though she could fly if she tried. There on the horizon was a big orange moon lighting up the sky, lighting her way to the hospital. Indeed it was an awesome night, an awesome time; it has always been so when a mother receives her first baby.

What should she call her little daughter? After a moment's reflection, Margo said, "I'll call you Esther. Esther Sue Jong, after my mother. Mom, can you believe it? I have a baby!" Oh, how she wished her mother were alive to be with her tonight.

In the quiet pre-dawn hours, Margo parked her car at Savernake County Medical Center. Riding the empty elevator to the top floor, she tiptoed down the hall, peering in all the dark rooms till she came to the nursery.

The nurse, seeing her in the doorway, walked among the bassinets to the far corner in which lay the most beautiful baby of all. "May I hold her in my arms?" gestured Margo.

The nurse brought the baby, wrapped in a pink receiving blanket, into an anteroom and said somewhat snappishly, "The doctor said you might look at her."

"But I've never held a baby. Please," Margo pleaded.

"Only for a moment. She's very tiny."

Margo carried the baby over to the large picture window

and showed her the moon. "Look, Esther Sue Jong—look out there. There's love out there. It's waiting for us, and together we're going to find it and keep it forever." Esther opened her eyes and looked up into the glowing face of her new mother. Then she wriggled and went back to sleep. It was the happiest moment of Margo Jong's life, for in that moment she realized she had found love. It lay in her arms.

All the way home through the dawn Margo wept tears of happiness over Esther and tears of sorrow for poor Bill, who stumbled along the rocky path of rejection when he could just reach out and touch love. "Maybe some day he'll do it," she thought. "I hope he will."

Surtsey's Decision

Surtsey hugged each of her children in turn. "How's Bucky?" she asked anxiously, looking in their faces for some sign.

"He's much better," replied Mark. "Carol is staying with him and they're doing more tests."

"The doctor says he might let him go home tomorrow," said Mary Lynn. "We think the pain may be psychological. Bucky didn't tell the doctor, but little brother is worrying about you and Dad and 04Y4. You see, Mom, rooming with Phlox in the hospital and all, he knows her pretty well. He feels responsible for Dad taking Phlox to that motel. That's what he told me."

So they all knew about that too.

Mark laughed. "He says he was going to take her home on his bicycle. How about that?" They couldn't help but smile.

While Surtsey was claiming her bag, Mary Lynn murmured to Mark, "He didn't come with her. See, he didn't come. Why didn't he come?"

Once home in the family living room, Surtsey gathered her children around her and told them she had something to say. They seated themselves on the floor beside her chair. "Now," she began, "I know what you are all thinking. Obviously, your father didn't come back with me today and you are wondering if the trip was a waste of your great efforts in our behalf." She looked at each of them in turn before resuming. "I think I owe it to you to tell you what it has done for me. It has done a great deal. For one thing it has made me see that your father and I must be alone more often to feel like a couple again. We need that more than I realized. Maybe your father is right when he says I am a better mother than a wife. If so, it wasn't intentional on my part. By the same token, when he injures us by his insensitivity to our needs, he doesn't really mean to. I wanted him to come back home with me today, but he has a sale he hopes to make to a wholesaler in Syracuse, and he considers that to be in the best interests of our family."

Surtsey saw the dubious expression on her children's faces and she had to admit to herself she was putting the best possible light on the situation. However, she had to say something more to convince them that the status quo was worth preserving. And so she continued. "Dear children, I can't thank you enough. I can't begin to tell you how you've helped me by giving me this trip. It has shown me that love is giving someone something you can't have yourself. You couldn't go, but you made it possible for me to go. Surely, by the same token, we can let your father free to be the way he is. Some people can't seem to help being the way they are and making others miserable along with themselves, and they may never change. Your dad is one of those. But on the other hand maybe he will. If we resolve not to let him make us feel defeated and if we keep trying, our love may succeed in helping him to care about us. Furthermore, if we pray hard God will help him change!"

"So, what you're saying is that you're going to give him

another chance," said Mary Lynn.

"It's not a question of giving him another chance, my dear child. I have already given him a thousand chances and forgiven him a thousand things, and I guess I can forgive him a thousand more! It's too late for me at my age to lose my bread and potatoes and my Blue Cross plan," she joked. "That is, if I want to go on doing what I do best. I am rather a pro at being a mother, you know, though I must say there are many who are working overtime to make me think it's unimportant—even my children sometimes! Rearing children can't be just a sideline activity to some other occupation. It takes too much energy and thought and care, things money can't buy. So as long as there are fledglings in my nest I'm going to keep this family together. That's my decision. Bless you all and thank you for my wonderful vacation. Now let's go see Bucky!"

"Bucky, my dear, what are you doing back in this place? Don't tell me," said his mother gaily. "I can guess, you wanted me to come home and go bike riding with you!"

"The doctor says no bike riding for a while," replied Bucky sadly, "till the pain's gone."

"Oh, Bucky!"

"It's gonna be hard to be a good detective if I can't ride a bike and have to use crutches. He says I can't even run!"

"Well, maybe you'll have to take up another profession," commented Surtsey. "How is your detective work coming? Have you filled up the notebook with clues?"

"You can look at it. It's on the dresser by those flowers the Saffies sent—they know I like phloxes."

His mother opened the notebook and her eye fell on "white Corvette parked outside Thorn Motel, voices, laughter, sounds like Dad."

She turned to him. "Yes, I know you do. And we all know how much you like Phlox Fontaine!"

"Dad likes her too!"

"Yes, Phlox is a very attractive girl and your father likes attractive people. We all do."

"But Mother, Dad loves Phlox. I heard him say so."

"Oh, Bucky!" Then she hastened to say, "Love's elastic; don't you know we can all love each other?"

"I know, Mother. It says so in the Bible but, Mom, you just don't understand," he said matter-of-factly, looking pleased that she had brought him new comics.

"No," she murmured to herself, "I can't understand. Some things one can never understand."

Two days later Surtsey was in a state of nervous suspense awaiting word from the doctor, still wondering what was wrong with her little son. Bucky looked healthy enough; he had mentioned pain only once since she came from Myrtle Beach. She remembered what Mary Lynn had said about it being psychological. Bucky had mentioned Phlox and it was certainly apparent that he was infatuated with her; in fact Bucky seemed jealous of his father's helping the girl. That's what it was: Bucky was growing up enough to be jealous. He had a crush on Phlox, but he didn't really understand!

Surtsey pushed back her brown hair. Why didn't the doctor call? The test results were to be back today. He should have made his rounds by now. The worried mother poured herself coffee and let it get cold in her cup; she forgot to pay the laundry man; she called her dentist and thought she was talking to the eye doctor. She cleaned a bureau drawer.

It was afternoon when at length the important call came. The blood tests and X-rays were negative. Bucky could go home. Apparently he had a virus, a little synovitis perhaps. He must use crutches, but it should clear up soon. What a relief. Surtsey hurried to the hospital to bring her little boy home. He was her pal and he was going to be all right. If only he wasn't growing up so fast.

Surtsey rushed into Bucky's hospital room. "The doctor says you can go home now, and when you get there I know you'll feel just fine. If need be, we'll find you a new profession that's even more fun than being a detective. Mark wants you to help him; he has some toys that need to be sanded. And Anna Maria has invited you over tonight to pull taffy."

Bucky smiled. "I guess her cake business is a flop without me. You know my leg doesn't hurt anymore. And Mom, guess who just drove down High Street in a great big yellow truck?" said Bucky as he put on his shoes.

"Who?" asked Surtsey.

"Dad! That's who. Gee, I always hoped he'd get a truck to haul our Little League team around in!"

"Good," commented Surtsey, not adding that Bud would never chauffeur kids to a baseball game. "I'm glad you saw him. That means he'll be home soon."

Bucky was searching under his mattress, in the drawer, under the bed, searching everywhere. "Someone stole my Laser-man comic! Oh, Mom, I can't go home without it."

"Come," she laughed, smoothing his blond hair and tucking his shirt tail in his jeans. "I'll buy you another." She smiled tenderly at her little son. Home just wasn't the same without him.

Purple and Yellow

Bud Sanders flew back from Myrtle Beach happy over the money he had won at golf and with a contract for twenty thousand plastic swords from a Syracuse toy wholesaler. Everything was going his way and now he had a special treat awaiting him at home. He taxied from the airport to the town of Duxbury to pick up a new yellow GMC truck he had ordered as a gift for a certain little treat. The pickup truck was a nice machine and it would bring him a warm reception at the Thorn Motel.

Bucky had indeed seen his father drive up High Street in the yellow truck. The older man passed the hospital without giving his ailing son a single thought. Bud pulled up under the pines at the Thorn and was about to honk the horn, when he decided not to. He climbed down from the cab and rapped on the door. Phlox answered his knock and, as Bud knew she would be, Phlox was enthralled at what she saw parked beside the cabin. When Bud handed her the keys and she sat on top of three hundred and fifty horses, she began to believe that at last she was somebody of power and standing—a "top dog" who couldn't be shoveled around and programed by everybody else. This vehicle would buy her prestige at the only place left for her to go—Safflower

Hill—from where she planned to launch further ambitious projects.

"Now, baby," said Bud, climbing in the cab beside her, "how about a little reward for me? Just put a little kiss right here, baby," he said, puckering his lips together and pressing her against the door.

"Don't baby me, Mis-ter Sanders," she retorted, shoving him back. "And don't kiss me either. I'm no fool. Now when do I get title to this truck?"

"Soon, baby, soon—as soon as we can sneak over to Duxbury and transfer it to you. Next week for sure. Aren't you glad to see me? Didn't you miss old Buddy-boy?"

"Yes, I did," she softened. "I really did. Now I'm going to drive you to the Royal Purple for a big celebration. I have a date to meet a friend there after a while. How about fetching my sunglasses and locking the door?" While he dutifully did as he was told, Phlox, her pretty pink face animated, investigated the glove compartment and the set of tools and noted with satisfaction the four-speaker stereo and the CB.

"Go back and get an eight-track," she commanded Bud when he reappeared. It took a few minutes until he climbed up onto the seat beside her with her tape deck. He sat offensively close and he smelled of some weird cologne.

"Oooh, you smell good," said Phlox, at the same time tuning the stereo to its loudest. She allowed him to take a few small liberties with her person because it wasn't far downtown and it seemed a minimum price for a new yellow truck.

They parked outside the Royal Purple and Phlox ostentatiously locked the doors of the truck herself for the benefit of the freaks who were lounging about watching her enviously, and she quickly pocketed the keys. Bud, looking anxiously up and down the street, hurried his young companion into the dark, sour-smelling basement known as the Royal Purple.

Bud's reaction was what any of his peers might have predicted. He sniffed, made a face, and began to wonder who might see him there. He certainly hoped none of his kids ever came to such a hole. It was probably filthy; he couldn't see a thing.

Phlox sat down in a booth. "Here," she said, handing him two quarters. "Put these in the juke box." He did so, pressing the very first button, and quickly sat down, carefully turning his back to the tiny dance floor. Black strobe lights flickered, reflecting off his shiny bald head. Then with a great crash the acid rock pinned him in the booth. Phlox wriggled her shoulders and snapped her fingers and Bud fidgited in the seat, trying to attract the waiter to order a beer. He could use a beer. While Bud's back was turned, a sleazy looking guy like a sewer rat, damp and sticky, oozed up out of nowhere and pushed in beside Phlox.

"Did he come across?" the rat asked in a loud whisper, nodding his head toward Bud. Phlox gave him a look poisonous enough to wither crab grass.

"Mr. Sanders, meet Crabbe Grass."

"Gee, the Poly-Toy manufacturer! How about that? And you a friend of Phlox! How about that? Guess you two want to parlay a little, so I'll float on by." He winked a knowing wink at Phlox and oozed on away to watch from a dark corner.

"I know what you're thinking, Bud," said Phlox. "What's a nice girl like me doing in a place like this? It just so happens this is one of those places we kids dig—even those kids from up on the Hill. Maybe Mark will come in! It's nearly five-thirty." Her mention of Mark had the desired effect.

"Five-thirty! Say I've got to cut out and catch a cab home. There's a thing at the club tonight in honor of us board members. I'll call you when I'm free and I'll get you to Motor Vehicles first thing next week—after we have our real welcome-back-from-South Carolina party!" He wanted to kiss her, but he didn't dare. This was blackmail country, and he went home and took a shower.

After Bud left the Royal Purple, Crabbe Grass crawled back into the booth, followed by Stevie Rivers from the Hill. "Oh, hi," said Phlox, "I was hoping you'd come. I have great news, so prepare yourself for a surprise. I'm moving up to your place in a week or two and I'm bringing something big. Just prepare to elect me president of Safflower Hill! Don't put me on your work list; I'm going to be an executive. But find me a corner where I can put my sleeping bag. It must be clean and have a window view!" she commanded. Stevie's gaze indicated that Phlox had found a new slave.

Crabbe was jealous. He wasn't welcome at the Hill for all his money, his ill-gotten gains. After Stevie left, Crabbe looked greedily at Phlox. "Why do you go up there, my little chickie? You and I could make sound together—the hungry hound and the rich bitch." He snarled and howled in a low, insinuating voice.

"You're revolting," she said, holding her nose, her pinky finger with its turquoise ring pointing right at him. But he was the only ally she had besides Stevie, so she said no more but left the Royal Purple hurriedly. Crabbe waved goodbye and went on looking for customers. If he had seen what she rode away in he would have been very impressed!

A few evenings later Carol came into her mother's sewing room wearing a new yellow cable-knit cardigan. "How do you like it, Mom?"

"Is that the sweater your father brought you?" asked Surtsey.

"Yes," replied Carol.

"It's lovely, dear. It's so becoming. You should wear yellow more often. Now you see, your father does do nice things! I hope you told him so."

Carol answered in a low voice, "It's a perfect fit; I've wanted one for ages. There's only one catch."

"What's that?"

"You'll never guess who has one just like it," Carol said angrily.

"No, who?"

"Phlox Fontaine, that's who!" exclaimed Carol, her eyes bulging.

"Phlox!"

"Yes, Phlox. The last person in this world I want to dress like!"

"You'll have to wear it anyway to show your father you like it," observed her mother. It was difficult for Surtsey to get out the words, but the mother in her managed to speak though her throat was dry.

"Oh, I will. But wouldn't you know, just when I get something nice—" Carol paused, a look of contempt on her small square face. "On second thought, this is what I think of his yellow sweater." She snatched up her mother's sewing scissors and before Surtsey could stop her, Carol cut the lovely sweater into four pieces. "He can give it to her to shine that new yellow truck! Liar! Hypocrite! Maybe you can take his insults; I can't." Carol stormed out of the room. She came back again. "Furthermore, if you want my opinion, you're throwing your life away out of loyalty to someone who doesn't even exist! All you do is cover up!"

Surtsey bowed her head. She felt like a stone. Deny it she might, but her worst suspicions were confirmed. She could almost forgive Bud for herself, but she was deeply pained by the hurt he was inflicting on their children by carrying on with Phlox Fontaine. And it was true: she did cover up for him to try to spare them all.

Sudden Manhood

Word spread far and wide that more action was planned at Glory Land Park by that guy in the tree, and kids showed up in record numbers for the impromptu concert on the bridge. Skip was a hit with his songs about loneliness and Penny had her hands full protecting him from his new fans.

An hour after the park closed, Penny and Freud huddled over a table behind locked doors." One thousand for you, one thousand for me, one thousand for Skip," counted Freud. "Here's for the Saffies, two thousand, three thousand for each of us. How's that for starters, my little tooth fairy? Not bad for a few months' work," said Freud. "What are you going to do with your money?"

He looked up expecting to see her smiling, but her face was covered with tears and the next moment she fell on her knees in prayer. "I'm going to thank God," she sobbed.

Emotional women made him feel helpless. He didn't know what to do, so he folded his hands and lowered his head. "Jesus," he said softly, as he closed his eyes. The next instant, in a moment of enlightenment, he realized he was no longer a boy; he was a man standing on his own feet financially, through his own initiative. Simultaneously, in one shocking second, his summer revealed itself to him as an embarrassing stunt at the expense of the most beautiful and desirable girl in all the world.

His need to prove himself to her was gone, replaced by a need to make amends by doing something of lasting value. He had a thrilling idea: he wanted to get married.

"Wow," he said to himself as Penny got up from her knees.

"I'm so thankful God helped us. I was sure we'd go to jail. Don't you pray, Freud?"

He just smiled and said, "Penny, have you ever thought of getting married?"

Penny was startled. She looked at him, but he was looking off into space. He didn't mean her. She no longer thought of him as a possibility, but it hurt anyway. "I don't think I'll ever get married," she said. "I'm not attractive to men."

"Come off it. I think you're attractive. Some guys prefer quiet girls. Would you believe it, my little tooth fairy, I'm thinking of getting married."

"It's a good idea," she commented. "Babies must be easier than business."

"Why do you suppose people want to have children, Penny? Is it to keep a part of themselves living on or what?"

"No, we don't get immortality that way. We already have eternal life from God if we accept His Son," she said, "But isn't human life a miracle? To think that two people can create life out of their love for one another is absolutely beautiful and God-given. For His purposes, I might add. It's worth covenanting for," she sighed. "Now you've made me wish I could get married."

"There's someone for each of us, Penny. Don't give up hope." Freud licked a large brown envelope and handed it to her. "Here's Skip's pay. Run it over to him, please. I have to be going. This may well be the most important day of my life."

Freud found Savy sitting alone on the beach. She had been swimming. "What are you doing?" he asked.

"Oh, hi. Well, I'm thinking about life. I'm restless, I guess." She paused. "I was thinking about you. How you came and moved into my tree. All my life I've thought of this place as mine. I'm even named after this woods." She smiled at him. "Most of the summer I've had to overcome myself to be civil to you. But—"

"But what?"

"Well," she laughed, "lately I've found myself beginning to like you. Not the way all your groupies do. Actually, I think you're a big show-off."

"And you're hoping I'll grow up."

"Exactly."

"Then what?"

"Well—"

"We'll marry and live happily ever after."

"Must you always joke?"

Freud moved close to Savy and put his arm around her shoulder. "Savy, something's happened to me. I've fallen in love." She turned to look at him and he kissed her passionately. "I've fallen in love with you."

Savy didn't say anything, but her heart was a battleground of conflicting emotions. Surprise. Lingering resentment. Delight. Hope. And even a tiny urge to flee. But most of all desire to love and be loved by this man at her side. For the first time he seemed like a man, strong and not foolish, someone to look to for comfort and guidance, someone to share with. But she wasn't ready to answer. Too much was at stake.

The harvest moon was rising over the river and Freud lay down with his head in Savy's lap. She stroked his short blond curls and ran her hand down his arm. Then she stopped, her warm hand beneath his sleeve, and after a few moments' silence she spoke. "What is there about moonlight on water that makes it so beautiful? It's like a path of golden feathers."

"Yes," said Freud in a husky voice full of longing. "They say Tatty lets down her hair and goes canoeing on moonlit nights."

"Sit up. Maybe we'll see her." They sat quietly watching the gilded ripples coming to them from across the water and then she came, silhouetted against the bullrushes in the moonlight. Her elm bark canoe glided noiselessly by.

"Isn't she beautiful? She seems to belong out there tonight. Is she crazy, Freud?"

"No, she's not crazy. She's struggling to hold on to a world no longer real to anyone else. It's our loss, not hers."

They watched until the canoe disappeared into the shadows. Freud embraced Savy tenderly. "Savy, I love you. I need you."

She pulled him close to her and looked lovingly into his eyes. "I'd like to hold on to this moment forever and listen to you say that over and over and never go home."

"Then stay, my darling. Stay with me here in the forest," he urged, holding her close and kissing her face. "I have to sleep by the lumber pile tonight. Someone's planning to steal it. Share my sleeping bag with me."

She hesitated, holding on to him, afraid to lose him. Though she yearned to say yes, something within her said no, not now, not here. Maybe someday he'll ask you to marry him. Reluctantly she freed herself from his embrace.

"I can't," she said. "This is not the place for anything casual or meaningless."

"Casual? Meaningless! Is that what you think of me?"

"No. No, I don't mean it that way," she exclaimed, seeing his distress. "Hold me close, John. I do love you. I do. But please understand what I'm trying to say. Tell me you do. You just have to understand me. I never wanted anything so much, but not now, Kingjohn. When I give myself it will be forever," she whispered. "That's the way I feel."

"But Savy," he interrupted. "I want you to marry me."

"You do!" she exclaimed. "You really do? When do you think it will happen?" She gave him a hug, a big bear hug.

"How about Christmas?"

"That's a beautiful time for a wedding. I wish it wasn't four months away."

"Then stay with me now. Let's go." He stood up and pulled her to her feet.

"No, I won't." She looked into his eager brown eyes. "But I'll marry you in September, after the signing ceremony."

"That's it," he exclaimed. "Perfect timing. We'll show everyone that our generation still believes in marriage!"

"September isn't far away—not with all we have to do. Kingjohn, I am so happy tonight!"

A Day by the Sea

It is not given to every man to work for a dream and see it fulfilled, but Brigham Bantley was not an ordinary man and neither was his aspiration to place in Glory Land a massive stone sculpture by Henry Moore.

The sculpture, the Family Group, arrived from England and was brought by helicopter from the railroad siding the day before and placed on a low stone pedestal by Tony and his crew. Today Brigham Bantley was going to the Garden of Contemplation to see the great work in its new setting, a place not unlike the fields at Hoglands in Hertfordshire from whence it came.

Brig was elated that the great moment was here at last. Would the work of the creative genius from Terry Green couple with that of the nature-loving man from Temagami Springs in a fruitful marriage? If they wedded as he hoped, their marriage would remind his visitors of the happiness children bring. It seemed a fitting theme for a family park.

The first visit to any new addition to the park was always a special experience. In past years Olivia had gone with Brig, but this time, mindful of her vote against buying the Henry Moore, he decided not to risk any criticism on an occasion of such importance. He wanted to see the sculpture with someone who would share his enthusiasm, and so he asked Anna Maria to go with him to the garden.

She was delighted to be invited, not for any lofty reason but because she wanted the simple pleasure of sharing her employer's excitement. When in his company she felt a new zest for life. So much so in fact that her own personal plans, which had nothing to do with him, were changing. She was reexamining her life style and looking for a way to break free from Cornwall House. For what she did not know, but she knew she needed a more fulfilling life.

In the depths of her heart she had a dream she had never quite laid aside. It was a dream she shared with a great sisterhood of souls, a dream to know a man, a companion soul, so strong, so compassionate and understanding, so absolutely faithful that she would be totally secure in his love. In other words, she wanted to get married.

It had not escaped her notice that most of her married friends had not found fulfillment of their needs for love. Though married they still retained a yearning for a greater love, for *more and more love*. Surely public law 04Y4 had stirred the depths of every married heart and revealed that the need was still there. Yes, said Anna Maria to herself, somewhere in every heart there is a need for an unconditional love that loves us as we are. Somewhere there must be someone to love each of us that much!

Where would Anna find a man? Someone like Brig. Her employer was a happily married man and his lovely children were her friends. It was not in her to be anything but careful in her dealings with him. She was not like Olivia! Olivia's idolatry was absolutely embarrassing. However, Brig didn't seem to notice. But then perhaps he did; maybe that's why he asked Anna instead. No matter, it was a pleasant invitation.

And on a warm day in August Anna Maria and her employer went together to see the Henry Moore. As they approached the garden between high cedar hedges, the sculpture came into view. Both of them stopped. "Sh-h-h," said Brig. They felt like they were intruding on a family who had come into the garden to play among the flowers. The garden was alive with their presence. The father and mother figures held in their arms a squirming baby and this lively child seemed to say, "Let me down to run in the park!" The parents were reluctant to let him take his first steps lest he run away from them. The effect was more than Brig or Anna expected and they shook hands and congratulated one another on this work of art. The marriage was a success. They turned to look again.

One of the many pleasures of looking at a great work of art is to be reminded of another time, another place, an earlier bliss. For the moment Brig was back in Sevilla in the Maria Luisa Park and Anna relived childhood moments around a village fountain in Switzerland. After they shared their memories, they walked slowly around looking at the Family Group from every angle, commenting on their impressions and sharing their perceptions. The play of light on the carved stone varied from moment to moment. There were patterns from the passing clouds; and the shadows of the stone figures created ever-changing designs. The flickering sunlight and moving shadow created special gifts for them, for what they saw might never have been seen in the same light by anyone else. Therein was the special delight of sculpture in the out-of-doors. Brig was thrilled; this wonderful piece of art placed in his garden was a celebration between man and nature to the infinite glory of an ever-creative God. It was a success!

They seated themselves before the great work and as

they looked at it in silence, a beatific peace came over the park. The bees buzzed, butterflies danced and birds sang. The gardeners arrived and clipped and sprinkled and worked happily while the newcomers on their low pedestal played in the garden. For a few moments this place was the whole world for Brig and Anna. They sat side by side and said very little for a long time.

At length the sky clouded over and the light changed from bright sunshine to a dull shadowless haze. And their minds wandered away to other things, to things of this world. And as usually happens, they began to dwell on their concerns.

Brig broke the silence. "Anna Maria, did you ever have a Slinky toy?"

"No," she said, "I didn't. What do they do?"

"This new law," he went on, "is like a Slinky toy. This little toy with which our men at the state capitol thought to amuse us, to keep us pacified and happy, arrived in our homes 'special delivery.' We opened their gift and it looked like a simple idea, this renew or divorce. It was even intriguing to see what the other fellows would do about it. But once out of its box it went this way, that way, each twist leading to the next, taking us along with it. And now we're all in a tangle we'll never be able to undo. When I was five I had a Slinky toy, and when it got all twisted up, I cried and cried because I was helpless to restore it to usefulness. That's this law; it makes me want to cry because it has the power to destroy us and it can't be defused. We're worse off with it than we were before! It's after us. We know it's lethal; we should confer on what to do about it, but our communications are paralyzed. So it's 'run for your life, save yourself, save your heart, spare your feelings.' Each partner is alone, afraid, sick, running this way and that, in aberrant directions like so many drugged spiders. What kind of example is this for our children?

"What, after all, is marriage?" he continued. "I believe it to be two people as one entity, of one spirit, with common commitments, who magnify and give security to one another. It isn't worth much if it doesn't do those things. But all that's been vaporized by the power of 04Y4 to divide us."

He shook his head. "At first, like everybody else, I thought it was a fairly simple law. But as summer passes, as I see what it's doing to us, I realize it is an act of Cain, alienating us from ourselves, our God, and one another. Yes, it is an act of Cain!" Brig sighed a sigh from the abyss and his usually animated face was long and drawn, his purple eyes black with concern. "Where will it all end?"

Anna understood what Brig was saying. She said nothing. 04Y4 sat beside them, ticking away. Brig was wounded; where would he run?

It was not long till her companion resumed speaking. "This sculpture means a lot to me. I chose it because it represents a family—robust and strong, together, steady, loving—like the families that built America. If one person sits here this summer and looks at it and realizes that this is what life's about, then it was worth bringing all the way from England to Savernake Forest. When I had the idea of acquiring this work it was a good idea, but now it seems a feeble weapon! It's rather easy to think of little ways to please the public; it's my own wife I can't satisfy.

"You know, Anna, my wife has run away from me. She seems to be searching for some satisfaction she hasn't found in our life together. I don't know what it is. I'd hoped we could talk and arrange for September 15, maybe go away together afterwards on a second honeymoon, but we're almost out of touch. Furthermore, it sounds like she's enamored of a young black man. If that isn't middle-aged madness I don't know what is!

"Before she left in May we had a quarrel. She wanted me to take a consultant's job in Saudi for my old company. Their headhunters have contacted me many times, and believe me the pay is higher than ever. But as I told her, this is *my* land, my glorious land. I've invested my life in it and I'm too old to be an *Auslander*. That's a trip for the young. I love this country—there is nothing like it anywhere on earth. Somehow we have lost our sense of direction; we are in the hands of unwise men, and I want to help people who are trying to save us from giving up our freedoms to men with no moral values. If I'm to do that, we can't live abroad!

"Then there's the fact that suddenly I realize time is my most precious commodity. I can feel it running out, and yet there's got to be more to life than I have ever tasted. I'd like to go looking for something more, something to hold on to, while I'm still young enough, healthy enough, to do it."

"You know," said Anna Maria when he stopped talking, "you remind me of Tolstoy, that great man who had everything and found out that it wasn't enough."

"I do?"

"Yes. He had what you have—a fine wife and lovely children, a high place in his society, many friends and honors. And yet, as I recall, it was from a lowly peasant farmer that he found that ultimate human happiness comes from none of the things that seem important; it comes from knowing God. The whole world needs Him, Brig. It's getting late for all of us. We need to accept His love and share it with others before it is too late.

"But instead of turning to Him we seek everywhere else for happiness, fun, achievement—belittling the other fellow, trying to feel more important because we really feel so small. But there is one to whom each one of us is very special. Before we destroy one another, each of us should ask a single question and seek its answer. 'Why am I, insignificant Anna Maria Abendtal, here? Why was I—with all the genes and other factors that make me *me*—why was I chosen to live on this earth? Why *me*? How am I, so blessed to be chosen, supposed to behave towards my fellow man, equally chosen? Am I to hate him, kill him, misuse and exploit him? Surely not. As soon as one asks all these questions, God comes along with the answers and life not only makes sense but is very beautiful. God will fill us if we let Him! He will sustain us through every ordeal!"

"Like you do me, dear Anna," murmured Brig. "You have helped me more than I can say. I think you're the greatest person I ever met." He looked at her and she blushed.

Just then Tony stepped up and, touching his cap, said, "Pardon me, sir, I hate to disturb you, but I'd like to finish the bench you're sitting on before I go home."

"Of course, Tony. The garden is beautiful. It will be a great place for our visitors."

"It's just magnificent," added Anna Maria. "I've never seen such beautiful stonework. It's like in the old country." That pleased Tony.

"Come along," said Brig to Anna, leading her away. When they were out of earshot he said, "Let's drive down to my place by the sea. I don't have a radio, a TV, or a telephone. I usually take off my watch when I'm there. All those things get in the way of my spirit! We'll spend the whole weekend swimming and talking like two high schoolers."

"I am in need of a change," said Anna slowly, considering the idea. It would be a welcome respite. "This has been a very demanding summer, hasn't it?"

"Let's leave right now. I'll get the Mercedes."

In a short time they were on their way. They drove along slowly through the hilly green countryside. The mid-summer air was pungent with a smell of heliotrope and clover. The grey-pink sumacs danced and swayed in the wind and red-winged blackbirds swooped across the road before them. Brig and Anna said very little, but the two-hour drive went quickly by and, in what seemed a few minutes, they were in their bathing suits on the sand.

A dozen sailboats, tilting with the wind, slipped smoothly past, each one a little island of tranquility. Fishermen sat in the lagoon in their heavy rowboats, and the breezes were fitful and cool. For a few hours there that afternoon it was a world without care, a tranquil summer's day, and they were absorbed in its bliss.

They lay on a blanket on the hot sand and listened to the sound of the surf. There was silence between them. Their thoughts flew outward, each on its own path, but the com-munion they shared, though silent, was rich in sensitivity to the beauty of this moment of rest and tranquility. Neith-er spoke; neither wanted to break the spell. As they lay side by side on the sand there came to them that sense of care-free happiness that belongs to youth, a sense of vitality in their being together, a sense of time without end. If they had been young lovers that beautiful afternoon they would have discovered that they were meant for each other and looked ahead eagerly to nightfall, to other days of exploring the depths of their love. But these two people, mature and middle-aged, had experienced life with many of its hard-ships and some of its rewards, and they knew that one searched for but seldom found moments like these. They also knew they didn't have long days to be with one another nor long nights of surrender. But as they lay there side by side, they knew that somehow during this day together, they were experiencing the essence of being. Brig and Anna Maria communed in silence, for they knew this afternoon was a precious God-given moment in their lives that might never come again.

The very trees whispered and sang, "Treasure it," and the breezes whispered, "Savor this moment in your lives. Hold it in your hearts; it is a bit of eternity. Hold it. Remember it."

Like every living thing is born, lives and fades, so did this precious afternoon. The sun went behind the clouds and the wind was chilly. "Anna Maria." Brig's voice sounded loud, self-conscious. He coughed and started over. "Anna Maria, let's play Frisbee!"

Anna Maria laughed her warm laugh. "Brigham Bantley, I'm not twenty, you know; I'm more like two hundred."

"Well, neither am I," he said, flinging the purple disc over her head. She chased it and brought it back. "Just for that I'll give you my famous side arm throw," and she sliced it towards him in a swift curve, which he barely caught. "That's a deck tennis throw from Temagami High!"

"Say, how about this?" Brig exclaimed, twirling it between his legs. The Frisbee caught the wind and sailed on and on, rolling away down the beach. They began to laugh and laugh until they were so tired chasing and laughing and never catching the elusive disc that they lay down on the blanket, all out of breath.

"Let's have some music," said Brig. "Some oldies for two-hundred-year-old Frisbee players. How about Rodgers and Hammerstein?" He put on a cassette of *The King and I* and they lay back to listen. When Gertrude Lawrence sang, "I've had a love of my own," Brig put his arm over Anna's back. "Anna, you've never told me. Have you had a love of your own?"

"I've had my children."

"I don't mean them. I mean a man."

She turned her head towards him and looked at him tenderly. "Yes, Brig, it was long ago and I've had years and years to ask myself if I did the right thing to let him go. Funny thing—04Y4 has made me think about it more."

"How did it happen? Who was he? Tell me—it's a side of you I haven't shared."

"No, no one has," she said, sitting up and leaning back on her arms. "No one has ever asked me before, but I'll tell you." She stared out over the sea and for a moment said nothing. Then she spoke, thinking aloud. "The pain is long since gone. It was in 1950 that I met Neal. he came to the army base in Brownfields to train and we became engaged before he went overseas to Germany. While he was abroad I inherited Cornwall House and all those early American ancestors I told you about. After two years Neal came home on leave. He wanted me to marry him at once and return to Munich. I can still hear his words. 'Maria, we've waited too long. We'll get married tomorrow and we'll sell the Cornwall House and invest the money in IBM and when we return we'll buy a ranch in Colorado.'

"Of course I know now he didn't realize the shock I experienced. I'll never forget it—his saying in that off-hand manner that we'd sell my precious house. He was going on about IBM being the company of the future and his dreams of a ranch, and all I could think of was his wanting to sell my precious inheritance. I realized he didn't understand the significance of Cornwall House to me." She shook her head back and forth, reliving that moment. "And he didn't know the real me at all or he would never have said that to me. So I sent him away and the last I heard of him he was working on a ranch someplace as a cowboy taking dudes on little trips. That was years ago and I sometimes wonder if he ever got his ranch."

Anna made a big pile of sand and patted it with her hands. Then she continued. "Often in the long lonely nights—and believe me, Brig, there are many when you live alone— often during the years which have passed, I've wondered if saying no was right after all. It was hard not to marry and have children, especially hard not to have children of my own. Do you think I was right?"

It was well she hadn't asked Bill Jong that question. He would have told her that a ten-thousand-dollar investment in IBM in 1950 could have bought her ranches and everything else that money can buy. But Brig knew Anna wouldn't have found happiness with an unloving man for all the money in the world. And so he answered, "I don't know, but I'm glad you didn't or I never would have had this day with you. Your friendship means as much to me as it has meant to Skip."

"Have you heard about his golden record?" asked Anna, glad not to talk any more about herself.

"He owes so much to you! To think that for years Skip was seeing you every day and I didn't even know you till this summer. I'll have a long time to regret that." The cassette played on. "Be brave, young lovers, wherever you are; be brave and faithful and true."

"That's too sad," Brig said, snapping off the machine. "Let's have a quick swim and go get some supper. And then tonight something beautiful will happen. We'll sit on the deck when daylight fades and we'll watch the stars together. I love the stars, don't you?" Without waiting for her answer, he continued. "It's August—there will be meteor showers tonight. How I love an August night!" He dived into an oncoming wave. Anna Maria, who was not much of a swimmer, floated happily in the waist-high water and rose up and down on the swells beyond the tiny breakers. She too loved the stars.

After a time they left the water, dried their wet legs, and put on their shoes. Gathering suntan lotions and towels to return to the house, they looked up to see a man riding towards them on a wheelie. As he came closer, Brig recognized him. "It's Mr. Sam from the General Store. He must have a telephone message for me."

Brig took a yellow paper from the man's hand, gave a brief nod, and the man rolled away down the strand. It read, "Grandma is dying. She's in a coma and an ambulance took her to the hospital." Brig looked out across the ocean for a long time. Then he said in a low voice, "Anna, it's bad news about Mother. She's dying. I must go."

"Oh, Brig, I'm so sorry," said Anna Maria, comforting him in her arms. "She means so much to you."

"Yes, she does."

"Of all the nights of my life, why did it have to be this one?" he cried, as he clung to Anna Maria. "I don't want to leave you."

"Brig, Brig, the Lord gives and the Lord takes away," she said. Why now—oh, why now? Both of them wanted the day to go on as it had. But it was not to be. Anna broke free and said quietly to her companion, "I'll be ready to go back in a few minutes and I'll make you a sandwich and a thermos of coffee. You'll have a long night ahead."

"Dear, dear Anna! I am desolated at being separated from you now. I'm not ready to say goodbye to this beautiful day. Let's stay a few minutes more." They stood side by side looking out to sea each with an arm around the other and then he bent down and spoke softly in her ear, "Thank you, my evening valley, for giving fresh meaning to my life and the courage to face what lies ahead. Will you let me tell you how much you mean to me?"

She looked up at him and smiled. "Dear Brig, you just needed a friend and I came along. That's what friends are for."

He drew her into his arms and they held each other close, and in their hearts they wept. They wept for dying mothers and lost wives, for old romances and for each other's sufferings, for human life and all its sorrows. And they wept because this beautiful day was drawing to a close so abruptly.

"Oh, dear evening valley, how I wish we could stay to watch the stars, but we must go. I will never forget this day. I think it will sustain me forever."

"Yes, Brig, it will sustain me too."

A short time later, as they drove home through the deepening twilight, the evening star appeared in the sky. Brig rolled back the roof of his Mercedes and they rode silently under the stars. Along the way, he drew the car over to the side of the road and they stopped to watch for meteor showers. Seeing none, it was necessary to press on, for much lay ahead. Brig drew his friend close to him, but Anna pulled away. Their day was over, and they were going back to reality. Sad as it was, there was a comfort: each was carrying something new in his heart, for something beautiful had happened that day by the sea and they would never forget it as long as they lived. They had shared together the wonder of being alive, of being a creature on a beautiful blue orb. In spite of sorrows and sufferings, it was wonderful to have been chosen for life on earth, and they both knew that it was so.

The Competency Hearing

Unbeknownst to the Filch brothers the competency hearing of Tatty Softshoe was called off thanks to the intervention of Harry Homer. On the twenty-eighth of July, Reed Filch, determined to get Tatty into the county home and in her absence search for the treasure rumored to be hidden on her place, was on his way to the hearing he had initiated. Knowing that the owner of Homer's Steel and Scrap was a familiar figure at the courthouse, he thought it might be politic to take him along to help increase the pressure on the judge to confine Tatty.

Harry Homer ushered Reed Filch into his cluttered office, which smelled of dust and engine oil, and they sat down. Harry pushed aside the invoices and dirty ash trays that covered his desk, and as he did so, he asked Reed what he had on his mind.

"Well," answered the storekeeper, "it's like this. I'm on my way to testify at the hearing to put Tatty Softshoe in the county home. She's not fit to be livin' alone. She charges at my place and never remembers to pay. Senile as they come, she is. Will you come along and help me?"

Harry Homer's sallow face went pale and the vein in his forehead swelled and pulsed. He swiveled away from his desk and got heavily to his feet. He was wearing bedroom slippers because he had a bunion. Saying nothing, he flapped back and forth, a deep frown on his face.

"We need your help to do it, Harry," said Reed Filch, prodding him. "Tatty's crazy as a loon!"

At that remark, Harry's eyes blazed. He drew his two hundred ninety-eight pounds up to full height and shoved Reed Filch, who was rising from his chair, back down. Harry picked up his telephone. "Now you listen to me. I'll dial the county home and make a reservation for a new patient and that patient is you." His voice was rising as he spoke. "Mr. Filch, Kaleri Softshoe is not crazy and she is neither incompetent nor penniless. Furthermore, she is my wife! As soon as I get that carload of scrap out there sold," he exclaimed, his arms flailing in anger, "we're going to the Fontainebleau on our honeymoon. I don't suppose you know where that is? Of course you don't," he added, scornfully.

"Now, you get out of here. I may charge you with slander. You'll be hearing from my lawyers. Get out before I throttle you. And I have Dobermans at our lakeside home in case you have any further good ideas!"

Mr. Filch, at the mention of lawyers and dogs, fled from the junk yard, his face quivering in shock and disbelief. What a story he had to tell his customers.

Every now and then something nice happens to a lonely person. Sometimes someone going down the street meets someone going up the street and they decide they can make a life together.

In some such manner it happened to Tatty and Harry that day he had promised Freud "to think of something."

That very day, far out on Big Bear Lake in an old row boat, a heavy man, his duck hunting hat pulled low over his ears and a Cuban cigar clamped between his teeth, cast his line down into the black waters of the lake, and when he pulled a fish into the boat, a wee person in an old velour fedora and a bulky fur coat put new worms on his line, and both of them had a very good time together. They shared a reverence for life—he for the work and the bread to sustain it, she for the soul to endure and magnify its purpose. And so the improbable pair, casting aside the conventions and wrongful judgments of men and relying on their inner promptings, found they could serve and elevate each other.

Not long afterwards, Kaleri Softshoe Tuttle married Harry Homer and the incompetency hearing was canceled. The only person who knew of this extraordinary union was John Freund III who stood up with the couple.

"At first," said Tatty to Freud, "we was just gonna live in sin. Harry said he figured we'd get more social security that way. But I went out in my canoe and had a long talk with Irv. He said, 'No, that wouldn't be right, Kaleri. I want my girl to get married. God will take care of you and Harry.'" She paused for a time as she thought about that. Then Tatty continued, "And Ruth must have said the same thing to Harry because the next day we just looked at each other and said, 'Let's get married.' What's five dollars a month, young 'un, when happiness is at stake? Do you suppose we'll have to come back from our honeymoon to sign that silly 04Y4?" She bit her lip and looked up at him out of her squinty eyes.

"You'd better come, Mrs. Homer. Irv wouldn't like you to get a divorce," laughed Freud. And Tatty laughed too as they gripped each other's hands in happy understanding that life is good indeed, no matter what! And that's how it happened that Harry Homer was so angry at Mr. Reed Filch.

Descent from Table Mountain

Word of Mother Bantley's death was bounced off a satellite to the office of Sinbad Ltd. in Capetown, South Africa, and delivered to Lucy Bantley on top of Table Mountain. Lucy left her friends looking at the magnificent view of two great oceans, and a few hours later she was aboard a Pan Am flight to New York, with a refueling stop in Dakar.

The trip home was a long one, with many hours to shed tears of sorrow that she would never see Mother Bantley again, never say goodbye to the dear old lady who had made her part of the Bantley clan. Brig's mother had presided over a family that was a family in the truest sense of the word—a tribal sense, people of all ages devoted to the well-being of one another. It had been a sustaining and satisfying thing for Lucy, who had lived in many places and had no real childhood home, to be counted a Bantley.

The old lady stepped down from her position of leadership when she became senile. No, she had not stepped down; she had slid away slowly, and since that time the children had gone their individual ways. Nevertheless there was a strong tie there, and now, with Mother Bantley's passing, it was the end of an era for the family. Lucy would miss her mother-in-law, who was as dear to her as a mother.

After she had recovered from her first shock, and after she accepted the fact that she had left her wonderful tour and was on her way home, Lucy Bantley began to think about Mamadoo. Here was her chance to get in touch with him. Maybe, if there was a delay, she could even see him. She would telephone the Teranga Hotel where the eleven o'clock show would just be ending. It would be fun to talk to that nice young man again and to ask him if he had written any new songs.

How good it was of him to come to see me off and bring me flowers, she thought. The picture of him was still in her mind: the deep blue robe, the black, black skin and the orange flowers. I wonder if he still dreams of coming to America?

When her plane landed at the Dakar/Yoff airport it was well after midnight. Lucy deplaned and hurried to find a telephone, rehearsing in her mind how she would address the operator in her poor French. As she rushed along she became aware of someone coming rapidly towards her. She looked up to see Mamadoo. He was strikingly dressed in his very best purple robe and hurrying towards her in great long strides. She noticed again how thin he was, like a Giacometti statue.

What a marvelous coincidence that they should meet here! Perhaps he was going on her plane. As it turned out he had come just to meet and be with her again. She was flattered he had come.

"How did you know I was on that plane?" Lucy asked eagerly. "I wasn't planning to be!"

Mamadoo smiled shyly and shrugged his thin shoulders. He had his ways; he had been expecting her. It couldn't be that he knew, and yet he was here. Lucy was delighted.

Could it be that her coming was relayed by jungle drums? She'd heard that in Africa messages are passed over great distances, relayed by jungle drums. It couldn't be that her coming was announced—or could it? Lucy loved mysteries; she might write an article about this one for *The Morning Republican*.

In fact she was so tickled to see him, she said impulsively, "Mamadoo, do you still want to come to America?"

"I do."

"But why with me?" she asked.

"Because I like you. I like you because you are an American," he said quite matter-of-factly. To him it seemed reason enough but not to her. She looked doubtful.

"Do you like all Americans?"

"No, just you. You remind me of a white mama in a song my mother sang to little baby Mamadoo." Lucy looked at him curiously. Imagine that; she was thinking she'd like to hear that song. Perhaps she could arrange to stop over when she returned to Africa in a few weeks. There were still the game parks to see; in fact they were what she wanted most to see. So she would undoubtedly be coming back to finish her trip as soon as the funeral was over. Why, she was just getting to know the most interesting people— that anthropologist from Berkeley and the ornithologist from Australia.

Yes, she would come back, and she would see Mamadoo again. Meanwhile, she was asking herself a question. Could this child of Africa make it in America? It would be difficult for him, but maybe he could if he had help—her help.

"I know nothing of this young man," said her rational mind. "I will find a way to help him," argued her emotions. "I have seldom used my partnership in Glory Land or offered any ideas. Perhaps it's time I do. This boy is bold and he's candid—both useful qualities in the complicated world back home. I like him and I'll trust him. With enough publicity, enough bally-hoo, I'm sure he will be a success—a modest success at any rate," said her practical business sense. "My children will love him and they will learn from each other." She talked herself into making him an offer right then and there, because if she went home first she knew what would happen. Someone would talk her out of it.

"If you really want to come to America," she found herself saying, "if you really want to, then let's sit down and talk about it." She looked directly at him. "You don't know anything about my land. It's very different. Do you understand that you might not be happy there, that in fact our ways might ruin you?" He lived in two worlds now, the city and the bush. Could he adjust to a third without losing his precious individuality?

"But don't you see," he answered, "I want to be ruined as you call it. I want to be a success in America. I have cousin in Detroit. I want to be American." He lifted his bony shoulders and made a French gesture with his arms. "After all, we are your ancestors." Lucy laughed. What a funny way to put it, but maybe he was right; some scientists were saying all life began in Africa, so maybe it was true! She stopped laughing.

"But what about your family, Mamadoo? Can you leave them?"

"Ah, there are so many of them. Of course they can't come with me. But I'll send back all my money."

She shook her head. "Not all. It costs much to live in America."

"Not the way I live—not simple."

Was anything simple at home anymore? No, nothing—nothing inexpensive or free or natural. Even simple living was dear. She suspected if Banter didn't get a job soon he'd find that out. Lucy Bantley didn't try to explain the complications to the Gambian. His ideas of America were based on what for him was reality. His cousin had sent dollars from America and so would he. That was what mattered, because money meant bread.

She looked at him again and he smiled. He was very thin; he never had enough to eat because he fed so many others. A good job was more important to him than all her theories about cultures. What is culture after all but peoples' ways—the ways they find their bread. Cultures span decades, even centuries. What do the starving care about culture? It was important that she help him in every way she could. He had the talent to succeed and if he went with her to America it would be up to her to sell that talent and at the same time protect his native spirit and strengths.

Yes, it was up to her to help and protect him. His future lay in her hands. Whatever was to be or whatever might have been, either way, she was now involved; she had to live with that realization. It was a heavy responsibility, but she suddenly felt very strong and very important to be undertaking it. "Mamadoo, listen to me. I'm going home to a funeral. I'll be passing through Dakar again in a few weeks on my way back to the *African Prince* and possibly I can change my plans to stop here once again later on. In any case, prepare yourself to go to America. I'll contact the United States Embassy; I have connections in our State Department. I will sponsor you and buy you a ticket. Do you need money?"

He looked at her carefully. Gone was his natural smile. He was afraid his answer might be misconstrued. He shrugged his shoulders.

"Your people will have to eat until you earn money. I will give you an advance on the pay you will receive for singing for my family in Glory Land." It was her commitment, and if he accepted they had a deal.

His face was somber and his black eyes brimmed like full cups of water. He was no beggar and it was hard for him to take money from a woman. However, it was necessary, and he snatched it and put it quickly somewhere inside his kaftan.

"Pan Am Flight for New York now boarding at Gate 1. All passengers report at once to Gate 1," said the loud-speaker.

"Now I must leave you, but I'll be back. Prepare yourself for my return," she called as she walked to the security checkpoint.

Later that morning the sun rose over the Atlantic and followed her across the sea, and Lucy thought a long while about her promise to the friendly singer. "How impulsive I'm getting in my middle-age." She reflected that as far as Mamadoo was concerned she had gone from "maybe I could" to "perhaps I should" to "of course I must" quite quickly for one of her disposition. She knew nothing about Mamadoo and was helping him out of faith alone. So what! It felt good, very good, no matter what anyone would say at home. They were all running everywhere doing their thing and so would she. They could like it or not. She had her Mamadoo and he would be a success in America. She would see to that!

Jail

For several weeks a peach-skinned girl with blue eyes and short, wavy wheat-colored hair, looking decidedly more animated than she had in many months, was seen driving around Temagami Springs in a new model yellow GMC pick-up. She was wearing tight jeans and a deep yellow cable-knit cardigan. When the truck needed gas she charged it at the Gulf Station on Third and Main where Bud Sanders had done business for thirty years.

Who was she? Where did she live? The gossip reached the ears of Mr. Freeroder at the Freeroder Bike & Cycle Shop who recognized her as the Fontaine kid, former house guest of the Freund family. Someone else had seen her in a white Corvette, which was frequently parked at the Thorn Motel. No one in town had a white Corvette but Bud Sanders; so the story was put together that the president of Poly-Toy had a twenty-year-old chick.

Actually Phlox was waiting for Bud, who was either working or playing golf at the Temagami Club, to come across with the transfer papers for her truck and it seemed like a long wait. Bud was keeping her dangling in order to reach a level in their relationship which satisfied him that she was his before giving up title to the truck. She seemed just a little too eager to have it. Meanwhile, Phlox spent her time sleeping and driving around town trying to arouse a little envy. Sometimes she parked by the dam to try breaker, one-nine on her CB and sometimes she lounged at the Royal Purple, which had become a pretty dull place what with all the kids gone to work at Glory Land. Things got going in the evening, but all in all it was a long day for a person with nothing to do.

With few companions to choose from, Phlox spent lots of time talking to Crabbe Grass about the rotten side of life, and she spent a lot of time thinking about her arrival at Safflower Hill. She would not give the Safflowers title to her truck; she would rent it to them for whatever privileges she wanted. Nor would she contribute any of the clothes she designed to their common pile. They could have her old stuff—the purple knit pantsuit her mother had given her, the yellow cardigan from South Carolina (it was really not in style), and a few other things, but none of her own original designs. She didn't want her designs modeled by farmers!

And now and then when Phlox had time, she put on lipstick, swiped from her mother's purse, and wore it just to please Bud. He liked women in lipstick and it was a kind of fun way to play dress-up. She regretted his giving her the pretty yellow nightie; it would go into the clothes pool too, and that couldn't happen soon enough!

Finally, she grew impatient when it began to seem like Bud was putting her off about the truck. At the same time she ran into Crabbe, also restless, and he suggested they plan a little caper together. They would drive her truck to the famous bridge, well after midnight when dumb ol' Freud would be asleep in his tree and Simple Simon in her tower, and they would steal a pile of lumber they knew was waiting there for some new building project. They'd take it up to the Hill, as a sort of present, and leave it at the farm just to see who accused whom of what!

It was a cracker-jack idea except that it failed. Someone tipped off Freud, still angry over the blue Honda, and he slept out on the bridge and watched Phlox and Crabbe—both of them physical weaklings—lift the boards onto the truck. When they seemed to be tiring of their little stunt and began arguing over how many to take, Freud telephoned the police.

By morning, Phlox and Crabbe were in the county jail. Phlox made her one call to her mother, who called Tulie, who didn't feel she could intervene on account of her position as a judge's wife, and so she called Anna Maria, who—as one might expect—was filled with concern for a young person in trouble and agreed to help Phlox if she could.

Anna Maria promptly dialed Jean Fontaine. "I've just heard about Phlox. That poor child in jail! How lonely she must be."

Jean answered, "It serves her right. Maybe it will do her good. It's so embarrassing!"

"Serves her right? Will do her good?" It will toughen her, thought Anna. Aloud she said, "If you don't mind, Jean, I'll go at once and see what I can do to get her out. She's too young to take such consequences. How lonely she must be. How very lonely."

"She's never been lonely in her life," answered Jean. "She's been supported and has everything!"

"I'm sure she has, but what comfort is that to her now? She's not a full-grown woman yet. Don't you see that all this nonsense that's been going on is just her cry for help. If you remain deaf to it she will be totally lost; of that you can be sure!" To herself she thought, You wouldn't step on a beautiful flower because it fell—you'd pick it up. Youth should be beautiful inside and out. I must tell her God loves her. "Why didn't you come to me before, Jean?"

It was comforting to Jean to have someone doing something even though she resented this woman, whom she barely knew from Lost Friday, acting like she knew more about Phlox than her own mother. It was insulting in a way; but perhaps Anna Maria could do something to mitigate this awful disgrace, which was even worse than that terrible happening in the tree.

Jean thanked Anna Maria coolly and put down the receiver. "I wonder what a man like Brig Bantley sees in her." Jean felt a headache coming on. With Phlox in the county jail she needed an immediate hour with her psychiatrist.

Anna Maria, on the other hand, hurried to the jail with her heart full of anguish for Phlox. It wasn't a great distance, so she went on foot. As she walked down the street she realized she had never been to the county jail nor met Sheriff Smith. He had been reelected twice; apparently the citizens were satisfied. She hoped he was kind and she also hoped the justice would either set a bail she could afford—or better still, dismiss the case. She wondered again about the episode in the tree. She had heard the stories that Phlox was found in her underwear, but she also had heard from Tulie that Phlox had driven Freud away from home. Anna had known Freud since he was a kid, and she knew he didn't need to take advantage of a girl like Phlox. Anyway, that was none of her business.

The more recent scandal about the Fontaine child and Bud Sanders was shocking, and so sad for Surtsey Sanders. It was said Bud kept Phlox and bought her the truck.

Maybe, thought Anna, he meant it as an act of philanthropy to a neglected child, but that was not what everyone was saying. Surtsey had confided in her that Bud met Phlox for the first time when she shared a room with Bucky in the hospital. Funny, the way hospitals were mixing the sexes. Short of nurses, they said—sharing expensive equipment, they said. But where was good judgment? There seemed to be no good judgment anywhere, so how could an institution be better than the people who ran it? Well, all that was water under the bridge and the world was full of people making mistakes, bringing pain to others. It was sad, but if she could help Phlox it would surely help everybody who knew the child.

What a summer it had been! So much pleasure and so much pain. She, Anna, had never really come into full being until this summer and now she was feeling love and pain as never before. She had experienced everything in life—joy, sorrow, passion, loneliness, friendship and pain—and she had found herself. She liked what she found. She was liberated, on top of it all, able to live with the pain and rejoice in being alive. She had her job and all her young employees, but she knew her new-found energy and sense of purpose came not from the job and the people but from something else, from her association with a man—a good man, a strong man, a man who was seeking to know the meaning of life. Her inner dependency upon him was as strong as her outward independency. Yet she could neither satisfy her need for him nor feel there was anything wrong about it. It was only a friendly relationship. They were friends, that's all. But what a pleasure to have a friend in a man. It was rather amusing. No one suspected and that was well. It could be misunderstood as something it was not and hurt others. That's what made it such a delicate matter, but it was delicious nevertheless and would end with the passing of summer. She sighed and hurried on. "Now I must see," she said to herself, "if having so much, I can make it worth something to this young girl."

After a few minutes walk, she was in the jail, looking up at the sheriff in his handsome purple and grey uniform with its silver buttons and big star. He looked down at her curiously. Everyone in town by now had heard that the museum lady was doing great things at Glory Land. So this woman had come for Phlox Fontaine, the spoiled brat. He hoped the judge would set bail and that she would take Fontaine away so the other prisoners would quiet down.

"Sheriff Smith, may I talk for a moment to Phlox Fontaine?"

"Okay, Miss," said the sheriff, who had taken a liking to this smiling woman. "Five minutes." He led her into the cell block and in a few moments he unlocked the cell door and Anna stood face to face with Phlox. How beautiful she is, how faded like a flower at the end of summer, thought Anna. There's so much hurt in those pale blue eyes.

"I'm Anna Maria Abendtal and I've come to try to get you out of here, but first we must talk so I can go before the judge. Tell me what happened."

"I didn't do anything wrong. Freud said I could borrow some lumber," she lied, "to take up to the Hill where I'm going to live! As for the truck, it really belongs to me, though I haven't got the title yet. Ask Mr. Sanders if you don't believe me. Someone just wanted to get me in here to pay me back for being François Fontaine's daughter— probably that snotty Penelope Dupre. She knows about Freud and me!"

"All right," said Anna, "I'll be back as soon as I can get proof for the judge of what you say. I hope I can help you."

Anna Maria walked out into the hot August sun. How should she proceed? It would be easy enough to handle Freud and Penny; they were her friends. But Bud Sanders was another matter. When a certain kind of woman hears certain kinds of things about a certain kind of man, she tries to stay away from him, especially if he is the husband of a friend. Ordinarily she would hesitate, but this summer Anna Maria had become an expert in handling people; so, summoning all her experience to her aid, she marched down the street and into the offices of the Poly-Toy Corporation and asked to see the president.

She was escorted into a very functional office and Bud rose to meet her, giving her the pleasant greeting one gives to a friend of one's wife.

"Bud," said Anna, sitting down in a brown leather chair near his desk and laying her white purse upon it, "I'll get right to the point of what I have to say because it is an urgent matter. I've come to see you in behalf of my friends and of Phlox Fontaine. As you possibly know, Phlox is being held for stealing lumber from young John Freund and Penny Dupre—and for stealing a yellow truck. She maintains that she did not steal the lumber—just borrowed it; and I think I can convince Freud and Penny to withdraw their charges. But what about the truck? Does it belong to you, to her, or exactly what is the situation? She said the truck is hers, that you gave it to her as a present, and that she's taking it to Safflower Hill."

Bud looked out the window. His round face had lost its smile at the mention of Phlox and he stalled. "My son lives up there, you know," he said slowly, looking at his fingernails. "We had a quarrel and I said I'd do nothing for him—that includes all those scruffy friends of his." He hesitated a moment. He had been disappointed in Phlox for not being more giving. The fact that he had taken from women all his life more than he gave was never recognized by himself. The same quality in Phlox was hard to forgive. He could certainly use the truck at Poly-Toy, but then again, he was still hopeful for an improvement in his relationship with Miss Fontaine. He said slowly, "Well, I guess I did tell Phlox I'd give her the truck." Then he had an inspiration and he added quickly, "She was so good to Bucky up there in the hospital. I didn't know she was going to the Hill."

"And did you tell her it was to be transferred last Monday, but you were playing golf till too late?"

"Yes, that's true."

"Then she wasn't lying! May I tell the judge you are going to give the truck to the Safflowers, through Phlox, as a present from Bucky?" That fact will spare Surtsey and also be of help on the Hill, thought Anna. "If this child goes up there to live taking a truck, she will be very important. She needs to feel important; we all do. Imagine me without my position or you without Poly-Toy Corporation!"

"I couldn't," he snorted, "it's given me everything." Cheeky sort of gal, this Abendtal woman, but it was a good idea about giving the truck to Phlox from Bucky. It was a perfect cover up. And if she took it to the Hill it would look like an act of charity on his part.

"Then give a little in return," Anna said. "You'll feel like a new person. And why don't you make friends with Mark? He's just like you—developing a business out of nothing. You must admire *that* in him."

"I can't."

"Yes, you can. Here's the phone," she said, reaching across his desk and pushing it toward him. "Call him up. He's at my house working. The number's 564-0777. Now,

I'll be going. Thank you for saving my day. I really must hurry; after I spring Phlox I have to help those kids prepare for the big celebration."

"Celebration?"

"Yes. September 15—to mark the remarriage licensing. You and Surtsey will be coming, won't you? No one should miss it; it will be a day to remember! Now before you get cold feet, please phone Mark."

"You won't tell anyone anything about Phlox and me?" he asked sheepishly.

"Of course not, but I can't speak for Phlox." She didn't tell him that his latest escapade was on every tongue. "That is, I won't tell if you call your son." It was akin to blackmail, but it was irresistible. Anna Maria watched Bud dial and when Mark answered, she picked up her purse and hurried away.

"Hello, Mark. How have you been? This is Dad."

"Hello, Dad. I'm okay."

"I hear there's difficulty over the truck Bucky's giving Phlox. It will ease her adjustment up there. She's used to better things, and it may be tough living like that."

Same Dad, handing me one of his backhanded insults, thought Mark.

"I hear everyone gives something to the Hill. A truck's a big deal, hunh?" There was silence at the other end, so Bud continued nervously. "Well, Mark, look after Phlox. She's as soft as a cashmere kitten, and as Bucky would say, 'hot as a jumbo jet with its engines on fire'!"

"Dad, haven't you heard that women are not sex objects?"

"That's what they think, son, but they can't censor a man's thoughts!"

Mark put down the phone, choking and coughing. Then

he picked up the phone again. Bud was still talking. "It was good of you kids to make Surtsey come along to Myrtle Beach. She never wants to go anywhere anymore—the change coming on, I suppose."

"Okay, Dad. Is that all?"

"Mark, how are the wooden toys coming?"

"Fine. Just fine."

"Maybe we could copy them at Poly-Toy sometime."

"Maybe. Bye, Dad."

Bzz-z. Mark had hung up.

Mark stood by the phone and looked out the window, thinking. Apparently his Dad was trying to make up, but the old man still didn't understand about plastics—suggesting Poly-Toy copy his beautiful toys in ugly, smelly plastic! What a peace offering!

As for Phlox, he'd do what he could to make her happy at the Hill—for his mother's sake. He owed a lot to his mother—at this point, just about everything.

"The Me in Me"

Anna Maria hurried back to the courthouse and after waiting a considerable time for a hearing with the judge, she finally was able to approach his desk and explain the facts of the case. He agreed that since Mr. Freund and Mrs. Dupre had withdrawn their charges, Phlox could be released.

"Thank you, judge," Anna said gratefully as she took Phlox by the arm. "Come, let's go to my house." It was hard to walk when they felt like running. Shouts and obscenities echoed behind them down the corridor.

Phlox stopped short, recognizing the voice of her partner of the night before. "Oh, dear, I forgot about Crabbe. Isn't he coming, too?"

"No," said Anna. "He's wanted on other charges. It seems the evidence was on his person last night." Phlox knew it must have been hashish and that it was in his shoe.

"This is an awful place for a human soul," whispered Anna. "Let's hurry away from here."

"Let's hurry to my house for a cup of coffee. Mark will be there. Do you know Mark, Bucky's big brother? He's just built a beautiful wooden bathtub; I don't know for whom, but he says they're the rage in California, and he's promised when his relief comes to drive me up to the Hill to try it. I'm going to take along my towel and robe. Then we'll go on to the Pink Pavillion. All right?"

"Sure," said Phlox, who was more quiet than usual, "I have nothing else to do." She was afraid to ask about the truck.

"You know," said Anna, "I need a receptionist at the Pavillion. Would you do me a favor and help me for a few days till I can find someone?"

Phlox nodded, "Okay, I have nothing else to do."

"We really have a lot of fun. It's hard work at Glory Land, but I try to make it a common effort worth doing. We all share the work and the joy of being where things are happening. And we have so many laughs!"

"I could use a few," said Phlox.

"I'll bet you could," said Anna. "Tell me now, what do you like to do most?"

"Me? Oh, I like to design clothes."

"You do?" exclaimed Anna Maria. "I didn't know that!"

"Nobody knows it but me and Freud and my roomie in Seattle."

"My, that's a wonderful talent. I don't suppose you could design me something for September 15—if you'd do it right away I could have my dressmaker put it together in a hurry."

Phlox looked baffled as she appraised Anna Maria. Finally she said, "Well, maybe I could."

"I know what you're thinking," laughed Anna. "I'm no fashion model! But I'd love to be seen in a dress designed by you. Just don't put me in pants," she laughed. "Seriously, I meet people from all over the country." Then she added, "Brig—that is, Mr. Bantley—and I are working on a display cabinet for the room in which our customers wait for seating. We're going to show original works by artists and craftsmen. Can't you see a cabinet displaying your sketches and a little photo of you along with your biography for people to read?"

Slowly the pink color was coming back into Phlox's face. "You know, Miss Abendtal, you're the first person who has asked for the *me* in me! Everyone else seems to want me for my looks. I can't help if I look the way I do!"

"No, nor can I help it that I look this way," said Anna smiling. "It seems that the face we show the world has to be lived down or gotten around. If I could have designed my face I'd have done a better job, that's for sure. On the other hand you must show everyone that you are not only beautiful but talented; and no one could ask for more than to be both!

"So I'll give up my tub bath today and when we get to Glory Land, you can go into my office and I'll get you some drawing paper. In an hour I'll send in lunch on a tray and you can work undisturbed on my dress for the celebration. I suppose it should be a long dress. Forget about the receptionist job—I'll get someone from the agency."

"Oh, Anna, I like you. What do you do at Glory Land?"

"What don't I do? I'm a cook, maitre d', general manager of the Pink Pavillion and head of the complaint department. And often I'm just someone who listens. It's amazing—I'm not young and I've never worked harder, but I've never had more fun than I'm having now."

"Than when you were my age?" queried Phlox.

"Yes, life gets better and better once you know who you are. I think you're making a real beginning. Oh, if I'd had your opportunities at twenty. Young people today have so many choices!"

Phlox spoke up. "There's another thing I like to do," she said. "I like to sing."

"You do? Well, now, we'll have to have you sing for us too."

Phlox began to sing, " 'Bring back the sunlight, I'll even take tears; oh, what has happened to all of those years.' " Then she commented, "My mother hates that!"

"I think it's beautiful," exclaimed Anna. "My dear friend, Skipper, wrote that song and to hear you sing it brings tears to my eyes. 'Sunlight and shadow,' that's what life is for all of us." Her face saddened, thinking of her little Christian godson who was killed in Lebanon. "Only for some there does seem to be more shadow," she said softly. They walked the last block up Main Street in silence until they came to Cornwall House. "Here we are. I want you to meet Mark." I hope he won't kill her, thought Anna, but they have to meet sometime if she's going to live at Safflower Hill.

NEW YORK (UPI)—It is expected that AT&T earnings will show a rise of ten percent in the third quarter and the company is expected to pay an extra dividend. Last week the stocks stood at an all-time high on the Composite Stock Index.

PART VII

The End of Summer

A Little Supper

Lucy Bantley arrived in Lake Placid from Africa one hour before Mother Bantley's funeral. She and Brig met after their long separation at a moment of great family grief. There was no time for private emotions or intimate communication, which in itself was injurious to the psyche of husband and wife for whom such a reunion is best spent in deepest privacy, a spiritual recovery from the wounds of separation. But it was not to be, for after the burial was over it seemed to Brig a travesty to argue with Lucy about her travel plans or their marriage, not at a time when they were reliving old memories, settling affairs, claiming souvenirs, rereading old letters—all the things one does when a loved one disappears irrevocably into the mysteries of the universe. And so Brig had kept silent and Lucy made no promises. Elusive Lucy. Yes, that's what she was and how hard it was to live with a noncommittal person. It seemed obvious that she was going to resume her trip. She had renewed her passport and gone to the doctor for a cholera shot.

It was very sad and very hard for Brigham Bantley to lose his mother, but it was not as devastating as it might have been had he not been separated from her by her senility for so many years. He had long since said goodbye to the person he would always remember her as being. And he felt also that she was not gone from him forever; they had shared too much and loved too long for that. This couldn't be all there'd ever be! He knew they'd meet again in heaven.

Brig arrived back in Temagami Springs in the late afternoon. Lucy stayed behind in Lake Placid to help his sister, Anne, dismantle the old house. It was a task from which Brig ran away; he couldn't bear to do it. It made him too sad. Luckily, the women understood he was needed in Glory Land, so it was easy for him to make his excuses and leave.

Arriving at his house, he went to the kitchen and was surprised to find taped to his refrigerator an urgent note from Olivia Dupre. "Come over to dinner tonight. I want to talk to you about Glory Land and I consider it *imperative* that you come." It was a curious message, but he would go right over to find out what was so urgent.

Before he could knock on her front door, Olivia came rushing outside and embraced him. "I'm so sorry, Brig, about your mother."

"Where's Rene?" Brig asked, not seeing Rene in his usual place at the window.

"He's in the hospital for tests. He said to express his condolences to you."

"Thanks, Olivia," Brig said. "I hope Rene is not worse," he added, stepping inside the front door.

Olivia shook her head. "He's no better. He's pretty bad, I'm afraid." She led the way into her small living room.

"Won't you sit on the couch, Brig? It's the only comfortable place. Rene's worn out this chair by the window—two or three of them, in fact."

Brig sat down heavily; he was very tired. He watched in silence while Olivia poured him a glass of Tio Pepe sherry.

"I'm sorry I can't offer you a cocktail."

"You know I don't drink them," he said brusquely.

"It would relax you, Brig, is what I meant."

"My dear Olivia, I don't need to be relaxed; I need to be comforted!"

Olivia immediately sat down close beside him on the couch and put her arm around his shoulder, "So do I, Brig. So do I." Brig sat inert but with a wan smile on his large handsome face. His sideburns were now completely white.

"Let's drink a toast," said Olivia, "to us, to our future." We are alone, at last, she thought.

"I'll drink to that, but when are you going to tell me what is so urgent? I got your message," said her employer.

"Well, it's serious enough," she replied. "But first let's enjoy our dinner. We're rarely alone like this." She led the way to a small table set for two. There were flowers on the table and she lit the candles and turned down the lights. In her white crepe lounging pajamas and gold jewelry she looked her most bewitching. Brig ate quietly, his mind on other things, not noticing that Olivia sparkled more than usual and looked very beautiful. When dinner was over and they were standing again, he said, "That was a wonderful treat, Olivia—very thoughtful of you. I've been kind of depressed, but I guess after this delicious dinner and a good night's sleep, I'll recover."

"Do you want to sleep here? I have Penny's room. Do stay, Brig. It would be fun fixing your breakfast. I'd like that!"

"No, no," he replied. "I have a lot to do before I sleep and even good moments like this can't last forever, Livy. If only we could hold on to them." He was thinking of the day at the beach with Anna.

"I'm waiting for a few good things to hold on to," sighed

Olivia.

"Don't be so cynical. You've had a hard life in many ways, but you have a lovely daughter."

"Penny! She's not much comfort to me now. I can't understand her. To think that after all I've done for her, she'd do what she did to me! It makes me very sad."

"Things will change," said Brig. "There's change in the air everywhere. The kids were the first to sense it. You'll see."

"Or maybe they brought it about! That, Mr. Bantley, brings me to why I want to speak to you. We must do something now. You and I. No matter what you say, the kids are taking over your place and you don't even see it!" Olivia stared at her boss accusingly.

"They are?"

"Yes, they are. Penny and Freud and that crowd from the Hill, and even Phlox Fontaine. They're taking it over and we have to do something about it, you and I. We made Glory Land what it is and they'll ruin it—treating it like some plaything. We must do something quickly," she cried hysterically.

"Now, now, Olivia. Things have been great this summer. Attendance is up and what's more important, everyone's having a good time."

"With 04Y4 hanging over us?"

"In spite of 04Y4. Why are you so worried?"

Olivia, seated now on the couch, put her head on his shoulder and began to cry softly, choking back sobs. "It's everything—Rene and 04Y4 and Penny and you and everything. I'm losing my grip. I'm not wanted anymore." Brig put his arm around her to comfort her.

"Yes, you are, dear girl. Your happiness is essential to all of us. I appreciate your long hours of work. Just remember our good times together." He patted her gently.

"No one asks for my ideas anymore," sobbed Olivia. "I'm an outsider. They didn't ask me to help decorate the bridge or anything. I could have helped with the concert for Skip. I'm full of ideas!"

Brig touched his head to hers. "I know, I know. I'll think of something I can do to help you. I really care what you think, my dear Livy. I always have. Believe me, I do. We'll plan something new together."

"Thanks, Brig. I thought you'd understand," she said, looking up at him with wet eyes. He handed her his handkerchief.

"Come see me alone in the office tomorrow," he said, rising to his feet. "Now smile for me. I love your smile."

She managed a smile and passion was in her eyes. Oh, Brig, if I could tell you how I feel, she thought. But did he know? How could he not feel her need for him? He couldn't be so good to her if he didn't love her. What did he mean when he said he'd plan something new for the two of them?

After he left, Olivia went at once to bed to think about Brig. She fell asleep wondering what he would plan for the two of them to do together. Did that mean that Lucy was leaving him for good?

"My Evening Valley"

As soon as the sun came up the next morning Brigham Bantley was on his way to the Peak of the Morning Light. The suddenness of his mother's death and the return of Lucy had proved almost too much to bear. If only Lucy had reached out to him, had greeted him after their long separation with the same eagerness as she showed in their early married days; but even in sorrow, they could not share, could not communicate. She was going away again soon and if she didn't return, their long union made with the blessing of God would be dissolved by default. It was time to force himself to face the truth, to settle the emotional conflict tearing him apart.

The more disturbed he felt about his wife, the more he comforted himself by thinking about Anna. He had been away only a week, a very full and poignant week, and yet he had missed Anna Maria every hour of every day. He was slowly beginning to realize how much he had grown to depend upon her, how he turned to her for answers to many things about the park and personal things as well. It was small wonder Olivia felt neglected; she had always been his foremost helper. He was almost thankful that she blamed the kids and not Anna for taking over what she regarded as her prerogatives. Let no criticism ever fall on his friend, Anna Maria!

Of one thing he was sure: he loved Anna in a very special way. This love permeated his being, filling his soul with a kind of happiness. It was a self he had never known before, but one he dreaded to be without ever again. Furthermore, this love he felt for Anna Maria was a mysterious sort of love. It wasn't exactly physical and it seemed to transcend the intellect. In Brig, this love reached the depths of his soul.

But what were her feelings towards him? He suddenly decided he had to know. His old life was dissolving; the summer was almost over. He needed to know that when the end of summer came there would still be someone near to care about him.

Somehow, thought Brig, he had never loved Lucy in quite this way. Oh, he had loved her passionately, had delighted in her as a person, in her lovely countenance and her deep intellect. But this special joy, this closeness he shared with Anna Maria, had never been his before.

"Lucy, Lucy," his heart cried, aching at the thought of her. "All those abundant years of child-rearing and nest-building and planning for the future are moving away like a train in the night, opening a distance between us!"

As he hiked slowly up to the mountain top, the sky darkened and a storm was imminent. Brig took refuge in a lean-to built by Skip and Banter many years before. In a few minutes the rain came, filling the air with ribbons of water. He sat in the shelter and watched the thirsty ground absorbing its drink. After a time of heavy downpour, the rain decreased in tempo and came down in a smooth fine mist. The tall trees swayed, their leaves dancing a dance of thanksgiving, and the birds dashed from tree to tree. Then once again the downpour resumed and blew in great sheets across the open fields, barely visible below him, dampening even covered places.

As the clouds passed on and the sun came out, the countryside looked happy and cleansed. Brigham too had been washed, freshened, renewed. There in the lean-to he made his decision, and it brought him instant happiness. Taking off his storm coat and throwing it over his shoulder, he ran downhill in great leaps; through fields and woods he ran, slipping and sliding as he went but smiling, laughing, rejoicing, for suddenly he knew what he was going to do.

Coming to the old fording place in the Big Bear River, he waded across, soaking his jeans to the knee in his eagerness to be on the other side, and he ran along the path of soft and slippery pine needles. Passing his favorite place where the river ran among the rocks, the water now lively and fragrant after the fresh rain, Brig saw the person he was hurrying to find. There on the great smooth rock that spread far into the river sat Anna Maria. She did not see him coming. The young white birches, bent by the rains, were blowing back and forth like a papal blessing over her brown head. He put his hand on his chest to suppress the thrill he felt at finding her there and, approaching quietly, he stood behind her on the smooth stones. The river swept and swirled around them.

He stepped towards her. "I'm glad you're here," he said.

"I'm resting," she replied softly, her heart quivering from surprise. "Shhh, I don't want to break the peace of this perfect moment. The river is beautiful when the water's high."

Brig was silent, looking down at her. After a little while, Anna drew a deep breath and got to her feet to speak to him. Quickly, before she lifted her head, he stretched out his arms and, before she knew what was happening, he pulled her close to him. "Anna Maria," he whispered, burying his head in her hair. "Oh, Anna, I want you as my valley in the evening of my life!" He held her in a tight embrace so she could not escape from him.

Stunned, shocked, overwhelmed—she said nothing but clung to him. Then she whispered, "It's not quite evening yet, Brig." Her voice was barely audible above the noises of the water.

"Well," he said huskily, "it's late afternoon. You know what I'm saying. I want you. I need you. I love you." He pushed her a little away from him and looked into her warm brown eyes. Then he pulled her close to him again. Anna Maria began to tremble, holding back tears. Her need for him was greater than his for her, and yet what could she say?

Finally she looked at him and the tears fell from her eyes. "What about Lucy?" she asked gently, breaking away and turning from him because she could not keep from crying.

"She's leaving, going back to the Serengeti in a few days. It's over between us."

"Oh, Brig, I'm sorry. But what can I say?" He took her by both shoulders and turned her to face him; then he kissed her tenderly on the mouth, seeking her reply.

She didn't respond but drew her face from his. "I'm afraid—afraid of myself, of my feelings for you. You know I love you. I love you in my very soul, Brig. But this is earth, not heaven. What can I say?" she cried, walking down to the edge of the water where it twirled round and over the rocks. He followed her and brought her back into the sunshine and they sat down side by side. Brig put his lips on her ear. "Say yes; you know you want to," he urged in a low voice.

"You know me that well!" she cried.

"My Anna, our love has made us new. When we are married we'll do great things together. We'll go to St. Catherine's in the Sinai and Mars Hill in Greece; we'll visit all your orphans and bring them home to live with us; we'll educate them in America. It will give me so much pleasure to use what I have to make you happy. Then all my hard work will not have been in vain! Anna!" he pleaded.

"Brig, Brig, don't tempt me so. I can't answer you now, Brig." She put her head on his shoulder for comfort and then continued. "But I will—after Lucy leaves, after you're sure. Promise me you'll come back to me then."

He put his arm around her and took her hand in his. They sat silently for a long time rejoicing in their love for one another.

"Do you know, my evening valley," he said slowly, "your name is very beautiful. It suggests sweet sadness, the sweet sadness of our love, for it is sad when things like this happen."

"I know, Brig. Sometimes I can't believe what's happening and I feel so confused. There's been so much suffering this summer and yet we've been drawn closer together here in our town. Where is there any comfort? We all have to cling to someone, don't we?"

"I think our real comfort lies in the future in knowing we will see God in His heavenly kingdom. It's thrilling to know we will have life without sin and suffering.

"My mother's death brought back memories of my childhood. Almost every night she tucked me in and then sat on my bed and said, 'Brigham, let's pray. Remember, you're saying this prayer with Jesus. *Our father who art in heaven.* . . . .' Sometimes I would ask her about heaven and we'd have a little talk about God." Brig sighed. "Now she's gone—but I have you, and I am truly blessed. Oh, evening valley, you are very dear to me." He was about to kiss her when there came the sound of hammering from the south pasture.

Brig looked up, startled. "Now what? What could they be repairing at this time of day?" He looked at his watch. His employees weren't due for half an hour.

The Surprise

No hammer ever hit a harder blow than the bang-bang-bang from the south meadow. It was a heart-breaking interruption for Anna Maria at the most profound moment of her life. "It's from the 'fane,' Brig," she said quietly. He might as well know.

"The what?"

"The fane, the new chapel."

"The fane? The new chapel?" he asked, releasing her from his arms like a mother dropping her knitting when the baby cries.

"Yes, in the old barn! It's a lovely surprise for you from all our young people. I must say I think this park needs a chapel, don't you? You said yourself there's never a dull day in Glory Land." She spoke faster than usual, running on to soften his reaction. "They've had more fun with this!"

"More than enough fun, I say. They cannot continue another minute without my permission. Olivia's right: they have taken over. These kids have taken outrageous advantage of me all summer. But to do it while I'm away for my mother's funeral is a little bit too much! It's outrageous and I won't stand for it." Anna Maria was alarmed. She had never seen Brig so angry. His mouth was set firmly above his strong chin and his eyes were almost black.

In fact it seemed to her his wrath was deeper than the situation warranted. Was he perhaps angry about something deeper? Was he troubled by what had just happened between them? Anna was holding the depths of her reaction to his proposal to herself until she was alone. Her nerves were quivering and she was barely under control. But she knew it was up to her to save the situation now. She looked at him pleadingly. He seemed unmoved. What tactic should she use?

"Please don't make trouble, Brig," said Anna, looking at him pleadingly. "Savy and Skip say they too own shares in Glory Land."

"Yes, that's right. They do," he conceded grudgingly.

"Then let this be their contribution to its future. Every undertaking, like every person, has to be renewed from time to time. Places, like people, can fall out of fashion. Maybe you should be grateful to them for preventing that from happening to this beautiful place."

"I've always hated that word gratitude and I've never felt it in any of my children. I guess it's our fault, Lucy's and mine; but I don't know where we failed. We've worked so hard for them," he said gruffly.

Anna defended the children. "It's nobody's fault. Gratitude is a very difficult thing to show," she said slowly and deliberately, as though she were a teacher explaining a math problem. "It is a very delicate emotion. If gratitude is overstated it's suspected of being self-serving. Anyway, it's more of an attitude than a statement. Your children certainly respect what you've done. Let them finish the chapel without your criticism. You're a very forgiving man, Brig. Don't forgive your children less easily than you do others."

"Since you're so excited by this crazy business, take me

there and show me what's going on!"

"Don't be angry, Brig, it's a church!" They walked without another word in the direction of the noise. Brig held her hand in a tight grip.

When they came upon the place, he let go of her hand. The building, which was alive with activity, had been the old English barn where Tony kept the lawn mowers. It was a sound structure, of mortise and tenon construction. The drawknife beams and braces were secured by oaken pegs. Marks of the broad-ax, which had hewn the timbers, were still visible on the old wood. The barn had stood for a century and a half in the little valley and been used as a stable by Tyler Lansdown. But because it was out of the way of the tourists and served a utilitarian purpose only, Brig had let it fall into a state of disrepair. The skeleton was strong and the roof still held out the rain, but as a building it wasn't much to look at. It had been a low priority on Brig's list. But now it had taken on a new and different look.

The carpenters had cut little windows of varying sizes in the newly repaired walls, and the sagging roof had been propped at an unusual angle. The results were reminiscent of Le Corbusier's Notre Dame du Haut at Ronchamp. In fact it looked quite remarkable for an old barn, but Mr. Bantley was too angry to appreciate the change. Indeed he seemed so vexed that Tony, who was showing some young men how to plaster the outside walls in the old-fashioned manner, kept right on working, afraid to look Brig in the eye. Tony DeLuca had been avoiding his boss by dealing through intermediaries ever since the tree trouble.

Brig Bantley grunted a greeting and went inside where workmen were planing the barn floor. He was utterly astounded by this new folly in the park. After what seemed an endless pause, he said, "Anna, tell me—don't you think the architecture's rather strange for a church?"

"No, I don't; all I see is love," answered Anna Maria, smiling around at the many busy people. Her back was straight and her chin held high.

Brig's feeling of opposition deserted him for a moment, but then it returned. "Nevertheless, Olivia is right. Absolutely right. She's our artist and she should have been consulted. I didn't realize what she meant last night. It looks like it was made by Tatty Softshoe!"

"By Tatty? Oh, wait till you see the cross Tatty's making with her own special stones! She showed up with them yesterday in her red wagon and volunteered. Lucky Tony was busy with the stuccoing—he doesn't like anyone but himself to do any stonework in this park," exclaimed Anna enthusiastically. "Not only is Tatty helping, but everyone in town is in the spirit of this thing. It's like building the cathedral of Chartres—a community enterprise! I'm helping too. I arranged for my Spanish seamstress to make ecumenical banners designed by—would you believe it—Phlox Fontaine!"

Brig seemed in shock to know the whole town was involved. He spoke aloud as though she wasn't there. "No! They've all gone too far without my permission. It will have to stop. There are many ramifications no one has thought about—things like liability insurance and workmen's compensation. The unions will be after me. No, I tell you, it has to stop."

"Brig," she shook him a little, "come to your senses. This is not a small thing; it's larger than you or me or the kids. No, I can't let you destroy the togetherness which has gone into this. You're absolutely right, we should have gone to Olivia first, but in her present state she would never have gone along with it. She's a veritable watchdog of your prerogatives. I'll go to her and apologize now."

"Not you."

"Yes, me. I encouraged it. I got carried away as the kids' official unmarried advisor for the celebration day."

"Celebration day? Celebration of what? What's happened to all of you?" he asked, amazed that there could be anything more of which he was unaware.

"Of the relicensing. EZ-OUT, as they're calling it. We're going to have it here so all the young peoples' parents will feel they'd be missing something if they don't come, as an added incentive to sign. It will be a joyous time; we're planning a marvelous party. So before you throw me another black Frisbee, my dear friend, let me tell you all about the celebration. The kids have elected old single me as their advisor and I speak as a person of standing here at the chapel."

Brig was caught up at last by his soulmate's joy and enthusiasm—maybe it was her mentioning the Frisbee; anyway, he began to think that he could probably fix up the legal side of this affair with a few phone calls after lunch. Let them have their way. If Anna was for it, all would be well.

"You win, Anna," he smiled. "Now show me around."

Anna stopped to talk to a carpenter and Brig went on inside and sat on a sawhorse.

"Who's paying for all this construction, miss?" he asked of the first Saffie who walked by.

"Everybody," she answered. "Tourists, townspeople, all of us. Offers to help are coming in from everywhere, Mr. Bantley. People are caught up in what this represents— a reemphasis of our traditional American values, of working hard together for a common goal instead of saying 'let the government do it.' We have to hurry to finish this chapel

while help is plentiful. Harvest time on the farm will soon
be here and we'll lose half our helpers; but we'll make it on
time. When the news spreads, no one in the whole country
will want to miss it. It might even save some marriages.
You never know, do you, Mr. Bantley?"

Anna, noticing his intent interest in what the girl was
saying, approached him smiling.

"Come down to the Pavillion and I'll make you breakfast.
But first, cross your heart, Brigham Bantley, and promise
you won't interfere."

He strode to her and crossed his heart. Then he bent
down and whispered, "I promise—because of you—not to
interfere. I love you that much! And I think you're beautiful
to let them do this; you knew you could bring me around."
He gazed lovingly at her from the depths of his violet eyes.

"You big-hearted man!" she exclaimed. And while they
breakfasted, Anna Maria told Brig about all the plans for
the celebration and for the fantastic party afterwards.
There would be music and dancing and singing—and signing, she hoped. Brig volunteered to pay for a feast, a real
feast for everyone who came, and Anna agreed to prepare
it. Then she said, "And one of these days you'll get your
invitation. My waitresses are doing them during their time
off." Realizing as she spoke the implications of her words,
her voice faltered and her face showed pain. Brig realized it
too. He got up, and after whispering something in her ear,
he left her to her thoughts.

My Love

After Brig had gone away Anna Maria went to the cabinet where the valuables belonging to the park were kept. Removing the silver tea service, she started for the art gallery, holding the large tray with its precious pieces in both hands. In her present state she felt almost too weak to carry it, but she hurried on. The local artists were holding a tea in the afternoon to mark the opening of their annual exhibit and their committee had already arrived. They'd be waiting for her.

As she staggered along the path through the pine forest, she met Olivia who was walking rapidly towards the administration building. How colorful she looks, thought Anna; one would never guess she has a daughter Penny's age.

Olivia stopped her. "Anna, I want to confide in you about something; it's very personal, but I know you can keep a secret." Olivia's hand gripped her forearm. "Please listen. I need your advice."

Olivia had been more than a little resentful of her prerogatives where Anna was concerned and certainly had never come to her for advice. Anna was merely the keeper of the kitchen. What was Olivia going to say? Whatever it was, she didn't want to hear it. Oh, why do people always confide in me, thought Anna Maria. It makes me nervous. She tried to break away, but Olivia wouldn't let her.

"What I have to find out," said Olivia, "is this. It's about Mrs. Bantley. You're such a friend of Skip's he'll tell you if you ask him. It's this. Is Lucy Bantley leaving? When is she coming back? I must know because just between you and me—now this is very secret. Don't tell a soul. I'm very much in love with Brig—I have been for years—but I've never let it surface in my consciousness till lately. But now I have real hope; this summer has drawn Brig and me closer than ever before. He named a road after me—wasn't that sweet? And last night when he came to my place he asked me to comfort him! He never sounded so intimate before. He was just beautiful!"

Olivia sighed, remembering their intimate dinner together and her being brave enough to ask him to stay all night. Repinning a lock of her hair which had fallen out of place, Olivia looked right at Anna and said, "I've heard Lucy isn't coming back, and though I don't wish her anything but luck, I can't help but think she couldn't care much for him and be away this summer. She's letting him know that it's all over between them. Really, she's not the woman for him anyway. Don't you agree, Anna?"

"I don't know anything about it," answered Anna Maria. "You'll have to ask someone else."

Olivia persisted. "I'm sorry, but I've got to get to the gallery," said Anna, "before I drop this silver." Her heart pounded as she hurried away. Why, oh why, did she say that to me, Anna cried out from the depths of her heart.

"I'm in a hurry too. I have a date with Brig," Olivia called after her.

Anna hurried on. I'm jealous, she thought, that's just

what I am. I'm jealous! She had barely recovered her equanimity when Skip overtook her. He wore his blue Dutchboy cap on the back of his head, which gave him a boyish look. Usually his expression was lively but not this morning. Anna knew he had something on his mind, and she was very glad to see him after her dreadful encounter with Olivia. Skip fell in beside her and took the heavy tea service from her arms. Anna Maria steadied herself by holding on to his elbow as they walked through the hemlock trees.

They walked along slowly, talking about Skip's latest lyrics, and Anna began to recover from her encounter with Olivia. She had purposely pushed Brig's proposal to the back of her mind to treasure it, to think about it later, alone. She was hardly able to believe it had happened: Brig wanted to marry her; he had called her his "evening valley" and it was from his heart. But Anna didn't want to think about that now, not while walking with Brig's son. She wanted nothing to diminish the thrill within her of what had happened that morning, and so she sublimated her reaction.

As she was trying not to think about what had happened at the river, her young companion said to her, "I must ask your advice, Anna. It's about Mom."

Oh, no, not him too, thought Anna, feeling a tinge of pain.

Skip continued. "Savy tells me that Mother is leaving for Europe and Africa and may not be coming back by the fifteenth. I want to tell Mother about the song I'm dedicating to her at the celebration, but Savy says not to tell her because it wouldn't make any difference in her plans. Will you ask my mother to stay home for my sake?" demanded Skip. He was one person who had absolute faith in Anna Abendtal.

She looked at him, forcing herself to look willing, but inside she felt strangely disturbed. They were continuing toward the art gallery, when suddenly she said, "She'll be back in time," and she was surprised when she said it. She had no idea what Lucy's plans were and it just popped into her head.

"How do you know?" exclaimed Skip.

"I don't know how I know. Don't ask why—I just know," she said slowly.

"Well, there's no hope unless you can think of something," said the fair-haired boy she loved so much. He looked down at his middle-aged friend and their eyes met.

"Don't sound so sad, Skip. You have Penny now. You can let your mother go."

He wondered what she meant about Penny. Could she mean that Penny cared for him? If she did, it would be great!

"I guess I'm a little sad because I just want to see some appreciation from my parents now that I've sold *Bring Back Those Years* and am making it on my own. Parents act like making money's such a big deal and the only thing that matters to them, and when you finally have some success they could care less." Skip held the tray up, balancing it like a waiter.

"I appreciate you, and Penny does too," replied Anna, "but please be careful with the tea service."

"Penny? How come you say that?"

She reached for the silver. "Go." She pointed along Way Dupre, glad to take the tea service from him. "Ask her. How would a middle-aged woman know what she sees in you?" laughed Anna Maria, giving him a hint of what everybody knew—everybody who saw the tender look in a young girl's eyes—that Penelope Dupre was in love with Skipper Bantley.

In love? What about herself. Was she really in love with Brig? Oh, fatal question, the one she refused to ask herself since that day at the beach, because she already knew the awful answer. Of course she was in love—in love like a young girl. Only now it was different. She was all alone with a burden of love and joy and pain such as she had never known before. She made up her mind in that moment to hold their love close to her while it was new and good, to treasure it in her heart, and ponder it for a time before offering it up. She needed to be alone with this new wonder, away from everybody; and so she decided to walk through the woods and over the bridge by the secret path that Brig had shown her, to the Indian cave, the same cave whose ransom she had received for Cornwall House so long ago. It seemed appropriate that she should go there with her thoughts, to a place which meant so much to her and Brig long years before they knew each other.

So after delivering the tea service Anna Maria Abendtal slipped away across the meadow and along the shore to the big overhanging rock. She spread her coat and sat down, dangling her feet in the water. Then she lay back against the warm stone to think about Brigham Bantley. A beam of late afternoon sun fell on her breast and made a spot of lovely warmth.

Then and only then, there alone in the cave, did she allow the magnificence of Brig's loving her to well up in her heart and diffuse through her whole being. It was the greatest thing that had ever happened to Anna Maria, something she had never allowed herself to think could happen. She had been very careful never to show more than a kindly interest in her employer. Now, what a glorious thing it was! He wanted to marry her and she wanted him with her whole being as she had never wanted anyone before. Anna Maria was flattered by his proposal, gratified that he, the handsome and wonderful pride of the town, wanted her, a middle-aged spinster of no consequence, to marry him. She lay a long time enjoying the warm, happy after-glow of his proposal of marriage.

If only they could be together all the time, loving and sustaining one another, searching together for the meaning of life and love, of joy and pain, of loneliness and comfort. Together they could do so much for others. She hugged her soft woven purse to her, pretending it was Brig, like a school girl kissing her pillow. And she lay there filled with bliss and overwhelmed by the power of love returned.

Me—Mrs. Brigham Bantley! Imagine that! As she lay there with that name rolling around on her tongue, trying to make it seem like hers, there came to her a soundless question from the great somewhere.

"Mrs. Brigham Bantley? How can that be when there is a Mrs. Brigham Bantley?"

"He wants me to be a mother to Skip and Bant and Savy!"

"How can that be? They have a mother; man can only have one mother."

"He wants me to own a share in Glory Land, to drive a beautiful new car, to travel and wear fine clothes—those are things which go with being Mrs. Brigham Bantley!"

"Nothing is worth those things if paid for by conscience."

"What then is worth the price? I know—to have someone to come to me in the evenings. He calls me his evening valley. He needs me. We'll share each other's company in the evening of our lives. Every one needs someone," she said to herself.

"I need you, Anna Maria Abendtal. I need you. I'll help

you. Trust me."

Anna Maria opened her eyes to see who was speaking. No one was there and yet she felt a presence. She knew who it was—she and Brig had talked about Him often.

Anna closed her eyes again and verses from the Scriptures began coming out of her memory. "Thy maker is thine husband; the Lord of hosts is his name"; "I am the way, the truth and the life"; "I have chosen you"; "I will never leave thee, nor forsake thee."; "Follow me."*

Anna Maria had never felt such love as she felt at that moment. She was bathed in a baptism of holy love and her heart was filled with compassion for everyone who hurts. She lay there a long time, laughing and weeping. God had work for her to do. What a joy to know that He knew her and He cared about her heartache for Brigham Bantley. This was His answer to her prayers. She knew what God required of her. There was only one answer for Brig and his heart was already prepared for it. That's why he had called their love a "sweet sadness." She would never become Mrs. Brigham Bantley.

She could go forward now without guilt, knowing she had been pleasing to a man and that her Maker was understanding of her heart's desire. In a way Brig had made her a gift, and like all gifts it had delighted the recipient, but she must give it back. She made her decision to obey God, and He would replace it with His gift of indwelling love. Now it was time for her to pick up her cross and follow Him.

And yet, woman that she was, Anna's pent-up emotions poured out and she lay on the sand and wept. What God now asked of her was hard, but she had to face it. Out of love for Skip and Brig and Savy she had to go see Lucy Bantley and somehow persuade her to stay for the signing.

---

*Isaiah 54:5; John 14:6, 15:16; Hebrews 13:5; Matthew 9:9.

All That Remains

Anna Maria set forth to do what she had to do. She left the Indian cave, and in a sweet and tranquil numbness went back to her automobile, and later only vaguely remembered stopping at the Pavillion and asking Phlox to be her stand-in. Bathed in a special awareness of the power of love, she went without hesitation, and it seemed only a few moments till she drew up in front of the old Bantley homestead in Lake Placid.

She knew the street from Brig's description of the elms—a gothic vault of sunlight and shadow—and she recognized the house by the pile of things on the porch waiting for the Salvation Army and by the vacant look of a house whose last occupant has gone to another world.

Anna Maria knew Lucy Bantley from card club, but she had never been to her home nor would she ever have dared to ask even a simple favor of Temagami's first lady; but today her burdens were light and she was joyfully approaching Lucy with a simple but perhaps useless request. She was going fearlessly, knowingly, even happily.

Anna Maria got out of her car and, as she walked up the porch steps of what had so lately been an old lady's castle, she suffered again Brig's pain when he first received the biting news of his mother's death that day at the beach. She was able to convey with heartfelt sorrow her sympathy to Lucy and Brig's sister, Anne, and while she was doing it she realized that her sensitivity to both joy and pain had been enhanced by what happened at the Indian cave. She beheld the world with new perspective: nature took on new hues and everyone seemed more beautiful, every pain and every burden sharper and sadder. It was like being someone else to feel this way, someone bigger, wiser; and life was somehow magnified and vibrantly meaningful. It was like being born all over again! I am now a new person; and if I ever needed proof, my being here is it.

Lucy Bantley was surprised to see Anna Maria and very pleased that someone cared enough to come to her with condolences, because most of them had been for the old lady's children; yet Lucy too loved and missed Grandma Bantley.

"How like you to come," she said to Anna. "Come inside. I'll try to find you a place to sit down. What a job this has been! And I'm in a hurry to get on with my trip. The auctioneer will be here tonight and then I can get ready to leave. In fact I want to leave by the afternoon plane tomorrow so I can have a layover of a few days in Geneva—to rest up after this awful ordeal. Losing Mother Bantley has upset me terribly and everyone here in the States is so nervous—I just want to get away. Then I have to fly thousands of miles to Capetown to catch up with what's left of my tour."

"Just so you come back home by celebration day on September 15," interjected Anna Maria. "Of course you've heard about our big party at Glory Land, haven't you?"

"Yes, I have heard via the Temagami grapevine. How like Brig not to have told me anything about it. But I'm not sure now when I'll be returning. I was to leave on September 10 for the Far East but I must visit Dakar first to see my friend, Mamadoo. Travel in Africa is not like here. Flights don't go every day. It will take time."

"May I ask, who is Mamadoo?" Anna was curious.

"Oh, yes," said Lucy, her eyes gleaming, "I love to talk about him. He's a darling young man from Gambia. I'm going to bring him to America as soon as I can. What an exciting person he is for me with my interest in African music and culture. He sings and dances and writes strange haunting songs—great songs!"

"He's like Skip then," said Anna.

"Well, yes, you might say so! They certainly do have something in common. Skip will love Mamadoo," said Lucy, retying the striped triangle she wore over her hair.

"Skip is most anxious for you to get back for the celebration," said Anna. "He's writing songs especially for it. Aren't you thrilled that *Bring Back Those Years* is a golden hit?"

"Of course I'm thrilled—it's on every station. 'Bring back those years'; yes, it's nice to look back, but I'm looking ahead to bringing Mamadoo home with me. You know, Skip has always been such a dependent child, being the youngest, I guess. He and I have been very close, but we also tend to hurt each other. I wish he'd get himself a girl."

"Are you happy about John and Savy?" asked Anna.

"Yes, indeed, I certainly am. From what I've heard of John Freund, Savy has met her match. It seems to me John will take over Glory Land completely the next time Brig turns his back and that will be a good thing too! Brig's been so tied down; but I'm not getting any younger and I can't wait forever for him to be free. I decided if I was going to study music all around the world, I'd have to go alone. There are so many music lovers and anthropologists on my tour! I'm really anxious to get back to them. In fact, I'm going to Geneva a few days early because I have a cold coming on. If it gets worse the family will urge me to stay home. The minute I returned they made all their old demands on me!"

It was obvious to Anna Maria that nothing was going to deter Mrs. Bantley from resuming her trip. And so she said, "I have been thinking of my mother so much since Brig's mother died. I said goodbye to her many years ago—and goodbye to my homeland as well. How wonderful that you're going to Switzerland. I'm wondering—oh, this is such a big favor, I hate to ask it, but could you—is there any way you could visit Zweisimmen for me? My old Uncle Werner is still living; I'd love to send him a little gift by your hands. If he could see his Anna now—Chef de Cuisine, Glory Land!" Anna Maria looked at Lucy to see her reaction.

Lucy continued to wrap crystal goblets in newspaper and said nothing at first. Then at last she said, "I've heard what you've done for the Pink Pavillion from Brig, of course. He certainly admires you; it's good someone loves cooking. I don't care one thing about cooking, I guess because in my home we always had a cook. My father was an ambassador, you know." She looked up from her work. "Those were the days when we lived well!"

"It's rather different in my country. We have a saying, *'E Frau e nie dahebsher als daheim,'* meaning 'a woman is never lovelier than at home'! Then there's the perfect woman— *'Kinder, Kirche, Küchen'*—children, church and kitchen!" Anna laughed while she repeated those old-fashioned Swiss sayings.

However, Lucy replied in a serious tone. "I don't buy that, Anna Maria. Not that there's anything wrong with my husband, but I'm a charter member of women's lib. I may even have founded it!"

Anna rose to her feet. "I wish I could stay to help you. Where should I put this?" She held out the Coke glass in her hand.

"Oh, just put it in the sink. Anne is going to have the place cleaned after I leave. You haven't told me where to find your uncle."

"You will go see him then? That's wonderful!" exclaimed Anna.

"He lives in Zweisimmen, a little crossroads village in the Oberland. Everyone knows everyone else and if you find Zweisimmen, you'll find my uncle and my cousins."

"I lived in Bern as a child. I'll find it, Anna. You're so kind to my children that I'll be glad to do this favor for you; and as it's for you, the children will be more forgiving of my whole trip; but even if I weren't going to Switzerland I'd have to go back to Africa. Help them understand.

"There's no way I can promise to return at any special time—who knows? When one is away, far away, this life here seems unreal. There's something so pleasant about the slow natural pace of foreign countries. Where are we Americans rushing? And who knows, I may get killed in a plane crash or catch a deadly fever."

Lucy brightened. "But I hope not; I have to go for Mama-doo, Anna. When I get him back here everyone will see why I have to help this special person. He has so much promise and no opportunities—just big responsibilities. Do you know, Anna, at twenty-three he supports twenty-one people including his brother's widow and all her children? I'm discovering it gives me more pleasure than I've ever known to help this poor child. Can you understand why I am compelled to go?"

"Yes, I can but—"

"But what if I don't come back right away?" Lucy interrupted. "If I don't return, I ask you to do me a favor." How could Anna refuse if she were going to Zweisimmen for her? "I ask you to stand by Brig's side. After all, he has 'his glorious land' and he has the children."

Anna Maria bit her lip and her eyes were moist, but Lucy didn't notice. She was busy wrapping plates. "Please do me another favor—for old times' sake. Go to an *alkoholfrei* restaurant and have a *schale* for me," said Anna to change the subject from Brig.

"It will be fun. What is it?"

"You'll find out," laughed Anna Maria. Then she drove back to Cornwall House, not sure whether she had helped anyone at all. But Uncle Werner would be delighted to have a visitor from the United States, and if Lucy put flowers on Elsa Abendtal's grave it would be a great comfort to Anna. Thirty years was a long time to be without a mother.

Bridges Are Made for Loving

One summer evening a few days later, when everyone had gone home and the bridge was quiet with only the gentle noise of ever-flowing water, Skip sat on a wooden post and Penny stood beside him, cutting his hair.

"Penny," he said. "What are you going to do after the fifteenth? Are you moving back to town?"

"Can one ever go back to the way things were after this summer? I don't think I can," she replied, not cutting but looking away, hating to think of summer's end. She turned back to her work. "Let me see how you look from the front." Cutting a little from his bangs, Penny continued, "Mother's pushing nursing school. I've finally come to realize that she's ashamed to have a daughter who's a baker!"

"Simple Simon is a pieman!" joked Skip, quoting a remark made by Phlox some weeks before, which had irked Penelope.

"Please don't rub it in. That's exactly it. After all, my mother is the Associate Director of Glory Land, so I can understand that as a pieman—maybe I should say a pie-person—I've been a disappointment to her! But sometimes she's a trial for me too," she added, clipping a piece of hair from the back of his neck. "I'd never have had The Sesame

Seed in the first place if it weren't for my father. In everything I've ever done I've had him backing me all the way. When I carried in his lunch last Sunday and fixed his water bottle, I told him Phlox said that I'm just a Simple Simon. He took my hand and said, 'No, dear, don't say that. You're Simon of Cyrene.'" She stopped to wipe tears from her eyes. And then she said, "That's my father—sitting there helpless in a wheelchair and sustaining me! What would I do without him to smile at my questions and listen to my problems?

"And he does the same thing for Mother. Whether she knows it or not, he's made it possible for her to have a career and bring up a child. Even now, he does a lot of little things for her and he never resents it when she's too busy for him. He folds all the clothes and cleans her glasses. In the morning he lays out her purse and car keys. Would you believe it—he even winds her watch!"

"Ouch," said Skip. "You cut my ear."

"I'm sorry, I didn't mean to!" said Penny, turning his head with her hand and giving him a little kiss to make it well.

"You're forgiven," said Skip, smiling his quick half-smile.

"Do you know," continued Penny, "when my father heard about the Way Dupre he had me drive him over to look at all the new signs even though he could scarcely breathe? He kept saying to me, 'They're for your mother, they're for your mother.' But your father says they're in honor of him too—because of the war," she added. "Dad was a war hero, you know, but he's very modest about it. It certainly was nice of your father to do that for them."

"Yep, I guess it was." Skip was thinking how nice it would be if his father did him a favor and listened to his songs once in a while. Aloud he said, "Mother's gone back to her tour. I have to conclude that since there's not much time left she doesn't intend to return for the fifteenth." He looked glum.

"Skip, I'm so sorry. You know," she commented, combing through his lovely wavy hair, "people their age have had a hard summer. Do you suppose our celebration day will save anybody's marriage? I hope so."

"Who can tell?" he answered. "In a day or two I'll sing you one of the songs I'm writing for it; it's shaping up—a little something called *The Ballad of the Big Bear*, about everything that's happened this unbelievable summer. Haven't we come a long way?"

For a few minutes all that could be heard was the clip-clip of the scissors while the young couple thought back over their summer. It had been an unforgettable time. Then Skip asked Penny what she was baking for the upcoming feast.

"I'm making the wedding cake with help from Anna Maria. She's using an old recipe of Monica's—cake with raisins and candied fruit and sugar icing. Doesn't that sound good? But what a job it is! I sure hope all the people we've invited will come, even the ones who won't sign." Penny examined Skip's haircut from all sides and smiled at the results of her handiwork. Skip looked darling, like always. "I hope Father can be here. It's touch and go whether he will be well enough to spend the day at the park. Of course he has permission to sign at home, but guess who's offered to go for him in her new truck?"

"Who?" There could be only one person who would fit the look in Penny's eye, only one person with such a truck. "You don't mean to tell me that—?"

"Yes, Phlox!" After a pause Penelope added, "You know I guess I'll have to forgive her that Simple Simon bit. My father says I must praise the Lord for everything—even for her! That's a very heavy idea but I'm trying."

"Phlox! I don't believe what's happened to that girl since she got out of jail! What a change. I can't believe that she could blossom like she has!" exclaimed Skip.

"Everyone blooms for Anna. Everything she touches grows into something beautiful. There, turn around. I've done a good job. Now it's your turn to cut my hair." She handed him the scissors. "Now only a little. Don't ruin me." Penny sat down on the post. "What are you going to do next, Skip? There's talk that you're getting a manager and that he wants you to take the Saffies on the road. You know, I'll miss you. It's been a great summer." She sighed and looked at him sadly—the summer was almost over. She was so much in love with Skip.

"No, you won't miss me," he said, taking her by both shoulders, the scissors in one hand and comb in the other, "because I'm not going anywhere. You can forget the rumors. Maybe I could travel around to nightclubs and sing for a bunch of potheads and drunks, but what kind of a life is that? No, I'd rather stay right here and let the world come to me. It's been a slow dawning, to be sure, but I'm beginning to realize how blessed I am to have this lovely park to work in—the river, the mountains, best of all, the freedom to be myself and control my own work. But I need a woman to help me!"

"I thought you didn't like women," Penny said, teasing him, so relieved he wasn't going away.

"I guess I did say that once—there don't seem to be many of my kind left anymore. Just look at the women I know. The Safflowers all want their togetherness. My sister wants a career. Your mother works; mine rushes around the globe; Freud's mother is moving to Santa Fe. Where would such women leave a creative man? If you meet one who stays home and takes care of a family, she apologizes for it. I'm not criticizing women, you understand. That's just the way it is. But you, Penny—you're different. You've been taking care of me this summer, cooking my fresh vegetables, remembering my vitamins—even cutting my hair; but best of all, you've given me support and direction!"

Penny smiled at this strange sort of compliment. After all, she was primarily a businesswoman. But she loved catering to Skip's needs. She waited on him like she waited on her father, because it made her happy and gave purpose to her life. There was no one on earth she would rather take care of than Skip Bantley. While she was musing over this, it came through to her that he was saying something else.

"What I'm asking is, Penny, will you marry me? Will you be my inspiration and helpmeet? Thanks to *Bring Back Those Years,* we can afford to get married. We'll take a long, long honeymoon and I'll make love to you in the morning and write about you in the afternoon and sing to you in the evening. How's that?"

"Stop, stop," cried Penny, jumping off her perch and knocking the scissors into the river. "Stop. Stop. Say that again!" she cried.

Skip put his finger on her mouth and said, "I'm going to learn all the answers to my girl's questions about God." He leaned down and kissed her on the mouth. "Will you be my Mina Edison?" he laughed. "Will you take care of me so I can write?"

"You're not afraid I'll be like Utrillo's Lucie Valore—let no one hear your songs unless they buy my cookies first?"

"Not you, not Penny Dupre. There's nothing selfish about you. You have a way of holding me up and showing me to God, which gives me light. Penny, I need you. There's no one like you!"

"You know," said Penny, smiling up into his twinkling eyes, "you make a better speech than a proposal!"

Skip looked embarrassed. "I was planning to ask you next weekend. Let's take a walk along the river and I'll start all over." He took her by the arm and they walked across the span in the direction of the hills, pausing to look down at the river running underneath their feet. Then Skipper drew Penny into his arms and, pushing away her long brown hair with his hand, he kissed her cool neck and backed her slowly up against the tower.

"Now, is this better?" he asked. "How's this for a proposal?" She opened her mouth to reply and he covered it with his mouth, kissing her tenderly and lovingly. Suddenly he stopped and began to hum. "Da da—dee da dum da da—brid-ges are made for lov-ing," he sang. "Pardon me a second, Penny, while I run inside and jot that down," he exclaimed.

"You come back here, Skip Bantley," she commanded, thunder and lightning in her eyes.

"But Penny, don't you understand, if I don't catch a song, it goes."

"Skip, if you don't catch me, I'm going." She walked away quickly toward the mountain path. He pursued her and in a moment she was in his arms.

"Pen-nee is made for lo-ving," he sang. "Da-da dee-da-dum-da da-da. Isn't that a good song?"

"There's a time to sing and a time to love," said Penny. "Take your choice."

"No contest," he replied.

Tulie's Windfall

The phone rang in the house of Judge John Freund. Tulie answered, "Yes?"

"Tulie, this is Margo Jong. Oh, the baby's fine. She weighs seven pounds six ounces already and she's sleeping through the night. I keep Esther right here with me in the office so I can continue to work. In fact, it's business that I'm calling about. Can I reach the judge?"

"No, Margo, I'm afraid not," answered Tulie. "His whereabouts are unknown. I don't even know where he is; and frankly, Margo, I'm glad I don't because I feel safer not knowing. May I help you in any way?"

"In fact, you can. It's your account I'm calling about," the broker replied. Tulie looked surprised; her account lay dormant, consisting, she believed, of a few shares of General Motors and General Electric.

"It's about your shares of AT&T," continued Margo. "It occurs to me that though the third quarter earnings will be up considerably, the market is obviously anticipating the news and the fourth quarter may see a reduction in earnings."

Tulie was puzzled. She didn't know she owned AT&T. "Usually the judge looks after my investments. Are you suggesting I sell?" asked Tulie in a timid voice.

"Well," answered Margo, "that's up to you, but I think the judge would be pleased that you've had a one hundred percent gain in three months. The taxes on short term gains would be offset by his losses. Think it over and let me know."

Tulie was flustered by this unexpected happening. A windfall—just in time for her trip!

"How many shares do I own?" she asked gingerly, hoping it would be a round lot of one hundred shares.

Margo answered in a crisp business-like tone ordinarily reserved for male customers: "Purchased May 15, one thousand shares, split two for one on July 7 to stockholders of record August 1—so you have two thousand shares. They've been selling today at 49 to 50."

Tulie was astonished. It was a fortune! The judge must have had a secret bank account for years to have accumulated fifty thousand dollars. Why hadn't he told her? He always said she asked too many questions; now she was silent.

"Tulie, are you there?"

"Yes, Margo dear, I'm just thinking how I'll spend my profits. Sell it all and I'll be around to your office in the morning to get my check. For once it seems the Freunds have made a good investment!"

"Yes," answered Margo, "who would ever have thought of buying AT&T? But John said you loved the telephone!"

"Did he?" said Tulie. Maybe I did, she thought to herself. "Goodbye, Margo. Take care of that precious baby!" Tallulah sat motionless for a long time. Her face was flushed and sweating. She took off her glasses and sat back in her chair and laughed and laughed—twenty-three years of pent-up laughter. "I surely underestimated my husband, and now he will find that he has underestimated me!" Oh, sweet revenge! It was going to be so sweet to open an account in Santa Fe with one hundred thousand dollars—a very good beginning for an antique business.

The judge would surely not return till after the ceremony and she would be gone by then. Tulie Freund smiled. Now she could indeed make a new life in the West. The sooner, the better, she thought.

The next morning it was raining when the offices of Anderson, Chase, Jong and McVay opened for business, and Mrs. John Freund II was standing at the door under an umbrella waiting for her check, which she mailed immediately to a bank in Santa Fe—the part of it, that is, which she did not convert into travelers' checks for her trip.

However, the day was not over for Tallulah Freund. She drove home to Pleasant Street on this beautiful morning. (Yes, in spite of the drizzle, the day one acquires sudden wealth is a beautiful day.) Tulie arrived home to find a further surprise awaiting her. There on the rug in the hall lay a long thin envelope, another letter from Frank Fontaine. With great curiosity Tulie opened it and read:

My dearest Tulie,

[Since when am I "your dearest," she thought?] I want to thank you for all you've done for Phlox. [Me! I couldn't do a thing with her. She didn't get up for breakfast. She hated antiques. She was never around. She was impossible—not to mention what she did to Freud in that tree!] I really regret what happened after she left your house—too bad she fell in with that blasted toy maker. He thought he had a real live doll to play with, but Phlox is smart—she took him for a truck! [Such a disgraceful child, thought Tulie.]

Now that Phlox is doing better, I've had time to think and I've been thinking a lot about us lately, about the good old days at The Grease Pit. By now you may have heard that I'm getting a divorce by default on September 15. I just couldn't go on with so much unnecessary pain and so little love in my life, not when given a way out!

I've even convinced myself that it will be better for Jean to be weaned from me now because—you see, just between us—I haven't been feeling very well lately. I may not make it to our twenty-fifth reunion—but on the other hand perhaps I will. I've been thinking maybe you and I could take up where we left off, now that I appreciate the way you are. You're what I really wanted after all, dear Tulie, but I was too young to know it. Let me hear from you soon. Could we go to our twenty-fifth reunion together?

All my love,
Frank

Tulie reread the letter again with a half-smile on her face and she thought to herself as she read: Frank Fontaine, you're twenty-six years too late! And you're just like all the rest of them. "Good old Tulie!" Well, I have a surprise for you, Frank; the Tulie in your head isn't the real me at all.

Goodbye, Frank. I wish you the best, you deserve it if anyone ever did. But good old Tulie is going away, far away, to a new life as somebody you've never seen, maybe wouldn't even recognize. Who knows—a man might come along with eyes to see the real me! But if he doesn't, at least I'll enjoy being myself for a change, and that will be something. Goodbye Frank!

The next day, Tallulah Freund received another call from Margo Jong. "Did you hear the news, Tulie? It's coming over the teletype now. Yesterday AT&T dropped six points for the sharpest one-day drop in several years. It is thought the company is having equipment problems and investors were taking their profits. Tulie, I'm so happy for you. I think you sold just in time! Aren't we a pair of experts?" said Margo.

"Yes, we certainly are," smiled Tulie. She laid the phone gently down on its cradle. Her new life had begun and it was already more exciting than she ever hoped it could be.

A Small Room in a Swiss Hotel

Swissair flight 212 from New York to Geneva droned across the North Atlantic. Economy class passenger L.L. Bantley rested her head against the cold plastic seat and shut her eyes. In the back of her mind Lucy knew if she didn't return in time she would be divorced, and a new set of complications would enter her life. And in a way she was indifferent; she was protesting this new law that was threatening to ruin her summer. It was time for a citizen to cry, "Enough! Let me be." That's how she felt in her rebellious spirit; but the government, the soulless machine, moved ahead. It had no heart. How could it care about the protest of Lucy Lorenson Bantley?

Lucy knew of course that her anger over 04Y4 was in vain, but Mamadoo would be worth whatever price she was to pay. For one thing her mission in his behalf was already changing her own idea of herself. She was amazed at her new-found perseverance in the face of so much opposition at home. This was the first time since her engagement to Brig that she had taken a giant step towards another human being, and she was surprised and pleased at her own audacity and at the warm and happy feeling it gave her. Even this little side trip to Switzerland alone, under no protective wing of a travel agency and over the objections of her family, was evidence of her new-found courage. There alone on the plane, she thought about the youth whose future she was taking as her responsibility. Why had she singled him out to help? He had appealed to her. But Lucy was not quite sure what there was about this young African that was so appealing. Was it his naïve faith in the U.S.A.? That must be it; his simplistic faith and hope had reawakened her appreciation of being an American. She wanted to show him that her land still stood for individual opportunity and the helping hand. She felt sure she could extend that helping hand to Mamadoo, who carried so much responsibility with such spontaneity and optimism. It was paradoxical that he fed twenty-one people and her sons fed only their cars.

Lucy removed her shoes and shifted her position in the narrow seat. If only she didn't have this miserable cold. The press of a button brought the male host with a blanket and pillow; nevertheless, she shivered as the long night dragged on and on. In truth she was far sicker than she acknowledged to herself.

Arriving in the morning at the Geneva airport, she went quickly through customs to a cab, which took her to a small hotel in a back street. Sinbad would have put her in the Intercontinental, but she chose this because she was watching her expenses. There was Mamadoo's ticket to buy. It had been rather a disappointment that her husband had not suggested that Glory Land pay for his ticket. Lucy never quite asked him outright, but when she hinted as much, Brig had commented that the season would be over before "the kid" could arrive. However, Brig also made it plain that if she wanted to indulge this middle-aged peccadillo he would not interfere. He had even added that perhaps she could present her new find at the dinner club in the Temagami Springs Motel. The nerve of him to suggest that! Mamadoo was much too talented for the motel restaurant. Her conversation with her husband had only made her more determined to bring back Mamadoo.

While the cab driver lifted her bags into the care of an Italian in a long green apron, Lucy stepped to the kiosk nearby and bought copies of *Paris Match* and *Sie Und Er*. She would lie down and read until she felt better.

But once in her tiny beige room on the fourth floor of the hotel, Lucy requested the porter to draw the heavy woolen drapes to shut out the hot sun. She would try to get some sleep right away. She washed her pantyhose quickly and hung them near the heater to dry. Then she pulled back the feather quilt, removed the wedge from under the mattress, and fell heavily onto the bed. It was as unyielding as every Swiss bed she had ever slept in, and its resistance did not help her aching head. If only she could tune out the clamor of the cars and cycles in the street below.

Maybe she'd awaken later and go down to the Rhône River to a little *Stube* she remembered from years before and have a *raclette* with pickles and Neuchatel wine. At any rate she had to be well by tomorrow for her trip to the Oberland, because the day after was her flight to Dakar. Mamadoo would be waiting at the airport. She knew he would.

But Lucy Bantley was too sick to sleep and she lay alone, aching and nauseous. As the hours passed, she felt worse and worse. When she opened her burning eyes, the huge brown armoire that stood beside the bed seemed to waver out from the wall and threaten to crush her. She turned over and over, her arms in the way, keeping her from finding any comfort. What was wrong? Probably some

African virus for which she had no immunity. Maybe it would kill her, and then what would happen to Mamadoo's dream?

Finally Lucy slept, an uneasy, dream-filled unpleasant sleep, full of frustration in foreign places. She shook herself awake from a bad dream only to fall asleep still dreaming the same bad dream.

Sometime in the night she heard the sound of her own voice calling, "Brig, Brig." She was looking for her husband. She reached out across the bed beside her. He wasn't there. Where could he be? He wasn't there and she needed him desperately. She was yearning for her husband and he wasn't there. "Oh, to have you here with me," she cried in her sleep. "To feel your soft sweet body next to mine. Brig, where are you?" she screamed aloud. She sat up, half-dreaming. He wasn't there. She fell back and hugged her pillow to her. Her auburn hair lay tangled damp upon it.

Fully awake now, she was all alone and she yearned for her husband as only a faithful wife of many years can yearn, yearning for the warmth and comfort and release of his embrace. And she knew then that this should still be hers to have, could still be hers. It was she who had been rejecting intimacy with Brig little by little; and she knew too that there had been a great loss. She had run away from his love and there was no one to help her and no one to care. And maybe she would die here in this little box in a little back street in Geneva. And no one would know.

After a time she slept, and when she awoke in the morning she had a fever of 104 degrees. Days passed in the tight little box high above the busy street. They were days of cold silence and grey light. Lucy couldn't breathe; she felt like a rock was resting on her spine. No position afforded her comfort. Her head ached as if she were wearing a tight helmet and her toes and elbows and neck were sore. Sometime during the week she staggered out to a clinic for Spanish workmen and found her way back with a bottle of Ampicillin and an envelope of green sleeping pills. It had been years since she was so sick, indeed if ever she had been.

This was different—her very life was threatened, and lying there alone, she was afraid of death. Floating through her semi-conscious mind came a male voice asking, "Do you have to go?" Someone had said that to her. Who? When? One of the children. She thought about them. It had been a long time since she had seen Banter. Now she would never see him again. Savy was engaged to marry Freud, and Lucy would never see her grandchildren. Skip was writing songs. Would he succeed? She'd never know. She cried and cried and she prayed, "Please God, let me see my grandchildren."

And then for the first time in her life she began to pray, "Lord Jesus Christ, have mercy upon my soul." It was the only prayer she could think of. Bant had given her a book when she went on a tour of Russia about an old pilgrim who wandered about Russia murmuring that prayer. At the time she wondered why Bant had given her that little volume, but the prayer was with her now. It kept going through her head like a broken record. It bothered her at first, but it became sweeter and sweeter and she clung to it, for it was all she had.

Look Up, Lucy Bantley

Lucy Bantley awoke one morning in her small hotel near the United Nations to find that she was alive and well. The fever was gone; so was the pain. She had very nearly died, but today she knew she would live. It was time to make fresh plans.

The veteran traveler was a little shaky in the legs, pleasingly slimmer in her green dacron slacks, and in urgent need of a hairdresser. The shakiness suggested that a train ride over the Alps was preferable to driving a rented car. The slacks responded to a bit of hasty surgery, and the hairdresser was found to be living next door. And so in a few hours Lucy stepped out into the sunlight of early September, a renewed woman, slender and pale and very grateful to be alive, and more eager than ever to visit Anna's uncle and to hurry on to Africa. She spent that day at the airline office and railroad station and window-shopping in Geneva.

At exactly 9:25 a.m. the *Bundesbahn* carrying Lucy Bantley pulled out of the Geneva station. It gathered speed with thrilling power, clattering over the rails at an ever-increasing tempo that made her heart beat faster. Bridges, walls, paths, and gardens screamed by as the train picked up speed.

At length the train settled into a steady motion and Lucy relaxed. The trip would be three and a half hours. She had looked forward to this ride on the train through Switzerland. She knew from past visits that around each bend and behind every mountain there awaited some visual delight, some small surprise or some great vista. But she had not considered that here, as in America, the ancient bucolic beauty was threatened by man's modern additions to the landscape. She was glad to see that somehow in this proud land the new and old suffered one another with more harmony than back home. And in spite of the changes, she was delighted to be back to this familiar place.

But in the landscape today everything seemed to say, "Cheer up! You are alive!" The red roofs pointed skyward, the peaks on the ancient castle of Rolle, the chimneys, the poplars and cypresses, the church steeple of St. Prex, all said, "Look up, Lucy." And so she did. She looked up at the ragged clouds sweeping the tops of the Jura Mountains, at the sun-streaked villages on the French side of Lac Leman, at the vineyards of grapes on the nearer slopes, rich and ready for harvest.

Time sped by and soon she was aboard a smaller train to travel over the Alps to the Simmental valley. It wound a zig-zag course through the little yards of Montreux, holding back red Volkswagens and grey camions at each little lane.

Further and further below was the great blue lake, and as they climbed she remembered an earlier climb on a Swiss train to *Wengen* when a little voice beside her said, "It is so beautiful I can hardly hold my heart." Who had said that? Ah, yes, it was Skipper speaking—a little tow-headed boy in high socks sitting with his face pressed to the glass, looking down into a deep Swiss valley so many springs ago. How quickly the little boy had changed into a man. It troubled his mother to think she had spent so little time with that sensitive child. She had missed so much and now she could never have it back.

"Yes, Skip, it's still beautiful—all of it—the old chalets of brown weathered wood, that farmer picking lettuce with his long crooked pipe hanging from his mouth, those children playing ball—why, if it bounced it would be gone forever!"

An old man stopped to watch the train go by, his tassel flying in the wind. Below them were cowpaths etched in the mountainside like contour lines, and a tiny chapel sat at the bend of a narrow road. Yes, Skip, I know what you meant; it is so beautiful that I can hardly hold *my* heart. All about lay moss-covered boulders and milky mountain streams, and the little villages far below trimmed the ridges like something on a Christmas tree. It seemed if she so much as wriggled in her seat the train would topple into the valley below. Her ears popped; soon they were on top of the Alps and the descent began.

Lucy waved to a logger beside his horse and a farmer with a big bundle of sticks under his arm. A little girl in a red apron who lived at the railroad crossing returned her greeting. It was fun to listen to the chattering children riding the train home from school for lunch. They wished one another, *"Bonne appétit,"* as they detrained. Then a few miles further down the track the conductor switched to speaking German, and it didn't seem long until at last there lay Zweisimmen in the green valley below at the juncture of two valleys. In a short time the train slowed to a stop under the roofed station and Lucy Bantley stepped onto the platform. It was 12:58 p.m.—time for lunch and a *schale*.

Lucy walked down the winding streets to a little tearoom on a triangular park lined with well-trimmed horse-chestnut trees. There she found an *alkoholfrei* tearoom. Seated inside beside the window she could see the shingled church tower. Behind it rose the *Rinderberg*. From half a world away, Lucy had come to this little Bernese village spread across the green valley and surrounded by great fringes of mountain forested in pine. And she was happy she had come here for Anna Maria Abendtal and eager to meet Uncle Werner.

Zweisimmen—Two Valleys

After eating a delicious yellow omelet with fine herbs handsomely presented on a deep blue plate and drinking a *schale*, which proved to be milk and coffee in a glass, Lucy asked the waitress where she could find Werner Abendtal and was directed to a faded-brown three-story chalet a few hundred yards away. It would be recognizable by its green shutters and the year 1808 painted in red over the front door. Like all the other houses, like the bread itself, it was *halb-weiss*—made of white plaster below and brown woodwork on the upper stories.

Lucy found the house with no difficulty. It wasn't far; nothing is in Zweisimmen. A stout middle-aged woman in a long white apron, her grey hair worn in a bun, was working in the back garden. Lucy decided to knock on the front door. After a time it opened and there stood the old man himself, his cheeks rosy, his eyes a dim twinkle. He wore so many layers of clothing she wondered how he could breathe. He had put on his coat over a sweater and vest, apparently in haste, and it must have been something of a struggle because he looked anything but comfortable. He peered at her inquiringly through thick lenses, his look conveying both curiosity and mistrust.

To allay suspicion, Lucy Bantley immediately said, "Anna Maria sent me to see you," whereupon he encircled her hips with a tight embrace and said in a quavering voice, "*Grüss Gott.* How is my Anna, my little Anna? Welcome to my house. Come in. Come in. How is my little Anna? You come all the way from America?" His head was trembling in disbelief.

Uncle Abendtal escorted her inside in a very courtly way, and when they were seated the old man talked about his niece for a long time without stopping. He talked slowly, remembering the old times: how sad it was for her when she lost her beautiful young mother and how grieved he was when his brother had emigrated to America and taken his little one with him. Little Anna was so gifted; she was known throughout the village because she sang wherever she went. Even in sorrow she sang.

Finally the old man stopped talking and, taking a large white linen handkerchief from his vest pocket, he wiped his red perspiring brow. "Ach, I talk too much! Tell me what brings a new friend from my little Anna." He looked at Lucy closely.

"I came to wish you happy birthday and I've brought you a present from Anna Maria. She's written something inside. I'm to tell you to read page seventeen," said Lucy all-in-one-breath as she handed him a heavy package. She was enjoying every minute of the happiness she had brought the old man.

Uncle Werner unwrapped the book with shaking fingers and looked at it in wonder, first holding it close to his face and then moving it away from him. It was a big book with special large-sized print and he handled it the way one would handle a precious piece of fine china. After he had examined the cover and the binding, he looked at the frontispiece.

Then he turned the pages carefully one by one to page seventeen and very slowly read the personal note from his niece written in Swiss German. It obviously touched him greatly and he read it over and over again. At length he took his white handkerchief out of his pocket and blew his nose loudly. "Did my little Anna ask anything else?" he inquired.

"Why, no—just to give you all her love."

"Ah, such a dear child," he said. For seconds he was still, his blue eyes full of memories. Then he remembered his guest. "Dear Frau, here in her letter my little Anna asks me to put flowers on her mother's grave. She says if I can't walk up the hill, maybe you would do it for me." He paused for breath, but before Lucy could agree, he continued, "It's just like her to know that an old man's legs are not so willing anymore. But maybe I could make it." He tried to get up from his chair.

"No, no," interrupted Lucy. "It would be a privilege to go. I want to go. I may not see Anna for some time, but I'd like to tell her I've been to her mother's grave." She stood up. "Just point out the way." Herr Abendtal got slowly to his feet. Walking was difficult for him, but he accompanied her to the door.

"When you come back, we'll have tea. Wait until my cousin, Teresa, hears we've a visitor from my little Anna! Come," he said. Lucy followed along. "I'll ask her to pick flowers for Elsa's grave. If I stoop too much I get dizzy, so Teresa won't let me do any work in the garden. She scolds me every day just like a mother. Here she comes now. The good woman is a little bit deaf."

Teresa, middle-aged cousin of Anna, appeared from down in the garden where she was picking lettuce and looked inquiringly at the slender, stunning Lucy in her long leather coat, green slacks and ankle-high boots. Teresa was

wearing a heavy, grey knit dress and hand-knit grey stockings, and she seemed a little embarrassed to be caught in
her work clothes.

"Teresa, this is Frau Bantley from America, good friend of
our Anna Maria. She came to bring me a birthday present."
He looked at Lucy. He couldn't take his eyes off her. His
own face was drawn up, smooth and shiny and full of happiness. "Will you pick her a bouquet to take to Anna's *Muti?*
Anna asks it."

Teresa, shy and a little flustered, but obviously excited
by their guest, went at once back down to the garden and
returned with an armful of white dahlias. "I'll show you
the way to the cemetery." Teresa thought she should go
along, but the old man detained her by taking her elbow.
He pointed with his cane. "It's up there by the church. You
can't miss it."

Word had spread through the village that an American
lady was visiting the Abendtals; more than one Swiss haus-
frau looked from her window, which just happened to need
washing that afternoon in September, to watch the beautiful foreigner with an armload of flowers walk down Farb-
gasse to Lenkstrasse and turn left on Kirchgasse.

Trusted with this very special mission, Lucy approached
the thatched-roof church slowly, trying to put herself in
Anna Maria's place. Lucy knew better than Anna perhaps
what Anna had missed by losing Elsa at such a tender age.
For a mother, any mother, to lay flowers on a mother's
grave is a poignant, bittersweet experience. Who knows
better than she what a living mother gives to her child
and how important she is to its life, how much is lost when
death is premature.

As she mounted the quaintly roofed stairway from the street to the churchyard, the clock on the tower wall below the peaked steeple chimed the quarter hour. Lucy Bantley followed the gravel path through an arbor of trees and came around in front of the ancient chapel. The building was simple, low and squat, whitewashed with a wooden shingle roof. It had stood at the juncture of two valleys for almost four hundred years and with its white tower and peaked steeple was a lovely sanctuary. Upon its face was painted an archangel with St. George and the Dragon and the dates 1590 and 1890. Behind the chapel rose a steep mountain covered with pines.

Lucy stepped down over the sunken stoop and into the tiny church. It was cool inside and smelled of must. The pews and pulpit were freshly painted grey, each wooden dowel-head blue. She stood for a moment and looked at the stained-glass windows and the very ancient green and brown paintings on the walls.

She turned and went out into the cool sunshine and walked through aisles of pines, looking at the gravestones lined along the gravel paths. Black shiny crosses marked the end of life of a dozen young men killed in an avalanche in 1970. Nearby stood a wheelbarrow full of hemlock boughs. A solitary gravedigger was placing pine branches on graves wherever needed, caring for his quiet burial ground in a way that was harmonious with the hills and fields around it. How very frugal and how very Swiss, thought Lucy.

The visitor from America sat down quietly for a few minutes under a big old tree at the back of the graveyard and laid the dahlias beside her on the bench of moss-covered logs. She sat quietly absorbing her impressions of the place in such a way that later she could convey them to Anna

Maria, because Anna would want to know how it felt to be there. And for quite a while Lucy watched school girls playing in the yard nearby. She was surprised when the clock on the church tolled three. It was time to find the grave and be thinking of her train ride back to Geneva. She walked along the neat rows of graves and looked at the wooden crosses under their peaked roofs, seeking the one she had come so far to find. Each grave had a pink geranium on it, which gave the cemetery a warm lively air. It was a pretty place. Lucy read the markers as she went, looking for that special one for Anna Maria.

"Liebe und Arbeiten," she read. "That means 'Love and Work.' How extraordinary! What a strange thing to put on a tombstone," said Lucy to herself. "Why, here it is again on another woman's grave. *Ihre Leben War Liebe und Arbeiten.* Here's another. The poor souls. Is that all they could find to say about them?" she wondered. "Oh my, here's Elsa's grave! 'Elsa M. Abendtal 1916-1945. *Mutter, Liebe und Arbeiten.'* " Lucy Bantley had found the stone she had come so far to see! She looked at it for a moment and thought of this mother's love and of her life, short though it was, a life of work for a grateful family who had never forgotten her; and then slowly, tenderly, Lucy Bantley laid the bouquet of white dahlias in front of the gravestone and rearranged the pine boughs around it.

As she stood up and looked lingeringly at this grave of an unknown girl, something happened to Lucy Bantley, something so unexpected and so precious it became a beacon in her life forever after. In that moment she received a bliss, a love, a warmth such as she had never known nor ever known could be. She was overcome by joyous rapture.

She clasped her hands together and knelt softly down, half crying and half laughing, and holy, unutterable joy filled her to overflowing. Never in her life's most treasured moments, not on her wedding night nor at Savy's conception in the forest, nor during her children's births had she felt such wholeness, such meaningfulness. The universe was hers and she was the universe. And in that moment the purpose of her life was crystal clear: *Liebe und Arbeiten.* She had been running away from the substance of life, from *Liebe und Arbeiten,* and from the people who counted most, her family.

Lucy Lorenson Bantley wept and wept, the tears of joy flowing down and splashing on her leather coat, and she was happier than she had ever been in her life because inside her the emptiness was gone, replaced by a great peace and a great love and an overflowing spirit. She wanted to tell the whole world what she had found.

At length she rose, her face shining with happiness, eager to go back home across the sea to begin to live her life at last. She must hurry—make up for all those years now gone— help everybody to know what she knew. Her fear of death was gone. She would never die. For the first time she understood the significance of the life and death of Jesus, Son of God, for she too could live forever, and the peace that filled her was the peace of knowing herself and others as beloved souls of God, precious crystals of His light. Now they were precious to her as well and most precious of all was her husband, Brig, her companion in life whom she had taken in holy matrimony in the presence of God. She needed to be with him and share what she had found, to love him and work for him and her family.

With light steps and head high she left the tiny cemetery and found her way back to the old man's house. Uncle Werner was sitting in the garden waiting for her. Teresa had been to the *Bäckerei* for a pie "beautiful enough for our guest from America," and she had come home with a special pie with rosy apples under a golden glaze set in a ring around the crust. They sat down to tea, and although the two Swiss had never seen Lucy Bantley before this afternoon, they saw that she looked lovelier upon her return from the cemetery.

All too soon it was time for her to leave. Uncle Werner fetched his two canes and put on his shiny black tie and his wide-brimmed hat. And cousin Teresali, who had changed into her Sunday dress, took off her pink apron, and together they walked slowly to the railroad station. Uncle Werner carried a book in his pocket for his Anna Maria. There in the station waiting for the train they held hands: the old gnarled fingers of the elderly man, the rough-red fingers of Teresa, and the soft white hands from across the sea were joined together in love, and their faces reflected their happiness. As the train got under way, Lucy lowered the window beside her seat, leaned out and waved her silk scarf at the two people on the railroad platform. She threw them kisses and in her heart she cried, "Farewell, lovely town. You sent us your daughter, Anna, and because of her another newborn spirit leaves your valley for the New World. Bless you, bless you. Goodbye, Uncle Werner. Goodbye, Cousin Teresali." And the train went around the foothills of the *Rinderberg* and they were gone from sight forever, but they would never leave her heart.

At ten o'clock that evening Lucy sat in the *première classe* restaurant in the Geneva *Bahnhof* having a raclette with pickles and drinking white Neuchatel wine, not because a slice of melted cheese on a boiled potato is so very special, but because it is so very Swiss—something one would have no place else. While Lucy ate her dinner alone, a wandering violinist came and stood beside her table playing Strauss waltzes and smiling from under his black brows. The old Lucy might have been a little too haughty to accept the intimacy of his serenade but not the new woman. She loved every note of the music and all the expressions on the violinist's face. She would always remember him as part of this memorable and very special day. She sat a long while thinking about her new self, about the disappearance of her fears, the flowering of new life within her, and she knew above all else that she must be home by September 15th. Lucy Bantley only wanted to be with her family, to hear Skip's songs, to see Savy married, and to share it all with Brig. How could she have been so cruel as to leave doubt in anyone's mind about that! But she had not forgotten the young Gambian to whom she had made her commitment. If only he could come to the celebration too!

Anxiously she consulted her airline schedule. If she were to wire him at once to meet her in Paris, in three days' time they could arrive home the morning of the 15th. The ceremony was in the early afternoon. They could make it in time if Mamadoo was ready—and she knew he would be waiting. She ran through the big old station to the Swissair office and was back in no time with it all arranged. She sat at her table and ate a Swiss pastry, and at her request the violinist played *Hello, Dolly*. Lucy was on her way home— back home where she belonged, back home to *Liebe und Arbeiten!**

---

*For God is not unrighteous to forget your work and labor of love. . . . Heb. 6:10

Sweet Sorrow

Anna Maria shivered as she unlocked the Pavillion door early on the morning of September fourteenth. Frost was late this year; she hoped it would hold off one more day. Buttoning her heavy Irish sweater to keep warm, she bustled inside the kitchen. There were many things to do to prepare for tomorrow's banquet. Mr. Bantley had spared no expense to make this a royal welcome; and the cooks, who usually returned to their distant homes after Labor Day, had volunteered to stay on to prepare the feast. It would be a very busy day and it was just as well for her; she would have no time to think of other things.

Anna removed several packages of meat from the freezer and then she went to her office to prepare her list of plans for the day. There on the desk was a note for her in the night watchman's handwriting.

"Mr. Bantley asks you to come to the garden as soon as you come in."

He's heard from Lucy, thought Anna Maria, with a touch of anguish in her heart. I must go to him now. "Oh, Lord, give me strength," she prayed. She went to her closet and changed to her tennis shoes, for the grass was wet with dew. She hurried to Brig in the garden.

Anna found him seated in the arbor. His face was lined with suffering and was pale after a sleepless night; but when he saw her coming his look changed to one of happiness. He rose to meet her and took her hands in his.

He looked at her tenderly, questioningly. "You've come. It seems like I've been waiting forever." He bent down and kissed her gently on the lips. It was the temptation of her life to throw her arms around his neck and pull his body to hers, but instead she turned her head away so he could not read her face. Oh, Brig, sweet, tender Brig, how I love you, she thought.

"Come over here. There's so much I want to say to you, dear Anna." When they were seated side-by-side he spoke again and he was looking off across the garden. "All my life I've yearned to find someone like myself, someone seeking the meaning of it all." He looked at her. "And I've found that someone in you. You and I belong together. Believe me, we do. I can't imagine any greater human happiness than a marriage of body and spirit."

She interrupted him quickly, afraid to have him continue. "Yes, Brig, that must be the greatest thing on earth; it must be perfect happiness."

"I wanted us to have that," he continued, taking both her hands in his and placing them on his knee.

"I, too, have wanted it." She clutched his hands; she had to say what was on her mind even though it was hard. "Dear man, how rarely are our dreams fulfilled in this world. It *was* a dream, an errant dream. We both know that." She looked away.

"Was it?" Brig asked, putting his head on her shoulder like an injured baby seeking comfort for his pain.

"Yes," she said, stroking his thick black hair. "It was a dream. Who can find happiness in taking someone who belongs to another? Brig, believe me, I love you. But I love Lucy too. I love your children; they couldn't be dearer if they were my own. Children want their parents to be happy together."

After a pause she said quietly, "We both know there is a higher commitment than the love between a woman and a man and that is to value one's self as a person ready to face judgment. And there is a greater love for all of us and that is the love of God. Do you know what I mean?" she asked, anxious for him to understand what was in her heart. He sat upright and looked at her with a look both loving and forlorn.

Anna hugged him to her for a moment. "Know, dear man, that this is the most difficult moment of my life, but we won't regret it, either of us. We must live within the will of God. And as you live out your life as a whole man, uncompromised, you'll appreciate what I'm saying and love me the more as men should love one another—because we stand for our values."

"But how can you go back to living alone? How can you face that emptiness after what we've shared?" he exclaimed.

"I'll never be alone again, Brig," she said softly. "I've learned something since that day on the rocks, something I've been wanting to share with you. You're the one person in all the world with whom I can share this." Slowly, in a voice full of wonderment, she told him of her afternoon in the Indian cave, she told him of her encounter with Him and His love. Her friend could only look at her in awe, grateful that all this had come to her in his beloved Indian campsite. "I now understand that He was born so that we need never be lonely. He is waiting in the depths of our despair to love us as we are and to show us our purpose in being, to show us the way to God. May I go on?"

"Don't stop. Tell me more," he murmured, his eyes on her face.

"I think," she continued, "that you and I and everyone who has ever lived has experienced from time to time a desolate feeling of loneliness, of separation from other human beings." He nodded his head; he knew that feeling.

"From my summer's experience with all kinds of people, it has come to me that it is not strange we feel lonely because each one of us is so singular. The inner essence that makes you, you and me, me is so unique and individual that not one of us can find total understanding from any other human being. But oh, how we all long to be understood! We search for it, dream of it all our lives, but very few seem to find it. If they do it is a magnificent gift. Somehow, this summer you and I found in one another that kind of sympathy.

"We met at a lonely time in our lives and discovered we were on the same quest—to find the meaning of life—to find out why we came into being, whether it matters, whether anyone cares. Before we met we had both decided life is more than an accident, more than a mathematical probability. We decided it was a gift and we were asking ourselves whether we were doing enough to justify our existence, whether somewhere there was something more for us. We shared our intimations about God and our understanding of what it means to be a human being; we revealed our lonely places to each other. And in so doing we found that rare person who seems to understand our individuality. So rare an experience of friendship is overwhelmingly beautiful. It explains why when we are together we feel such deep companionship, such inner excitement. At least that's how I feel." She smiled at him and he squeezed her hand. This strong man seemed to find no words, but there was an intensity in his violet eyes, a look of adoration.

Anna Maria was not finished speaking. She felt she must express herself to him, to let it all hang out so that there would be no pain between them in the future. "We call this mutual feeling love, for what else could it be? And it is love, human love—and yet somehow it transcends what we have known before. It is God's love! He is giving us His understanding. You and I want more of it, we can't get enough of it. Somehow we feel that through an earthly union between us we would have more of what life's all about. Oh, Brig, there must be such marriages on earth, though I suspect they're few indeed. But the answer for us lies beyond human relationship; in fact a tie between us now would be bought at the price of losing everything. In our hearts we both know that!" Brig nodded his dark head.

She lowered her voice. "My love for you has been a lonely love. I could share it with no other person, not even you. For a few moments there on the rock when you came to me from the mountain, I had everything I've ever wanted; but even as I received it I knew it was not mine to keep, and after that I knew the very depths of loneliness. When I reached those depths the other day in the cave I learned to my amazement that God knows all about me; He knows I'm lonely. He is aware that all of us are lonely, and so He gives us the Comforter, His Spirit. When we meet Him we find what a precious thing life is, that we do indeed matter to God in a very personal, very individual way.

"And so let me tell you, dear Brig, that our association has brought me more than I can say. Knowing you has been a deep abiding gift, which I will always treasure. I didn't know I could ever find such empathy, that what we've shared could happen between two people. Now that I do, I am happier than I have ever been!

"Though we will suffer a great loss, heavenly understanding will bring joy! He will help us overcome our pain. Do I reach you, O my beloved soul? I have never been happier in my life than I am here with you at this moment. It is for me a moment of sweet sorrow!" She fell silent and Brig sat with his head against the arbor, looking at her from under his dark brows with a look full of heartbreak and understanding.

They sat for a long time in silent communion. Finally, Anna Maria took a deep breath and made herself look Brig in the eye and smile. "All children want their parents to live happily together. Did you know that Skip begged me to ask his mother to come home?" Brig looked surprised. "You didn't know that, did you?" He shook his head. "And she is coming home, isn't she?" Anna picked pine needles from his sweater, waiting for his reply.

Brig looked startled. "How did you know? Yes, she's coming home. She telephoned me from Paris last night. She'll be home early tomorrow bringing her African singer. She sounded changed somehow—elated, happy, very eager to get home!"

"I'm so glad for you. I'm so glad," whispered Anna Maria, hugging him to her. Then, looking deep into his eyes, his heart, his soul, she added, "And we'll all go on being happy, all of us. Promise me." She smiled a knowing smile and said to herself, I knew He'd bring her home!

As the strong shadows of a bright September day fell in patterns all around them, Anna Maria Abendtal and Brigham Bantley—who recognized each passing moment as precious, who knew there is an eternity and that they were parts of an everlasting whole, beloved of God—these two sat silently side by side in the Garden of Contemplation and shared the very essence of life, a reverence for God.

They had shared it since the first word was spoken between them. Now it was a silent communion; and there is nothing between man and woman to equal what they shared.

Anna was the first to break the silence. "Oh, my, I've learned to hate clocks when I'm with you, but have you forgotten, there's a feast to prepare?"

She would have stood up but he held her back and pulled her close to him. "Oh, evening valley, I love you more today than yesterday."

"And I love you too. Let's share this happiness we've found with others so that it will grow and spread. His love can change the world! We must tell everybody about Him." Brig hugged her to him and then, letting go of her gently, he said, "I brought the frisbee. Let's play." He made a sidearm throw. The disc whirled round the sculptured figures and landed in the father's lap. Brig climbed the pedestal to retrieve it and put his arm around the mother figure. He patted the mother's face and, laughing like a child, he tossed Anna the plastic platter.

She leaped in the air and surprised herself by catching it. "I think I'll try for the Olympics," she said. "Or do you think I'll be too old?"

"Never. You're timeless. In fact I've just named that figure up there after you. Meet *Anna Maria avec famille* by Henry Moore." Anna looked upset. "Don't worry, I won't put a sign on it!" She smiled at him from the depths of her warm brown eyes.

Brigham Bantley and Anna Maria Abendtal walked back to the Pink Pavillion together, back to their preparations for the big day. They walked across the fields laughing and tossing the purple frisbee between them like two carefree children with nothing to do but play, like two children on the last day of summer. Tomorrow it would all be over and they knew this was to be their last game.

The Fifteenth of September

At three o'clock the next morning Brigham Bantley awakened. He got out of bed and drew back the draperies. A great orange moon shone across the valley. It was a beautiful sight.

Brig stepped to the table and snapped on the radio. A young male voice was singing, "Bring back the sunlight, I'll even take tears; light up the darkness and bring back those years." It sounded familiar somehow, but Brig didn't really listen. He was in a kind of shock, so much had been happening. Brig thought he'd heard that voice somewhere, but he didn't recognize it until the disk jockey said, "This is station WAMY, Temagami Springs, bringing you the top twenty. For the first time ever we've played you a tune by one of our own: Skip Bantley singing his new hit song, the new number one! Let's play it over again!" "Bring back the sunlight. . . ."

Did he say Skip Bantley? Yes, that was Skip's voice. Did he say top twenty? That must mean Skip had made the big time! How could that be? Brig shook his head in disbelief that his dreamy kid with no ambition had made something of himself. He hadn't helped him at all, so how had it happened? Who would have thought it possible? As he reflected on this piece of news about his youngest child, Brig Bantley remembered that someone had believed in Skip. His evening valley had believed in Skip from the beginning. Thinking of Anna Maria gave Brig a heavy heart. He snapped off the radio.

There would be no more sleep for him this night: he would go for solace where he had gone so many times before. Brig took his walking stick and set out for the mountain top by the light of the big autumn moon. Across the fields of Glory Land, past the infamous oak, across the bridge—its young habitants asleep in the twin towers—and through the dark woods he hiked, out upon the rocky meadow at the mountain top. He climbed to the pinnacle and there alone in the moonlight he thought back over the incomparable summer fast departing into fall. There was frost on the ground.

He stood watching the moon set and the rays of the rising sun come over the eastern mountains, highlighting the rock on which he stood—the Pok O'Dawn as the Indians called it, his Peak of the Morning Light. Brig wondered who had given it its beautiful name. Probably some early riser like himself, a red man, a visionary, a God worshipper. For a time he stood watching the sky, watching daylight come to his glorious land, and while he watched the sun rise, he began to feel strangely remote from the scene below. Glory Land seemed unimportant to him, and in that moment he knew that he was ready to let go.

"It's time I give it up. I never thought I could, but now I can," Brig said. "I'll give Glory Land to my children to make of it what they will. What Glory Land has been to me no one can take away, but now I must move on. Lucy is coming back and she has worlds to share with me. Perhaps we'll find other places where, because of us, people will find meaning in being and working together and I'll be free to go on sharing what I've found."

His wife was right, he had been tied down for too long. But everything was about to change. Tonight there was the wedding. His daughter, Savernake, was going to be married and it was gratifying that she had found someone capable of taking his place. Young John had a lot to learn. He was a little too bold and presumptuous, but his zest for life and his ambition would keep Glory Land alive, and that was all that mattered to him now.

Lucy would be home in a few hours on the commuter plane from New York, bringing her young friend from Africa. Even before they arrived, Banter would come on the early bus from the city. When Lucy had gone away again after his mother's death, Brig had wired his eldest son a ticket home from India, to have at least one special guest for his daughter's wedding, and so today his wife would find a big surprise awaiting her arrival. Brig knew it would make Lucy happy, for she and Bant were very close. It would be a heartwarming day for his family and he was glad.

Only lately Brig had come to see that all of them, each pursuing his own individual course, had lost sight of a very important source of strength—togetherness as a family. It was up to him to assume leadership, to keep them close as his mother had done for him and his sisters. It was time for the Bantleys to realign their priorities, to pool their strengths and share their discoveries, to enrich one another. Life was short and it was time to come together and celebrate.

Even while he rejoiced, his eyes searched the tree-tops below for the tin roof of Cornwall House. Somewhere down there in the valley Anna Maria was preparing to go to Glory Land—she who had helped him realize what life is meant to be: a testament of love. He owed his calm heart to her; even his fresh feeling of happy expectation over the reunion of his family he owed to her. And his heart ached because she had no beautiful homecoming awaiting her. It would, he knew, be a bittersweet day for Anna Abendtal. If only he could do something for her. "God be with you all day long, my evening valley," he prayed.

And as he lifted his eyes from the valley he saw a jet far away, making a trail across the horizon above the mountain tops, and in that moment he knew what he would do for Anna. He could bring her orphans to her so that she too would experience a happy union with those she loved.

With joy in his heart, he leaped up and descended the hard stone pinnacle and, throwing his suede jacket over his shoulder, he hiked briskly down through the forests and fields, past the seven little forgotten graves in the tiny overgrown cemetery, and back to the Valley of Springs.

It was the fifteenth of September come at last. The bright morning star was just above the horizon.

Freud moved back home to get ready for Celebration Day and for his wedding. Primitive living was too difficult for a man with so many projects and responsibilities. The job of Ben Franklin had been a success and through it he had made many contacts for his bright future, most especially one with the Harvard historian, Arthur Longworth, collector of Franklin memorabilia.

Tonight Freud and Savy would be married and his life would have new purpose and take new directions. Because of this and because his mother was leaving, he had deliberately devoted as much time as he could after the park closed to being her son.

He helped oversee the packing of her treasured antiques and now they were gone from the house. Most of its contents had come down to Tulie from her parents and grandparents. She was taking them with her. The old home on Pleasant Street, where John III had grown from babyhood to manhood, stood almost empty after all those years. Freud didn't know he'd feel so much pain and he didn't even know how to define for himself why he cared that almost every material thing he'd grown up with was gone.

Strangely enough, his father had come back unexpectedly from Lake Abitibi. He appeared the night before, gaunt and haggard, his jowls dangling, his bleak eyes lusterless. The judge returned as he left, without a word to anyone. He had come back to sign EZ-OUT. Instead he found that his wife of twenty-four years was leaving him.

"Come and get your breakfast. John! Children! It's only cereal and toast. I hope you don't mind paper bowls, for there isn't much time," called Tulie from the kitchen. "I must get an early start. Freud, Linda—before you sit down, just help me get these tables and chairs into the trailer."

The elder John came, as he always had, when he was called. "No, don't take that chair, son," he said gruffly as Freud was about to pick up the bentwood rocker. "It's mine." Judge Freund pulled his rocker over to the window and sat down, rocking back and forth. "Tell mother I don't want any breakfast." Today was a public holiday, but tomorrow he would sell his AT&T stock and invest in a gold mine in Quebec. That was some comfort! He half smiled and puffed on his briar pipe with the green shamrocks. The judge was lost in dreams of what he would do with great riches and only half aware of the bustle around him and the empty house.

Meanwhile Tulie Freund went upstairs and took a last look at the things she was leaving behind: old flannel nightgowns and worn out blankets and all the other worthless "old lovables" associated with a thousand good times. While she was upstairs Freud went into the kitchen and made his mother, as she had so often done for him, a bag of peanut butter and jelly sandwiches. He also put in a carrot stick for her teeth and a couple of Oreo cookies.

The rest of her life Tulie (who eventually married again, a manufacturer of TV dinners) told anyone who would listen about her son who loved her so much he made her peanut butter sandwiches on his wedding day. She invariably felt a little heartbroken when she remembered that day.

However, this morning Tulie was in wonderful spirits as she finished her packing and hurried to depart. Linda brought the grandchildren to say goodbye. They were on their way to swimming lessons at the YMCA. Tulie kissed them and hurried them quickly toward their car, while Linda wiped her tears on a towel.

Tulie was getting into her own car when her grandson came running back. "Are you going to telephone us, Grandma?"

"Why, of course I am. And you phone me too." Tulie smiled broadly. She had told no one that the telephone company was more than a link with home; it was her gateway to a new life in the West! Instinctively she opened her purse to assure herself that the fat books of travelers' checks were safe inside, bought with her profits from AT&T. "Well, I have everything. I guess this is it," she said, looking at her son. "You understand, dear—I have to go."

"Yes, Mom. I understand." She clung to him for a moment and then got into her car and shut the door.

"Happiness is a bright day, a trip ahead, and a son who makes peanut butter and jelly sandwiches! And I want to hear that you and Savy are being married by Christmas. I'll fly home for your wedding. Oh, Freud!" She kissed him tenderly; she was leaving her little boy, her baby.

And so on September 15, Tallulah Freund drove away from number ten Pleasant Street for the last time in her life, pulling a U-Haul-It trailer.

Judge Freund rocked in his rocker and Freud, holding back a tear, said to no one in particular, "Am I hallucinating? For a moment those silver fenders looked like wings!" He shook his head. "It's really too bad she can't be here for our wedding. Maybe I'll ask Dad to take part in the ceremony." Strangely enough, the judge agreed.

"I went away one woman. I'm coming back another. I hope they recognize the new me," Lucy said to the young man at her side as the plane descended over Temagami Springs. The plane circled low over the terminal and Lucy looked down. "Who are all those people? There must be some VIP aboard!" She looked about at the passengers and looked down again.

"Why, there's Skip and Brig. Look, Mamadoo. There they are. Praise God—there's Banter! He's home!" She was overcome with joy. "And Savy and Freud. They're holding hands. How cute they look together. There's Surtsey. And look at that crowd of young people. They're the Saffies I was telling you about."

The plane banked for a landing and was on the ground, taxiing to a stop in front of the crowd. As Lucy Bantley stepped back onto American soil tears rolled down her cheeks, but her smile shimmered like sun after a long rain.

Brig dashed through the gate, and when Lucy saw him she ran like a bride to embrace her husband, and he was filled with a youthful happiness. She was younger and more radiant than he had ever seen her. As he swooped her slender body into his arms Lucy whispered in his ear, "Brig, I've come home to help you with Glory Land." He carried her across the ramp and set her down at Banter's feet. "Oh, Banter, my darling, it's been so long!" Everyone standing around was caught up in their joy and clapped and chattered.

Freud pulled out his Jew's harp and Skip strummed his guitar. Mark beat on a drum and together they sang the last verse of *Bring Back Those Years.*

"Mamadoo, come. Meet my people." Mamadoo had been holding back, watching this strange scene. Summoned by his benefactor, he walked slowly forward. He was as black as a wet elm and his eyes and smile were radiant like the sun. His big eyes searched their faces. Her people shall be my people, he said to himself. He was happy, but he was very, very homesick. The banks of the Big Bear River were very different from the banks of the Gambia.

While the Saffies rushed to shower love on the African youth, Lucy turned again to Bant who had come from India for this great day. They looked at each other appreciatively. Banter's long white garments gave him a holy look. Lucy scarcely knew her son with his long brown beard and dressed in these strange robes. Banter bowed from the waist, his hands in prayerful salaam. "Mother, *namaste,*" he said. "I salute the divinity within you."

She grabbed him to her. "Oh, my dear, it's Jesus who lives in me. I didn't remember that you have such deep blue eyes. Oh, Banter, how I love you!" They clutched one another for a long time; it was so good to be back home with the family, with the only ones in all the world who really cared. It was a joyful occasion.

Olivia looked around the sick room to see if Rene had everything within reach. "If I'm going to the ceremony I'll have to hurry. Here's the form for you to sign, Rene. Mrs. Lovall said I could bring it home if we don't tell anyone. And I'll put a glass of water here for you." She arranged his bedside table. "Are you sure you don't mind if I go? Oh, how I wish you could come along. I'll stay home if you want me to." She would really have preferred to stay home now that Lucy Bantley had come back, but Penny would be upset if no one was there to taste the Swiss cake she had made for today.

"No, no, what would Penny say? Fetch me the pen. This is a joyous day for our town and I'll be right in the church with you. When I hear the carillon peal I'll sign at the same time you're signing, my dearest. And I'll be thinking of Paestrum, won't you?"

Olivia smiled at him. He always said that, the dear man. What she wouldn't give for a cigarette. Rene went into a spell of choking and coughing. "I'll stay."

"No, go. You must go."

"I'll come home early and bring you a piece of wedding cake." She hurried out.

Rene lay back on the fresh linen pillows; he was grey and exhausted from coughing. As he lay there he wondered if he had much time left—a few years at most. It was good that Penelope was getting along so well with The Sesame Seed; if only her mother could accept that. And now she was engaged. He was happy the kids told him their secret. Skip would make a good husband because he had sensitivity;

Penny needed an understanding man.

While Rene lay looking out the window in the direction of the park his whole life passed before him—his mother and father struggling to survive on their land grant in Canada, emigrating to the States, the track meets in high school, placing second in the state in the one-hundred-yard dash, the war in Korea, his injuries, and every one of the long years as an invalid passed in review. He thanked God for his wife and daughter. Olivia and Penny had been good to him during those years of helplessness, but it had been hard to lean on them for everything.

"Oh, God," he cried silently. "You alone know how I've suffered. The physical suffering's been nothing compared to my helplessness, to the lack of consequence of my life. What was I meant for? Why was I born? There must be meaning to my life—if only I could find it."

Slowly it came to Rene that there was still some purpose to his existence. He could repay Olivia now—today—for the best years of her life. He picked up the telephone and made a call. Soon someone would come to take him. He had it all arranged that they would come whenever he called. Dropping the receiver on the hook, he reached for a tissue, choking back tears. He picked up the pen and wrote.

My darling, goodbye.

I want you to be free, so today I'm going to move to the Old Soldiers' Home. I know I won't last long after I get there and when I die I want you to take my G.I. insurance and go to Paestrum and Portofina and all those other places just like we planned, because I don't want you to think this great country is ungrateful for the wounds we've suffered. Our dreams were postponed, that's all. Thanks for waiting. I'll be with you all the way.

I am yours always,
Rene

P.S. I'm not signing EZ-OUT. I want you to be free.

It was not enough to give her, but it was all he had. Rene began to choke, again and again, and then he fell back on the fresh linen pillows as the carillon began to play. EZ-OUT lay on the floor where he dropped it. Shortly, Rene heard the ambulance come up the drive.

The Rebirth of Love

The citizens of Temagami Springs rose early on the morning of September fifteenth and ran to their windows to see what kind of a day it was. It was beautiful, sparkling and blue, perfect for their celebration. The town council had declared it a holiday and many had the afternoon off. Who would want to miss a parade, free food, and music? Indeed, no one knew what to expect on such an unusual occasion.

For the people concerned, the day arrived as inexorably as income-tax day. Those forty-five years of age and older had made their decisions. For richer or poorer, for better or worse, their choice was made. There were, to be sure, those who welcomed with joy the chance to be free. They didn't bother to say goodbye. Some citizens just disappeared. Others, depressed and unable to face living alone, sought death as the only way out. But there were others, men and women who pondered together the meaning of matrimony and found it to be a God ordained holy and blessed, albeit mysterious, spiritual relationship in which the two become one, and in so being, they receive strengths and satisfactions and an abundance of life, which make their relinquishment of self worth the sacrifice. These latter people, the survivors, were coming in great numbers from all over the state to register their decisions at Glory Land.

And at Glory Land all was in readiness for their coming. Around the fountain at the front gate and in the many flower beds Tony's crew planted fall flowers—thousands of red and yellow and white chrysanthemums to enliven the mellow brown buildings with splashes of color.

Brig had finally convinced Olivia to join the spirit of the occasion, the spirit of togetherness that prevailed among all the many townspeople who volunteered to prepare the park for this great day. Under Olivia's watchful eye and at her direction, the park was adorned as never before; the carousel had a new coat of paint and its horses wore necklaces of flowers. When Livy wasn't looking, someone made garlands for the sculpture—for the mother, father, and child in the Garden of Contemplation. Bouquets of fresh flowers were in every building. Even the fireplugs wore fresh paint. The park sparkled as never before for this very special day.

At high noon all over town the church bells pealed to summon everybody to the celebration. People hearing the dissonant chorus ran out in the street to watch for the beginning of the parade. And in a few minutes, round the corner onto Main Street came the sleek silver Bantley Bentley, driven by a man in white garments and a curly brown beard. He drove slowly, and when he waved and called them by name, they recognized Banter Bantley, home from India.

Close behind the B.B. followed a new and shiny, yellow truck. It was driven by Mark Sanders—dashing Mark with the jet-black hair and wavy beard, the town's musketeer. At his side was a beautiful girl with short blonde hair and pale blue eyes. Behind them in the truck The Saffie Group played merry music as they rolled along.

Next to come around the corner were Savy and Freud in his ancient Buick convertible of uncertain hue. Savy was sitting close beside her fiancé and talking all the way—after all, it was her wedding day. Behind them came Skip and Penny in The Sesame Seed delivery truck, followed by Tony DeLuca and the Vietnamese gardeners on the Glory Land flatbed. Bumping along behind them was a big, yellow school bus bringing elderly couples from the nursing home, followed by mountain people in sports cars. Everybody rode along, waving and calling to their friends on the sidewalks. In back of the motor-driven vehicles followed farmers on horseback and children on bicycles—Bucky Sanders in the lead. Those on the sidewalk fell in behind to march in the parade to Glory Land. Last of all marched the prize-winning Temagami Springs High School band playing patriotic tunes.

Only one vehicle didn't make it. Tatty's vintage Chevy had suffered a flat tire and was parked somewhere on Route 9 waiting for a mechanic from the AAA. Its occupants settled for coming in their new car, a wedding present to Tatty from Harry—a Cadillac sedan.

The leaders of the processsion traveled slowly in first gear so the walkers could keep up, and in half an hour arrived at the gates of Glory Land where the parade halted while the Saffies climbed down from their trucks and made a line on both sides of the entrance. A bugle blew, Tony opened the gate, and the people of Temagami Springs proceeded down Way Dupre, past the theater and through the fields, to the little valley at the foot of the high hill where stood the newly built chapel. The unusual chapel, set amidst beds of multicolored flowers, gleamed white against the green foothills beyond.

Those who were signers went inside to sit, and the spectators spread their blankets and opened their chairs on the surrounding hillsides. Everyone was looking at everyone else and all were talking at once.

"Look who's back—Mrs. Collins. She's that cook whose husband ran away with the go-go girl—but she brought him back!"

"There's Mama! Mama DeLuca. How thin she's grown!"

"No wonder—all that wailing!"

"Who could that trim young lady be with the little baby?"

"Don't you know who that is? That's Margo Jong, the wealthy stockbroker, and she's not as young as she looks!"

"But that baby she's carrying—it couldn't be hers?"

"It must be! Look how she's showing it off!" (Margo Jong was holding Esther up for everyone to see—the dearest little baby with a cap of black curls.)

"But it couldn't be hers. It's black!"

Three large families of Vietnamese, chattering to one another in their native language, jostled their way through the throng to make a place on the stone wall for their old grandma and grandpa to sit.

But the greatest stir among the crowd was the arrival of Harry Homer, who had come in a new red Cadillac Eldorado. Out of it stepped a woman in a long pastel mink coat with silver slippers and white bobby sox and on her dark head above her white, powdered face she wore a rhinestone tiara—or maybe it was diamonds! Twenty paces behind them with its head down walked a weather-beaten dog, blacker than ink, a white satin bow around its neck.

"Who could that be with Harry? Am I dreaming? It's Tatty Softshoe, the rock lady! She looks like she's wearing a mask!"

"Aren't we all wearing masks, my dear? Who knows what we're really like?"

"Get a look at that coat! It's mink—real mink."

"Don't you think it's a little too long?"

"How come she's with him? I can't believe my eyes!"

Everyone in the throng was occupied with looking at everyone else and no one missed Anna Maria Abendtal who was over in the Pavillion putting finishing touches on the buffet. She was alone with her thoughts. The summer was over. A long, bleak winter lay ahead. Tomorrow she was going home to Cornwall House to her lonely rooms and her memories, and she felt sick at heart. Years before when she had given up Neal she believed the right man was still to come. Now she wondered. There could be no other like Brig. She knew she must not think like this, not today, and yet she could think of nothing but him. Her decision had been the right one, the only one. There had never been a choice. That was that; but she felt so heavy-laden and distressed.

Perhaps it had been a mistake to come to Glory Land for the summer. No, no, she exclaimed to herself. That's not true. This was the best summer of my life! Then why am I so sad and depressed? Why am I thinking tempting thoughts of what might have been? It was a dark hour for Anna Maria, this eclipse of her happy spirit. If only she could talk to someone—to Tulie; but Tulie was gone. Anna's eyes filled with tears thinking about her friend.

She went to her office and opened the desk drawer, removing a tissue. Her Bible was lying there. She picked it up. "God," she said, "help me or I can't go to the ceremony. Everyone will notice that there's something wrong with me."

She opened it to the book of John and her eyes were drawn to Chapter 15, verses 16 and 17. "I have chosen you, and ordained you, that you should go and bring forth fruit, and that your fruit should remain." The same message! "I command you, that ye love one another."

"Love—that's it," she exclaimed. "The message is always *go* and *love*. I will, Lord, I will."

The heavy dark feeling left her. Her spirits soared. She remembered the morning on the rocks with Brig talking about love and the day by the sea when she and Brig shared their awareness of the eternal purposes of God. What they shared was *agape* love. (Because they were man and woman, they confused it with their own loneliness and need.) But what they shared would still be part of Brig and Anna, forever helping them to serve others with true and unselfish love. How few understand, she thought, that real love is never wasted; it doesn't destroy lives, it creates, and it never dies. It passes its blessings from generation to generation.

The summer had been a great success. Lucy was home with her family; Glory Land was at peace; the Safflowers had jobs and a place in their community and even Phlox was changed. And today—well, today there was the excitement of the big celebration prepared by the young people of Temagami Springs. Anna walked among the tables making sure everything was in place.

Yes, everything was ready for the guests. Big bouquets of yellow and rust mums brightened the long tables. A special buffet supper was waiting to be served after the ceremony. There were many coming, some out of curiosity, some for the signing and some for one last good time at Glory Land. Anna surveyed her preparations and was pleased. It would be a good day after all.

Just then a cannon went off and the door burst open. "Anna Maria, hurry. The ceremony's beginning," cried Phlox, fluttering with excitement, her porcelain skin flushed. She was radiant in her pale lavender chiffon dress.

"I'm coming, I'm coming! Just let me wash my hands," said Anna Maria, taking off her big white apron. "This dress you designed for me is beautiful, Phlox. I feel so thin." She smoothed her long rose-silk gown appreciatively.

Anna Maria followed Phlox through the swinging doors. The female Safflowers, dressed in pale green dresses and with dark green ribbons in their hair, were waiting to escort Anna to the ceremony.

"How lovely of you girls to come for me. I hope I'm not part of the show," said Anna Maria, giving each one of the jumping girls a little hug.

"Of course you are! You're Queen of Love and we are your court. All the signers will walk past you."

"Why, I'm not even married!" exclaimed Anna Maria.

"No, you're our vestal virgin!" commented one of them innocently, a former Latin student.

"Oh, my!" said Anna Maria, thinking it was all too true. "Just so I don't have to say anything!" she observed out loud, smiling inside at the innocent remark.

"No, Freud's doing all the talking and I think Skip is making a dedication of some kind. He's written lots of new songs just for today."

"And the Bantleys have brought their house guest along. He's come all the way from Africa."

"Margo Jong brought her new baby!"

"And you should see Tatty and Harry—they're all dressed up and they came in a new red Cadillac and Shadow's wearing a big bow tie!" Everyone talked at once.

"People are pouring in two by two, like Noah's Ark! Isn't

this fun?"

They hurried together through the park, and as this beautiful group of young women approached the chapel, they lined up in pairs behind Anna and whispered to her to walk down the aisle ahead of them and sit in the rattan fan-chair upon the dais. There was no turning back for Anna Maria Abendtal. She was pushed along with the clapping approval of the smiling crowd. The Saffie band played for them as they came down the aisle and "Old Glory" flapped vigorously on the nearby hill.

The group stopped playing when Anna reached her appointed place; there was an air of expectation as Freud, wearing a tan gabardine suit of European cut and an open-necked shirt, stepped up to the microphone. He was wearing his Ben Franklin wig!

Freud grabbed the mike with his usual confidence and, looking back and forth at their upturned faces, he spoke. "I'm glad you all came here today to celebrate with us the rebirth of love on earth. Let there be a new beginning as we join hands and thank God for the blessings of this hour, which seemed so long in coming." The Bishop of Brownfields stepped forward and everybody joined hands in prayer.

After a moment of silence Freud resumed speaking. "I want to introduce to you Temagami Springs' famous songwriter, singing his album of new songs. Singing with him is a young lady from Safflower Hill. Ladies and gentlemen, Skipper Bantley and Phlox Fontaine."

Skip ran down the aisle of the full-to-capacity church and up onto the stage. He was wearing a white suit with a pale blue shirt. Phlox, breathtakingly beautiful in her lavender gown, stepped out from the Queen's court. She had been carefully schooled by Anna and as she passed Freud, she paused briefly to say under her breath, "Forgive me. Let's be friends." He smiled—it was a day for forgiveness. Then Phlox joined Skip at center stage, and she smiled down at her father who was seated in the front row. Frank had come to hear Phlox sing and there was peace in his heart now that his only child had found purpose in her life. It had taken a certain strong-mindedness for both of them to reach their new state of being, but happiness was their reward. Somehow the pain in Frank's heart was gone and he felt younger than he had in years.

Skip Bantley spoke softly into the mike. "I want to dedicate this song to my mother." He sought out Lucy in the great sea of faces and smiled his twinkly smile. "To my mother, whom I love, I sing, *Return to Me Tonight.*" When he finished, the audience refused to stop clapping till Skip held up his hand. "Just to be on the safe side, I wrote one for my girl too. It's really a new version of a song I sang the day I fell in love with Penny!" Penny, seated with the court, was not prepared when he and Phlox began to sing, "I was just a homeless waif a floatin' on the stream." They'd scarcely met when he sang that song; did he really fall in love with her that day? Penny began to cry softly but dried her eyes and joined in when everyone else began to clap and sing along.

At that moment, if anyone had taken his eyes off the singer, he would have seen a very smartly dressed woman come down the aisle on the arm of a short suave man who looked like a stevedore, but was in fact a jewelry salesman. In her calculating way, this woman, who was Jean Fontaine, arrived deliberately late—almost too late to hear Phlox sing. She had come with one idea: to show off the ten-carat diamond ring on her third finger left hand. But no one looked around, not even François Philippe Fontaine, who was up front smiling with pride at his only daughter.

Everyone was charmed by the young singers on the stage, and no one looked around.

"My friends," declared Freud, after the singers had sung an encore, "don't anybody leave. We can't wait any longer for what we came here for: the rededication and signing of—whatever for?" He pretended he had forgotten why they came and everybody laughed. "Oh, yes! The famous 04Y4. Oh for, why for, Senator Paddock, did you do this to us?" The crowd hooted and howled and hissed until Freud raised his hand.

"Come here, Miss Lovall. Ladies and gentlemen, this is our beloved Clerk of Courts. She is celebrating her retirement by helping us today. Please come two by two to her and put your names on the marriage register. May I call to your attention that the state symbol for this legal license is EZ-OUT. Has it been easy?"

"Nooo!" roared the crowd as the band began to play happy music. There was much laughing and joking while the couples came down the aisles and signed the registry.

After some time the line was growing short, when a baby-faced man pushed his way through the crowd and down the rows till he found Surtsey Sanders. "Come along, my steaming volcano—let's sign that form." Surtsey looked at him with fire in her eyes. "You knew I'd be late," he added nonchalantly. "I had a big deal cooking."

"Yes, I know, one hundred thousand plastic pistols."

Bud looked surprised. "Yeh, I just sold them. How did you know?" Surtsey gave him a knowing look and they walked together to Miss Lovall.

If she can walk up there with that man, thought Margo Jong, I guess I can do it by myself! Margo Jong was in her glory now that she was a mother and she wanted everyone to see Esther. She got up from her seat and toured the dais like Miss America. She was carrying Esther in a sack next to her breast so the baby could find comfort in the beat of her heart. Everybody jumped up and gave her a standing ovation. Mothers wept tears. But way back in the back row a very intoxicated man rushed out to get himself another drink.

Not to be left out, a tiny woman plucked at her husband's sleeve. "Come on, Harry. Irv says we should sign even though we just got married." Harry had gotten used to Irv's advice and so he humored his princess. "Yes, my dear, let's not take any chances." Whereupon up the aisle to the tune of *Walk With Me Into the Future* marched Kaleri Tuttle Homer on the arm of her new husband. Harry smiled down at her and escorted his woman with style, happy he was able to afford her a costume suitable for this occasion. Tatty Softshoe was resplendent in her pastel mink coat, and in her black eyes she wore a smile as old and wise and knowing as the earth itself.

They moved to the table and the undertone of chatter continued. "Look at that pair. Why that's Harry Homer— the fat man with the boutonniere."

"Is that the rock lady on his arm? I don't believe it!"

"He was lonesome—just looking for a wife."

"I didn't know he was *that* lonesome."

"They say she's a princess!"

"Look, look! Here comes Mrs. Bantley. Isn't she lovely in that white chenille knit? I'm glad she got back. She was away all summer, you know. Touch and go."

"Who's that fellow with her in the nightgown?"

"Why it's Bant—Banter Bantley. It is! I don't believe it, but it is!"

"Where did he get those funny clothes?"

"I wonder what kind of a holy man he is?"

"Aaahh," a ripple of approval went through the audience. "There's our Brig. Isn't he a man though!"

"Who's that black fellow with them? He doesn't look like an American!"

Their comments were interrupted by Freud. "And now, ladies and gentlemen, now that everybody's signed, if you'll all be quiet for a few more songs." The noise subsided. "I would like to introduce our very special guest on this wonderful afternoon, who has come all the way from Africa to sing for us: the Bantley's houseguest, Mr. Mamadoo."

The drummers accompanied him in the African manner and Mamadoo came forward, trim and proud, wearing his very best western-style clothes. With a look of eager wonder on his face, the tall youth from across the sea looked down at the faces below him and smiled like the newly risen sun. Then he fumbled with his thin black tie, loosened it, and reached under his white shirt. Everyone was silent, almost aghast; what was he doing? After much fumbling, he pulled out a leather sack that was tied around his neck.

"Is he going to do some kind of magic trick?"

"Is it a fetish?"

"What's going on?"

Lucy looked at Brig and nervously fingered the beads at her throat, realizing that she didn't really know this young African. After what seemed a long moment, Mamadoo took the bag from around his neck and pulled from it two things, a tattered dollar bill and a long string of photos encased in plastic. Everyone was in suspense; why was he taking so long?

"I have here my first dollar tip from the Hotel Teranga, a dollar-down on my trip to America." He held it up, smiling.

"And I have here photos of all my family." He held them up and looked at them. "At the top is my mother and my dead father and then there's my godmother who is an American." He turned to look at them. "I expect to invest this dollar and get rich; I also expect to find this lady. To her, and to all of you, I dedicate my song!" Everybody loved him. Where but in America could this be happening?

Mamadoo looked at the crowd in the fane, then closed his round eyes. When the waves of clapping receded out over the hills, he stepped to the mike and sang a simple song in his dialect.

The music was stirring and strange; the listeners fell silent, not understanding the words. Then he began to sing it over again in simple English.

"In a poor little land by the sea far away
Lived a poor little boy who loved to play.
One day he fell sick and would surely have died
But for a gift of love from the other side.
Now he's gone across that big wet place
To find his white mama and kiss her face."

While Mamadoo sang he walked around the stage carrying the mike, and when he finished singing a murmur went through the crowd. Something was wrong with Mamadoo. He was crying. He wiped his eyes and everyone smiled because Mamadoo was smiling again. Mamadoo whispered something to Freud who looked startled.

Then the young black man turned and stared at all the people seated behind him, one by one; and while everybody watched him, he raised his arms on high and his sunrise smile grew and grew into a veritable beacon of light. His tall, slender body trembled all over. Was he sick? They watched in rapt attention as he turned, his face all aglow, and walked slowly, shyly, over to Anna Maria Abendtal

who had been innocently watching the strange scene.
Then, reaching out his trembling arms to Anna Maria, he
pulled her from her peacock chair. "White mama! White
mama! I've found you at last! I knew I would if I could get to
America. It's me—Isaiah!" he cried, tears streaming through
his smile. "Don't you know me? I'm the little one who got
sick. You saved my life. I'm little Isaiah!" He fell to his knees
and embraced her feet. Then he stood up and clapped his
hands, very nearly falling off the dais for joy.

Anna Maria was stunned, electrified. It couldn't be that
this long, lanky youth was the little boy with the swollen
belly and stick-like limbs, that this handsome man was her
Isaiah, the tiny five-year-old child who had died. Was he
alive and here and holding her hand? "Isaiah!" she cried,
hugging him to her, then pushing him back to look at his
eyes, then hugging him again. "You can't be Isaiah. But you
are! Yes, I see that you are. I recognize you by your smile—
that same smile you had as a baby!" Her little one, her first
godson, whom she had long believed to be dead, was alive!
Anna Maria began to tremble. She blushed and her face
shone with joy.

"Yes, ma'am, it's me. I've grown up."

Lucy, by this time, was on her feet and running to the
stage with her husband following close behind. "Is he
Isaiah? Really Isaiah? Your first orphan? Oh, Mamadoo,
you are a gift from God! I knew you were special from the
beginning. To think I was the one who found you! You see,
Brig, you can forgive me; my trip was not in vain, I found
Anna's Isaiah!"

While Lucy was fussing over Mamadoo, Brig helped a
staggered Anna Maria back to her chair. He gave her his
handkerchief and stood beside her protectively with his
hand on her shoulder, murmuring so only she could hear,

"Steady, my evening valley; it's wonderful, it's wonderful; there—there, my evening valley," and fanning her with his program. Anna sat limply, smiling blissfully, and murmured to Brig, "Isaiah didn't die. He's alive!" Her hand was on her heart, which was beating very rapidly.

Half the audience, those who could see what was going on, were in tears. Freud assembled the Saffies behind the commotion on the stage and with one shout they burst into song, "Break forth into joy, O my soul," and, linking their arms, they swayed back and forth behind the new mother and her godson.

Finally, Freud held up his hand, gesturing that there was more to come. "Mark, will you introduce our last song?" Mark Sanders, in clean blue-jean jacket and clean patched pants, a red bandana around his neck, stepped out from the singers.

"I'm not much good at public speaking, but I have been asked as president of our community to make a little speech and I can't refuse. We who live at Safflower Hill didn't have a very easy time of it at first. We wanted to live and work together, in a bygone way perhaps, but in a way in which we each contributed to the commonweal with what we had to give. We were trying to live on love and hard work, and now after many shaky months we've made it, thanks to all of you—to the understanding and the jobs you've given us.

"However, there were dark days when no one had any faith in us and we almost gave up; but it only takes one candle to light the world and when the days were darkest, we found that one. She came to our rescue with every penny she had and paid our mortgage. She just happens to be my mother, Mrs. Surtsey Sanders. Thank you, Mom, from all of us Safflowers. And now Skip sings to you, *We*

Owe It All to Your Love. Surtsey stood there and received everything she ever needed—loving thanks from her eldest son—and her heart was full. Little Bucky at her side, looking darling in his brushed denim suit, jumped up and ran to the stage and sang along with the Saffies. And Bud Sanders looked at his wife and said, "Well, I am surprised. I wondered why you were so poor."

"Dear friends," said Freud, "just one more thing. Tonight Savy Bantley and I will be married here in the new chapel. We'd like you all to come to our wedding and be with us while you wait for the fireworks, which my dad is providing as a special surprise for this great occasion. And now it gives me great pleasure to invite you to follow Anna Maria and Isaiah to the Pink Pavillion for our wedding reception."

The guests lost no time in accepting his invitation. They spent the afternoon eating from the most beautiful buffet they had ever seen. When supper was over someone started a snake dance, which grew into a column half-a-mile long. They snaked down the Way Dupre and through the sculpture garden, past the theater and the art gallery and around the oak tree, coiling over the bridge and back again through the green pines and around the cooks' village. Finally they were exhausted. They sat down under the maples and the elms and on the great lawns and rested for the wedding at eight o'clock. Old men lay down on blankets and babies slumbered in their strollers; neighbors chatted to each other and a few couples just sat and held hands.

Sometime during the day a message came for Olivia Dupre and she slipped out unnoticed and went home. She was met at the door by the Anglican pastor. She could tell by his face that it was Rene. Sometime during the ceremony her husband had been taken by ambulance to the Old Soldiers' Home; there, a short while later, after twenty-four years of suffering, the emotions of this day were too much for his tired heart to bear, and God had taken him. "He has gone home to glory," said the priest. "Shall we pray?"

After the priest had prayed, Olivia staggered into the little alcove of her tiny salt box to Rene's room where he had lain just hours before. On the floor near the empty bed lay a crumpled paper. Olivia, numb and in shock, picked it up and unfolded it. It was EZ-OUT. "He didn't sign. He didn't sign," she murmured, sinking to her knees in desolation. Rene had rejected her as his wife and now he was gone. And in her heart she knew Brig was gone as well. Olivia's two worlds, the one so hard and so demanding, the other, her consoling dream, lay in ruins around her; this woman who had labored so long for her men collapsed in shock and sorrow.

Sometime later, Olivia lifted her head and saw the note on the table in Rene's handwriting. She picked it up and read it slowly with tears streaming down her cheeks. "Yes, Rene, I'll go to Paestrum, I'll go. He wants me to be free! Isn't it strange, I've wanted that for so long and now that I am, I don't want freedom at all. Oh, Rene, they were good years, they were. I never wanted you to go to the Old Soldiers' Home!"

Olivia laid her head against the bed, murmuring between sobs, "Why didn't you sign? Why didn't you, Rene? Both gone, both my men gone. I've never been so alone in my life!" she wailed.

"No, Mother, you're not alone," said Penny, as she ran

into the room and sank down beside her mother on the floor. Skip came in quietly and stood above them. "You have us. Let's tell her about us, Skip. We're engaged, Mother. We're getting married soon. You'll always have us! We'll take care of you." Seeking comfort in each other's arms, Penny and her mother rocked back and forth. At length it came to Olivia through her agony that Penny was going to marry Brigham Bantley's son, and she realized that what she had lost, her daughter had gained. Penny would be called Mrs. Bantley. Ironic as it was, it comforted Olivia to be connected in some way to Brigham Bantley.

She stood up and wiped her eyes and tried to smile. "Skip. You're going to be my son! Isn't that wonderful?" She took his hands and Penny's in her long fingers and looked into their beautiful young faces, and then she laid her head on Skip's shoulder and sobbed and sobbed while the young people suffered in silence with their arms around her.

After a time Penny spoke. "Mother, would you be very brave for us? Skip doesn't want to miss his sister's wedding. Let's not let our sorrows hurt the others on this special day. Let's go back to Glory Land as though Dad was still with us, because he really is, you know."

Skip coaxed her too. "It would mean so much to us Bantley's to have you there—particularly my father. Judge Freund is coming to conduct the ceremony even though Mrs. Freund has gone away."

Olivia seemed doubtful that she could pull herself together.

"Dad would want us to go. You know he would, Mother," said Penny.

"Yes, you're right, he would," said Olivia slowly. "Take me by the arms, children. Lift me—help me—sustain me— and then I can do it." To herself she said, I owe Brig this. He and Lucy must be happy tonight. She sighed heavily; it would be her wedding gift to them. She went to her bedroom and changed her clothes, putting on her Mexican wedding dress and fresh make-up and a dab of perfume. Then she came into the room and said, "Come, children, we have walked in the valley, now let us lift up our eyes to the sun."

Penny hugged her mother close. "You're very brave, Mom, and we love you so." Then, with their arms around each other, the three of them left for the wedding as the church bells rang throughout the town.

The news of the marvelous doings at Glory Land was telephoned all over town, and as the bells tolled seven, those who had not gone to the celebration abandoned their TV dinners in their microwave ovens and turned out for the wedding.

It was a momentous occasion when under the stars of the universe, in the forest of his early love, and from the depths of his own being, Brigham Bantley gave his only daughter, Savernake Bantley, to John Freund III in holy matrimony. The matron of honor was Kaleri Tuttle Homer and the best man was her husband, Harry. The service was performed by Judge John Freund II and Rev. Z.B. MacMorlan.

And the people in Glory Land went on celebrating with sound and light, with love and laughter, far into the night, for it truly seemed to them that there had been a rebirth of love on earth.

The Wedding Night

After their wedding the bride and groom slipped away unseen into the woods and crossed the Big Bear River to the old logging road which led to the Indian cave.

"It's only six-tenths of a mile further; can you make it, Savy?"

What a question! She didn't reply that it was six-tenths of a mile she'd gladly walk with a full backpack if need be. How many times had she taken this trail since she was a child? But there had never been a time like this time! Savernake led her husband along with the light-footed speed of an Indian guide.

While they paused for breath and were admiring the moon, they heard the sound of something coming down the trail. What was it? What was coming? They stood to one side as round the bluff came an old Chevy with one headlight. It was Tatty with Shadow on the seat beside her.

"Want a lift? I thought maybe you might be tired. You gotta save your energy," she said, squinting gleefully. "Harry woulda' come, being best man and all, but he's a real nut about fireworks and I didn't want him to miss anything so Irv said I should come."

Just then the first rocket flew into the sky over Big Bear

Lake and cascaded down in a burst of shattering brilliance. Tatty was awed. "Ya can see 'em from here! Ain't they beautiful? It's like they're just for you two young 'uns—hot and burstin' like you two are burstin'! Ha-ha," she chuckled, knowin' all about that kind of burstin'. "Well, if you don't want the ride, I gotta be goin' back to my lover or Irv will say I neglect Harry." She gave them a knowing wink and drove jerkily away into the night.

When John and Savy neared the cave, a sheltered place beneath an overhanging rock, they found a campfire burning. Coming closer, they saw that Tatty had fixed it up into her idea of a honeymoon suite, a thick pile of hemlock branches for their bed, and next to it a wedding bouquet of cattails in a rusty milk can. On a faded manila tag was a message from Tatty in Harry's fine handwriting. "Like Irv said to us, 'Now you're hitched, enjoy yourselves.'"

The young pair stood looking at this love nest, deeply moved by the old Indian's kindness. Then, as the fire blazed and crackled, they turned to one another and embraced in a long hungry embrace. "Oh, Kingjohn, take off that funny wig," said Savy from the depths of his kiss. His reply was unintelligible so she snatched it off and threw it in the river. "Now you look like my man."

"You've thrown away my treasured hairpiece!" cried Freud, about to dive into the river to retrieve it.

Savy held him back. "Let it go. I didn't marry Ben Franklin!" They ran to the river edge and watched the silver wig float downstream where it lodged on a rock for a time and then floated away, revolving slowly in the moonlight until it disappeared in the dark.

"We can't stay like this," said Freud, stripping off his coat and shirt. Savy looked at him like a woman in love. His blond hair lay in ringlets around his face and his tan chest shone in the moonlight.

"You look wild and beautiful, my love," she said, putting her arms around him, "but you're cold. Let's get into our sleeping bag." With his arm around her shoulder John led Savy back to the cave towards the pile of hemlock branches, which was covered by an old buffalo rug. They halted, looking down at the matted fur. "It looks like a dog blanket to me," said Freud.

"Poor Shadow. I wonder where he'll sleep tonight," said Savy shivering. "Don't laugh, John—Shadow's slept at the Fontainebleau!"

"He can have the Fontainebleau. I like this place better," said Freud as he vanished into the night to get more wood for the fire.

While he was gone Savy picked up the rug from the bed. Lo and behold, it was not Shadow's rug at all, but Tatty's well-loved, well-worn, muskrat coat! Savy quickly changed to dry jeans and put on the old coat. When Freud returned, she expected him to flip but he didn't even notice; all he had eyes for was his bride and the fact that she was dressing.

"Why are you dressing?" he cried.

"Because I'm an old-fashioned girl, silly. I want you to undress me on our wedding night. Besides I was cold, but now that the fire's hot I think I'll take off this coat." She laid it gently in the far corner of the cave.

"Savy, m' love. You are so funny." Freud kissed her a quick kiss. "Come, woman, I've been wanting to get you into my sleeping bag for a long, long time. Now I can hardly wait."

"And I've been wanting you to want me for a long, long time."

"Now," he said, looking at her with adoration, "it's time to undress the bride." Slowly, tantalizingly, he undressed his bride; it was better than the five-pound Sampler. Then, taking her in his arms, he said, "Savernake Freund, I love you, I love you." They sank down and gave themselves to one another with complete abandon, loving one another utterly and forever, until in a whirling helix of delight, husband and wife swirled into one indivisible, fathomless being.

The fire flickered and burned low, and Savy and Freud lay wrapped together in beautiful weariness, listening to the soft rush of the river. From time to time a skyrocket burst into a giant flower in the sky. Eventually the celebration at Glory Land ended and all was peaceful in the forest. The campfire went out and the dew began to fall. Savy and John lay in close embrace, whispering tender words, making warm promises, and giving themselves completely— utterly ravished with their love for one another. Overhead a meteor streaked across the sky and vanished among the stars.

And God who "maketh Arcturus, Orion and Pleiades" looked down upon this man and this woman who by their marriage covenanted with Him to bear His godly seed. And in return He blessed them with unutterable bliss. He put His trust in them to renew the earth. Would they keep covenant with Him? Would they serve Him and His seed forever?

The pale light of dawn peeked over the foothills. They were dozing off when Savy spoke. "Kingjohn, what about us when we're forty-five? We'll never be separated, will we?"

"Never, my love. Now go to sleep," he whispered.

"Kingjohn? Will you sleep with me tenderly all of my life?"

There was only the sound of rushing water and the

whisper of wind in the oak trees.

But over the horizon twinkled "the bright and morning star" with the promise of more love, *everlasting and perfect love* for everyone willing to receive it.

Postscript

High overhead, Weatherbird satellite, a complex creation of the minds of men, revolved soullessly in the heavens and peered down on the happenings in Temagami Springs and on the newly wedded couple. If on this night it had been able to record emotions in the human heart as it recorded storms aloft, if it had been able to measure in micrometers the ebb and flow of human joy and pain, of life's sweet sunshine and swirling storms, it would have focused its lenses on the young couple at the peak of their confidence in one another as the answer to everything, at a moment so precious that in years to come they would look back on it in wonder at their innocence and trust.

If, as the days pass and sorrows come, they find themselves in a cold house, dwelling in pain, without comfort may they remember that there is One waiting with joy and warmth and blessings for their home.

There is one who overcomes pain, softens sorrow, calms all fears, heals wounds, sustains hope, provides comfort, energizes love, beautifies existence, forgives everything and endures forever.

May they reach out to Him, for He is Love.